A FAMILY OUTING
IN THE ATLANTIC

Jill Dickin Schinas

with illustrations by the author

"Roll on, thou deep and dark blue ocean, roll,
Ten thousand fleets sweep over thee in vain.
Man marks the earth with ruin. His control
Stops with the shore."
(Byron)

For Jim, who gave the boat to Nick; for my parents, who thought we would come back home to start a family; for Roxanne, who wasn't born but wishes she had been; and for Caesar and Xoë, who have forgotten all about their first outing in the Atlantic but who still live with Mum and Dad on the deep and dark blue ocean.

Published by *Imperator Publishing*
109 Esmond Road, Chiswick, London W4 1JE
www.imperator-publishing.com

Text and illustrations copyright © Jill Dickin Schinas 2008
www.jilldickinschinas.com
www.yachtmollymawk.com

First edition published in the United Kingdom in 2008

ISBN 978-0-9560722-1-4

A catalogue record for this book is available from the British Library.

Printed and bound in Great Britain by *Lightning Source UK Ltd*
Chapter House, Pitfield, Kiln Farm, Milton Keynes MK11 3LW

A FAMILY OUTING

In the Atlantic

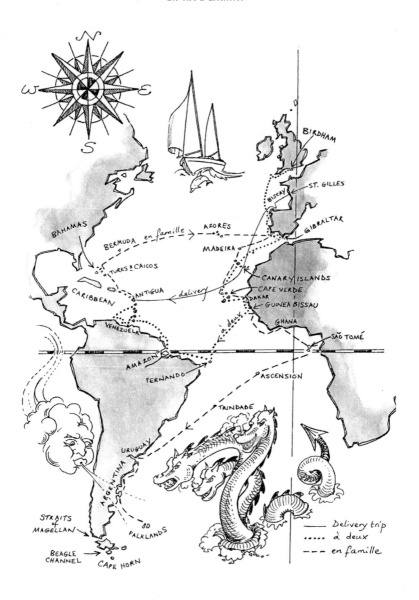

CONTENTS

Foreword *by Tom Cunliffe*   **7**

1 *Once Upon a Time, in El Ferrol*   **9**

2 *Round the World or Round the Bend?*   **27**

3 *And All I Ask is a Merry Yarn*   **57**

4 *Into Africa*   **75**

5 *Worlds Apart*   **93**

6 *The River of Life*   **119**

7 *Hurricane Caesar*   **143**

8 *Baby on Board*   **169**

9 *Oilskins and Nappies*   **195**

10 *From Santa Cruz to São Nicolau*   **215**

11 *Desert Islands*   **243**

12 *Crooks and Crocks*   **265**

13 *Fish and Ships - with Chicken*   **295**

14 *Be the Current Against us*   **321**

15 *Stepping Stones*   **349**

16 *Mollymawks*   **371**

17 *Silver and Cold*   **389**

18 *They That go Down to the Sea in Ships*   **411**

Epilogue *And They All Lived Happily Ever After*   **437**

Glossary *of Nautical Jargon*   **449**

FOREWORD

By Tom Cunliffe

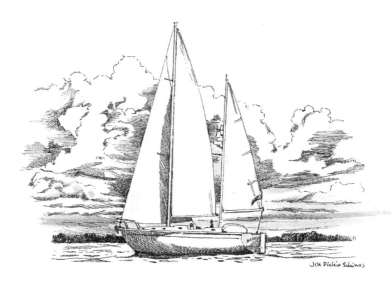

Jru Pickin Schinas

When I first gave up the rat race to go cruising with my wife, it was early in the 1970s. In those days, young people could still dream about the life of a sea gypsy without being heckled by political correctness, calls for more and more safety (whatever that means) and being cross-examined about where the money was to come from. We had grown up on the great sea stories produced by the likes of Eric Hiscock, Peter Tangvald and Bill Robinson. None of them dwelt much on the question of finance, so we just assumed that somehow they had the money organised. The fact is that many of these heroes had no special arrangements and neither did we. What we did have was a sound little ship, the boundless optimism of youth and a determination to work wherever we found the chance of paying our way.

It is progressively more difficult for today's adventurers to follow this route. Propaganda abounds that would steer us all to sea in brand-new production craft bristling with expensive kit. The cost of this approach puts such projects off limits for ordinary people, unless they have inherited, sold a business or retired. Others have their endeavours funded by sponsors as they dance in the media spotlights, desperate to be the first or the fastest. Harbours are becoming more crowded, local folk in what were once faraway places have realised that yachts can mean money, and bureaucracy is proliferating. Casting fate to the ocean winds without visible means of support in the third millennium demands a lot more guts than ever it did thirty years ago. Keeping going, despite producing three fine children and surviving a capsize off the Falklands that ended on the winch cable of an RAF helicopter, shows the true spirit of seafaring.

The Schinas family are talented people. There's nothing on the planet that Nick can't fix, while Jill is an artist of character. The children are developing in the same mould, but the overriding feature of all their lives and the guiding spirit of this book, is their self-sufficiency and courage to make their own choices, come fair weather or foul.

Setting off for Tierra del Fuego, they detour to the Caribbean to top up the cash. Their wanderings also take in West Africa, the Amazon, Southern England and South America. One-year voyagers can't do these things. They are in thrall to the next hurricane season, the need to return and probably mainstream economics as well.

If your own wealth and security are not measured in terms of creating the leisure to reflect, to laugh and sing, to paint, to enjoy the world around you, and sometimes to be truly afraid, take a few moments to ponder the nature of riches. To be free of time's ever-cracking whip and still make ends meet with dignity is treasure indeed. Jill's book shows a balance in life's bank that is far into credit. Read it if you dare, but leave it out if you fear you may lack the nerve to cut loose and live.

Tom Cunliffe
October 2008

1

ONCE UPON A TIME, IN EL FERROL

In which our fate is sealed.

Stretched out on the pilot berth in the main cabin I listened to *Maamari* crashing through the waves and with each rise and fall of the boat felt my stomach lurch. My back sagged into the slack lee-cloth, set up to stop me from rolling out of the bunk and onto the floor, and my head lolled uncomfortably against the wooden rim of the cot. For the past four hours and more I had lain here, shifting my body from side to side as I searched in vain for the luxury of my familiar bed. But that bed was now many hundreds of miles away.

Oh, for some respite from the unceasing motion, the continual bucking and plunging and crashing. I opened my eyes. The cold, grey light of early dawn had already seeped into the cabin and I knew that it must be after six o' clock. Feelings of dismay washed over me; Monday morning feelings exactly like those I used to know as a child, when I woke with the dread of going to school. As Nick dropped down into the cabin I closed my eyes again, but there was no escaping it. Another hour of tossing and turning would not bring me the sleep I sought - and besides that, it was my turn to take the watch.

The skipper peered in at me. "Happy Christmas", he said, with what seemed to me to be quite inappropriate good cheer.

Yes, it was December 25th. And here we were, the two of us, crashing about in a gale. This was not the life I had dreamt of when we set off to go cruising. Struggling out of the bunk I was hit by a wave of nausea and had to grab for an empty saucepan.

"Nick," I sobbed, as he wrapped a comforting arm around me," I don't want to live on a boat. Please, Nick. I want to go home!"

A few chance words, spoken to a friend - it was these which started the ball rolling and turned my world upside down.

Before I was born my parents were already sailing and so, inevitably, I received a saltwater baptism and cut my teeth on a warp. However, the boats that my family sailed were just little ones, and for us the horizon was a far off place. I, alone of my family, had notions of exploring beyond that rim. I can recall watching Clare Francis, on the TV, as she sailed single handed across the ocean. I must have been about eight at the time and my chief memory is of her sobbing into the camera, yet in spite of this I decided that I would like to do the same thing one day. For years the dream of venturing afar under sail lay buried beneath a host of other ambitions and activities. And then I met Kay and Sarah.

Actually, it was my parents who met them first – newly-weds, with the words "Just Married" daubed on their boat. Wherever they cruised that summer Mum and Dad kept bumping into the happy couple, and after the holiday and the honeymoon were over the four of them decided to get together for a meal. I just happened to be around that evening and thus it was that I came to be introduced.

One thing leads to another. I forget how it came about, but one day I happened to mention my sailing ambitions to Sarah: "I want to cross the Atlantic," I said. They were words proclaiming an ambition rather than an intention but no sooner were they spoken than Sarah cried, "I've got it! There's someone you simply must meet."

A few days later Sarah phoned to suggest that we get together in the local pub. With her came her husband, Kay, and one of Kay's old school friends.

"This is Nick," they said. "He's a yacht delivery skipper." And with that, and some feeble excuse about feeding the neighbour's cat, they abandoned the two of us.

"Want a drink?" asked Nick. He was wearing a red nylon shirt and flared nylon trousers. His shabby jacket had lost its zipper and the man himself seemed to have mislaid his brush and comb. Frankly, I was not impressed, and I would have hit the road after the first half pint had it not been for Nick's next remark. "I'm looking for crew," he said, and then he explained that he was about to take a brand new Beneteau from the factory in France straight across the Atlantic to the Caribbean.

It transpired that Nick regularly delivered yachts to the Caribbean, but this was to be his last such voyage for the time being. When the job was done he planned to set off in his own yacht - and not, I learnt, for the first time. He and his parents had already circumnavigated the globe via Panama and South Africa, taking six years to complete the tour. This time Nick planned to do the job properly and go around South America, too, and this time he was going to "take it easy". If it took the rest of his life that would be about right, I gathered, for in what better way could one spend those three score years and ten?

I studied this 'old salt' closely. With his public school accent and the sartorial style of a tramp he cut a curious figure. I had sailed with enough incompetent captains and lascivious skippers to be wary of shipping with a stranger, but Nick seemed straightforward enough and his credentials were impeccable. The opportunity to cross the Atlantic with someone of his experience might never come again.

And so the deal was made and the die was cast. A few weeks later I packed my bags in preparation for what, at the time, was envisaged as no more than a brief diversion from my life's usual course.

That morning, early in April, I awoke to find a patch of warm, yellow light shining through the forehatch and brightening the cabin of the little boat which I called home. As I lay in my bunk the pool of sunshine danced around, moving from my face, where it warmed but dazzled me, to the mahogany planking of the bulkhead. To and fro it swayed as *Serenus* rocked gently on her moorings. I lay and drowsed, soaking up the peace of the beautiful morning, until the sound of footsteps on the jetty outside told me that I ought to be getting up. The manager of the boatyard beat its bounds each morning and I could just about set my watch by the time he passed by. It was a little before eight o'clock.

Serenus was moored on Birdham Pool, a marina dredged in the 1930's from the pond of an ancient tide mill. The mill itself was heading towards dereliction but there were places within the rambling edifice which still kept out most of the rain and the wind, and it was my good fortune to have been given the use of one such place for an artist's studio. Reminding myself of all the little jobs that had to be done before I set off that evening for France, I pushed away the blankets and scrambled out of bed.

Outside, the old jetties were still slippery with dew. Yellow lichens and velvety green moss sparkled as if bedecked with sequins. A few slippery steps on the wet planking took me onto the ancient sea wall whose chaotic rubble of rocks held captive the waters of the pond. This morning a faint breath of wind ruffled the surface of the mill pool, fragmenting the colourful image of 300 smart yachts which the sunshine had painted on the black water.

Turning away from the forest of aluminium masts and dazzling white paint, I looked out over the harbour. It was low water and acres of glistening mud stretched from the foot of the sea wall towards the copse on the opposite shore. Far away in the distance a line of hazy clouds hovered above the ridge of the South Downs, and I could just make out the Goodwood grandstand. Only a couple of miles away across the mudflats was Dell Quay, the place where I had spent so much of my childhood messing about in boats.

I stood a while, as I did each morning, and listened to the birds and to the curious sound which the water makes as it seeps down through the mud. As I gazed out over the harbour I felt certain that I would never be happier than here. Our trip across the Atlantic was scheduled to take at least four weeks, and I was sure that even in that short space of time I would be homesick for Birdham Pool. As for the mill itself, certainly I would never stay away long from this wonderful old building.

I knew and loved every corner of the half ruinous mill, for I had explored it all, from the sack hoist in the rafters of the bin-floor right down to the dark and muddy depths where the lower water wheel should have been. In the course of days and weeks spent in the County Record Office I had unearthed every written detail of its history, too. The things that I had learned brought the place alive in my mind. If I closed my eyes I could see the miller, in a jacket white with flour, and hear the stones roar as they spun around.

Now the mill stood silent. It was used only as a store, and although many passed it by few people came inside. Only one corner of the old place still breathed life, and this was the small room that the owner had kindly lent to me. My studio clung to the seaward side of the building. It was an after-thought in timber tacked onto the original brick shell, and it perched precariously above the mud and water on stout but worm-eaten stilts. From my lofty garret I could look down on the lock gates and when the tide allowed would see the yachts passing in and out of the mill pool. The opposite window overlooked the sea wall and my own boat, whilst a third gave me that marvellous view of the harbour. It was a perfect set up. No artist could have had a better studio and I looked forward to many more happy years of living and working at Birdham Pool. These were my thoughts as I set off for France, that evening in April 1989.

Finding crew for a delivery trip is not as easy as one might imagine. There are plenty of people who say that they would love cross the Atlantic, but when it comes down to it most of them are too busy. Nick had therefore been only too pleased when I asked if I could invite along a friend of mine - a young fellow named Andy. This would mean that he had only to find one other crew member.

Nick had travelled ahead of us to the Beneteau factory in St. Gilles Croix de Vie, and when Andy and I arrived we found that the boat was already on the water and the skipper aboard. Of the fourth crewman there was, however, no sign. "He dropped out," Nick explained casually. "No matter; we don't really need him. And there'll be all the more for us to eat."

To one whose experience of yachting was gained in cramped family-cruisers and mouldering old-gaffers, the Beneteau 50 which we were to sail across the Atlantic was absolutely palatial. Fitted into the ample hull were no less than four double cabins, each with its own private bathroom! I had never before seen such luxury in a boat. Intended expressly for the charter industry the yacht was, from that standpoint, quite wonderfully well appointed, but to the sailor who wants to venture offshore a surplus of 4-star accommodation is somewhat irrelevant. He has very different priorities. At the time I knew nothing of these either, but I was soon to learn.

Given a yacht which will hold a course without constant intervention from her crew, a man may cross the oceans all alone. Generally speaking, one can easily balance the sails of a boat so that she will behave herself when heading into the wind, but rare indeed is the yacht which can be persuaded to sail downwind in a straight line. For the steadying hand of a man the long-distance single-handed sailor must therefore substitute either an electronic pilot or a wind operated steering device. In the absence of any such aid the helm cannot be left unattended, and this gives rise to the need for extra hands.

Our Beneteau carried no self-steering gear, and so for the duration of the voyage her crew must take turns, day and night, to guide her over the waves. I began to see that this was not a 'pleasure cruise' I had embarked on - and I began to wonder whether we really could manage without a fourth crew member. Certainly, Nick, Andy, and I were all going to have to work our passage.

Nick had been contracted to deliver our yacht in pristine condition, without a mark to tell of the 4,000 mile passage through fair weather or foul, and with no sign of anyone having ever lived aboard her. In consequence, our preparations for the journey were mostly concerned with wrapping the fancy, white leather bunk cushions in sheets of polythene, covering the teak table tops, and placing aluminium foil on top of the cooker. From a navigational point of view our only preparations were to rig the sails and make sure that the anchor was attached to the boat.

According to Beneteau's representative it had taken the factory just three weeks to get the new boat from the drawing board to the water, and it seemed ironic that it would take at least twice as long to deliver her to her destination. No time was allowed us for any kind of a shakedown sail, and on the morning after our arrival in France, without any ceremony or formal hand over, we untied our mooring lines and set off for the open sea.

Andy and I had both crossed Biscay before, but in heavy, long-keeled yachts quite capable of riding out a gale at sea. Our present charge did not quite fit this bill as Nick was quick to explain when, two days out from France, we picked up the forecast for a blow. By the following afternoon the wind had risen to force six and was still strengthening. Prudence suggested that we put into La Coruña, on the north-west corner of Spain. Nick rapidly quashed some gung-ho muttering from Andy, who was in favour of pressing on, by informing us that he had already turned one Beneteau upside down off Cape Finisterre! He had no intention of repeating the experience. In the rising gale and driving rain we pressed southward, then, and by midnight we were safe within the port.

For three days, while the gale raged, we lay snug inside our bolt hole, enjoying the seafood tapas in traditional spit and sawdust taverns, and passing the wet and windy nights in jazz bars and rock'n'roll clubs. But after three days we were all itching to get underway again. Although the forecast was still bad the glass was rising and the sun shone. A discussion with some local seafarers reinforced our feelings about the notorious cape, which the Spanish know as the Costa del Muerte (or Coast of Death) but after a couple of beers in the sailing club we had talked ourselves into a quick trip across the bay to the adjacent harbour of El Ferrol.

"Is there a marina there?" we asked the local sailors. It was important to us that there was a marina, because our yacht did not carry a tender.

"Marina! Si, si!" the Spanish chorused in reply.

The sail across the bay was delightful, with the wind just for'ard of the beam and our yacht romping along, kicking up sheets of white spray. It was for days such as this that she was made. Arriving at El Ferrol we found a pretty harbour whose narrow entrance was overlooked by forts perched on rolling green hills. Once inside the estuary we looked about for the marina. On the southern side of the harbour a forest of grey cranes lined the quay, and there were warships moored alongside. We passed close by, and a little man in a big hat came running down to greet us.

"Donde está la marina?" we called out, but in reply he only waved his pistol angrily.

At the head of the bay we overhauled some racing dinghies, and again we made our enquiry. This time our question met with riotous laughter. The helmsman simply doubled up in the bottom of the boat, but his friend, when at last he was able to reply, said, "Allí", and pointed back down towards the warships.

Finally, having explored every inch of the estuary, we decided to tie up in what seemed to be the fishing port. It was all a bit of a puzzle but there was certainly no marina in El Ferrol. As we entered between the two walls of the port we spotted a club house with a floating quay.

"Well, this must be what they were talking about," I suggested. Certainly it was the most obvious place to moor, and so we went alongside at once and made fast our lines. It was only after we had made the boat fast that we troubled to look up at the crowd which was gathering on the quay. When we did, we found ourselves face to face with half a dozen bewildered Spanish soldiers, all armed with submachine guns and all with their weapons trained on us. Yes, it was the marina alright, or so they said, but clearly it was not open to visiting yachts.

We eventually found a berth alongside a dumb barge in a small, commercial dockyard. It was rather an incongruous spot for a well-bred charter boat to find herself but, as it soon transpired, no less unsuitable than the district was for her crew. The first bar that we walked into that evening seemed a little odd. The second did not feel right either. As I led the way into the third Nick said, "We're having a drink here whatever it's like."

Stepping inside the gloomy den we were at once confronted by two scantily clad girls who eyed us, and me in particular, with a mixture of contempt and embarrassment.

"Nick, are you sure you want a drink here?"

But he and Andy had already fled.

Stumbling around the red light district we came, at last, upon a regular establishment whose landlord happily plied us with wine and brandy until the very small hours of the morning. While we were there, I dug out the Spanish dictionary which Nick habitually carried in his pocket. I couldn't understand why our request for the marina had been so strangely received. The answer, once I had checked the words, was all too obvious. "Donde está la marina?" means "Where is the navy?"

An evening in the red light district may be an unusual starting point for romance, but nevertheless, it is from that evening in El Ferrol that Nick and I date our beginning. Thereafter my fate was sealed and my beloved Birdham Pool belonged, at once, to a previous lifetime. And henceforth Andy had to resign himself to the role of gooseberry, a role which was no easy one to play within the cramped confines of a yacht on the ocean.

On the 28th of April the gale finally moved north, away from Biscay. In the calm that it left behind we motored for the corner with our mainsail slatting, and we rounded awesome Finisterre in the shadow of the tall cliffs. From here our destination lay to the south-west – but of course, the sailor must pay little heed to the naïve instruction which the map, on its own, suggests. Rather, he must follow the guidance of the ocean. Unless he wants a hard time he must follow the ocean quite literally, in fact - and that was what we now did. The winds and currents in the North Atlantic blow around in a clockwise direction, and to head straight for the West Indies would have been to buck the system. Instead, we set course for the Canary Islands.

Now that we were properly underway life slipped smoothly into a steady routine - and this was absolutely necessary, for with only three of us to run the ship we needed the discipline of a timetable. Day in, day out, we followed a rota of three hour watches. The boat was so light and lively that she could not be left to manage by herself for even a moment, and the task of keeping her on track was quite taxing, especially at night. As the end of our stint drew near we would wait eagerly for our replacement and if, as often happened, the next man failed to appear at his appointed hour, waking him up was quite a business.

Standing for'ard of the wheel, but still clutching it, one would wait until the boat seemed to be holding a steady course in roughly the right direction. This having been achieved, the next thing was to dive below and burst into the offender's cabin, to shake him violently and turn on the light. Without waiting to see what effect this achieved, one then had to scurry back up on deck to rescue the boat from an impending gybe, or to haul her off the wind. And as often as not this performance had to be repeated two or three times before it achieved its end.

Naturally, our duties did not stop with managing the boat. Someone had to feed us and wash the dishes, and somebody had to keep track of our progress across the wide, empty chart. With so much to do there was no time to be bored.

As we made our way steadily south the days grew warmer and the ocean became an almost luminescent blue, until its colour seemed to me to be more beautiful than any precious gem. Above us the sky was a vivid cerulean, and where its rim met the sea there lay a necklace of soft clouds. We were at the centre of the world, and already the days spent shut away in Birdham Mill seemed a lifetime ago.

Two days away from the Canary Islands we sailed into a shoal of turtles which lay scattered about the water like giant lily pads. There must have been hundreds of them. There was hardly a breath of wind so that, in order to keep up with our schedule, we were obliged to motor. Thus, we found ourselves dodging amongst the serene reptiles. For an hour or two we wended our way carefully through the flock, until at last they began to thin. Eventually we thought that we had seen the last.

"'Should have picked one up," Andy said, and I nodded agreeably.

"Too late now." It was my turn to take the helm and I settled myself behind the wheel and leant back on the guard rail. This was all rather pleasant. If only there were just a little bit of wind so that we could shut down the infernal combustion engine...

At that moment my reverie was interrupted abruptly by a shout from Andy. "Turtle!" he cried, as if it were the first we had seen all day, and then he plunged over the side.

As we turned the boat around Nick and I watched our crazy shipmate's progress. Andy had already shown himself to be utterly fearless and completely insane. He perpetually climbed the mast for the fun of it, and he also enjoyed streaming along behind the boat on a line.

As Andy approached the turtle it raised its head, looking for all the world like a cartoon character. And then it dived. That seemed to be the end of the game. But, no; to our surprise the foolish creature surfaced again. Perhaps it had not had time to fill its lungs, or perhaps, having never seen a man before, it mistook Andy for something benign. With great presence of mind, Andy grabbed the turtle by its back flippers and propelled it towards the boat. As he clambered onto the transom, hauling his prize behind him, Nick and I leapt clear of the snapping beak.

"What are you going to do with that?" I asked innocently.

"Don't you want to paint a picture of it?" Andy replied. Only that morning I had done a little watercolour of a flying fish which had come aboard in the dark.

"I'm going to eat it, of course," continued Andy. His appetite was already legendary amongst us.

The turtle lay gloomily on the cockpit floor as we discussed its fate.

It looked most unhappy.

"Aren't turtles rare?" I asked. I now know, for a fact, that all turtle species are endangered.

"They aren't rare around here," came the retort.

Nick suggested that the animal might be a protected species, but the hunter affected a knowledgeable air.

"It's just a common turtle," he said, and with that he went below to fetch a knife from the galley.

We watched squeamishly as our savage companion rolled the turtle onto its back and sawed off its head. Soon the immaculate teak grating was blood-stained and gory.

We stewed the poor old turtle in red wine. It had the colour and texture of pork but it tasted more like beef. Judging from the size and weight of the beast we had expected to have enough meat to last several days, but in fact we ended up with barely two pounds.

"Not worth the trouble, really," said Andy, and much to our relief he decided that he would not bother catching any more turtles.

On the 5th of May, having spent the previous night ambling along its shore, we arrived at the southern tip of Gran Canaria. The sun rose to reveal a barren, rocky island decorated with hundreds of little white cubes. I was appalled and yet at the same time fascinated by the sight of these ugly little chalets and hotels clinging to the grey cliffs, and I shot almost a reel of film as we approached.

We made our way to the holiday village of Puerto Rico and moored the boat in a marina. Although it was still early in the season the adjacent beach was already thronged with tourists, and time-share salesmen, like hungry sharks, cruised amongst them picking off the weak. For us Gran Canaria was no more than a well-placed stepping stone. We took on fuel and water and then, the very next day, we set off across the Atlantic.

Leaving the last outpost of Europe behind him the yachtsman is once again faced with an apparent dilemma. Whether to take the "short cut" and head straight for the Caribbean – that is the question. Many do succumb to the temptation to follow the great circle route, but Nick reckoned he knew better.

"This breeze is just a local one," he said. "If we head west straight away we'll soon lose it."

Instead we must go down to the 18th parallel where, the captain assured us, we would pick up the genuine tradewind. For the first couple of days his crew seriously doubted the wisdom of the exercise. In heading south we fell straight into a band of absolute calm and our faith in Nick's discretion was sorely tested. Once again, we were obliged to motor.

I had imagined that the Atlantic Ocean was perpetually wild and tempestuous, and on that second day out was actually quite disappointed to find that it could be as flat as the old mill pond at home. Towards supper time, as the sun was setting, we switched off the engine, and for an hour or two we enjoyed the silence and solitude. Occasional swells heaved the horizon and rolled towards us, gently lifting the yacht as they passed beneath her. We peered down at our reflections, perfectly mirrored in the darkening water. We were all alone.

Or were we? As we sat and watched we realised that there was quite a bit of life close at hand. Just a few hundred feet from us a petrel rested on the ocean. Then, as we hung over the rail, we noticed tiny insects skating on the surface of the sea. I began to think of the world below and imagined the mountains, valleys, and plains which lay two miles under the water. I tried to picture the hidden world and the shoals of strange fish; the whales, and perhaps the giant kraken who might be swimming about down there. What did our boat look like to the shark as it floated across his sky?

Nick appeared at my side. "Do you know what these are?" he asked, and looking up I saw a number of curious, pink bubbles dotted about on the water.

"No. What are they?"

"Portuguese Men of War." He fetched a bucket and lowered it over the side in order to scoop up one of the odd creatures as it sailed past. We studied the translucent, pink balloon. It was clam shaped and gently corrugated by four or five spars. Beneath the air sac a mass of inky, mauve and blue streamers writhed up and down.

"Don't touch it," Nick warned. "They can give you a nasty sting." Indeed, the multiple stings inflicted by a Portuguese Man of War can kill. We watched with great respect as the deceptively beautiful organism tacked to and fro across our bucket.

"Look here, Skipper!" Andy bellowed from the opposite guardrail. "We're being over-taken by the bloody jelly fish."

He was right, and it was time to start the engine once again.

On May 13th, at 20° north, we finally picked up the wind which was to send us rolling on our way to the Caribbean. And roll we certainly did. Nick suggested that we sleep athwartships on our over-spacious double beds. It took me some time to get used to feeling myself tipped up and down like a see-saw, but I had to agree that it was more satisfactory than being forever thrown to and fro across the bunk. Andy gathered up all the spare cushions from the empty cabins and built himself a sort of padded coffin in which to sleep.

As our course took us still further south the days became hotter and our attitude to the individual watches changed. The once popular midday slot became an ordeal of survival beneath the fierce sun, which was now almost directly overhead. At this time of day we could feel the black stripes in the teak-laid cockpit seats burning our bare feet. The poor unfortunate whose turn it was to take the wheel needed to wear a shirt to keep his skin from burning, and in spite of dark glasses and a sun hat he would usually finish the session with an aching head. Oh, for a tree to sit beneath! When the boats reached the Caribbean they would be fitted with biminis, but there were no such luxuries for us.

Nor did we have the benefit of electronic aids to navigation. Every morning Nick took a couple of sun-sights with his sextant, and then, at midday, he did a noon-sight or meridian passage. As he plotted our progress across the empty chart he willingly shared with us the secrets of the navigator's trade, and hours which should properly have been spent catching up on our sleep were now spent fiddling with the sextant or thumbing through the almanac and the sight reduction tables.

Nick carefully went through the theory of celestial navigation with each of us in turn, explaining how, using the tables and the black art of trigonometry, we could calculate our distance from the sun's known position. Two circles around the sun's position, appearing as lines crossing on the chart, were then intersected by a third - our latitude. This was easily learnt, with the help of the almanac, by observing the precise time at which the sun achieved its zenith.

That was the theory, and I was surprised to discover how simple it all was. However, with my head full of declinations and degrees I found it easy to lose sight of what all the numbers actually represented. The addition and subtraction were straightforward but long-winded, and one tiny error in the calculation could put us hundreds of miles away from our true position.

The days rolled by. Our lives were running around a routine based on the clock, and yet time was no longer of any consequence. We had long ago forgotten how long we had been at sea - we seemed always to have been at sea - and five days or five weeks were all the same to us. Ironically, our navigation depended on a fastidious knowledge of the date and time, but although we carefully counted each second of the hour as we took our sights, the figures were as meaningless as a phone number.

Each evening we watched the sun fall behind the sea and saw the last rays painting the clouds. Even as we sat looking at them the clouds began to fade, the lurid pinks and the golden orange glow slipping away. While we ate our evening meal in the cockpit the sky grew pale and the first stars appeared. Darkness crept up from the sea behind us and the night took over.

As night fell, the heavens were suddenly decorated with a thousand bright stars printed in unfamiliar patterns above us. If the moon rose its sharp light would soon obscure the stars, but at other times we would lie in the cockpit and gaze up at the bewildering forest of beacons. The night sky was a chart. If we could only decipher the patterns and learn to recognise the stars we might steer by them, or at any rate use them in plotting our position.

Nick pointed out a few of his old friends. Aldebaran drew circles around the mast head and Antares led Scorpio slowly out of the sea. Gradually, I learnt to untangle some of the ancient constellations.

"Centaurus doesn't look much like a centaur," I said to Nick. I was lying with my head in his lap as he sat behind the wheel. "I'm beginning to recognise them," I said, "but I'll never remember them when we finish this crossing."

"You'll see them again soon," he answered. "There will be other crossings."

And so we began to plan an itinerary. The sort of itinerary that could take a lifetime to fulfil.

Nick, as I have mentioned, had already sailed around the world. He and his parents had followed the tradewinds to the Caribbean, had cut across the Americas at Panama, and had then let that steady, reliable wind ferry them right across the Pacific and the Indian Oceans. In short, they had sailed what is known as the milk run. Now, Nick wanted to do something different; he wanted to do the thing "properly". And then and there I found myself signing on for a voyage which would carry us far south, to the most remote tip of the American continent and to that notorious landmark, Cape Horn.

"Well, in fact, we might not actually round the Horn." But we would travel through the Beagle Channel, a channel carved by snow and hail and the vicious winds of the Southern Ocean. Named for the ship which first explored it - the same ship which carried Charles Darwin on his voyage of zoological discovery - the Beagle Channel threads its way through the fractured tail-bone of the spine of South America. It passes only a day's sail to the north of the actual islet of Cape Horn.

"So, in fact, we might as well nip down and take a trip around it, while we're there."

It was easy to make such plans while we lazed along under the glare of the tropical sun. They were nothing more than pipe dreams. The future was to hold many adventures, and most of them were to be wild diversions from the proper plan, yet still we would always hold fast to the dream: from now on, the Cape Horn peninsula was our lodestone.

The tradewinds continued to blow steadily, and the ocean rolled and danced around us. By now the never ending round of watch keeping was beginning to wear me out. Sleep was becoming an obsession, and yet I still found it difficult to relax in my bed. My subconscious seemed to think it hardly worth going to sleep for just three hours at a stretch, and as a result I was so exhausted that I would frequently nod off behind the wheel. Paradoxically, I often used to wake up in my bed believing that I had nodded off in the cockpit. Sometimes I would wake mumbling, "Where's the wheel?" and at other times I would go blundering up on deck believing that I must have abandoned the helm. The boys, of course, found all this hilarious.

Our cockpit was equipped with two wheels, side by side, in imitation of a racing yacht. In the early days Andy and I had developed the routine of "handing over", like pilots in an aircraft. "You have control," I would say, and long after the joke had worn thin Andy would wake me for my watch with the same words. One night, after I had twice woken with a start and a cry and reached out

for the wheel, Andy appeared in my cabin at the appointed hour.
"You have control," he said as he shook me. Then he handed me the unbolted, second wheel. Lucky for him that I did not just grab it and go back to sleep!

One afternoon while I sat at the helm and Nick sat nearby, our shipmate suddenly burst out of the cabin and began to search the horizon.
"Where's the ship?" he demanded.
As watch-keeper it was clearly my responsibility to keep a look-out, but we had seen no ships since Gran Canaria disappeared a fortnight earlier. Engrossed in conversation, neither Nick nor I had looked around for some time. Now I glanced over my shoulder. Sure enough there was a black and white dot creeping up on us from astern.
"It's over there," I said, affecting a casual air. "But how did you know....."
Too late. Andy had ducked back into the cabin. We heard him chatting on the radio. "Hello, Ship. This is the yacht that you were calling."
    We were now just three or four days out from Antigua, and now that our solitude had been broken we began to think of the landfall ahead.

At dawn on the 25th of May we took star-sights. This is a matter which requires careful timing; the horizon must be sharp, but if one waits until it is perfectly clear then the heavenly beacons will have faded away. The sights put us thirty miles from our destination and – sure enough – later that morning the faint grey outline of an island appeared on the horizon. We two novices felt like explorers discovering a new world!
    The ocean was shallower now, and with the proximity of land the erstwhile barren waters brought forth life. There had been very few birds out in the Atlantic, but now shearwaters and frigate birds went wheeling through the sky, and a white tropic bird shrieked to us as it circled the yacht. If there were birds then there must also be fish, we concluded.
    Ever since leaving La Coruña we had towed a fishing line, and Nick had promised that his ridiculous home-made lure, fabricated from a plastic bag, would one day bring a nice, fat dorado

to our table. However, the only fish we had seen over the past few weeks had been flying fish. Frightened at the approach of what they no doubt took to be the world's biggest tuna, these little creatures often hurled themselves into the air ahead of the Beneteau. In ones and twos and in vast flocks of perhaps a hundred fish, they skimmed and skipped over the water with their membranous fins outstretched. Gliding over the wave tops, using their asymmetrical tails as rudders, flying fish can travel for up to 200 yards. Flitting about just above the sea they look like huge, iridescent dragonflies. Flying fish are good eating but they are tiny. We wanted something that would fill the pot, but nothing had ever shown the least bit of interest in Nick's unorthodox fishing tackle.

My watch was over and I went below to rest. As I drifted in and out of wakefulness I suddenly became aware of conversation in the cockpit above me, and there was a distinctly fishy smell. Yes, that was it! It *was* the smell of a fish. We had hooked one at last. Wide awake now, I tried peering out through the nearby port-hole which opened into the cockpit at knee height.

"Let's see this fish," I said. "Pass it down to me."

"I don't think it will fit," answered Nick, and as he spoke an enormous fish head dangled before my eyes. I was on deck in a moment.

The fish was a Spanish mackerel, or wahoo, and it measured at least three feet. I had never seen such a big fish.

"It's huge!"

"No, not really," said Nick. "There are yellow-fin tuna almost as big as the boat out there."

He set to work, cleverly cutting all the flesh from either flank of the fish, leaving only the head and tail and the belly full of guts attached to the bones. There was enough meat for at least three meals. Anticipating a dinner ashore this night we bemoaned the fact that the fish had not turned up sooner.

As the day wore on the grey shape on the horizon grew larger and greener. Gradually we began to make out houses and trees on the gentle slopes. Then, as the sun sank towards the sea, we made our way steadily along Antigua's south-east coast; past an old sugar mill, past a white hotel, beneath Shirley Heights. Finally we arrived at the wave-carved columns - the so-called Pillars of Hercules - which mark the entrance to English Harbour. We motored past the end of a reef and entered the famous, historic port, the best hurricane hole in the Caribbean. To our left a small, derelict fort perched on a rocky promontory in the harbour mouth, whilst on our right hand side the trees rolled down the steep, hollow slope from Shirley Heights. Waves slapped gently onto a white sandy beach. Ahead of us was a forest of yachts gleaming in the evening light and - we had made it! We had crossed the broad and briny Atlantic Ocean.

Unabashed by the indifference of the resident yotties, for some of whom our achievement is a bi-annual event, we manoeuvred with the maximum of fuss into a vacant berth on the quay. The nearest watering hole was so near that we had to tie our mooring lines onto their veranda. 'Happy hour' was in full swing and reggae music thudded from the speakers.

After 19 days on the waves we stepped not so nimbly ashore and jostled our way to the bar. "Mine's a rum punch, Skipper," Andy cried, "In fact, I think you owe me a double!"

We lost track of Andy over the years, but when last we heard of him he had just been chosen as one of the skippers for the BT Global Challenge, a race which is run "the wrong way" around the world. I can picture the scene now, with the yacht surrounded by ice floes and smashing its way through 50 foot waves - and with Andy up there on the spreaders, laughing his head off or singing a sea shanty. He has all the credentials for the job.

2

ROUND THE WORLD OR ROUND THE BEND?

In which we prepare for a life all at sea

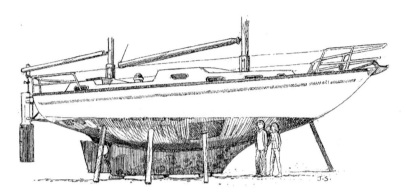

By a relay of float-planes and Boeings we made our way back home to England, and now dawned the moment of truth. Giddy with romance and without another care in the world I had happily thrown in my lot with Nick. Would I like to sail around the world? You bet I would; crossing oceans is addictive! Was I happy to head for Cape Horn? Sure! I was happy to go anywhere. The lure of the sea - and the charms of the skipper - had ensnared me utterly. But like so many sailors of yore I had signed on for the next voyage without seeing so much as a photograph of the vessel which would carry me.

All I knew of *Maamari* was that she was a 44 ft, centre-cockpit ketch built, sometime back in the early seventies, on Australia's Gold Coast. I suspect that had she turned out to be a rusting tin bath, with a towel for a sail, I would still have gone ahead - for by now the dream was firmly planted in my heart - yet, still, I was a little downcast when I finally saw the boat. Nick had warned me that she needed a bit of work, but I was not prepared for the sight which met my eyes on that first acquaintance.

Maamari had been laid up for the winter in a boatyard on Hayling Island. By the time we returned to England, in early June, most of the other yachts which must once have crowded around her were back in the water, and so I had a clear view of the hull. With a beautiful sweeping bow and curved, slightly raked transom the boat was certainly pretty - but even from the ground I could tell that she had been neglected. When I climbed the ladder to the decks, strewn with old wood and oily jerrycans, I began to have some reservations, and when I looked below I almost despaired.

Unwitting of my concern Nick hopped gaily down into the cabin. "Welcome aboard," he said. I climbed down into the saloon, a beamy, open space smelling of mildew and littered with grimy bits of engine. Beneath them, covering a patch of filthy, paint-splattered, plywood flooring, was an object which resembled a long-dead, furry animal but which Nick called a rug.

The paint on the deck head was nicotine stained and the cabin sides were lined with cork tiles dating to about 1972. The bunk cushions would have looked decrepit even in a third-class railway carriage, the galley was rotten, and something green and slimy was living in the fridge. A tacky cross-section of the Victory was nailed to the main bulkhead and to this, for some reason, I attached the brunt of my despair. "That thing will have to go."

Nick could not have cared less, one way or the other, about the decor. Of far greater concern to him were the major repairs and adaptations planned.

"There are one or two things to do," he repeated, with what seemed to me to be incredible good cheer, and then he proceeded to list them in full. The hull itself was heavily built and sound - no cause for alarm there - but from what I could gather just about everything else on the boat needed attention of one kind or another.

"I'm in the middle of rebuilding the engine. And then there's the rudder to see to. The rig is too short, so I mean to change that, and then there's the antifouling. We need a new prop. The fresh water pump is on the way out, too, and, as you can see, the bunk cushions..."

"But, Nick," I interrupted with a wail. "You said we had to be out of here before the autumn gales. You said we had to leave England in August."

"September at the very latest," he said.

"But that gives us only..." I began to count on my fingers.

"Six weeks, or maybe eight," said Nick. "We'll just have to do the best we can. As I always say, if you don't leave before you're ready, then you'll never leave - and one thing's for sure: I'm not spending another winter in England."

With so much to do it was difficult to know where to begin, but we decided that the priority should be to get *Maamari* afloat again. She was not yet habitable (in my opinion) and as things stood we would be spending half our time in the motor car, travelling to and from the yard. Once she was back on the water we could take her up the harbour to Birdham, where I kept my own little boat.

While I set to work on the hull, with scrapers and scrubbing brush, Nick began work on the engine. He had had the gear box reconditioned and the main problem now was the heat-exchanger housing. This was a hollow, metal box measuring about twelve by four by five inches. Its end faces were pitted beyond repair. We got a quotation from Volvo for the necessary part and then, when we had stopped laughing, we found someone who could make one up for £90. Even this seemed a little over the top, to me, but it was a £640 saving on the cost of the mass produced part.

The rudder was the next item on the list and the main problem here, Nick explained, was that it was hanging in the wrong place. All logic suggested that it ought to be at the back of the boat, to give the maximum advantage, but instead the design placed it at the end of the rather short "long keel", just beneath the mizzen. Technically, therefore, *Maamari* was a yawl.

"What I'd really like to do," Nick explained, "is to move the rudder to the back and extend the keel to meet it."

"What! And you still plan to be out of here this September?"

Even he was doubtful about achieving that deadline, and so we settled for increasing the size of the rudder. This would help somewhat in the solution of the problem, but it would also put an increased strain on the steering cables and was to cause us many a fearful moment in the years ahead.

The next chore was the antifouling. As a result of my labours, the ground beneath the boat was now speckled with chips of old paint and littered with the debris of some most impressive, inch long barnacles which I had discovered on the underside of the keel. We slapped on four coats of unbelievably expensive paint - the label said that it contained copper but I felt that, for the price we were paying, it ought to be liquid gold. Unfortunately the week we choose for the task turned out to be the windiest of that summer and so, inevitably, we coated ourselves and the gravel below with about twenty quid's worth of the precious stuff.

While all this was going on we were also trying to sort out the rig. Nick said that he had always been dissatisfied with *Maamari's* performance. What she needed was a taller rig, and so he had decided to add ten feet to the main mast. But - a new mast! Where were we going to get the money for that? The only answer was to extend the existing mast, and so each afternoon that week, as soon as the new coat of antifoul had been applied, we downed brushes, hopped into Nick's old banger, and set off on a tour of the adjacent boatyards. At the end of four days, having searched every yard for forty miles around, we had still failed to uncover any section which matched *Maamari's* Australian spars. It seemed that our plan would have to be scrapped. And then one day, while we were sitting in the cockpit, it suddenly dawned on us: *Maamari* had matching spars! The mizzen, massively oversized, was identical to the main. We could use the one to extend the other!

Now it only remained for us to find a new mizzen, and this proved to be quite simple. I almost fell over it as I was crossing the yard that same afternoon. The local yacht broker had possession of a brand new, 45 ft spar of the type used by Beneteau. Somehow, it had been damaged in transit and was crushed at either end, but there was a good 30 ft of spar which was clear of damage – and 30 ft was all we needed. The poor broker nearly collapsed when we had the nerve to offer him a mere fifty quid, but luck was on our side. "My loss will be your gain," he said graciously.

Our next problem was getting the three spars round to Emsworth and to the workshop where John Powell, designer and manufacturer of the very first aluminium spar, had agreed to do the necessary cutting and joining. Without further ado Nick strapped the 45 ft write-off directly onto the car roof, lashing it through the open windows. It stuck out by a good 15 ft at either end.

"Surely this can't be legal," I said, but Nick was unconcerned.

It was almost dark now and so, by way of a sop to my anxious entreaties, he lashed a torch to the after end of the mast. Negotiating the junctions was the most hair-raising part of the journey. The tip of the mast was already 12 ft out across the road before we could see around the corner, and I had visions of impaling a passing motorcyclist. We managed the eight mile expedition without incident and although we attracted plenty of attention from other road-users, two police cars passed us by as if we were invisible. Powells very kindly fetched the other two spars with their trailer.

Work aboard *Maamari* continued at a manic pace. During the day our attention was mostly given to the hull and its fittings, but the drab and dirty interior which had so depressed me on first acquaintance was not being neglected. Evenings and the occasional wet day would find me cleaning and painting the deck-head, or measuring the cushions, while Nick ran bits of wire here and there or tinkered with the engine. Days spent away from the yacht were rare - we begrudged even the odd few hours spent elsewhere - but when Nick's brother, Johnnie, wanted some help with the launch of his boat we naturally felt obliged to provide it.

The boat had just been lowered down into the water when someone craned his neck out over the quayside and said, "D'you wanna buy a carpet?"

"A carpet! We could do with a carpet for the saloon," I told Nick.

Encouraged by this news the salesman said, "Brand new carpet. Come and have a look."

We scaled the ladder set into the wall and followed him round to a Transit van, parked behind the nearby pub. Another man was sitting in the driving seat and the engine was still running. Our fellow had a half-empty pint pot in his hand.

"'Been doing a job the other side of town," he explained, "and there was one roll of carpet left over. The boss said we could flog it and split the dosh between the boys."

He threw open the back door of the van to reveal a couple of dozen rolls of wall-to-wall type carpet. "What colour d'you want?"

Just the job for a boat," Nick said, fingering the material.

"Yeah, durable," said the man. He began to look a bit fidgety and the driver revved his engine.

"I thought there was only one roll," I said in surprise.

"This lot's for a bank job."

"What?"

"It's for the NatWest."

We bought the carpet and without bothering to finish his drink the vendor dumped his glass on a nearby crate and leapt into the van. In a cloud of exhaust smoke it disappeared along the quay.

By now *Maamari* was just about ready for the water, and so we made our arrangements with the yard. The following morning a little toy road crane came trundling towards us and parked up in the shadow of the yacht.

"Is that the crane that lifted her out?" I asked Nick.

"No," was the curt reply.

I crossed my fingers and prayed that our luck would not run out today. The little crane extended its jib above us. The strops were put in place, the slack was taken up - and the alarm bell in the cab began to ring. *Maamari* was not even off the ground, yet!

The boat was right beside the sea wall. It was just a matter of lifting her up a few inches and swinging her around, but would the crane be strong enough? Would it be possible, or would we end up with the crane lying across our deck as it toppled onto the boat? The driver pressed the crane to try a little harder, and with a creak and a sigh *Maamari* left the ground. Without further ado the man swung her around and put her quickly into the sea.

Now that we were afloat it was immediately apparent that we would not be so for long, unless we moved. We had only a few inches to spare under the keel and the tide was falling. This was the big moment for the engine. Nick turned the key and it answered with a meaty roar. All was not quite as rosy as it seemed, however, for as we chugged along the newly-assembled machine spewed out all its cooling water into the bilge. We made our way gingerly up to Birdham Pool with the chief engineer all the while tipping jugfuls of cold water into the heat-exchanger.

Once in the marina *Maamari* started to attract attention, and the comments began. In theory the Pool is a private place, with no access to the public, but in practice every ambling rambler is led by curiosity to stroll along the peninsula quay which points towards the old tide mill. And *Maamari* was berthed right beside this quay, in the most public place of all. The most frequent and disconcerting remark directed to us was, "What happened?", but somebody even asked us if we had had a fire on board. We soon became reluctant, when faced with the usual barrage of questions, to mention the fact that we were just about to set off into the wide blue yonder. Even our nearest and dearest were sceptical about the self-imposed deadline, which was now just four weeks away.

Aware that we were pressed for time, John Powell and his right-hand man, Roger Plumb, took just two days to make up our new main mast. Using the hand crane, in the corner of the marina, we raised it into place that same evening. To the horror and disbelief of our friendly neighbourhood chandler we turned up on his doorstep, the following morning, demanding an instant supply of 12mm rigging wire and numerous Norseman terminals.

"Impossible!" he cried, but by lunchtime he had fulfilled our needs – wonderful man – and we had beaten him down to the lowest possible price.

I lost count of the number of times my friends and I hoisted Nick up and down the mast over the next couple of days. There were no winches fitted at this stage and so it was a tedious business. Nick generally likes to be aloft, but with the mast held in place only by bits of rope he felt most insecure. His mood improved gradually as those ropes were replaced, one by one, with the new rigging, but after two days spent cutting and swaging that strong, stiff wire his hands were scratched and cut and he ached all over.

I took time, in between back-breaking sessions at the halyards, to paint the name and a broad, blue stripe on either side of the boat. While I worked a Belgian woman from a visiting yacht came to stare. She was a strangely masculine creature, topless but flat-chested and bony. Between lips painted white with sunblock she smoked a fat cigar.

"Beautiful boat," the woman said at last, and my opinion of her changed in an instant. Here was someone who could see beyond the superficial chaos which, after all, was only skin deep. Perhaps it explained her own appearance.

As soon as the main mast was secure we decided to take a well earned break and pop over to Cowes. We would call it our trial sail. 1989 was a Fastnet year and the start of the Whitbread Race too, so that along with the usual flotilla of sails, skipping like butterflies over the Solent, there were assembled in those sheltered waters some of the finest racing yachts in the world. The royal yacht, *Britannia*, was there, and the river was as solid as a car park with one-design Sigmas, Contessas, and a host of other sporty yachts. Swallows and Sunbeams lay anchored in ranks in the river mouth, and Redwings flitted to and fro.

In spite of our incongruous appearance amongst this illustrious company not one derogatory remark was made as *Maamari* drifted up the river. The old mainsail barely reached to the spreaders of our new mast, and there was no mizzen because we had not yet had time to step that mast. The hanks on the old, diminutive headsail jammed on the new, fatter forestay, with the result that the sail hung in bags, like a scallop-edged curtain.

Actually, the fine folk of Cowes did not see this latter sight since, although the breeze was light, the ancient headsail tore asunder before we made it into the river. Perhaps the only remarkable thing is that we did not have to endure the embarrassment of being rescued when, just after the sail split, the steering cables also parted. While Nick fiddled with them, for the best part of an hour, I endeavoured to reach to and fro and so save us from drifting onto the Brambles Bank. The racing went on all around us and ships slid in and out of Southampton water, but – mercifully – no one paid us any mind. God help anyone who needs assistance during Cowes Week. Men have fallen overboard and drowned while their colleagues rush headlong past them, and all in pursuit of line honours and a tarnished silver rose bowl.

Back at Birdham we finally got the mizzen up, and the compliments began to flow. Yachting "experts" in general had been sceptical about Nick's plan to extend the mast, and certain wise men had shaken their heads and muttered in scorn. It had taken an act of courage and self-confidence on Nick's part to defy them. Now that the poles were both in place the full effect could be seen and even the worst doubters had to admit that it was a vast improvement over the original rig. It just looked right.

This was all well and good, but there was no use in sticking an extra ten feet on the rig unless we could find the sails to fit it. Buying brand new sails was out of the question, and so an hour was spent in phoning around all the local sailmakers to see whether anybody had anything of the right size. Having investigated various unsuitable wedges of rotten canvas we finally located what seemed like a perfect suit - in Cowes. Back we went - on the hydrofoil this time. By a strange coincidence it transpired that the sails had come from a Swan 38 which Nick had brought back from Turkey the previous year. He greeted them like a long lost pair of trousers: "There's that patch I sewed on in Gibraltar."

Both the main and the genoa were a perfect fit for our new spars, and since Nick knew the owner we got them for next to nothing. Somebody else kindly gave us an ancient, rather rotten spinnaker.

Now it only remained to sort out a roller-furling - and, of course, we were not about to part with a thousand pounds for a pukka, custom-made job. At this stage, indeed, we did not have a thousand pounds to our names. What we did have was two old bangers and my little yacht, *Serenus*. Getting rid of the cars would be no problem, but yachts are not so easily moved. If we did not find a buyer then we would we have no money in our pockets when we set off. Moreover, we would also have the burden, in our absence, of her mooring fees.

The deadline had now been firmly set for August 21st, and this was less than two weeks away. Life assumed an even more frantic pace as we hurried to be ready. Work aboard the boat began to take second place as we sought to tie up all the loose threads of our existence. Nick and I were freer of commitments than would be most intending voyagers, but still there were plenty of things to sort out.

Every now and then I would be called away from the task in hand to unlock *Serenus* and display her to idle enquirers, but no one seemed to be very interested in a cosy old wooden boat. Then, with just ten days to go to our deadline, along came a little family who fitted her perfectly.

"She's lovely," said the woman who, as far as I could gather, had never set foot in a boat before in her life. "Nice and snug. Nice and safe for the children."

And that evidently clinched the deal. Dad had been an expert dinghy sailor in his time but with admirable patience, and not a little cunning, he was luring his wife gently towards his first love. Meanwhile, we were rid of a potential burden and gained enough money to finance the first year of our travels.

With four days to go we were still without a furling system for the genoa when, as luck would have it, we came across an old, slightly bent length of Rotostay extrusion. It was being used as a ridge pole for an awning, but its owner was easily persuaded to swap it for a length of timber. Clutching our prize, we rushed off to the Rotostay factory. We asked them to bodge up something for us using the second-hand section, a new length, and our old, Australian roller-furling drum. Oh, and could we please have it in two days time?

Truly, the gods were working on our case. They must have been. Not only did Rotostay comply with our eccentric request, and within the specified time; they also jettisoned the old, warped extrusion and replaced it, at no extra cost, with a new piece! The assembled stay was delivered, in the evening, two days after our enquiry. We fitted it there and then, by torch light.

Finally, the morning of our departure dawned. At first light we were up and on the go, fitting cushion covers, newly made with the help of a friend, and frantically trying to stow several hundred pounds worth of tinned food. We missed the midday tide and by late afternoon Nick was still trying to find homes for two windsurfers - and a tandem, would you believe? - while I scurried around the mill gathering up a few of my favourite things. As day turned into night piles of our belongings still lay scattered all over the deck, and a mountain of books and clothes and stores blocked the saloon. Friends and relations arrived to see us off and were ignored as we struggled with the chaos. By two-thirty in the morning even my mother had given up and gone home and we, too, had had enough. Forsaking the mess in the cabin, we cast off our lines and locked ourselves out of the marina.

Any excitement or exhilaration that we might, or should, have felt over our departure was crushed by exhaustion and, for my part, by the despair which overwhelmed me when I surveyed the pile of junk in the middle of the saloon. It still had to be stowed - somehow, somewhere, sometime. Nick, in a zombie like trance, motored *Maamari* straight into a channel beacon, but fortunately no harm was done.

Leaving Chichester Harbour we headed west, gradually sorting ourselves out as we went. Dartmouth was our first port of call. It was dark when we arrived and as we opened the river-mouth the town looked like a cluster of jewels nestling in the dark cliffs. We knew that the following day was the day of the annual regatta, and we anticipated some difficulty in finding a place to anchor. To our surprise we found a prime position, in the middle of the river, right in the heart of the action.

Dartmouth is one of the most beautiful and quaint towns in southern England. Its position, on the steep side of a narrow valley, has afforded little opportunity to despoil it with encircling ring-roads and other hideous, modern contrivances. Raft-like ferries, able to carry no more than eight cars apiece, shunt to and fro across the stream - for mercifully there is no obscene concrete bridge spanning the gap.

This is a town dedicated to the river. An old fort guards its mouth, and an imposing, red-brick naval college overlooks the inner reach. On one side of the water, steam trains with shiny green and black paint roll in and out of the railway station, panting and gasping clouds of white steam. On the other side, in the town itself, cobbled streets crawl from one 'olde pubbe' to the next and then suddenly stride up the hillside, leaving their follower struggling for breath.

Now, in the time of our visit, the river was thronged by hundreds of craft, ranging from day-boats and four-berth cruisers through to ocean-going yachts like ours. Dominating, and lending a kind of picturesque grace and nostalgia to the scene, were a British Navy warship, dressed overall, and the "world's oldest sailing ship", *Maria Assumpta*. The square rigger's presence in this ancient port was especially suitable, and when she went alongside the cobbled quay, with its backdrop of charming period cottages, cameras all over the harbour were clicking. (A few years later, *Maria Assumpta* was wrecked, alas, and with the loss of two lives.)

As for the regatta itself, its agenda escapes my memory entirely for the highlight of the show, without doubt, was the aerial display given by the Red Arrows. This was what we had all come to see.

The Royal Air Force aerobatics team in their Hawks is unequalled throughout the world, and Dartmouth is said to be their favourite venue. One can easily see why this might be. At one moment we were gazing vaguely around the sky, saying to each other, "They should be along soon," and in the next split second nine red darts came screaming down the valley out of nowhere. They seemed to pass below the height of our mast.

Pulling back sharply the planes fanned out and up, into the sky, leaving three contrails each of red, white and blue. And then they were gone.

"Where have they gone?" we all muttered, peering around.

As if in answer, from the rim of the valley on either side, the red

Hawks screeched over us again – vrrip-vrrip-vrrip... They crossed the river in quick succession, and then all was silence again; and so the show went on.

Arrowheads and diamonds passed up into the bright blue firmament and fell away to leave those nine strand, patriotic patterns printed temporarily above us. Time and again the planes disappeared as suddenly as they had come and then reappeared just where we least expected them. Yes, we could well see why this river valley might be the pilots' favourite venue. They were having a wonderful time.

I am told that for photo fanatics the hill overlooking the town is the best place from which to view the action - and truly it must be quite something to look down on nine red planes flying in perfect formation above the yachts - but for the ultimate in spectator thrills nothing beats a jet flying a barrel roll over your mast head. Or was it through the rigging? At least two of them passed behind the funnel of the warship – in opposite directions, at the same time - and I have a photograph to prove it.

After the drama of the air show the evening's fireworks display on the quayside was a paltry affair - but those of us who were viewing it from the water managed to make the event twice as exciting by gathering in our dinghies just beneath the podium. Orange sparks flew off into the night and turned to liquid fire in the black water below. Above the vrrip, screech, whirr and tac-tac-tac of the rockets I distinctly heard the hiss of flames hitting the water, and the light thud of sticks falling back.

"They're falling back on us," I said to Nick, but he, as usual, was unconcerned.

I kept my head down - not an easy thing to do when the sky is full of glorious green and red meteorite showers, but I had a vision of getting a rocket stick in the eye. In the morning I found three burnt-out fireworks in our dinghy.

From Dartmouth we moved on, out to the Scilly Isles – but why, you may ask, were we bothering with these native lumps of rock when the wide world beckoned? Were we not bound for Cape Horn?

Cape Horn, the pre-eminent symbol of seamanship, and the sailor's Everest. The early explorers named this region Tierra del Fuego - the land of fire - but rightly it should have been called the land of ice and fog and tempestuous storms. What made us think that we were fit to sail here? And what images did the name conjure up in our minds?

Gaunt, grey, cold-hearted mountains rising up out of a cruel sea. Stern, grey skies, aloof and angry, pressing down on a vengeful land. The wind, a mad devil shrieking with insane glee as it swoops down the barren cliffs. And below the pitiless skies, in a narrow corridor between the towering mountains, a winding path which leads from one ocean to another. A sad place. A cold, grey place. I found it impossible to imagine the Straits of Magellan bathed in sunshine. But sad, grey, cold, wuthering places have their own melancholy beauty.

We also pictured the man himself; the fearless, determined explorer, Magellan. In him the cold, cruel sea and the mad wind found their match. Relentless as they, he drove his ships on - unheeding of the pleas and the mutinous grumblings of his suffering, frightened men - and fought his way through ice and storms and blizzards into the Pacific. The summer of 1520 was a particularly bad one in the Southern Ocean, it would seem. Ice hung all over the ships' rigging and lay in sheets on their decks. One man actually lost his nose. It was frostbitten and when he blew it, it came off in his hand.

Now, why, in the name of heaven, did we want to go to this place, above all others? Some sort of prove-yourself masochism? No, not at all. In fact, I believe that those of us who interest ourselves in this kind of remote place suffer from an inability to realise, at a *physical* level, the misery involved in being painfully cold - or, for that matter, unbearably hot, tired, or thirsty. We are *drawn* to these places - by what, I cannot really say - and we build in our minds, and more especially in our hearts, an image which I can only describe, somewhat feebly, as romantic.

Fog is dangerous; ice floes more so. A combination of the two contains the greatest potential for tragedy. But we dismissed such images and pictured *Maamari* determinedly fighting her way through the strait; our valiant little craft defying the might of those grey cliffs; braving the devilish williwaws which tear down from on high; tip-toeing, like a mouse, along the grey corridor, beneath the sad, steely, louring clouds.

Besides the melodrama, we also pictured scenery incomparably grand. The mountains with their peaks hidden by cloud; the glaciers with their snouts in the sea; the sheer cliffs beneath which we would anchor. Of course, it is not possible to anchor beneath sheer cliffs, because the water is too deep, but we had some vague notion of tying up to the shore, or perhaps to the kelp forests which are marked on the charts. We saw ourselves accompanied by dolphins and seals while watching penguins bob up and down on the waves. And in the evening the aurora australis would paint fantastic, coloured patterns in the sky to the south.

After we had fought our way through the straits, then we would turn our faces again towards the sun and would make our way up the backbone of South America. Running northwards from the islet of Cape Horn is a vast archipelago arranged like so many vertebrae in the continent's spinal column. Like a worm eating into a ship's keel the sea has chewed the land, riddling it with narrow channels, and we dreamt of exploring the labyrinth.

Yes, we were bound for Cape Horn - or, at any rate, Patagonia. In as much as we had a destination, this indeed was it. But we were in no great hurry, and even this goal was viewed as little more than a staging post on our journey, for we meant to journey indefinitely. Truly, it was not a place but a *lifestyle* which we were setting forth to find. There was no desire to go dashing around the globe just for the sake of ticking it off on a list of achievements. Just as the true craftsman enjoys the act of creation quite as much as he enjoys the end product, so each step of our journey would be an experience cherished in its own right. We were not content with the idea of merely travelling from A to B. We were voyaging for the sake of voyaging. On our passage to the Caribbean I had caught a glimpse of the life which Nick knew well - the life of the idle wayfarer, carried along on the waves - and now I was abandoning the somewhat uncertain existence of an artist for the still more precarious one of an ocean-going hobo.

We were heading for Cape Horn, and we would never let go of that goal until we reached it, but our wanderings would be more like those of the honey bee than the crow. There was plenty of time for detours. In fact, our first detour had already been thrust upon us: the money which we had got by the sale of my little boat would not last us long, and so we needed to stop and earn some more. The most obvious place for us to do that was amongst the charter yachts in the Caribbean, and so our travels must begin by retracing our previous journey. This time, however, we could move at our own pace - or so the theory went.

But why start with the mundane? Why, with the world our oyster, did we want to bother visiting Devon and the Scillies? Well, in reality the seafarer seldom can travel at his own pace; he is bound to follow the rhythms of the season, and the season was moving on. Winter drew nigh. We were determined that, if the worst should come to the worst and the weather strike us hard in Biscay, then at least we would not become embayed. Miles to the west were money in the bank - and hence our sudden interest in the Scilly Isles.

For now, at any rate, the summer weather held, and we drifted lazily along through the glassy water under main and spinnaker. We tossed the mackerel line over the side and immediately hooked four fine specimens. Within half an hour there were nine in the bucket and, not wishing to be held guilty of wanton destruction, we forced ourselves to call a halt. Three more fish ensnared themselves while I was streaming the line to sort out its tangles, so that the final count was twelve. It is always the same story with mackerel: all or nothing. They are either there in their hundreds, or they are not.

The spinnaker collapsed in on itself, a bundle of shiny, yellow tissue, and a fulmar swam past and overtook us. This time we need not start the motor; there was no schedule, except the one set by the weather gods. Razorbills bobbed about in the distance on the mirror-flat surface. A while later I saw some fins - or perhaps they were flippers? They circled in the water, but not as a shark checking out its prey; this was a tight circle, made by floppy fins - or flippers. Was it a turtle, performing some strange revolution?

We drifted towards the creature, and I now saw what looked like the disembodied head of a dolphin eyeing us eerily from just below the water. A spastic dolphin! That was how it struck me at first. We looked through our array of textbooks and discovered that the animal was actually a sunfish.

Except for the fish and the birds we had the sea to ourselves, but not the sky. The Ministry of Defence were doing strange things in the sky and the most peculiar of their creations was even more strange than the sunfish. It was some kind of unmanned missile; a cigarette-shaped thing which flew past with a low whistle in distant pursuit of a four-engined jet. This beast made several passes over and around us during the course of an hour and leant a sinister air to an otherwise glorious afternoon. I have since been told that it was probably a prototype Scod missile.

We reached the Scilly Isles the following day and anchored in Hugh Town, on the island of St Mary's. It was a pretty place, but pretty windy too; we woke one morning to find that the hook had dragged. Meanwhile, life aboard ship was running to a course which I soon discovered to be the norm. The electric pump which raised our fresh water from the tanks had given up the ghost. By astonishing good fortune we found, in one of the island's few, ill-stocked shops, a little foot operated water pump. For want of anything better, we fitted it as a temporary measure. Seven years later it was still our only link with the water supply and the pressure system remained unrepaired.

On the 11th of September we finally took our leave of England's shores, discovering at the moment of our intended departure that the anchor winch, too, had packed up. Now, when it comes to anchoring, weight is the chief requisite. Better an engine block, or some other lump of iron, than a cunningly engineered but all too dainty creation. To this end Nick had chosen for our main anchor an 80lb CQR. More weight was added to this substantial mass by the use of half inch diameter chain, and 15 metres of this chain now lay along the sandy bottom of Hugh Town harbour. (I apologise for mixing my measures, but our chain and anchor are sized according to the imperial system, whereas we lay the gear out according to the advice given by our modern-minded echo-sounder.) Altogether, we were now faced with lifting around 200lbs (or 90kgs) of iron by hand.

Electric anchor winches are a wonderful boon while they are working, but they are far too prone to failure. Not for the last time was I to curse the contrivance. By running a line back to one of the genoa winches we managed to lift the gear and haul it aboard, but it took us more than an hour. And then we were off. We were leaving England. At last.

During the two short months of our frantic preparations I kept a diary, and when I read through it now and recall the chaos of those days I find myself thinking of Donald Crowhurst, whose ill-fated voyage began along similar lines. Like him we were pressed for time and like him we set off with much still to be done, but there was one fundamental difference: whilst Crowhurst was an inexperienced sailor, leaving to race around the world in a new, untried vessel, we were setting off in a boat which had already circumnavigated. Beneath the peeling paint was a seaworthy ship. She had been proven. And so, too, had her skipper.

Maamari was far from being a dream yacht when we left, but she was ready enough and her crew were more than ready. Even so, I cannot pretend that I did not, on the day of our departure, have any fears or misgivings. It was beneath a grey and oppressive sky that we headed south from the Scillies. The air was damp and cold. The wind was light and not in our favour. Until this moment thoughts of our journey had filled me only with impatient excitement, but now I was suffused with a kind of dull panic. That ever watchful sentry, the Bishop Rock, faded slowly into the murky haze and with it went Merry England with her green and not-unpleasant shores. The despair which suddenly washed over me, and the strange dread, imprisoned like a coiled spring just beneath my breath - these were not concrete things that I could grasp or explain. All that I could identify was a seemingly inexplicable depression and an anxiety which made me restless. Sleep did not come easily on that first night at sea.

Sleep is, in fact, one of the greatest problems when sailing short-handed and this I already knew from our recent Atlantic crossing aboard the Beneteau. Then, there had been three of us. Now, we were only two. Concern about how we would cope was undoubtedly one thread in the knot of my muddled thoughts, and so it was ironic that the concern should help to bring about exactly that which I feared.

Maamari differed from the delivery yacht in many respects, but one of the most crucial was that she could be left to take care of herself. She had a self-steering system. The most versatile and least reliable self-steering system is the auto-pilot, an electronic apparatus into which one simply programmes one's intended course. Far more appropriate to a cruising yacht are mechanical systems which steer the boat according to the wind's command, and ours was one such – a fantastically Heath Robinson gadget consisting, in essence, of a wind-vane perched above an auxiliary rudder.

When the helmsman was at the wheel and steering the boat by hand, the self-steering rudder was lashed amidships. But with the main rudder lashed and the wind-vane in charge, this second rudder did the work. The man on watch had merely to align the wind vane so that it would be luffed (that is, so that its leading edge would be facing into the wind) when the vessel was pointing in the hoped-for direction. This having been done, the vane would then be blown over to one side or the other when the boat veered or luffed away from the intended course. A wonderful bodgery of rods and linkages connected the wind-vane to a trim-tab, on the back of the rudder below, so moving it, and so steering the boat.

On board the Beneteau I had felt imprisoned on watch; for all the freedom that I had, I might as well have been manacled to the wheel. The self-steering rudder relieved us of the need to be perpetually at the helm – but someone still had to be about, tending the sails and fiddling with the vane when need be, and keeping track of our progress across the featureless sea. Moreover, we had to keep a constant look-out for other traffic.

For the time being autumn hovered, like my fears, just beyond our sight. The lazy dog-days of summer had slipped away, but the sun seemed reluctant to take his leave of us. *Maamari*, too, was slipping along quietly. This was not the Biscay that we knew and dreaded. Perhaps, if we tiptoed thus, we might even slide unobserved past the angry god of the Bay. I pictured him in my imagination: a troll-like creature raised to wrath by anyone who dare go trippetytrapping over his head. Right now he seemed to be taking a nap.

Four days out from England, on the 15th September, we sighted the high cliffs of Northern Spain, just ten miles away in the haze. We pressed on for the cape, ever watchful now, for this corner is one of the busiest shipping lanes in the world. At this rate it looked as if we might be round and snugly tucked up in a sheltered harbour by breakfast time next morning. However, if we really thought that we were home and dry and free from the clutches of The Bay, then we had another think coming.

That evening the wind died altogether, and the coast of Spain disappeared into a murky haze. By nightfall we were wrapped in a thick, damp, blanket of fog. While Nick slept I took the first watch, peering over the rim of the sprayhood and straining my eyes into the void to try to catch sight of a ship bearing down on us. All around us I could hear the deep reverberations of engines and the noise of fog horns. At times the sound seemed to come from somewhere above us. I tried peering a little higher above the imaginary horizon but still saw nothing. Was there any point in sounding our own, reedy horn? It was so feeble that the officers on watch would hardly be likely to hear it from the cosy sanctuary of a ship's bridge. I could only pray that they had their eyes glued to the radar and that we showed up on the screen. From some points of view it was not such a bad idea for us to be sitting in a crowded shipping lane. At least they would be looking for each other.

The radar! Of course! I hurried below to switch it on, cursing myself for my stupidity in having overlooked its aid. I had never used a radar before. A flick of the switch and... nothing. When I woke Nick, he said that it was the first time that he had sailed *Maamari* in fog and the first time, too, that the radar had ever failed. Mere coincidence or the work of Biscay's troll? There was no doubt in my mind which was to blame.

I started the engine, to give us some last minute, last second manoeuvrability, but as I resumed my stance, peering out over the sprayhood, it occurred to me that this and my intensive watch keeping were a vain effort. The fog was so thick that from time to time I lost sight of our own bow. Really I might as well have gone below and read a book or slept.

By nine the following morning the fog was beginning to lift. The first vessel I saw was a big cargo ship about a mile away to seaward. I could not hear his engines, which suggests that he was further away than the ones who had passed in the night. The next thing to appear out of the murk was a dirty great box, huge and grey, bearing down on us from ahead. I altered course smartly and by almost 90°, but it still passed close enough for me to see two men up in the bridge and to note that they were wearing white T-shirts. Four minutes after appearing, the ship had disappeared into the gloom astern of us.

For the time being we pressed on under engine, but by midday the fog had been burnt off, the sun was shining down, and a steady breeze had arisen. True, it was blowing from the west, but at least it gave us something to play with and we began a lovely beat, thrashing along the coast about four miles off. Ahead of us we could make out four headlands, the last of which was Finisterre, just 16 miles distant. Things looked good - but still the evil troll had not finished with us. First, the new genoa split along a line of stitching. Then, during the evening, the wind increased. By nightfall we were beating into a good force seven.

As the wind rose we had taken down the mainsail, leaving *Maamari* to do the best she could under mizzen and her old, well-reefed genoa. Close-hauled in the lumpy, green-grey waves the boat reared and bucked, her bow now reaching for the sky and then crashing down into the trough beyond. Her progress was like that of a drunken cripple as she staggered along, picking up way for a moment only to lose it abruptly as she slammed into the wall of the next big wave. Solid water swept the decks. All night long we tacked to and fro in the shipping lane off Finisterre, keeping the sentinel light in view, keeping good watch for the ships and managing, just barely, to keep from losing ground.

The following morning the wind began to abate, and by eleven we had the main back up and were able to claw our way steadily passed the cape. We were finally free of Biscay.

The weather along the Iberian coast is fickle and unpredictable and can be absolutely awful at any time of the year. Autumn, with its inevitable savage gales, was snapping at our heels and we knew that we must hurry along; but betwixt the gales come equally halcyon days, and it was our good fortune to enjoy many of these as we trickled south. Our trials on the remainder of this leg of the journey seldom came from the weather.

Having crossed the Bay we gave ourselves a short holiday in Muros, a fishing village which hides in a ria just south of Cape Finisterre. From there we decided to make for the river Vigo, thirty miles further on. The trip should have been an easy one - and it would have been if we had not got a rope around the prop.

The day was warm. The sky was blue. But the forecast was for more fog. Having drifted along idly all morning we eventually decided to crank up the iron stays'l. All went well for a couple of hours and then the steady rattle and roar of the beast was interrupted by a loud thud from beneath our feet. We knew at once what had happened and Nick stopped the engine.

Since Nick could not swim it fell to me to investigate the matter, and so I hauled on my wetsuit and donned a harness. In spite of the suit the water was icy, and when I stuck my head below the waves the skull-shrinking cold took my breath away. The boat rolled and lunged in the light swell. Now, how was I going to get down there, under the hull, without being brained by a 16 tonne sledgehammer? The water was quite clear and even without diving right under the boat I could see the tangle of colourful net which had somehow managed to knot itself in a cat's cradle around the propeller. An hour was wasted in trying to hack it away with a kitchen knife lashed to the end of a deck broom, and then I gave up.

Experimenting with the engine, Nick found that it could still provide some propulsion and so we motored on, at barely one knot. It was not until we reached Vigo, at two in the morning, that we discovered that the gears would not disengage. Consequently, our arrival into the crowded marina was a somewhat lively affair and we were rather glad to have the cover of darkness.

The next day a Norwegian yachtsman, hearing of our plight, kindly lent us a vicious tool which he called his boat hook. The item had a large, curved knife in place of the usual hook and another one, sharp and pointed as a dagger, where it ought to have had a knobbed prong. With this offensive weapon we were able to clear the fouled propeller from the comfort of the jetty and in the course of an hour we amassed two carrier bagfuls of assorted nylon string and net.

Immediate concerns having been resolved, we now turned to general maintenance. First on the agenda was the radar, and Nick quickly traced its demise to a fault in the wiring. Next he gave his attention to the engine. This still needed regular drinks of cold water to replenish the stuff it was spewing into the bilge, but what it really required was a new cylinder head gasket. The engineer got to work. Within a couple of days the job was finished and he was feeling pretty pleased with himself - but the same could not be said for me; I had managed to pick up salmonella and spent two miserable days wishing and waiting for death. The doctor at the hospital whence I was carried by Nick assured me that I would be in bed for another two weeks yet. However, on the third day I recovered sufficiently to stand on my feet and so we were able to leave.

We set sail for Porto. Or rather, to be more precise, with Porto our destination, we motored off down the river in a flat calm. We had hardly lost sight of the marina when the engine began to fade intermittently. Dirty fuel was the diagnosis, but a minute later there came a loud bang and the engine stopped abruptly. A cloud of smoke rushed up out of the cabin.

In disbelief, we stared at the temperature gauge. We were used to watching that particular needle, for it told us when the beast needed another glass of water, yet on this occasion the needle was as low as we had ever seen it. What could have happened?

Hastily unfurling the genoa, we turned the boat around and struggled back upstream. Cangas, on the opposite shore of the river, was closer at hand than Vigo. On the last, faint breaths of a feeble evening breeze we limped into the harbour and dropped the hook.

Our worst fears were realised: the engine had seized. Only that morning Nick had filled the sump with oil but in the space of scarcely half an hour the machine had managed to shed ten pints of this, its lifeblood. How had it happened, we asked ourselves? How could an engine lose ten pints of oil in thirty minutes? Nick traced the leak to a tiny, pin-prick of a hole in a copper feed pipe.

There was no point in wringing our hands or crying over spilt oil. The only thing to do was to get on and fix things up again. We took the offending copper pipe ashore with us that same evening. The first male we encountered was accosted and asked if he knew the whereabouts of a welder. Even in the midst of our grave misfortune luck was still with us, for not only did this chap happen to know the whereabouts of the man we needed; he actually took us there, straight away, in his car. The pipe was re-soldered while we waited - but that was the easy bit. Now we had to mend the engine itself.

Having come to terms with the disaster we set about devising a means of lifting three hundred weight of engine out of the bilge and into the cabin, so that Nick could work on it. Again.

First we took down the plywood wall which divided the engine room from the adjacent passage. Then we fastened pulley blocks to the beams above the engine and by a system of tackles were able to raise it, inch by inch, out of its hole. This took a whole day to achieve. For the ensuing week the engine blocked the passage and obstructed the galley, so that our only access to the aft cabin was by way of the cockpit. For meals we were forced to go out on the town. We bore the hardship bravely and soon became well known figures in the local bar.

Dismantling the engine from the sump up, Nick found that the white-metal shells of the crankshaft bearings had melted. The steel beneath them was also damaged. Facilities in Cangas being strictly limited, Nick tucked the crankshaft under his arm and we hopped on board the ferry to Vigo. There, we were able to get the crankshaft reground. We bought new shells, and Nick fitted them - and less than two weeks after the misadventure we were shipshape once again and ready to depart.

It was mid October now and our sail along the coast to Porto was a chilly one. Though the sun shone from a clear sky, it could not induce us to pull off our jackets and woolly hats.

Nick's father had spent quite a bit of time in the town of Porto and had made it sound quite delightful - hence it came to be on the itinerary - but when we reached the river mouth we were quite alarmed by what we found. Great, white-capped waves were rolling and breaking across the greater part of the narrow entrance.

With hearts in mouths we crept cautiously forward, hugging a small rocky wall which juts out into the sea on the northern side of the river-mouth, to port. The wall looked rather unfriendly, and I imagined rocks just beneath the water's surface, but the rollers confirmed the information already gleaned from the chart: the water to the south was choked with sandbanks. The stream was sluicing out at about four knots and sending us all over the place, so that I needed full power just to keep the boat inching forward in a straight line.

"Closer!" Someone in uniform was shouting to us from a little white hut on the wall. "Get away from the shoal. Come closer to the wall."

The words were in Portuguese, but the gestures were unmistakable and the man looked as if he knew what he was talking about. Later we heard that a French yacht had gone down in the entrance just a few weeks earlier.

Porto was quite as charming as Nick's father had portrayed it. It is a town steeped in history of a unique flavour. Blended with the native culture of Portugal are influences from England - for, indeed, it was the English who established the port wine cellars which are the town's raison d'être. Dominating the town is an old bridge – a magnificent structure, wrought in iron and spanning the narrow valley at two levels. Having safely negotiated the river's entrance we wound our way upstream until we discovered this great arch and found a handful of yachts lying alongside the adjacent quay.

By now the sun had set, but streetlights on the quay cast down a familiar putrid orange glow. We got ready our lines and fenders and then, announcing our arrival with the thud of sea-boots on the deck, made fast to the outermost yacht. A figure appeared in silhouette in the cockpit of the moored vessel, and from the tone of his greeting we gathered that the gentleman would have preferred that we had not turned up.
"I'm leaving at first light," he warned, seeming to hope that the news might send us scurrying away to who knew where. He was one of that strange, irrational breed who have no qualms about mooring alongside another boat but who are offended when someone else turns up to do just the same thing. There was nowhere else to go, and so we resigned ourselves to rising early.

As it turned out we could have lain in bed till midday, or the next day, or the following week, for during that entire time no one was able to get out of Porto by sea. Under cover of the night, the wind got up. It was not blowing a hooley - it was probably not blowing more than force six - but it was blowing straight onshore. When we cycled down to the entrance on our tandem, we found the river-mouth completely cordoned off by rollers taller than a man. Signals had been hoisted outside the little hut on the wall, to tell any would-be visitors or departing guests that the entrance was closed, but one would have needed to be a half blind half-wit even to have considered the matter.

While others fretted, Nick and I took advantage of our official stormbound status and spent the week sampling late-bottled vintage port. On the hillside just across the river there were fourteen different "caves" from which to choose, and when we tired of visiting these there was the town itself to explore. Porto was our kind of place and we could have easily have stayed for a month. Sometimes, indeed, I wondered if we would, for the season was marching on and rumour was circulating amongst the yachtsmen of a boat which had once put in for a night and been stormbound all winter.

On the 24th of October the weather cleared, so enabling us all to escape from the river. We turned south, with the chart for Lisbon spread before us. By now most of our teething troubles aboard ship had been resolved and this little hop looked like being an easy one.

Outside the river we found that instead of merely shifting a few points, or easing up a little, the wind had faded to a feeble whisper. It seemed unable even to decide upon a direction from which to sigh. All afternoon and throughout the night we gybed to and fro and round about.

The next day the wind continued fickle and light, but that night's shipping forecast gave news of a gale to come. Soon the calms had given way to a light south-easterly and before daybreak on the 26th the wind had risen to about force five. It was a pity that fate could not send us a northerly, but still we preferred this thrash to windward over the frustrating calms.

Evening found us south of Cabo Raso, and having got this far we gaily assumed that we would be spending most of the night in port. The wind had never reached the threatened gale force and it now began to moderate. At eleven, with the lights of Lisbon on the near horizon, I went below for a kip.

I seemed hardly to have lain down before *Maamari* was thrown onto her beam ends. I struggled back out of the aft cabin. Nick was fighting to drop the mizzen whilst also trying to keep the boat off the wind (so that the sails wouldn't flog and split). The main had already been stowed – it is not needed in anything above a force five, and so we had not used it at all that day - and the skipper had managed to reduce the genoa so that it was now only a tiny pocket handkerchief.

I grabbed the wheel. Rain flew past us horizontally and seeped around the edges of the oilskin I had scarcely had time to fasten. Lightning slashed jagged scars across the sky. Illuminated by the flashes the Atlantic looked like a field furrowed all over by rows of white foam.

Nick put the wind strength at 60 knots, but there was little danger because it was blowing us offshore. *Maamari* ran before the storm. By midnight we had been driven far out to sea and there, when the wind's first fury had passed, we tacked to and fro, fighting to hold our ground. Whenever the wind allowed, we hoisted the mizzen and unfurled a little bit more of the genoa, but the gale kept returning to assault us again. Volleys of hail rattled like machine-gun fire on the decks, and rain, like a sniper's bullets, stung our cheeks.

The sun eventually rose to shed a wan yellow and pink light over the aftermath of the storm. Battered cumulus straggled across the sky, and two prisms of colour hung down side by side, like battle flags, from the belligerent steely clouds to the north. The tyrant was moving away. Like the shocked survivors of a blitz, we gathered ourselves together and moved quietly back towards the coast.

In the entrance to the Rio Tagus we came upon the noble *Sagres*, pride of the Portuguese nation and in particular of her navy. The sailing ship had evidently passed the night at sea too - and a fearful night it must have been with 60 knots tearing through all that top-hamper. Now, in the calm, she was setting all sail in order to create a stylish arrival up-river in the city. We followed in the lady's wake as headsails, fore-course and main-course, then lower and upper topsails were all spread out. With that lot pulling her along, the ship left us as surely as if we had been anchored.

On we went, up the River Tagus, looking for a place to moor. The first two marinas were full and we were turned away. As we entered the third tiny haven the engine quit, but somehow we managed to grab hold of a buoy and get a line ashore. It was midday but, exhausted by the previous night's activities, we fell straight into bed and slept soundly through the afternoon.

Sometime after dark I awoke with a sudden start. Something - some animal - was sitting on my chest! Was I dreaming? Still barely awake, I let out a yelp of alarm - and as I did, I felt the creature flee down to my feet.

"A rat! Nick, there's a rat in the bed."

"Go back to sleep," mumbled Nick. "You must have been having a nightmare."

Instead, I turned on the light. And there, cowering at the foot of the bunk, was a tiny grey kitten with big frightened eyes. It had evidently clambered across from one boat to the next and made its way into our cabin through the open porthole.

Lisbon was full of grand reminders of Portugal's glorious past; full of statues and monuments, palaces and forts. Trams whirred and rattled by in the cobbled streets. Pigeons clattered up from the pavement. We could have stayed and got to know the place - but we had to be pressing on. However, being still open to any kind of distraction from the greater goal we now hit upon the idea of a quick detour to Seville. Ferdinand Magellan sailed from here, and it was to here that his ship returned after having made the first ever circumnavigation of the world. For me the visit would be a kind of pilgrimage, offering the opportunity to recreate the historic scene in my mind. For Nick it was Seville's situation which appealed; the ancient city lies fifty miles inland and is reached via the River Guadalquivir.

Leaving Lisbon and the Tagus, we nipped around the bottom corner of Portugal, trotted along past the Algarve, and arrived off the entrance to the Guadalquivir just as dawn was breaking. A big fleet of fishing boats was pouring out into the sea, like a flock of Valkyries riding out to war. We pressed on, against the flood and amongst it, and were soon within the river's mouth.

The land on either side of the river is flat and low, so that we slid through it studying our surroundings as if from a slow train. An osprey perched on the flimsy topmost twigs of a scrub tree. Marsh harriers flapped across a field. There were dozens of herons, and little white cattle egrets adorned the bushes like huge blossoms. A flock of avocets took to the air and flashed across our bow. Deer on the riverbank twitched nervously as they nibbled the grass. To travel in this manner was a new experience and contrasted markedly with our recent adventures.

Late in the afternoon we came suddenly upon a lock. It had an abandoned appearance, but while we were considering what to do the gate suddenly opened. Entering through this aquatic portal was truly like entering the city gate, for afterwards we found ourselves passing through an industrial region on the outskirts of Seville. Soon we reached a bridge. It was far too low for us to pass beneath, but the middle section was designed to lift. We sounded our horn and waited. Traffic roared across the bridge in either direction, and we must have waited almost quarter of an hour, and sounded our horn half a dozen times, before the bridge keeper saw fit to stop the never-ending flow and let us by. As we approached the gap the man glowered down at us, and then, when we were actually between the pillars, he began to lower the bridge again!

We later found out that the bridge only opens twice a day - at ten in the morning and six in the evening - and that the lock, too, operates to a strict timetable. All in all we had been rather lucky, as usual.

Seville quite lived up to my romantic expectations, and we spent a pleasant few days visiting ancient landmarks such as the Moorish palace, the cathedral, and the Golden Tower where Magellan's ships were moored. A week later we left on the evening tide.

By the time we reached the river mouth it was five in the morning and a cold, grey and blustery day was dawning. Setting out into this suddenly-miserable weather was like stepping from the cosy warmth of a parlour into the street. By seven, the wind had reached force five and the glass was still falling. By nine it was blowing a gale - from the south, of course - and although our proper destination was Gibraltar we decided to put into Cadiz. There seemed little point in thrashing about all night; it would gain us absolutely nothing.

All day long we zigzagged to and fro, fighting for every inch of the twelve mile distance between the mouth of the Guadalquivir and the entrance to the Bahia de Cadiz. It took us eight hours to reach the harbour entrance.

We had no chart for Cadiz and on entering the walled port within the harbour were quite relieved to find a small marina. Its opening lay directly down wind and so, with our usual panache, we plummeted through the little gap and piled up alongside another, rather smaller yacht on the wall. Here we spent the next three days, not through any love of Cadiz but through the dictates of the wind. On the day following our arrival the local yacht club were recording gusts of 70 knots on their anemometer.

While we waited for conditions to improve we wandered aimlessly around the ancient town, searching for its soul. Cadiz was founded by the Phoenicians and is the oldest European town in existence, so that I expected to find something special here. We came upon some sort of street performance: a whole chorus of men was standing in a line across the street and each individual was singing and miming, with tremendous passion, words which were evidently meant for a lone hero. To this day I cannot hear this type of Spanish music without thinking back to this bizarre choir, but it is the only memory which I carry from that oddly characterless place.

As soon as the gale abated, and in spite of dire predictions from the local folks, we hurried away from Cadiz. Another deep low was forecast, but before it came through we had turned the next corner and reached the relative sanctuary of Gibraltar. Stage one of our journey had been accomplished. The next step would carry us out, away from Europe, and across the Atlantic again.

AND ALL I ASK IS A MERRY YARN

from a laughing fellow rover

The plan was that we should spend a week or two in Gibraltar sorting out some of the chores on our increasingly lengthy list and getting the boat up together.

The first item on the list was the purchase of a wind generator. This provides free electricity and no cruising yacht is complete without one. After much research we had decided that the best one on the market was the Aerogen, and this was easily and speedily acquired. Then followed the real work: the various items needing repair. The genoa must be sewn, and there were several deck leaks to be seen to, but top priority for me were the water tanks. Most of *Maamari*'s tanks were built of fibreglass but the two side tanks were made of steel and during her three year long lay-up these had sat half empty. The result was that as soon as the boat started to move, and the contents to slosh about, we ended up with water the colour of tomato soup. And I do not like tomato soup. Faced with a glass of this potion when already feeling under the weather I was sure to throw-up before it even passed my lips.

Two weeks were all that we had allowed ourselves to undertake these and several more tasks, but the gods had other plans. For almost six weeks we were held prisoners of The Rock while a perpetual series of tightly coiled lows chased each other along the Strait. And the wind was only the gaoler. Our chief tormentor was the rain. The Gibbos, as they are pleased to call themselves, boasted of their wettest December on record.

If there is one job which is impossible in the rain it is mending leaks. To test them one is always glad of a good downpour, but to mend them the wood must be bone dry. Gibraltar was so damp that the boat was going mouldy again, and after I had scraped and painted the water tanks I had to place lighted candles inside them to get the paint to dry.

Thwarted by the weather from attending to the yacht's maintenance, Nick turned his attention to her wardrobe; he decided that we should take this chance to get a new mizzen sail made. The mizzen we take for granted aboard *Maamari*; it is always up, come rain or shine or anything up to storm force. It never gets the glory; it never gets our gaze. If we think of it at all it is as just a balancing sail. Yet the mizzen is always the first to go up when we raise the anchor and the last to come down if the wind is up. The sail that had helped *Maamari* around the world was as patched as a pair of old jeans and a new one was definitely called for. What better opportunity than this, our enforced confinement?

"Make it good and strong, and make it quickly, please," we told the husband and wife team who were Gib-Fast Sails.

They shook their heads and tutted. "It will take a week, but don't fret. You'll be here for longer." And they were right.

Our budget did not run to paying marina fees and so throughout our stay in Gibraltar we were obliged to anchor. The anchorage lay north of the airport runway and so every time we went ashore we had to tackle a mile long row in our rubber dinghy. There were nights when the wind was so strong that we could scarcely make up on the upwind leg of this journey but equally memorable are the rare, still nights when the anchorage was on fire with phosphorescence. Every stroke of the oars then sent brilliant green "flames" through the inky water. When we lifted the blades, liquid green fire streamed and dripped from them, and astern of us our wake was a long green streamer. On these nights we would play for hours, tossing bucketfuls of water from the deck and never ceasing to be thrilled and astonished by the dazzling result. On one strangely calm morning, in the all too brief interlude between two gales, I looked down into the water and saw a little razorbill flying back and forth beneath the boat.

Sights such as this were marvellous, of course, but on the whole our stay in Gibraltar was anything but wonderful, and we felt that we were being made to waste time in this miserable anchorage with its pestilential weather. Nor were we the only ones. Many of the charter yachts which ply the Mediterranean by summer and then move off to the Caribbean had somehow got themselves holed-up in Gib, and they were desperate to be off. From time to time, on what seemed to be a less unpromising day than usual, one or other of these yachts would make a dash for it, but each and every one returned a few hours later and often with torn sails. Gib-Fast were having a field day.

Eventually, we too decided to give it a try. We were fed up with gazing every day on the grey cloud which capped the rock. After twenty-four hours spent slogging into a force seven we had made absolutely no progress and so we put into Ceuta, the Spanish enclave on the opposite shore from Gibraltar. Well, at least we were in Africa - sort of - and we took the chance to take a day trip into Morocco. It was my first visit to this land and one day running the gamut of pickpockets and hasslers in Tetouan was enough to put me off for life. After a couple of days we had another go at getting out of the Straits and ended up back in Gibraltar with a torn mainsail.

We limped back into the old familiar anchorage just in time for the biggest blow of the winter. At its peak this storm registered a steady 70 knots on the airport anemometer, and it wreaked havoc amongst the yachts. First to go was a Bulgarian vessel which let off flares in the night when it dragged. A police boat arrived just in time to pluck it from the rocky wall. On the following day the skipper of another yacht called up the commercial port, and they sent a huge ship's tug to come and get him. That left just two of us. Everyone else had fled into the marina. For a night of peace we would gladly have forked out the twelve quid fee and joined them, but we left it too late; by the time we decided that we needed to get out the wind and waves were such that we could not motor into them.

Needless to say, when things began to look bad we had put out a second anchor but at midday both anchors began to drag. We started the engine and Nick went for'ard to set a third anchor. This one was an 80lb Fisherman and it had never let him down. While Nick worked on the foredeck I struggled to keep *Maamari* head to the wind; if she fell off – if her bow dropped away to one side or the other - the extra windage would certainly make her drag much more quickly.

With all three anchors out and the engine going at almost full revs we could just hold station, but what if the Fisherman dragged? What if the engine chose this moment to throw in the towel? Behind us and on either side were nothing but rocky walls.

The bow plunged in and out of the waves. Never in all my life had I been so frightened aboard a yacht. Never before had I needed to wear a harness and tether while at anchor! But we survived the ordeal intact and, in the wake of this hurricane force wind, were quite blasé about the "mere gale" which followed it.

On Christmas Eve the long awaited "window of good weather" finally arrived. A disparate and desperate flotilla of yachts left Gibraltar with just one objective: getting out of the Straits was all that mattered. The caravan streamed westward on a sea as flat as the desert sands. By dusk we had made it - we were out on the open sea - but that night brought another gale and the east wind roared in manic glee as he made sport with the ones who had been lured out from their haven.

So it was that on Christmas morning I awoke with a leaden heart and within minutes of rising was hanging my head over a saucepan and vomiting last night's meal. This was decidedly not how I had envisaged the life on the ocean waves.

Assuming my place in the pilot birth, Nick slipped at once into a blissful sleep. I donned my oilskins. Outside, a lurid orange glow was seeping up from the horizon astern, and soon a tiny sliver of fire peered over the distant rim. Above us the sky was uniformly grey, and a light rain had begun to fall, but up ahead a huge rainbow, like none that I had ever seen before, formed not just a crescent but a hoop so nearly complete that it almost encircled the bow. At the same time it reached so high that it was almost at the masthead. Somehow this symbol in the sky seemed vaguely appropriate to Christmas morning. Uninspired by the wonder of it all, I staggered over to the lee rail and retched again.

With her wheel lashed and her reefed genoa balanced by the mizzen *Maamari* continued on her way without any interference from me. For a couple of minutes I stood peering out over the sprayhood. Then, after a brief glance at the compass and a thorough scan for shipping, I slumped down onto the hard, wet cockpit seat and wedged myself into a corner.

Christmas. It was the first one that I had ever spent away from my family, and so it was bound to feel odd. From where I sat I could see my little makeshift tree, its silver ornaments bobbing and swinging as the yacht galloped along. I was determined not to let the day pass without some kind of celebration, however token it might be. Lights and coloured banners had adorned the streets of Gibraltar and the atmosphere had been electric with excited anticipation. Swept along on the wave of enthusiasm I had bought all the necessary ingredients for a pukka Christmas dinner, but now the thought of preparing turkey and all the seasonal trimmings made my stomach turn. I decided to shove the whole lot into the pressure cooker.

"Glass is still falling," Nick observed cheerfully as, some hours later, he tucked into the strange mess of pottage. I ate my portion without much gusto and within ten minutes was passing it onto the fishes.
"More wind to come," Nick said pointedly, in case the message had escaped me. He went on deck and, hauling on the reefing line, furled a little more of the genoa around its supporting stay.

The storm hit us about six hours later. Under mizzen and partly furled genoa we still had too much canvas, and as Nick called to me from the companion way a rogue wave smashed down onto the boat. Its force was such that I thought the deck was splitting. Stunned for a moment, we watched in dismay as the sea poured down like a waterfall through the dorade vents and through the open hatchway. Then I tumbled out of the sea-berth and, blundering about the pitching and rolling cabin, struggled into my oilskins, wellies, and safety harness.

Up on deck, Nick shone a torch around and surveyed the damage. He found the genoa flapping madly, like an enormous wild beast struggling to get free. The wave had evidently landed in the sail and the clew had torn out. Beneath the sail, the pulpit was bent and the wire guard-rail had broken in two places. The chain locker hatch had shifted a good six inches, so that the locker now gaped open, and the box newly-built to house our windsurfers had been smashed to pieces. Studying the damage I was only surprised that the boards themselves were still with us.

While Nick lowered the mizzen I tried to hold *Maamari* head to wind until suddenly the weight beneath my hands disappeared. When I let go of it, the wheel spun freely. The steering cables had broken again. Fixing them was not of primary importance right now; it would have been handy to be able to put the waves on the stern, but at least we were miles from the nearest hard rock. Our attention was called far more urgently to the genoa, whose frenzied flapping made the whole boat shudder and threatened to bring down the mast. Together we hauled on the reefing line - and the line promptly broke.

From the safety of the cockpit I watched anxiously as Nick crawled forward along the deck. His aim was to reeve another line through the roller-furling gear but as he worked the bow plunged in and out of the waves and the sea sluiced over him. After ten or twenty minutes he gave up the impossible task and came shuffling back to the cockpit.

The shriek of the wind and the bestial roaring of the sail had drowned out even shouted communications between the foredeck and the cockpit, but now we put our heads together and tried to decide upon a course of action. We had to get rid of the sail, somehow, and if we could not furl it in the usual manner then we would have to lower it. But to do that we would have to completely *unfurl* it from the stay - and unfurled the sail would be more than three times its present size. The thought made us hesitate. Suppose the sail stuck in the metal luff-groove and could not be pulled down? Then our problem would be three times bigger and three times more dangerous. Such a monster, unleashed in this storm, would be sure to bring down the mast. While we were contemplating the dilemma *Maamari* was suddenly lifted and pitched onto her side. Water flooded over the lee rail and over the broad, high coaming and gushed into the cockpit.

"Let's get it down," cried Nick. "We've got to get it down." Never, in all his years spent at sea in *Maamari,* had he seen the cockpit coaming go under the waves.

"Go into the forepeak and unbolt the hatch. I'll pass you a line from the tack." So saying, the skipper crawled for'ard again and released the remaining dog-end of the reefing line.

At once the sail unfurled, spinning out from the rotating stay to dance and fight in a kind of hysterical panic. Beneath the beast, our little boat trembled. I swung myself down into the cabin and, with gritted teeth, went for'ard into the foc'sle. *Maamari* was bucking and plunging like an unbroken horse and I knew that for me to go and stand right in the bows would be inviting personal disaster. There was, however, no choice. Nick had already begun to yank the sail out of the luff-groove. My job was to stand beneath him and haul it into the cabin. If I failed in my half of the deal, the sail would be whipped off the deck and stolen by the wind and sea. Quickly, I unbolted the forehatch and then stood beneath the gaping hole, expecting at any moment to be swamped by a cascade of water. Nick threw the tack line down to me and I tugged, shaking with exertion and scarcely aware that I was throwing up all over myself. To my relief the sail at once began to flow down into the cabin and gradually the little wedge-shaped space was filled with wet, stiff canvas. The monster was slain, and we were safe.

The following morning the storm had abated and Nick woke me with the news that he had managed to bodge up the steering cables.

"I've made a start on the sail, too," he said, handing me the twine and a sailmaker's palm. "It has five open seams and the leech is completely shredded."

Although we could not know it at the time, the rest of the fleet setting out from the Straits with us suffered a worse fate than ours. They took a direct line to the Canaries and in the middle of that same stormy night passed through an oil slick. We had decided to check out the Selvagem Islands en route, and so we passed just to the north of the oil.

The gale continued to blow throughout Boxing Day, and on the 27th it occurred to me that we were now sailing through the same waters which just a few months earlier had been littered with sunbathing turtles. It hardly seemed possible. Still suffering from mal de mer, I was by now feeling thoroughly exhausted and dehydrated, and the anxiety that I felt on leaving England had returned to weigh me down. We had left in such a mad rush that I had not had time to prepare myself mentally. Everything and everyone that I knew and loved had been given up on a whim.

The future filled me with fear but it was not the fear of storms. Something far less tangible bothered me. I felt the need for some kind of path across that vast, frightening unknown of the future. Perhaps I had finally discovered why it is that perfectly sane people ensnare themselves in mortgages and insurance policies. Life is a great, empty, trackless ocean. What I needed was not security for my old age, however, but an itinerary telling me what to expect, so that I could chart my life's course. I have always taken great comfort from plans, although I am generally very happy to change them on the spur of the moment, but Nick would own to no plan - except that distant one of reaching Patagonia - and so I went comfortless.

On the 3rd of January, just as day was slipping into night, we sighted the Selvagem Islands. Unwilling to approach in the dark, we sailed to within a mile and then, for the next few hours, reached to and fro under mizzen and stays'l.

The Selvagems are a tiny group of uninhabited islands claimed by the Portuguese. As the sun rose we got our first proper look at Selvagem Grande, the biggest of the group, and I thought of the mountain rising two miles up from the seabed - a mountain twelve thousand feet tall, or thereabouts. Seen from down there it would be quite something, but for us it was just a dull, green mound.

According to the pilot book we could "effect a good landing" on this island and, sure enough, we soon came upon a couple of huts and in front of them a little concrete ramp. But the weather of the past few weeks had set up a great swell, and even to anchor was out of the question.

We turned away from Selvagem Grande and headed for Pequeña and Fora, the two islets which complete the group. Bottle-nosed dolphins were lunging about purposefully in the big waves and a cloud of gannets flew around, shrieking and hurling themselves repeatedly at the sea. The islands might never have provided man with a home, but for the creatures of the deep they were clearly a great metropolis.

I cast my eyes over Selvagem Pequeña, a low sliver of an island surmounted by a tumble-down castle of rocks. Its most distinctive feature was the prow of a large ship which sat rusting in the surf. The sight of a wrecked vessel always sends a cold shiver through other seafarers. Seeing a wreck is rather like seeing a ghost. As we passed along the narrow channel which separates Pequeña from Fora the ship seemed like a siren, luring us to share her fate. The air was filled not with singing but with the roar of mighty waves striking mighty, unyielding rock. Surf rolled past on either side of us.

Suddenly, as we surged onward through the pass, the sea beneath us turned from steely grey-green to deepest blue and then to turquoise, and then I could see the bottom. Rock, sand, and stone flashed by.

"Shallows!" I cried out in alarm, for we saw them all as clearly as if the water had been only two feet deep. I was sure that we were running onto the reef. I could hardly believe that we were not, even now, tearing our keel through the seabed.

"Gin clear," Nick said complacently, and he pointed at the echo sounder. We had 36 feet of gin clear water between *Maamari* and the bottom.

With our curiosity satisfied we now turned south towards the Canary Islands and that same night we sighted Tenerife. The next morning we were off the island's capital town and with the arrival of dawn we began our usual search for somewhere to moor. Eventually we spotted masts in the fishing port, just to the north of the town. At the far end of a long, narrow basin a row of yachts was moored stern-to on the wall - but there was no space for us. We considered going alongside the sea wall, where the ocean-going trawlers were berthed, but it looked rather unfriendly. We were stumped. And then we spotted another yacht which was tied, not to the wall itself but to one of those big trawlers. It was the Bulgarian yacht which had so nearly come to grief in Gibraltar and it was tied up next to a Russian.

I suppose we could have made our own arrangements - perhaps with one of the Korean trawlers - but our Korean is not too good, and besides that, the Bulgarians were already beckoning us alongside. Soon we were joined by an American yacht, and then by a Scot, so that by the end of the day we were a little international community within the greater village of Darseña Pesquera.

The Bulgarian yachtsmen were a friendly crowd. They had waited ten years for permission to leave their country and sail to the Caribbean, and they told us that they would be the first Bulgarian yachtsmen to cross the Atlantic.

"Perhaps you will be the first from a communist country to cross," we suggested, but they smiled confidently.

"By the time we have crossed, Bulgaria will not be a communist country anymore."

At the time this remark seemed to us to be nothing more than a fantasy.

The Bulgarian skipper, Ilia, proudly showed us around his boat. Her name was *Lady Day*. She was about 30 feet long but very narrow in the beam and with no standing headroom. It scarcely seemed possible that her crew could all fit into the cabin at once, still less lie down to sleep, for there were six of them. Ebullient with the joy of their newfound freedom, the Bulgarians themselves had no complaints.

After our recent trip across from Gibraltar the camaraderie of this little community in the fishing port was just what I needed to set me on my feet again. By day we worked on deck alongside one and other - for we had all suffered some damage in the storm - and each evening we got together for a meal and a sing-song. One of the Bulgarians was a young welder called Zlotti - a lovely man with not a word of English or Spanish but with a sparkle in his bright blue eyes. He had brought with him his guitar. George, the Scotsman, had a squeeze box, and he knew how to play it. The blend that the two musicians could produce was quite wonderful. First George would treat us to a little ballad or a jig while Zlotti strummed along as best he could. Then the Bulgarians would take over with a glorious rendition of some traditional folk song. Often tears would fill their eyes as the words and tune evoked some ancient memory of what their country once was and what, they so firmly believed, it soon would be again. After a time, the liquor having been flowing freely, the songs would become more bawdy and perhaps a little less tuneful, until by midnight we were reduced to howling out the chorus to 'The House of the Rising Sun' or 'The Drunken Sailor'. After a little while we achieved a certain notoriety amongst the main core of yotties, berthed on the quay, but it was one based largely on envy.

When we tired of singing the same old songs the talk would move, inevitably, to a discussion of our seafaring exploits, for when sailors cross paths they like to compare notes. Mike, the American skipper, had colourful tales to tell of cruising down the Pacific coast of Mexico and Guatemala. The Scotsman told of how he had lost his mast off Madeira and then, on reaching the island, built a new one from a tall, straight tree. Although they had begun their travels only a few months earlier, the Bulgarians, too, had yarns to spin, but the story which topped them all was undoubtedly Nick's tale of capsizing a yacht in Biscay. It was a tale which made the others all stop and think. They wanted to know every detail of how such an unthinkable thing had occurred, for each one wanted to be sure that it could not happen to him. As for me, I had heard the bare bones of the story before, of course, but never the full account.

"The forecast was good," Nick began, "and so we left St Gilles-Croix-de-Vie and set out across the Bay. It was my first delivery job, and the crew were not my own choice. They were straight off the company's list and I had only met them the day before. One was an American hitchhiker called Paul; another was an Aussie named Pete. The third was a girl called Debbie who boasted that she had never set foot in a boat before. And I don't suppose she will ever want to set foot in one again."

"So, we set off, on a lovely, still autumnal morning - but by the following day the wind was up, and by nightfall it was blowing force eight."

"Full gale," murmured George. "But the boat oughta ha' been able t' handle that."

"Yes. It wasn't much fun," Nick said, "but we pulled through. We were crashing along, and it felt as if the boat would fall apart at any minute. Some of the furniture shifted and we took on a lot of water, but we pumped like mad and when the pumps jammed up with sawdust we bailed. And we pulled through. The problem came the next day."

"While the gale was blowing I had been making for La Coruña, but when it dropped to about a force six I thought we might as well press on. The sun was shining and everything looked good. There was a rather lumpy left-over sea, but we were having a nice sail and our spirits were up. It was a couple of days since we had seen the sun, and so I was not too sure of our position, but I did know that we were some miles to seaward of Cape Finisterre. I knew that, because we'd crossed the shipping lane a few hours beforehand. With that in mind, I'd turned downwind and dropped the main. We'd got about a third of the genoa out - that's all - and we were surfing along nicely."

"And then what?"

"It was a glorious morning. Even Debbie was beginning to enjoy herself. She'd spent the past two days throwing up, of course. We had the hatches open to let the wind blow through the boat and dry things off. Everything was perfect. I was sitting behind the wheel, just getting ready to take a sunsight. I was just about to ask for the sextant. And then, all of a sudden, I was thumped in the back and hurled forward by a solid wall of icy-cold water! It just burst over us! It gushed into the cabin, where the boys had laid out all their gear to dry. And the first thing I can recall is the sound of Debbie screaming in hysterics".

"Well, I picked myself up and Pete appeared in the hatchway, saying, "Are you okay, Mate?" There was blood pouring from my face, where I'd hit the wheel, but I didn't even know it. I just yelled, "Bail!" - and they bailed. We all bailed. The water was above the cabin sole and the boat felt dead. The wave had simply swept right over us and, I tell you, the force was truly amazing. We'd had four 30 gallon jerrycans of water lashed into the cockpit, and they were gone without a trace! And the companion hatch had been hauled right out of its runners and curved back on itself."

"Well, after that I decided to quarter the seas and, at the same time, close with the land. I was keeping an eye over my shoulder now, of course, but nothing seemed amiss. Just a lumpy sea, that was all. I couldn't understand where that thing had come from!"

"By midday the boys had finished bailing and Paul joined me in the cockpit. We were waiting for the meridian passage but, once again, I'd decided to leave the sextant down below until the last minute. This time the hatch was closed. We'd managed to uncurl it and bash it back into place. We were taking no chances, but really everything looked fine. Paul had just lit up a cigarette, I remember, and I was just about to hand over the helm. We were chatting away. I stood up and glanced over my shoulder... and blocking the horizon astern of us was a wave the like of which I have never seen before or since. It was monstrous! And it was coming straight for us. Its crest curled and foamed, and it rolled down towards us as if it were possessed by some kind of deliberate, malicious intent. We were completely helpless. We could only stand there, gazing up at this wall of water, knowing that, in just a few seconds, it was going to smash down onto us and capsize the boat. There was no way we could avoid it."

"I told Paul to get under the cockpit table and I crouched behind the wheel, desperately trying to keep the boat pointing down the rollercoaster. Then the cockpit turned upside down and I was scrabbling about in the water."

"And he can't swim," I interjected.

"I don't know how I got out from under the hull but I found myself at the surface, at the transom. I groped about and found the toggle on my Crewsaver lifejacket and the thing inflated around me. God, that was a relief! And then, there I was – hanging onto the transom, looking up at this shiny, white hull framed by the blue sky. It was ludicrous! The day seemed so placid. And the boat just sat there, rocking gently on the waves like a big, fat, white duck."

"My lifeline was clipped onto the compass binnacle, which didn't give me any scope at all, and every now and then I'd be swamped by the waves. I had my hand on the lifeline clip but I didn't dare undo it; I was saving that for the moment when the boat sank."

"After I'd come to terms with my own situation I started to wonder about the others, and when I looked down I could see Paul's legs under the cockpit! I could even touch his legs with my foot, and at one stage I even found his hand and started to yank on it. I can remember wondering if I was liable for manslaughter but it all seemed a bit academic. The boat must have been upside-down for about two or three minutes by now and it was obvious that it was completely stable. I couldn't see any reason why anything should change. In the end it would sink and the others would all go down with it. I'd be left, on my own, thirty or forty miles offshore in this frigid November sea. I didn't really fancy my chances."

"And then, all of a sudden, there was a yank on my lifeline and I found myself in the clear air, dangling over the transom, with Paul splashing about behind me. And we were upright!"

"And Paul. He'd held his breath for more than two minutes? Ah dinna think... It's impossible!"

"No. Paul had found himself with his head inside one of those enormous cockpit lockers. It had fallen open when the boat went over, and there was air trapped inside. But he was in a real state. He hadn't known where he was at all, nor even if the boat was still afloat. And that goes for Pete, too; for all he knew the boat was on the bottom of the ocean. He burst out of the cabin with Debbie close on his heels and sobbing wildly. He'd had to hit her because she was having hysterics again. It turns out that they'd spent all that time desperately trying to open the hatch - which really *would* have sunk the boat!"

"Anyhow, there wasn't much time for rejoicing. There was so much water on board that the foredeck was submerged and only the voluminous, buoyant cockpit was keeping us afloat. We had to do something, fast. The buckets had been lashed into the chain locker, and so I went for'ard to get them. As I passed the mast I can remember noticing that it wasn't there anymore. I found it dangling over the side, suspended by the rigging. Later on I realised that it was only thanks to the mast breaking that the boat came up at all, because while the mast stayed there, in one piece, it was like a gigantic keel keeping us steady."

Ilia began to ask questions about a jury-rig but that, Nick told us, came much later.

"By an absolute miracle the buckets were still with us, and so we bailed like mad. The three of us formed a chain. I guess someone ought to have been comforting Debbie, but there was no time for that, and when her sobs had died down a bit I got her to pump the loo. I don't think she had any idea why she had to pump it - she probably thought I was just taking the mickey - but as long as the water level was above the pan the loo pump was emptying the boat. And it was above it for a long, long time. It was nightfall before we even got the level down to the cabin sole. Then we just curled up in a miserable, wet huddle and slept."

"When we woke up, our first priority was to get the stove going, and that was easier said than done. The inside of the boat was utter chaos, as you can imagine. Well, no, you really can't imagine quite how bad it was. Everything that was made of paper or cardboard had fallen apart and completely disappeared - there was no trace of any of the charts, for instance - and as for the matches... In the end we found half a dozen wet ones and the sodden striker from the side of a box. We checked the electrics and found that one lamp in the aft cabin was still working. It must have been just about the only thing to stay clear of the water. Pete spent the best part of a day with the matches and the striker pressed up against the bulb, trying to dry them out."

"Boy! He must have been desperate for a cuppa," quipped Mike.

"He was desperate to stay alive," Nick explained. "It was the middle of November and we were all soaked to the skin. The biggest threat to us now was hypothermia. When Pete got the stove going I knew we would be okay. From that moment on we kept it burning, day and night. And then, yes, *then* we began to think about a jury-rig.

"For some reason the mast was made in two pieces, sleeved together, and it had broken at the union, only three feet above the deck. Well, I couldn't do much with the pole itself but I managed to retrieve the boom, and the mainsail, and all of the sheets and halyards; I got them all up out of the water. I wanted the genoa too. It had also gone overboard, of course, and it was still attached to the roller furling stay. So I lashed the tack of the sail to the boat and then I undid all of the rigging screws, expecting that, as the mast sank, the sail would slide out of the roller-furler."

"What happened?"

"I'm not quite sure, but it went down with the mast and the stays. Rather embarrassing."

"So, you were able to make a jury-mast using the boom," Ilia said.

"That was the plan," Nick agreed. "I planned to stand the boom up inside the mast stump, but by now it was evening time again. To be honest, the others hadn't taken much interest in the project. The main preoccupation for them was being rescued. They'd had enough, and they wanted to call for help. I was dead against it, of course - I mean, we weren't in any danger now that the stove was going - but that evening we saw a ship. It was obvious that it was going to come quite close, and the others decided that their salvation was nigh. They tried the radio but couldn't raise him, so then they let off a flare. He was so close that we could read his name, but he just steamed on by - thank heavens. After that experience everyone was a bit more enthusiastic about the jury-rig."

"You'd think that it would be pretty straight-forward, wouldn't you, shoving the boom into the mast stump? We tied a couple of blocks onto it and reeved halyards for a main and jib, and then we tried to stand it up in the hole. But the boat was flicking to and fro like billy-oh, in the waves, and we blundered about like a bunch of comedians. It was like trying to pot the black with an 18 foot cue!"

"Well, we managed it in the end. Then we cut up the mainsail - brand new mainsail, it was, but it had to be done. We ran

the foot up the track in our little mast and stretched it out towards
the pushpit. Then we cut off the head and, since it didn't have any
eyelets, we just bunched up the corners for the tack line and the
sheet."

"How did she go?" asked Ilia, and I could see that he was filing the
information away, against some future rainy day.

"Amazing!" said Nick. "It went really well. Now we knew we were
going to make it to dry land. We just weren't sure which bit it would
be. We'd lost the charts, we'd lost the almanac. We'd still got the
sextant but that counts for nothing on its own. The next day we saw
another ship. Well, I looked at the VHF and it had water sloshing
about inside the little window with the digital display. No chance! I
looked at the ship and it was a really massive one - a super tanker -
and it was coming very, very close. So I gave it a go - I called him up
- and to my astonishment he answered. I was so surprised that I
hardly knew what to say! There wasn't much point in asking for a
position, because a position is no use without a chart, so I explained
our predicament and asked if he could give us a list of the lights and
harbours for the stretch of coast that we were approaching. I didn't
know that coast at all at the time."

"There was a pause, and then the captain came on. He ran
down the Admiralty list of lights and I jotted them all down with the
"ships pencil" - the only one we'd been able to find. He suggested
that I make for Vigo, and he gave me a bearing, and then he started
to go on about the entrance to the river. But by now he was about
half a mile past us and his voice was fading. That's about the range
of a VHF without an aerial.

I thought, "Well, that's that." But when I went on deck I
found that he was coming back again! I don't know what it costs to
turn a supertanker around, but it doesn't come cheap. This guy was
going beyond the call of duty and I was really glad he hadn't been
around when the boys let off that flare!"

"He brought the ship back. It was simply immense. As it slid
past, alongside, we saw that they were towing three plastic barrels on
a line. As they crossed our bow they let them go. Pete tied a coat
hanger onto one of the table fiddles - he was a smart lad, that one,
with a quick brain - and we fished the barrels out."

"Whisky in one," said George, with a grin.

"Cigarettes in the next," his wife suggested.

"No, they all had charts in them," Nick said. "They each had a photocopy of the Admiralty chart, with our position plotted."

"Why did he need to send you three?" asked Ilia.

"Western bureaucrats do everything in triplicate," Mike interjected quickly. "You'll soon get the hang of it."

"We were sixty miles offshore," Nick went on, but the others were cracking jokes and filling their glasses, and I was the only one still listening. "We made for Vigo, and when we got there we found some fishing boats. They gave us a tow up to Muros."

"And what did you tell your boss? Did you get the sack?" asked Mike.

"No, he's all right, is Alan. I called him up and said I'd had the boat upside-down for four minutes. He said, "That's nothing, Mate! Last one I turned over stayed on its back for 18 hours." He gave me a £2,000 bonus."

"What? He gave you a bonus for wrecking the boat?"

"Well, not until I'd finished the job, of course. Not until I'd taken the boat over to the Caribbean."

"You got it there?"

"Of course. But that's another story."

"We don't want to hear it," Mike said.

It was well past the witching hour and time to be heading home. As we clambered through the cockpits in the dark, Ilia's voice came to us.

"What about the wave? What caused the wave?"

"I don't know. It was just a freak. I think perhaps it may have had something to do with the edge of the continental shelf."

We stumbled down the companion ladder and flicked on a light to guide us to bed.

"Would it have knocked *us* down?" I asked, as we lay, side by side.

"It would have knocked a house down," Nick replied with a yawn, "but *Maamari* would have come up again straight away."

"Are you sure?"

"Quite sure."

"How can you be so sure?"

No answer. He was already asleep.

4

INTO AFRICA

on the strength of a whim

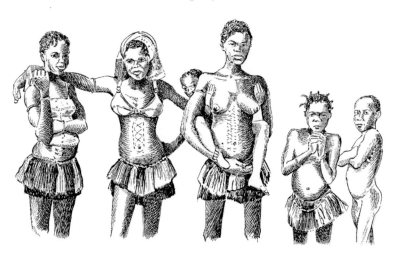

After a few days of our company the Russian fishermen asked us all to go away. Remarkable as it may seem this was not because they were fed up with us but because they wanted to paint their hull. They could not do so while there were four yachts tied up to it.

Was this to be the end of a beautiful relationship? Would we now be scattered around the port? We all hoped not and so we set off as one, with the four yachts still tied together and four engines tapping away. At first there was some dissent, both verbal and physical, about which way we ought to be going. The Bulgarians tried to take us over to the quay, in order still to be near their Russian friends, but the American skipper had his helm the other way.

Finally we picked on a Korean trawler and, to our surprise, were received with tremendous enthusiasm. Within minutes of our going alongside there were Chinese fishermen all over our boats, gesticulating wildly and helping themselves to the Spanish brandy. They spoke all the time but never in English. Eventually, after two thirds of a bottle of cheap Spanish brandy and much incomprehensible sign-language, they disappeared only to return moments later with an enormous, unidentifiable, frozen fish.

That night we had 17 seafarers of seven different nationalities for dinner aboard *Maamari*. Amongst them was the captain of the Russian trawler, *Elektron*. He wrote in our visitors book: "I was very pleased to get acquainted with you, dear English friends. Here in Santa Cruz de Tenerife I have now met English, Americans, Germans and Bulgarians. They are all wonderful people. I can feel that our relations are improving..." We were left feeling that the Cold War might have ended a lot sooner if matters had been left to a handful of sailors chatting over a glass or two of liquor.

All good things must come to an end, they say, and in our case it was certainly true. Already our pleasure in each other's company had encouraged us to remain together for almost a fortnight, but warmer weather to the South was beckoning. The Scottish couple were bound for The Gambia and suggested that we all meet up there. The Americans thought that it would be marvellous if we all stayed in Tenerife for the Mardi Gras. The Bulgarians were running out of money and needed to cross to the Caribbean before they ran out of food. Our destiny lay in that direction too, and our next stepping stone was the Cape Verde archipelago, 600 miles to the south. Indeed, we had planned to spend Christmas Day in the Cape Verde Islands, and were now many weeks behind with our schedule.

Together, the gang held a final party beside a barbecue bonfire on the quayside and then, over the next couple of days, we each set off to pursue our different dreams. As they cast off their mooring lines the Bulgarian crew thrust precious tins of feta cheese and helva into our hands, refusing all our efforts at reciprocity. They were right about the state of their nation. In the middle of the Atlantic they celebrated the final collapse of its Communist regime. We heard from them once, via some folks who had a Ham radio, but we have never seen them again. Perhaps the greatest disappointment of the cruising life - perhaps the only one - is to be forever parting from new friends.

After a brief trip over to Las Palmas for fuel, *Maamari* left the Canaries on the 20th of January. All went well for the first two days of our passage south but then, in the middle of the second night, the self-steering gear packed up. Checking it over at dawn we discovered what a torch light inspection had failed to reveal; namely, we found that the leading six inches of the rudder were missing. For three hours we fiddled about with the sails, trying to find a way to balance the rig and persuade the yacht to fend for herself, but with the wind on the stern it was quite impossible.

Since we were sailing for our own enjoyment, rather than to win any race or prove our muscle, we decided that we would henceforth steer the boat only by day. During the night we would still keep watch, after our usual fashion, but *Maamari* would lie ahull under reefed genoa.

Helming a little boat is something that I enjoy very much, but *Maamari* was not so little. She was hard work. When Nick steers a yacht he sits down and takes it easy - he can steer for hours and hours - but when I am on the helm I like to see where I am going. I stood astride *Maamari*'s cockpit, with one foot on the seats either side, and like a charioteer I urged her onward.

As I stood at the helm I watched the sea and studied its movement, later recording what I saw in the log:

"January 24th. *The sea is big today; dark blue flecked with dazzling white. The waves rise and rise and roll; then they sink quietly down again. All around me the ocean heaves up and down; rising, falling, rising again. It is relentless; tireless; forever striding past.*"

I wrestled the wheel to and fro. We wanted to steer 245°, but the wind was almost on the stern, and it was blowing force seven. If I lost concentration for a moment and let Maamari have her head then she rode up into it. Once she was facing 200° the waves would meet her on the quarter, instead of the stern, and as they smacked into the boat I would get a sudden, cold soaking. If I let her roll the other way, down to 255°, then the headsail slammed across in a gybe. And so I fought to keep Maamari rolling down the line. It was hard work but thrilling too, and my joy overflowed into song. Sea shanties, folk songs, love songs... everything I could think of. I sang at the top of my voice, with only the sea to hear me.

Always, when we put to sea in *Maamari*, we trailed two fishing lines astern of the boat, and that evening, just before dark, we caught a nice little tuna. The tackle which we used for this game – the same which we still use now – invariably makes a true fisherman laugh, for we have no fancy, high-tech lures nor even a reel. We are not interested in breaking records or being sporting - we are only interested in getting dinner onto the table - and so we use the strongest mono-filament line that we can find: line with a breaking strain of 250lbs. At our end, the line is joined to the boat by a piece of strong bungy. This takes the shock of a bite nowhere near so well as a reel, but then it costs nowhere near as much. At the business end of the line there is a 4" hook, clothed in shreds of blue and yellow plastic. A round, lead weight wrapped in the silver lining of a wine box provides the head.

With twenty dollar lures and all the proper tackle we could probably catch twice as many fish, but as often as not our lures are taken by sharks, which bite straight through the hefty, wire leader. Sometimes we lose as many as five lures on a passage and if each of these cost us twenty dollars we would not be half so keen to try our luck.

On the 26th the sun rose to reveal *Maamari* covered in a thin layer of rust-coloured slime which had evidently fallen in a rain shower during the past night. Right now, the sky above us was clear and blue so that it was not until later in the day, when a huge tanker appeared from nowhere, that we realised how bad the visibility had become. The air was filled with harmattan dust, blown from the Sahara.

Three days later we sighted land and I found that I had mixed emotions about the prospect of bringing our voyage to a close. Naturally, I was curious about the islands which lay ahead of us, but the sea had hypnotised me, so that I felt drawn to continue on and on. Time had again lost all meaning. Position, too, was of no relevance. Every day, when the sun was visible, we would get out the sextant and hunt down our position with painstaking accuracy, recording the precise second at which the shining orb was exactly so many degrees, minutes, and seconds of angle from the horizon - but whether we were off Africa or South America meant nothing on an emotional level. It is interesting to note that an obsession with minute divisions of time, expressed through complex calculations, is sometimes a feature of an intelligent but isolated mind on the verge of breakdown. I am thinking of Donald Crowhurst, entrant in the first single-handed round the world race - who devised an intensely complicated method for calculating the precise time at which he must step overboard and end his life - and also of the Nigerian political writer, Wole Soyinka, who was imprisoned in solitary confinement for more than a year and who later found that he had written page upon page of indecipherable mathematical calculations concerned with time.

Then again, perhaps it is only the dutiful concern with such things as time and position which keeps the long distance sailor from disappearing over the edge. It is the "frail thread of gossamer" which links us to conventional reality. Sometimes I wonder whether there might not be single-handed sailors whose failure to return to shore could be attributed to their abandoning that handrail of duty. Bernard Moitessier was so strongly lured that instead of finishing (and winning) that same singlehanded race around the world he just kept on sailing. The might of the sea is in more than its physical strength.

But islands too have a magical allure. It was evening time and so we got out the chart and looked to see what lights we might expect to find, come darkness.

The Cape Verde Islands lie in a half circle, like a necklace spread on the blue cloth of the sea. In the north-west is Santo Antão; in the north-east is Sal. Between them sit the islands of São Vicente, Santa Lucia and São Nicolau, and it was these last which we had glimpsed. According to the chart the light we were most likely to spot was an occulting white on the tip of Santo Antão. It blinks once every 58 seconds.

"Well, how on earth are we going to distinguish that from all the other lights?" I asked.

"Or from a fishing boat dipping on the horizon," Nick agreed. Nearly all the other navigational lights were shown on the chart as being fixed whites with a range of two miles, and we wondered how we would distinguish them from the streetlights.

Oh, we were very ignorant about the land to which we had now come! When darkness arrived the islands slipped away and were gone, and there was not one light to be seen. Not one! We stood off until daybreak.

In the first pink light of the morning the islands of São Vicente and Santo Antão re-emerged as jagged shapes softened by the mist of a light haze. Ilha Santo Antão is a massive, powerful rock whose grey-brown peaks and ravines were dramatically lit by shafts of sunshine playing like spotlights from the clouds above. Beside the great Antão, the island of São Vicente is a mere rubble heap - an assortment of low peaks thrown together - but this island and its harbour of Porto Grande was our destination.

As we approached the channel between the two islands the fishing line suddenly went taut, and hauling it in we found that we had caught a three-foot-long dorado. Could there be a more beautiful gift from the ocean? The meat of the dorado is delicious, but better still is his quite glorious colour. As he hit the deck the fish was greenish gold all over his belly and had a dark blue back. He was freckled with dots of electric blue. Finding himself suddenly stranded the dorado thrashed about, arching his body and slapping his tail up and down with tremendous strength. Then, after a few seconds, he lay still.

"Watch this," said Nick, and as I watched the magnificent gold suddenly faded until the fish was an iridescent silvery-white. Even the eye was now white, and the blue freckles had become black ink spots. The back was still dark if I viewed it from above but seen from a lower angle it was a shimmering Oxford blue. Could the camera capture this? I hurried to fetch it but was too late. After just a minute or two the fish began to tremble all over and then, as he died, the green-gold seeped back in to colour his skin.

Before the strong and steady tradewind we bowled down the passage between the islands of Santo Antão and São Vicente. With each craggy rock or headland that we passed some new nook or cove was opened up, and we explored them all with our eyes. Not one trace of verdure could we find but only orange-brown and grey-brown rock. At the time we supposed that the islands must once have been green – for why else name them so?

The bay of Porto Grande takes a big, neat bite out of the west side of São Vicente and makes an excellent natural harbour. On its northern, windward shore stands the port and town of Mindelo, and it was here that we threw out the anchor and came to rest. I cast my eyes over the scene before us and decided that it was not particularly African. Along the seafront a line of colourful, old-colonial buildings looked like cardboard cut-outs, and the backdrop of orange-brown hills just behind the town lent strength to the illusion of a film set, perhaps for a cowboy movie. Beside the painted buildings stood a miniature concrete replica of Lisbon's famous Torre Belem. Dominating all were the naked brown mountains to the north of the town.

Our time in São Vicente was chiefly spent in buying a piece of wood - no easy matter in a country without trees - and in repairing the self-steering rudder. That having been done we set off for the island of Santiago which lies about 120 miles to the south.

We set off from Mindelo into a good force seven, with the sun shining down onto blue waves and white spray. *Maamari* pounded along, close on the wind, and I was quite cross to find myself soon feeling very ill. How could my stomach let me down on such a splendid day as this? I spent most of the journey hanging over a bucket. We were going too well for me to hang over the rail.

By daybreak the following morning we were off Santiago, and for the next eight or ten hours we reached down the island's west coast. As a result of my earlier incapacitation, Nick had been up all night. Now, in the lee of the big island, the sea was relatively flat and I made a complete recovery. While the captain slept, I sat and studied the landscape. Sailing as a couple can be quite lonely, because for much of the time one or other of you is asleep, but it can also be fun to be a temporary single-hander and "own the whole world". Today I had both the ship and an island all to myself. I watched Santiago go by, mentally ticking off the salient features as they trickled past, and tracing our progress along the chart.

In fact, the salient and conspicuous features on the west coast of Santiago are few and far between. By far the most outstanding feature is its unutterably barren state. Dry, brown rubble climbs all the way up from the deep blue of the sea into the azure sky. Steep-sided ravines carve deep, jagged scars down through the sterile, lifeless rock. Halfway along the coast I saw a village of tiny stone huts standing right in the mouth of a huge, sheer-walled canyon. Or had my eyes deceived me? Surely, I thought, one would have to be crazy to build a village in the very mouth of a great waterway, however ancient and dry it may be. Someday we would return and take a closer look at that.

Now the wind began to falter and *Maamari* grew sluggish, but up ahead the sea was a field of little, white crests. Whether to reef, and wallow in the shadows behind the great peaks, or to press on under full sail and risk breaking something in the brief, fierce squall? – that was the question. Fortunately, Nick emerged from his slumbers in time to take over this responsibility. We reefed and regretted it - but not so much as we would have regretted breaking the mast.

So it went on. All day the massive orange rock slid by beside us. In all that time, and in all those miles, we passed only one green oasis - Cidade Velha, a village which the pilot book said was the first European settlement in the tropics. One day we would visit this "old city" but for now we rolled on past, skirting the nibbled edge of a dry, rubble-strewn plain. Then, in the midst of this desert, miles from anywhere, we came upon a white church within a white-walled cemetery. It was like a ship - one white ship - anchored in the expanse of a vast, orange-brown sea.

At the end of the day we reached the end of the island and found anchorage off Praia, the capital of the Cape Verde Republic.

With little money in our pockets Nick and I had planned, on leaving England, to take a fairly direct route over to the Caribbean. Four months on, and with our money dwindling day by day, we still held on to that objective - yet it seemed crazy to go dashing back across the pond without so much as sampling West Africa. We fetched down the atlas and thumbed through its pages. And, once again, the whim of a moment took over from our well-laid plans. Senegal was so near. And what was this archipelago just to the south, off Guinea Bissau? The matter seemed worthy of investigation.

We left Cape Verde on the evening of the 10th of February and had an effortless, uneventful sail to Senegal. The wind was east-north-east and was laden, as usual, with murk from the Sahara. Everything on deck - every stay and every stitch in the sail - grew coated in a film of orange mire. When the boat lunged into a wave, throwing up a sheet of spray, the film of dust became a coat of muddy slime. We set the sails and lashed the wheel and for the next three days had no need to lay a hand on either. *Maamari* strolled along casually, her pace lessening as we neared the continent and the breeze fell off. Shoals of flying fish skipped from under the bow and a pod of pilot whales moved aside in their lugubrious way.

Off Dakar the wind died completely. Some fishermen in a strange v-shaped canoe came across the glassy sea. They asked for water. We gave them some and then traded cigarettes for fish. I have never smoked and Nick had long since kicked the habit, but we always carry a carton for just this purpose. For some strange reason, fishermen always prefer cigarettes to money. Give them money and they think they've been diddled; give them cigarettes and they grin and toss over another couple of fish.

The current was dragging us south, away from our destination, and so at midday we fired up the engine. When we were three miles off, the tip of the Dakar peninsula and the off-lying island of Goreé emerged from the murky haze. Now, what should we make for? Someone had warned us against using the port. Eventually we identified a tight cluster of masts some way beyond the city, at Hann, and on approaching we found upwards of thirty yachts anchored off a beach. This was quite unexpected. We had seen only two other yachts in Mindelo and none at all in Praia.

We dropped our own hook on the edge of the flotilla and looked around to see if there was anyone we knew. There was something a little odd about the company. Ah, that was it - there were no dinghies, chattering to themselves at the end of their tethers, and the hatches were all closed. There was no sign of life whatsoever. Some of the yachts looked as if they had been sitting here for years; green seaweed fringed their waterlines and their spars looked strangely naked without the familiar bundle of canvas hugging the boom. These were not cruising yachts; they belonged to settled expatriates.

Dakar is a city without comparison. It is a vibrant termites' nest in the sparse savannah. Its pace is that of any modern conurbation, yet the influences which have been taken from the West are purely practical and functional. Islam is the dominant culture here, but even Islam has been softened and shaped to suit the African tradition and temperament.

From the anchorage at Hann Plage a road leads into town, cutting directly across a sandy, semi-industrial suburb. Relays of semi-derelict, blue and yellow buses tore up and down the road in fits and starts, weaving their way around horse-drawn carts. Arabic lettering in praise of God curled around the Renault logo on each radiator grill, and paintings of flowers, horses and Muslim gurus adorned the sides of the bus. Turbaned heads looked out from windows whose glazing was removed long ago. Hard-faced youths in T-shirts and jeans hung out of the open back door and touted for trade.

The pavements on either side of the road into town were ankle deep in soft Saharan sand and thronged with workers and businessmen. Vendors wended their way amongst the bustling crowd, touting oranges, towels, and toothpaste. Young and old alike, most of the men wore the traditional Muslim attire of a flowing, ankle-length shirt above matching, silken trousers. Bright blue, pale blue, yellow, brown, green, and even shocking pink - the gowns flapped, and the men tweaked them about self-consciously. Heads were held proudly high. Patterned, woolly skullcaps bobbed past red or grey felt fezzes from Morocco. Pointed white slippers slapped the ground beside cheap flip-flops.

And though they are probably the most lavishly dressed in all Africa, the men of Dakar by no means outshine their women. In this city even the meanest market vendor is draped in a gown of vibrant pattern and colour; even a beggar woman picking through piles of rotten garbage dresses in style. As for the ladies - with their flowing silk robes garlanded by gold embroidery, and their tall matching turbans these mesdames, who stride with majestic hauteur along the hectic pavement, could take the role of duchess in a theatre production. Indeed, in any other town they would look as if they had just slipped out of the back door from the stage. Only in Dakar, where everyone dresses in like manner, can such outrageous style and pomposity be above ridicule.

Friends who had been to Dakar had warned us that the place is a den of hustlers, thieves, and pickpockets - an accusation which is justified - but back at Hann Plage we were having problems of a different sort with the hoity-toity management of the local yacht club. Tramps like us were not welcome within the portals of this expatriate institute, and when the woman who ran the place caught Nick filling our jerrycans at an outside tap she hit the roof.

"Who is going to pay for that?" she demanded. "You think we have water to give away?"

Her house boy was standing close by, washing her shiny Citroen with a hose, and rivulets of the precious water were winding their way down towards the beach. Nick offered to pay, of course, but Madame sent him away with a flea in his ear. So much for fraternity amongst seafaring folks.

We weighed anchor and headed south for the Casamance. This river lies on the far side of The Gambia, in the southern third of Senegal, and to reach it from Dakar in one day is quite impossible. This would be no cause for concern were it not for the "pirogues".

We had now had the opportunity to make a close study of these curious v-shaped fishing craft, for there were scores of them drawn up on the beach at Hann. Some were tiny – barely big enough for their lone occupant – but some could accommodate a crew of twelve men. All were built along the same lines and consisted of a stout, curved keel to which were fastened two immense planks, one on either side. In the case of the bigger boats, a second plank butted onto the first, giving the boat a bit more freeboard.

To get their net into the sea the men have to tip the boat right over onto its side, and while most of the crew are shoving the gear out, one bails frantically to keep the boat afloat. The design of the Senegalese pirogue is testament to the fact that there is never any weather off this coast, for regardless of the quite remarkable unseaworthiness of their craft the fishermen will journey as much as twenty miles offshore. And - unbeknown to us, as we left Dakar - they will sit on the sea, in the immense blackness of the night, without a single light to betray their presence.

We drifted southward from Dakar on the gentle breeze and the current. The day dissolved into night and I took the first watch, as was my habit. I stayed on deck, for I could hear the distant drone of outboards, but there was nothing to be seen. There was no moon and the sky was overcast so that the night was as thick as mud. Then, all of a sudden, away to port, I saw a bright orange fire.

Fire? On the water? Fire is an International Distress Signal.

It was impossible to judge how big, or how far away the flames might be. Perhaps they were from a coaster, distant on the horizon. I altered course to put the conflagration on the bow wondering, as I did so, whether the vessel would still be afloat by the time we arrived. Then I darted below to turn on the radio, so that I could listen out for the mayday. On reaching the deck again, only seconds later, I heard cries of alarm and the sound of someone trying to start an outboard motor. Meanwhile, the conflagration, now plainly no more than a little bonfire, slid down our port side in the blackness. I suppose that a fire makes quite a good navigational beacon - but only when everyone understands the message.

Like many another river whose effluent spills into a shallow sea, the Casamance is surrounded at its mouth by treacherous shoals over which the sea rolls and crashes. The white foam and thunder were daunting, but the river is used by commercial traffic and the tortuous channel amongst the banks and breakers was therefore well marked. Once safely through the maelstrom and within the entrance we found ourselves floating along on a placid, brown river. It was surprisingly wide – or, at any rate, it seemed wide. The land hereabouts is low-lying and utterly flat, and this makes it hard to judge distances. Tall silk-cotton trees standing as much as 20 miles away looked like towers in a city, and there was nothing else but the trees to be seen.

As ever, we had been drawn to visit the Casamance on the flimsiest of notions. A short way up the river is an island called Karabane and on this island, according to our ancient chart, we could expect to find a church. Somehow this seemed an unlikely feature for an island which was sure to be undeveloped, in the Western sense of the word, and peopled only with native Africans living in flimsy huts. But our pilot book, which was of a similar vintage, confirmed the existence of a church and made casual reference to a Roman Catholic mission. White robed nuns, parading amongst the palm trees? This we had to see!

Beneath the expected line of palms which fringed the beach at Île Karabane was a short row of low, but rather European-seeming buildings. Just beyond the strand, hidden by the palms, we found a small village of sparsely thatched, wattle huts, each one lying in the fractured shadow of an ancient baobab or a silk-cotton tree. Amongst the trees there was one immense specimen whose roots, tall as walls, would almost have provided a dwelling place. This tree, the people told us, was more than one thousand years old. We decided that it must once have held some sacred significance as the abode of a deity – and it seemed no coincidence that immediately behind it stood the Roman Catholic church. Yes, it really did exist!

We were standing by the ju-ju tree, looking up at the church, when a very small boy arrived and, quite unprompted, began to give us a guided tour. Into the big, half ruinous building he led us, to stand in an aisle carpeted with white sand. Who had worshipped here, we wondered? There were seats enough for more than one hundred souls. Weeds now grew amongst the pews.

The boy took us through an open doorway and into the bell tower. At some stage the roof had fallen in, bringing down with it the old, bronze bell, and that bell still rested where it had fallen, with its supporting beam wedged across the corner of the tower at about head height.

"It is still used to summon the people to church," said the child, and to drive home the point he took up a piece of timber and struck the bell hard.

"Clank," said the bell.

"It's still used? Do you mean to say that the people here are Christians?"

"Of course not! Mon Dieu!" The boy scowled contemptuously. "We are Muslims here and we worship the one true god. But every other Sunday a priest comes from Ziginchior, and he rings the bell, like this..."

"Clank, clank, clank, clank."

If he continued in this way the whole tower might fall around us, and so we led the way out, across the rubble strewn floor. Next, our guide beckoned us back towards the beach. Hidden beneath the trees and shrubs were the burnt-out ruins of another old building. Was this the convent, perhaps?

"L'ecole Especiale," the little boy informed us, and he pointed up at the words emblazoned on a big arch above a doorway. The special school. But a school for whom?

"For the slaves, of course!" Our ignorance was clearly astonishing to this child, but there we had our answer: the Mission was nothing but a euphemism for a slaving station, and the special school was the place where the slaves were licked into shape and taught to recite their catechism, before they made the awful journey across the ocean to join others of their ill-fated race.

Trees had now taken root in the tiny, cupboard-sized cells which, like chapels around a cathedral knave, lined either side of the classroom. Before the French came it was the Portuguese who ran this operation, perhaps on less hypocritical lines but with seemingly equal inhumanity. The boy took us to see a crumbling edifice, measuring about 12 feet square and standing on the margin of the sea. He recited the patter, obviously learnt word for word from a professional tour guide:

"Here the Portuguese held captive the African men, women and children, until a ship arrived to carry them away. Sometimes there were more than one hundred slaves forced together in this one, tiny room. At high tide the sea would pour in." It was all strong stuff, intended to consume the audience in misplaced feelings of guilt. "Ah, my poor ancestors," he ended, sadly.

"*Your* ancestors!" I said. "Your ancestors were doing the selling!"

"Et alors?" He dropped the act and shrugged his shoulders. "Do you have something for me?"

Sixty miles upriver from Karabane is Ziguinchor, the regional capital of the Casamance and a town much acclaimed amongst backpackers. Rather than toil all the way upstream with *Maamari* we decided to leave her at anchor and catch a bus. To do this we had first of all to take a pirogue-ferry to Elinkine, but from there the journey was straightforward.

Ziguinchor was not much to our liking, being a featureless, sprawling town of low, modern buildings. Nevertheless, Ziguinchor is popular with the French and so we decided to pay a visit to the port and see if there were any yotties of our acquaintance.

Seething around the iron gate which barred the entrance to the quayside were scores of men and women who jostled each other for a place at the front, but on our approach the crowd melted aside - perhaps believing us to be from one of the yachts whose masts we could now see - and we were admitted unchallenged. None of the boats was familiar to us and having inspected them casually we turned to go; whereupon we were accosted by a most officious little man of severe countenance and speech. Were we from a yacht, he demanded to know? Where was the yacht? Had we cleared customs and immigration?

In an effort to satisfy his enquiries and take off the heat we said that we had cleared customs in Dakar but, regrettably, we had done no such thing. Fresh from the continent of Europe, where such protocol is nowadays regarded by officials with disdain and disinterest, we had not bothered to go looking for the customs and immigration officers in Dakar. In consequence, we were now illegal immigrants sixty miles within the national borders of Senegal. Out of the frying pan we stepped, and into the fire.

Where were our passports, our inquisitor demanded to know? Then, mercifully, fate intervened. "Wait here," the man barked - and as he marched away to sort out a fracas on the quay we turned and fled.

This experience coloured our entire impression of the town of Ziguinchor, and thereafter every trader that we met seemed intent on causing us the maximum aggravation. Perhaps they sensed our vulnerability, for while we waited impatiently for the bus which would carry us home the vermin of this place gathered about. When we turned down their poorly made souvenirs they rattled them in our faces and uttered taunts. Of all our experiences in many different countries this one stays in my mind as the most horrid.

Finally, the driver decided that the miserable crowd waiting in the sweltering sun was enough to fill his bus and we packed in. But whereas we had planned to lose ourselves in the scrum at the back, the man insisted that we two – the only tourists - join him in the cab.

"Have your passports ready," he said. "There will be a checkpoint along the way."

What had seemed like the end of our trouble was thus only a new beginning.

Sure enough, on the edge of town a soldier stepped out into the road and the bus drew to a halt. The door at the back was thrown open and the passengers were ordered to disembark, which they did, clambering over their seats and their possessions. What would happen when the soldiers asked to see our passports? Illegal entry is a serious crime in any state, and at best we would be thrown into prison. There was even a possibility that the boat might be confiscated. My heart was pounding fit to break my rib cage - but, again, the angels intervened; we were overlooked, and with the payload herded back into their fold the bus moved off.

I relaxed my tense mind and limbs, and my heart began to slow its beat. But not for long. The southern-most region of Senegal suffers from a blight calling itself the Casamance Separatists. To this day, the murderous minority who go by this name cause havoc in the region, stealing, setting off bombs, and murdering tourists. Since our visit we have been told that the Separatists had just recently killed two British tourists on the same route that we were now travelling, and for this reason the army presence was high. They were not through with us yet.

The soldiers at the second checkpoint wore semiautomatic rifles and mirrored sunglasses, a combination which suggests the influence of American movies and which always causes me to fear. As the bus stopped, the driver hopped down to inspect a front tyre which, being bald and threadbare, was now almost on fire. Seeing his chance, Nick stepped down and crouched beside the man. That left me alone in the cab.

The people in the back of the bus were once again made to get out and their papers were again examined. Then the lean, loose-limbed soldier commanding the unit poked his gun through the window of the cab and said... something that I could not understand. I gazed back at him, appalled. It was plain that he wanted my passport, or so I imagined, yet he had spoken not in French but in Wolof. Suddenly the man burst out laughing and his colleagues joined in. Nick and the driver got quickly back into the cab - and we were on our way.

There is very little traffic on the roads of Senegal, and when we saw a car approaching from the opposite direction I knew at once, intuitively, that this was yet another police check. By now I had been so long in a state of suppressed panic that I was on the point of collapse. In true American TV style, the car slewed to a standstill in front of the bus and two uniformed officers leapt out. This time there was no messing. They marched straight towards the cab... and asked to see the driver's licence.

We reached Karabane and the sanctuary of our boat without further ado, but the incident had left us badly shaken. We resolved to get out of Senegal the next day. That night I awoke, sweating and trembling, from a dream in which we had been pursued to the river's entrance by a warship. When the sun rose I was eager to be away directly.

On the first feeble breaths of the morning breeze, beneath the suffused glare of a hazy sun, we motored downstream. As we emerged from the calm cloister of the river and slipped out into the serpentine channel I cast a glance astern – and my heart gave one almighty thud before its pace instantly doubled.

"There's a warship following us."

"Don't be daft," Nick feigned nonchalance but his brow was creased. He glanced over his shoulder. Then he tapped the throttle lever with his foot, urging the engine faster.

Out into the channel twixt the dangerous sand banks came the warship, smoke trailing from its funnel, a bone of white foam in its teeth. The gap between us closed. Twisting and turning along the narrow passage like a rabbit before a hound, *Maamari* reached the final marker just as the ship began to overhaul us. We turned south. The warship rounded the buoy – and turned to the north. Truly, if there is a god, he has an evil sense of humour.

5

WORLDS APART

*In which are glimpsed the Old, the New,
and our own, very private world.*

In the lazy wind, on the back of the current, we ambled down towards Guinea Bissau. This was to be the last item (or so we told ourselves) on our detour from the direct route to the Caribbean. Guinea Bissau was a country of which we knew absolutely nothing except that it had some islands; islands clustering in a bunch - like nuggets fallen from a gold panner's purse - at the edge of the unknown shore.

Yes, islands on the map have all the allure of precious stones but these, which seemed from the image in the atlas to be clumped offshore, are actually uncut diamonds washed down into the mouth of the river Geba. A study of the relevant chart reveals all - but, indeed, the merest glance at this same chart ought to be enough to persuade any but the most eccentric explorer to give the place a very wide berth. Writhing amongst the low-lying alluvial islands is a tangled knot of narrow, shallow channels, cordoned with acres of drying mud or sand. The seaward area, which has never been

surveyed, bears the legend "Danger zone with rocks and shallows."
Merchant ships give this notorious coastline a good offing.

Night had fallen before we came within the influence of the
Geba, but a good wind had arisen from the west. The tide was also
in our favour, and this was not something to be overlooked or
ignored since, according to our old trusty pilot book, it could flow at
up to five knots. Using the radar to measure our distance from the
island shores on either side, and with a bearing on one light, blinking
at us from a buoy, Nick plotted our position and then came on deck.
"We're going along nicely. We might as well keep going for another
hour or two."

Because the river is broad but shallow we needed only to
pull over to one side in order to drop the hook and take our ease for
the night, but whilst we had the advantage it made sense to press on.
I glanced at the echo-sounder which had for some time been reading
12 metres and was shocked to see it suddenly crash down to only
three.

"It can't be right," said Nick. The electronic dashes on the little
screen flickered and then reformed in the shape of 2.6. When they
read 1.1 we were going to run aground. Nick was incredulous. "But I
just plotted our position! We're in at least 12 metres."

Our chart was new but it was based on a survey made forty
years earlier, and a river's entrance is notorious for the shifting shoals
in its mouth. Much could have changed in forty years. I dived below
to grab a torch and waved it over the water. The sudden brightness
emphasised the black cloak of night. We were alarmed to see that the
blue of the ocean had given way to a brown murk, such as one
would expect to find over shallow mud banks. And we were
galloping towards our fate at a good six knots, with the tide adding
further to our speed.

"Cast off the genoa!" I cried, doing so in the same instant. The
echo-sounder was now showing just 1.9 metres. Nick hurried to get
the lead line and ran about ten metres of chord off the drum. Then
he swung the lead.

"No bottom."

Well, of course there was no bottom! We were still doing
about four knots, so that the weight simply streamed in our wake.

"Again!" I said, this time bringing *Maamari* up; up towards the shore
I feared, but up regardless now, until she faced into the wind and the
sails stalled. The lead flew out, the boat caught up with it, but the

line running out through Nick's hand was already taut.

"No bottom," he said. "That confounded machine!"

If ever we had need of an echo-sounder it was now, in this river estuary, but such is the way of machines: they always betray a man's trust and let him down in the hour of his utmost need.

Working the tides we headed upstream towards the town of Bissau, and as we travelled we began to notice a certain constancy, or predictability, about the winds. From mid-morning until midday the wind invariably blew gently from the north-east. Then it seemed to break for lunch and an afternoon siesta. Towards late afternoon it filled in again from the west, gradually increasing in strength until by midnight it reached a good force four. Then it turned in for the night. All in all this was a very civilised wind.

In this part of the world there are three distinct seasons: the wet, the dry, and the harmattan. The wet season runs between June and October and during these months the skies dump around 140 inches of rain on Guinea Bissau. This deluge is equivalent to Britain's entire average rainfall for almost four years. The harmattan season is the time of dust-laden winds and sea breezes, neither of which bring any rain. Temperatures are a bearable 85 to 90°F. In contrast to the wet months, the dry season is so unutterably dry that mud-walled houses - and lips and heels - crack open, and the ground is so hot that one can feel the heat coming up through the soles of one's shoes. To quote our old friend, the Admiralty pilot, "...relief from the damp sultry heat (of the wet season) acts first as a tonic, but the adverse effects outweigh any beneficial ones." The author was clearly not much enamoured with Guinea Bissau. He writes at length also of mould and disease, and he manages to make the place sound like hell on earth. On our second day on the river I began to think him right.

It was early in the afternoon and we were at anchor, watching the water sluice by and congratulating ourselves on having chosen, for this little jaunt, a week when the tides coincided with the evening breeze. Lunch had been consumed and we were idling in the cockpit when a big brown dragonfly alighted on my hair. Then another one landed on the seat beside me. Another appeared on the rail - and another - and more, and more.

Next there came large black flying ants, which swarmed through the rigging with the whine of fighter planes and rushed to

invade the deck. And then, all of a sudden, we were under attack
from the heavy bombers: menacing black wasps, two inches long,
with the six black and yellow striped legs of their undercarriages
dangling below in a message of intimidation. The squadron bumbled
around our heads - engines droning, weapons primed - and I went
berserk.

Left, right, and centre I swatted, striking especially at the
angry-coloured wasps but sparing not even the dragonflies, whose
big eyes now seemed to me to be lit with psychopathic intent. I
swatted all and sundry, but the blitz continued. Shiny, black wasps
lunged towards me. Beetles in orange or metallic-green armour
plating went scuttling around my bare feet, antennae waving. For
half an hour the hostilities continued, with new combatants arriving
all the while to take the places of their fallen comrades, and then we
finally had the sense to start the engine and out-run our assailants.

The death toll had been appalling - half a hundred tiny
cadavers littered the deck - yet our side had suffered no loss. Not one
bite had the enemy inflicted. Surveying the carnage in a more
rational frame of mind I now felt more than a little ashamed, but my
near hysterical panic had drained me utterly. I wanted only to sleep,
and my principle emotion was one of dread. Would every afternoon
bring such an infestation? Fortunately, word of our unkind reception
got around the insect world and they never extended to us the
courtesy of another visit.

Wending our way slowly up the river we were increasingly fascinated
to think of the islands, so low that a hazy smudged line floating on
the soft horizon was the only symptom of their being. North of the
channel lay islands hardly divided from the shore. To the south, the
Bijagos islands were so near yet still so wholly unknown and
mysterious. Who lived here, disclosing not even the merest trace of
their presence? We saw no smoke, nor any lights at night, and the
swift, sullied waters of the river were ours alone. But before we
could explore the islands we were required to clear in, in the city, and
after our experience in Senegal we were not going to skip this duty.

Arriving off Bissau in the morning we anchored in what
seemed the most suitable spot, off a ruinous but still much
frequented iron pier. Tied up alongside the pier was a vessel entirely
decorated with the brown and purple stains which are wrought to
metal over time, and at first we took it for a wreck. Then we realised

that it was actually a ferry. It came uncertainly out towards us, its decks entirely packed with travellers. We launched the dinghy and went ashore to make the acquaintance of the place to which our curiosity had led us.

Bissau has gone to seed since the Portuguese were kicked out in 1975 - but then this little one horse town was never more than a claim, staked out with the inevitable pink and white palace, on the edge of an unassailable forest. The colonists never came near to taming this land, yet still they hung on to it with their teeth when the time to leave was long overdue.

Wandering up the main street, we took in the scene. The grand old buildings left by the Portuguese were decayed and mouldering, and Bissau was anything but affluent - this must be one of the smallest, most languid capital cities in the world, with no commerce and no shops to speak of - yet traffic scurried up and down the broad Avenue Amílcar Cabral as if on a race track, and although half the vehicles were battered old taxis, minus their windscreens and with their doors tied-on with string, the others were fancy new jeeps and Mercedes.

"There's something funny going on around here," we told ourselves.

Further observation revealed that the jeeps were driven by white folks and bore cryptic legends or acronyms, such as UNICEF. The Mercedes were driven by fat black men in designer sunglasses, with chunky gold jewellery encircling their fat wrists, necks, and fingers.

Here was the sordid truth about foreign aid made manifest. More than sixty organisations were at work within this little town, their employees serving as the emissaries of half as many alien powers, all of whom sought to gain a neo-colonial toehold in the country. Something like 2,000 foreigners lived here - witting or unwitting servants both of capitalism and communism - at the expense of the tax payers back home in Sweden, China, America, Russia... It seemed that everybody had an embassy or a consulate here.

And who can blame their quisling compradors - ministers and others in public office - who grow fat off the juicy chunks of slush money passed their way? Such behaviour seems even to be applauded by local society: "Get what you can grab - you're an idiot, to be despised, if you pass it over - and we'll sit at your feet and pick up the crusts which you toss our way." Foreign aid, in Guinea Bissau, is undeniably a disruptive and therefore a negative influence, undermining an otherwise admirably strong society. One suspects that this might be one of the primary objects of the exercise.

Guinea Bissau is a country of only half a million souls, yet its people belong to more than 14 different tribes. Nevertheless, this did not seem to us to be a nation divided by its ethnic and linguistic variety. The great majority of the people live in a style which is largely traditional, and they continue to worship God according to their ancestral, animist ways. Many of the city dwellers follow Islam. Fewer than ten percent of the people are Roman Catholic. Be that as it may, when the time arrived for the annual Mardi Gras there were plenty of revellers on the streets of Bissau.

The religious aspects of the Lent festival had no place in Bissau, and the carnival was given over to children and youths. Boys strutted up and down the avenue in a jumble of fancy dress, carrying masks of their own making. Young girls danced in the traditional manner. They wore skirts made of African cloth but had tinsel garlands on their heads.

This was a spectacle which presented a marvellous example of cultural cross-pollination. It was a window on the development of erstwhile pagan celebrations, such as Christmas and Easter. The legitimate parent to the carnival in Bissau is obviously the "masquerade", or masked-parade, of Roman Catholic Europe - a parade which, itself, almost certainly has origins in the pagan past - but the masks which the young Africans carried were huge creations, sometimes three feet high, and they bore a strong resemblance to the ceremonial masks of the local, adulterating culture.

The carnival masks were made only of papier maché and mud, and they were astonishingly light, but like the magnificent wooden initiation masks found anciently throughout this region, they sat not before the wearer's face but upon his shoulders - sometimes they were even held aloft at arms' length - and as the dancers swung and pirouetted down the road, the grotesque faces towered above the crowd.

Like the old wooden masks, these pseudo-traditional ones were portrayals of intimidating monsters or spirits. Many of them were coloured red and green and they generally had fearsome teeth. Like the traditional masks, these, their offspring, were very often ornamented with a symbol or figurine on the top. Yet the emblems used were not ancient relics but contemporary commentary. Many of the masks that we saw carried a little model of the pope, who had just visited the town, but one showed a white man in a pin-striped suit giving American dollars to a black man.

"They are not ashamed," said the man who walked beside us in the throng. He was Bjorn, a Swedish economist in the pay of one of the aid organisations, and he had come here "to sort out the treasury." According to Bjorn, the government had kept no accounts for the past ten years, and he labelled them incorrigibly corrupt. As for the people, they were nothing but idlers.

"On the edge of town there is a brand new Volvo factory, but will they work in it? Pah! They are happy to take our money - oh, yes! - but one cannot persuade them to work."

So far as I could see this was quite understandable. Unlike the peasant folk of nineteenth century Europe, the people here still have their land. Naturally, they are quite happy to receive cash handouts - most people are - but, work? Why should they want to work? Peasants do not give up the luxury of their ancient lifestyle until the land is stolen from them - and then, of course, they have no choice. All this was lost on Bjorn who could not comprehend that there are people in this world who are happy with their lot, and who do not wish to join the rat race.

"We are too quick for them. They just cannot catch on," said he, who even after two years had failed to come anywhere near to understanding the West Africans. His kind are still out there, trying to hammer in their we-know-best policies. Fortunately, the ground in Guinea Bissau seems to be pretty unyielding.

We left Bissau on Ash Wednesday, with the ship's compliment increased by a factor of two. Alain and Veronique were a French couple running a charter yacht in the Mediterranean, and they had come to see whether the Bijagos would be suitable for the same kind of venture. Nobody in town seemed to know very much about the islands ᴗ nobody we spoke to had even visited them - but the rumour was that on some of the outer islands the people had not seen a white face in more than fifty years.

We set off for one of the more accessible of the outer islands. The plan was to approach via a narrow channel shown on our chart as lying between this and the neighbouring isle.

Unfortunately this channel seemed to have silted and we could not enter. Instead we had to anchor more than half a mile off the coast, miles from any settlement.

Alain and I went overboard for a dip, but the water was so murky that we could not see our hands in front of our faces. There is something slightly unnerving about swimming blinkered, so to speak; or did we have an intuition of something sinister? At the time I thought that our fear of crocodiles or sharks was really quite silly, but now I know that both are to be found here in abundance.

We rowed ashore and spent two unproductive hours hunting for a path through the dense forest, wondering all the while what reception four white faces would get when they suddenly trespassed into a stone-age village. Our apprehension was further increased when Alain almost stepped on a snake, and we decided to call it a day. While we were retracing our steps, following the marks which we had left, the French man suddenly let out a cry and announced that he had seen a naked man rushing into the bush. "Ou peut être c'était un gorille."

At the back of my mind was the thought that the very first white visitors to these shores had ended up in the stew-pot.

After this abortive debut we studied the chart more closely and having identified the few anchorages accessibly close to a shore we chose a place called Cahabaque. Between the main island of Cahabaque and two much smaller ones we found a sheltered pond which seemed ideal for our needs – but, as it turned out, even here the matter of dropping the hook was not easy. Here there was either too much water or else not enough. The transition from one situation to the other could be described not so much as a gradient but as a vertical line. The bottom shelved so quickly that instead of running aground *Maamari* bumped the leading edge of her keel against a cliff of mud.

That night we slept in the cockpit and I awoke in the morning at dawn. No sound came from any of the three islands and there was no sign of life on the shores; there was nothing to be seen but trees. About halfway between the boat and the beach, a log floated in the muddy water but the surface was otherwise without a mark. There was not the slightest breath of wind. I considered taking an early morning bath but, serene though the surroundings were, the water was not inviting. And then I noticed that the log had suddenly gone, so that settled it. I had thought that it looked rather reptilian.

This time our foray into terra incognita went rather well. On the beach we encountered our first natives - a small boy, naked but for a string around his waist, and his mother, a woman who looked to be about fifty but whose belly was swollen with the next child. Although somewhat alarmed on being suddenly confronted by four strangers, the woman did not actually flee. After Alain's 'take me to your leader' pantomime had failed and his houses, sketched in the sand, had likewise brought no response, I then thought to utter the word, "Inorei", recalling the name from the chart. The woman at once pointed in the direction of the village. It was almost too easy.

There was no trouble this time in finding a path through the trees; we followed a well-worn track, as obvious as a pavement. After wandering for a mile beneath the high verdant canopy, we came around a corner and upon a cameo of thatch-roofed cottages framed by overhanging branches. My heart began to beat a little faster.

On the edge of the village we sat down in the shade of a tree. Before too long our view of the orange-brown, mud-brick houses was walled off by a crowd of little children and young girls and old men, who all gawped in silence at the intruders. Doubtless they wondered whence, and why we had come. As a welcome it was lacking in smiles, but at least no one was waving a spear in our faces.

The men of the village were clad in shorts or in a cloth worn like a sort of miniskirt version of a Roman toga. When we arrived the girls were wearing nothing but the briefest of "grass" skirts - garments which are actually made from the dyed and plaited fibres of a tree - but in our honour they began to don grubby white bras or corsets, doing this at a leisurely pace whilst standing in a row before us. Their bellies were scarred in an ornate pattern not dissimilar to embroidery.

By way of a tribute or peace offering we handed out cigarettes, and these were eagerly pocketed, figuratively speaking. After a while, since no one had taken the initiative to send us away, we got to our feet and embarked on a tour of the dwellings. Their occupants trailed along behind us.

The village consisted of a closely packed group of perhaps as many as fifty buildings, all of them constructed from large mud bricks which are laid in place whilst still wet. Tiny square huts squatted, like granaries, on steddles of the same sun-baked clay. The trellis-work of an old, round roof, now naked of covering, cast a spider's web pattern on the ground. We had no way of discovering the purpose of either of these two types of small building but have since realised that the "granaries" were indeed used to store the local grain, which is rice.

Black windows watched from the crazed walls of the bigger buildings. These were each set on a mud-built plinth and shaded by the ample overhang of a flimsy thatch. In the middle of the village was an open kitchen, set beneath the circle of a round thatch. At the side of an empty, well-trodden plaza another thatch shaded two wooden drums.

By no means could the earthen houses of this village be termed "mud huts". Some of them were quite large buildings, built on a fairly high platform fitted with mud-bricks steps, and with an ornate parapet wall along the edge of the shaded veranda. Pictures, letters and symbols were painted on many of the orange-earth house fronts and in most instances the pictures were of animals and birds, but on one wall I was shocked to find drawings of a jet fighter plane and a helicopter. Were these relics of the war? The Portuguese certainly did drop bombs over the forests - they even dropped napalm bombs as they tried to annihilate the foe who were, at one and the same time, their own colonial citizens. Whether they ever bombed the Bijagos I doubt, but just the sight of these astonishing machines over the island must have been awesome for a people who have still not even seen a car.

The Bijagos islanders are necessarily quite self-sufficient, needing and taking nothing from the civilisation of the mainland; needing no matches, no clothes, no fuel, no soap, no food... but needs and wants are a very different matter. The Bijagos enjoy a quality of life that many of us, who boast a much higher standard of material living, find very enviable. Theirs is a lifestyle entirely free from hunger and homelessness, and at the same time wholly ignorant of additives, pesticides, mortgage repayments, and electricity bills. Theirs is a society where crime is almost unheard of, for its penalty of ostracism is entirely prohibitive. It is a lifestyle where loneliness, even in old age, is impossible to conceive of; a lifestyle where social security is a family concern. But all is not entirely well in the Bijagos, for the whisper of material possession is in the air and glimpses have been had of a seemingly superior civilisation: that of the T-shirt.

Was it only a forceful few who pestered us continuously for the very shirts on our backs? At times it seemed as if the whole of Inorei was after us. Tiring of their attentions we bade the villagers adieu and set off down the long path to the beach. The children came too, but on reaching a certain point, which we took to be the limits of their village, the majority turned back. We continued along the way with our retinue cut to three young lads. Two came with us out of curiosity, but their companion and leader was the very incarnation of greed and covetousness. First it was our shirts that he kept tugging at; then he pestered Alain and Nick to surrender their shorts. After that he had a go at pulling Veronique's wedding ring off her finger, having, I am sure, no idea of its financial or its sentimental value. Finally, he reduced his demand to five biros. If we had thought to bring any biros we might even have paid him off, but as it was our pockets were bare.

Still with this thorn in our flesh keeping constant pace and continuing his harassment, we reached the dinghy and lifted it down into the water - whereupon, on climbing in and turning to wave goodbye, we found that the boys had picked up rocks. We were, as yet, sufficiently close that they might stone us; and naturally, we had no weapons of our own. With tremendous bravado our French friend leapt to his feet and gave a wonderful impression of a fierce, angry Neanderthal. The boys dropped their rocks and slunk away. Decidedly, Alain concluded, this was not the place to run a holiday business.

Back aboard *Maamari*, we now saw signs of life on one of the two smaller islets. A dug-out canoe was drawn up on the sand and below it, beyond a band of slimy mud, a woman was at work, washing something at the water's edge.

By the time we had got back into the dinghy and rowed ashore, six children and a man had come out of the trees. Hesitantly, we strolled towards them and they, with equal uncertainty, came to shake our hands. The family lived alone on the island and had, for their accommodation, the most pathetic of homes. It was just a collection of branches leant up against a flimsy framework of coppiced sticks and it measured perhaps four feet square. A child builds a better playhouse in the garden.

One was inclined to feel sorry for this family, whom western charity would doubtless have wanted to bless with corrugated iron sheets and PVC, but - then again - had they wanted to, they could very easily have built something better. In such circumstances benevolence is invariably destructive. (One is reminded of the way in which well-meaning Victorian tourists completely destroyed the unique, stone-age culture of the island of St Kilda, off Scotland.) In a climate where life is no struggle houses tend to be small, being built as much for privacy as for anything else, and for these folks, who had a whole island to themselves, this was obviously not a concern. Presumably they lived elsewhere in the rainy season.

The children and their father were most eager to show us their domain and the tour took us past the 'house' and past six pits dug in the ground. Here the four older children and their parents would apparently tread palm berries to make oil. Close by was an iron press of the type formerly used for printing relief. The finished product, red and full of sediment, is bought by a factor and taken to the market in the city. It is good, flavoursome stuff, hopeless for frying but ideal for soups and stews.

Evening found us lounging on the beach with the little family, swigging their palm-wine, each in turn, from their one plastic cup. When the man asked if he could visit *Maamari* my heart sank. After such hospitality, how could we refuse? - yet we knew that to have him aboard would be a mistake.

Darkness was approaching, and with its cover for our ally we shut the cabin from his sight and welcomed this yeoman of the Palaeolithic into our shabby but undeniably techno-aged cockpit. It was a disaster.

Our wine was sour to the visitor's taste. Peanuts he had never encountered and refused to even try. But the china mugs - which we had chosen to use to express the minimum of ostentation - were admired as if they had been finest porcelain, and the man's eyes widened in astonishment as they explored the boat. The shiny, chrome winches he touched and tapped shyly, no doubt wondering from what they could be made. The compass was an astonishing jewel; a crystal dome reflecting the light of the flickering candles. As his gaze roamed around the Aladdin's cave which had happened to arrive on his doorstep, the look of wonderment hardened to a lustful, all-coveting gaze. He wanted everything. Finally, his eyes lit on the outboard motor, hanging on the pushpit, and he demanded that we hand it over. It was plain that even if we did so there would be no smile of thanks and satisfaction, for this was a hunger and greed which *knew* no satisfaction.

Early next morning our friend arrived in his leaky old canoe, and began hammering on the side of our boat. Relations had become strained and we began to see how it was that Captain Cook ended up with a spear through his heart - and all because he would not let the natives steal his dinghy. It was time to be moving on.

Even after the anchor was aweigh the man still held tightly to our guard-rail. We spotted some fish lying in the bottom of his canoe and saw a chance to put this clash of cultures onto a better footing. Could we buy the fish, please?

The fish? He seemed amazed. He and his people were entirely self-sufficient and so it had never occurred to him that anyone could need to *buy* food. He had no idea what to charge, for in his culture fish had no value. Would he like to exchange them for one old, but still very serviceable hunting knife? Indeed, he would! The smile returned to the man's face and we parted company the best of friends.

By now we had all had quite enough of the Bijagos islands. Our French companions found that the palm oil merchant was expected from Bissau that same day and that they could travel back to the mainland with him. When last we saw the couple they were standing on the beach near Inorei, amidst a throng of islanders, and as we rowed back to *Maamari* the half-strangled utterings of Alain's saxophone came to us, over the still water, like the cries of a far off whale. The noise chased us from the anchorage - and we were on our way. Ahead lay nothing but the vast Atlantic and we ran eagerly into the ocean's embrace.

It is funny how small this big world is. You can sail for two days in the lightest of breezes and still make an impression on the surface of a child's globe. Trickling down the coast of Spain or Africa we used to mark off our progress each noon, and it was always quite amazing to see our little bunny hops make a mark half an inch long. But the ocean is a different matter.

Of course, the lines are still there - those imaginary lines which form the net to calibrate and contain our world - but when the land is so many hundreds of miles away it might as well not exist. Its existence has no meaning and the lines are betrayed for what they really are: just a figment of mankind's neurotic desire to keep everything under his control.

I think that I have never been happier than when we sailed across the Atlantic from Africa. On that crossing my mind reached a place of perfect tranquillity and absolute contentment, such as some people are evidently able to achieve after years of yogic meditation. But although it came without any such effort, this state of mind did not come to me overnight. To get to that place I had to cross a frontier.

Somewhere, deep within my being, I dread long-haul passages. Outwardly, I look forward to the voyage, but in the hours before we weigh anchor and sail my pulse rate increases and my breathing becomes shallow and dry. This is not a fear of storms, nor any kind of concrete fear at all, but perhaps there is, at the very core of man's existence, some primeval force which dreads the wrench from Mother Earth. One experienced cruising man of our acquaintance often gets a fever on the day of his intended departure.

For me, the first two days at sea are usually miserable since I am generally feeling sick. There is an element of the vicious circle here. Tension undoubtedly plays a considerable role in seasickness, and the fear of such suffering certainly adds to my apprehension and tension. The attitude of a sailor heading out to sea ought surely to be that of a bird uncaged and allowed the infinite freedom of the air, but often when we set off I feel more like a convict condemned to endure a sentence! My eyes are on the calendar and even on the clock. And then the third day dawns.

Is it really only the third day? Surely we have been at sea forever? The land is but a dim memory, on the shores of another world. The past is just a shadow, and the future is a nothing. Time has no meaning: there is only now; there is only here; there is only is. The cord which bound us to our mother has once again been severed, brutally severed, but now all that is forgotten - I can no longer hear her voice - and I am in the power of the sea.

L. Ron Hubbard, founder of the Moonies, could take some lessons from the sea - but perhaps he already knows them. Charismatic religious movements of this sort operate by removing the novice from his familiar environment and denying him the handrails of accepted knowledge, which are a man's only hope in the darkness. Then they satiate him with their own existence. Such is also the way of the divine and mighty ocean.

So much for philosophy. We had plenty of time for it on that lazy passage across the ocean. We had time for anything and everything it seemed, and the world really was our oyster. People generally have a very definite idea about where they are going before they push off into the wide blue yonder, but we were making it up as we went along. Having detoured so far from the milk-run route to the Caribbean we now thought that we might as well go the whole hog and visit Brazil, too.

The passage from Guinea to the corner of Brazil takes one south, over the equator and through the broad belt of the doldrums. This is a place which most sailors dread, for here the winds are light or altogether absent and it is possible to be becalmed for days on end. However, on this passage we never experienced even one hour of calms. The wind and current nudged us gently along. We took down the mainsail and spread butterfly wings, with a lightweight triangle of blue and gold stripey cloth balancing the genoa. Dolphins came to greet us; fish offered themselves up onto the deck or bit the hook. The brown fin and long back of a big shark sidled past silently just a few feet from the hull.

We showered in the sunshine, baked bread, read, and lay about. Once again we were, of course, peculiarly obsessed with the merest fractions of time as, with utter detachment and out of a sense of duty alone, we measured our exact position in relation to the sun. The land was so far distant that our chart was a blank page – a sheet made meaningful only through the numbers scribbled along each edge. This was our last link with sanity. Or was it the only vestige of insanity?

Such was our joy and sublime contentment on the ocean's expanse that we talked about turning away from South America and just circling around on the infinite blue. If a man had a yacht big enough to grow onions, yams, and coconut trees… but without such sustenance one grows dull - nature's bounty tinned and processed is no substitute for real food - and although our fruit and vegetables were lasting well they would be gone long before we tired of circling the deep.

By way of a compromise we altered from the direct and easy course to head north again, by a few degrees, and investigate St Peter and St Paul's Rocks. On the chart they looked like our kind of place – a tiny plateau of grey stone flung some 500 miles out from the coast of Brazil. Their appeal is even greater than that of other islands because they are uninhabited – but new lands are never as we expect them.

From an uninhabited rock standing solitary in the ocean one gets a peculiar but strong sense of being watched. There is an almost tangible aura of power, as if the mass were a lodestone sending out waves to create an invisible, as yet unidentified, field of force. Do man's footfalls erode some ancient, energetic property of the earth? To invade the sanctity of a mountain summit or a stack marooned at sea is surely an act of sacrilege... but here at the rock of St Peter and St Paul there was not the expected feeling of awe. Was the rock, physically, too lowly, we wondered?

As we came around the northern edge of the rock we were astonished to find a fishing boat anchored close in its lee, within a stone's-throw of the islet, and our own sacred seclusion was suddenly tarnished. We have since heard that there are often half a dozen long-liners here.

We turned south, and throughout the night the arc lights aboard the fishing boat cast a bright loom on the sky. In the smudgy grey light of the new day we found that we had a guest aboard *Maamari*. A big, brown noddy tern had passed the night on our pushpit. The bird was not at all shy; I sat so close that I could have touched him, but he ignored me. When the first long fingers of sunlight poked up above the horizon he yawned, stretched his wings wide and stepped out onto the air.

With almost too perfect synchronicity, we crossed the equator on the equinox - the day that the sun runs its orbit precisely above that latitude - and moreover we crossed it at precisely the hour when the sun was overhead. Our position lines were therefore two parallel ones, almost overlapping each other, intersected at roughly 90° by the latitude of the sun's meridian altitude. (Naturally, this applies whenever and wherever the sun is overhead the observer at precisely the time of the meridian passage, or local midday. Had our measurements been perfect the position lines would have lain precisely one on top of the other, and the intersection with the line of latitude would have been *exactly* ninety degrees.)

Three days later, at first light, we reached the island of Fernando do Noronha.

Cast adrift 190 miles from the mainland, Fernando is simply beautiful. For a time it was a penal colony, and I can think of no lovelier place where to be banished. Nowadays the island is a conservation area and it is rigidly protected. Although they seem to be unable to stop their wealthy vandals from destroying the rainforest, in other respects the Brazilians take ecological concerns very seriously.

There is a hotel on Fernando, but it is not the kind found in holiday brochures - in fact, the hotel buildings looked as if they were probably the old prison buildings. Nor was this an eco-tourism venture, for the visitors were all bronzed hunks in surfing shorts and golden-limbed babes wearing "dental floss" bikinis.

Only a very few tourists are allowed aboard the island at any one time, and they have to mind their environmental Ps and Qs. So, too, do the yotties. There is no choice of anchorage - one anchors in the appointed place - and, like the other visitors, yachtsmen must pay a daily fee. At this time inflation in Brazil was running at around 2,000 percent... and, as a result, the several thousand cruzados of this daily fee now amounted to only three pence a day.

For two days we roamed and rambled freely over Fernando. The glorious arc of sand below the tiny village was without the blemish of seaside cafes or pleasure boats, and hardly a car travelled the one, winding road. Indeed, the other tourists must have been *exceedingly* few in number, for we hardly ever encountered them.

On the western side of the isle, in the bay where they were born, a hundred young spinner dolphins splashed and jumped and played follow my leader. They were entirely safe from harm, for these waters were off-limits to mankind and even the adjacent shore was out of bounds. Would-be intruders, such as ourselves, were relegated to the cliff-top, 200 feet above the sanctuary. Here we sat, sunning ourselves in the company of a dozen lizards. Little, white fairy terns fluttered amongst the green leaves of the trees above our heads, and red-footed boobies squatted on the branches and watched us watching the wildlife. Tropic birds shrieked to one and other as they reeled around the bay.

If this was not the garden of Eden, it was something pretty close, but even paradise cloys after a time - rather like a surfeit of rich chocolate pudding - and when we had had our fill we went in search of some "action". Fernando do Noronha has that to offer, too. A few miles beyond the anchorage, on the island's northern shore, a megalith known only as Pico thrusts upward from a grove of orange-flowered flamboyant trees. This is a gigantic rock whose stature tells of an enormous ash and cinder cone once clothing the phallic core. At the very pinnacle of the rock there is a light, and because the face of the Pico is even more forbidding than the Matterhorn, a ladder has been set against its side.

A ladder. Does it sound as if the rock has become a child's climbing frame? This is a ladder 1,048 feet tall, ascending without hesitation in a vertical line – although some who have climbed it swear that in certain places the ladder is inclined slightly backwards. As if that were not enough - and even the thought of it is enough for one who cannot scale the mast as far as the spreaders - but as if that were not sufficient challenge, the rock itself is not entirely true. About halfway up there is a kink. At this point the ladder just carries on regardless, leaving the hapless mountaineer trip-trapping up the rusty steps with a gaping chasm of emptiness between himself and the rock. It was at this point that even Nick got cold feet. It was not just the gap and the wind blowing around him, he said, but the ladder seemed to sway. It is a very old ladder and some of the fastenings are worn thin. Nowadays when the bulb on top of Pico goes ping, the engineer who must fit the replacement gets to the top in a helicopter.

With a list of do's and don'ts as long as the seed-pods on the flamboyant trees, Fernando do Noronha is really for the birds and the fishes, but still we planned on staying a while. The plan was adjusted swiftly when the Brazilian government re-evaluated their currency, and the conservationists, in the same instant, decided to index link their charge to the minimum wage. (The minimum wage was an ever-changing figure, published daily in the newspapers, and fines had always been tied to this datum.) Overnight the fee for the two of us went from three pence to £24 - and, overnight, we quit the island.

At the corner of Brazil the ocean current divides, and so we faced a choice. We were of half a mind to turn left and head straight for Patagonia, chancing to our luck to bring us jobs and money sometime soon. Had we known, then, how many years we would be putting between ourselves and our avowed goal we would never have turned, instead, to the north. As it was, we bowed to what seemed like common sense: the Caribbean was the place for yotties to get rich quick. We had phoned Nick's parents to arrange a rendezvous in the Amazonian town of Belem, and now we set off in that direction, heading along the north coast of Brazil. As we left Fernando, a chain of two hundred dolphins went past at a brisk pace, leaping nose to tail.

The morning after our departure we sighted a curious apparition: rock spines, or the spires of half a dozen churches, poking up out of the sea. They had us puzzling. Ahead lay the coral atoll known as Atol das Rocas, but we were not expecting to find it covered in churches! In time the strange grey "rocks" evolved flimsy trunks, as they rose above the horizon, and eventually they were seen to be a line of palms straggling along a narrow sand strip.

Atol das Rocas is another conservation area, as taboo to man as a sacred isle, but a lowly stone hut amongst the trees tells of the era, not long past, when a lighthouse keeper lived here. According to legend, the fellow had not just one daughter but seven. Whether their mother lived here also history does not relate. For their sustenance the lighthouse keeper and his family were dependent on ships from Natal, 140 miles away, and when, on one occasion, the supply ship failed to arrive they found themselves with nothing to eat but fish and coconuts. The people of the Tuamotos, in Polynesia, survive very nicely on fish and coconuts, but the lighthouse keeper and his daughters apparently found the diet inadequate. After some weeks they grew thin and ill. The island had now become their Alcatraz.

In desperation the prisoners cast a bottle into the sea, with a message describing their want. Like a carrier pigeon trained to the job, the sea carried the prayer directly to Natal - or so the story goes. A ship was at once sent to the rescue, and the lighthouse keeper and his seven daughters were taken to Fernando do Noronha. Here the girls all died of smallpox. Apparently, it was the first time they had ever left the atoll.

Whether there is a shred of truth to the tale, I seriously doubt, but one thing is for sure: the bottle could not possibly have gone south. With ease and alacrity the currents carry their cargo north along the coast, and so they ferried us.

Up we went, through the heavy heat of the doldrums. We were on the heels of the sun and its searing rays scorched the deck. After ten in the morning we would creep into the shelter of the cabin, or else the unrelenting glare and torrid heat were enough to bake the brain. Thunder squalls passed and we caught rainwater off the sails. Far away on the horizon, a whale breached. Dolphins came to play at the bow.

We had a date with the Amazon - but as we drifted along the coast I wondered if we really dare go anywhere near this, the mightiest of rivers. The very mention of its name conjured up pictures of fallen trees swirling downstream on the ferocious current; of crocodiles lurking on muddy riverbanks; of all kinds of fearsome biting bugs, carrying fever and death on the wing. And on the day that we first drew near to the river the image was almost realised.

In the mouth of the Amazon sits Ilha Marajo, an island the size of Switzerland. Strictly speaking, the river which flows around the southern shore of Marajo is called the Para, but the Amazon is the chief tributary of the Para - so, effectively, they are one. Our plan was to reach Belem by way of the Para's entrance and then, after spending some time with Nick's folks, to continue around the island and leave by way of the Amazon proper. On the chart it was not an ambitious project, but the chart does not show the tides and those fallen trees. As it turned out, the chart does not even show all the sand banks.

We were a day's sail from the Para when the crystal-clear, turquoise waters of the Atlantic turned a sinister greenish-black, and we knew that we were now venturing into the no-man's-land which ocean and river both struggle to control. Two channels lead through the sandbanks splattered across the mouth of the Para, and to judge by the chart we reckoned the more westerly to be the main channel. Thus it was that, with the wind and current behind us and the tide just beginning to flood, we tore on past the first channel, where the local boats were plying, and were swept towards the main channel beacon.

All at once the black water was patterned with muddy, yellow-brown patches, and the massive tree trunks of my imagining came surfing towards us on the breaking swell. Our sturdy craft suddenly seemed as frail as an eggshell. And where was that beacon? That was no beacon! It was the mast and bridge of a wrecked ship! Ahead of us the water was marked only by breaking seas and they seemed to form a solid wall across the supposed channel. It was time to turn about and beat a hasty retreat - and beat we must, for the wind would now be against us - yet already the Amazon held *Maamari* in her jaws. For hours we writhed to and fro, clawing to hold our own, until at last the beast tired, the current slackened, and we were able to fight free. It took us the rest of the day to tack back up to the inshore passage.

Our first taste of the Amazon had knocked the little faith that we had in the buoyage and the charts, but leaning on instinct and the lead-line we managed to work our way up to the city of Belem, 18 miles upstream. Here we found anchorage off a place pleased to call itself the yacht club, although it was actually nothing more than a fancy social club where tramps such as we were barely tolerated.

Belem bustles with life, like an overgrown market town, but its commerce comes not so much from its surrounding hinterland as from the river. Only recently has man managed to cut roads, with his machines, and scar the rainforest. Before, the river was the only highway, and for Belem it is still the river of life and the raison d'être.

Buses, vans, taxis, lorries - they all come down the Amazon. The mail vans are big, yellow-liveried boats which depart from the city each morning for the five day journey upstream to Manaus. Others who trudge to and fro, making nothing of this epic journey, are the ferries: sturdy, white boats with names such as *God is with us*, or *The good Jesus of Belem*, emblazoned on the bow in scrolled, fairground letters. Between their twin decks hangs a brilliant pattern of swinging hammocks. In the streets of Belem the shelves of many a store are piled high, all around the room from floor to ceiling, with nothing but the colourful bundles made by rolled hammocks. Travel without your hammock and you are condemned to sleep with the roaches and rats, on the hard deck.

Each time the tide turned to flood a rush of traffic, newly favoured, would set off past us up the river in a sort of Le Mans style, panic start. On the last of the ebb a stream of boats would come trickling into Belem, panting like cyclists relieved to sight the finish line. Besides the ferries and the mail boats there were tugs; tugs like terrier dogs, which would rush about madly when let of the leash but which were otherwise to be seen grunting and growling as they tried determinedly to push an immense barge along with their mouths.

Apart from all these bigger boats, with their business in a far off city, there were little, local traders plying between the outlying villages and the metropolis. The biggest of these traders were ornate craft which looked like a cross between a fishing boat and an Elizabethan galleon. They appealed to my artistic sense, and the image rests in my mind of two traders bowling down towards Belem, in the pink light of early evening, with the wind in the pregnant bellies of their dumpy, brown sails.

Quite the most ubiquitous craft amongst all the river traffic around Belem are the boats which fulfil the role of taxi, minibus, and Ford Escort van. We named them shed boats because that was what they were really - just floating sheds. From their design it is plain that there is never any "sea" on the Amazon, for they often have barely nine inches of freeboard. A small wave would send them to the bottom. On top of the shallow hull, and all but covering its entire length, stands a tall, planked shed, which is similar in construction to the wooden houses strung out along the riverbanks. A couple of the shed boats even had thatched roofs, like the houses.

Although we hardly rated them as being worthy of the name of vessels we quickly became quite fond of the shed boats, and this was because of the highly original manner in which they are steered. The captain, or navigator, sits in the bow, but the helmsman-come-engineer sits at the other end of the shed. The distance between the two is not great, but the shattering tat-tat-tat of the one cylinder engine with its dry exhaust makes any kind of verbal communication between them completely impossible. Instead, the captain signals his desire to his mate by tugging on either of two chords, held in his hands. A tug on the left-hand string, and the helmsman pushes the tiller to starboard. A tug on the right and they turn, just so, to the right. With the same strings, the message to go either faster or slower is sent.

Nick and I were accustomed to signalling to one another from the foredeck to the helm and we had established a perfect rapport, yet for the life of me I could not see how this trick with the strings could possibly work. The potential for disaster seemed enormous, and every time a shed boat hove into earshot we would pop our heads up through the companion way and watch - but we never saw any collisions.

Day and night, the river traffic bustled around us, and there was always something to look at, but watching the world whirl by was not our only pursuit in Belem. We had an activity of our own planned. Nick's parents having gone to all the trouble of flying out especially to join us, we decided to make the most of the situation and become legally and decently wed. In Spain the authorities had told us that we must be residents; in Africa they had wanted to see our birth certificates and "a letter of introduction"; but in Brazil nothing is ever impossible.

To be fair, we did not organise the show ourselves but when enquiring at the British Consulate for some assistance and advice we encountered our representative's lawyer. The consul himself found the task beyond him (or beneath him) but Acy Marcos dos Santos took us under his wing and directly to a back-street registry office. Here the lawyer filled out a pile of papers on our behalf - "Sign here... and here" - and then he waylaid an old lady, passing innocently on the street, and despite her considerable initial reluctance persuaded her to witness that we were young free and single and without just cause or impediment. He never troubled to ask us whether we were all these things. I suppose he deemed it impolite.

The wedding would take place in a fortnight's time, Acy announced, and then he cast a critical eye over Nick and said to me, "He must be properly dressed, and see to it that he shaves and combs his hair." Nick was greatly offended. He had shaved and combed his hair just a week before.

By an extraordinary oversight we had neglected to pack a morning suit and a bridal gown amongst our shorts and T-shirts, and at first it appeared that the only tie Nick possessed was a plastic, clip-on one, shaped like a dolphin. However, whilst sorting through his underwear I came across my beloved's old school tie and this inspired him to dig out his old, stripey school blazer - won for rowing, or so he said. How this came to be aboard I cannot imagine.

The great day dawned, and Rosemary, my soon-to-be mother-in-law, eyed her son disdainfully. Her expression alone made clear her disapproval of the jazzy blazer and the almost-matching, fluorescent-yellow shirt. As for Nick's father - Jim's eyes lit up when he saw the groom, and he cried, "That's *my* blazer, damn it! I won that at rugby." (That is, rugby as it is played in the mud, and not with a capital R.) Fortunately he was persuaded that the man of this particular match was the more deserving cause.

We planned to go ashore at eleven and so at twelve-o-five on the dot we bundled into the rubber dinghy. Now, the tide on the Para flows at quite a lick, so that although *Maamari* was anchored only 50 or 60 yards from the shore there was plenty of scope for disaster. Generally speaking, we avoided anything too dramatic but used to drift a couple of hundred yards down current whilst paddling madly against the force. Then we would drag ourselves back towards the jetty in the slacker water close to the bank. The journey was a race against time also, for there were several holes in the 17 year old pneumatic dinghy, and the glue needed to fix them had set to a lump in the tin.

On the occasion of our wedding we had not only to contend with a four knot stream and the usual soggy floats; as we embarked into the boat we discovered that there was now a gash in the floor too. The river had ingress. Hobbled by pencil skirts, Rosemary and I slithered inelegantly into the stern of the dinghy. Nick rolled his trousers to the knee whilst Jim - who was at the oars - decided to undress and row ashore in his Y-fronts.

The stuffed shirts in the yacht club lined up to peer from the window. The English reputation for eccentricity was much strengthened by what they saw. Incredibly, we arrived ashore more or less dry - and then, whilst we sat on the jetty rearranging our dress and putting on shoes (and trousers), the heavens opened to drench us in the usual afternoon downpour.

"Time for a quick beer?" Nick wondered.

"There's always time for a quick beer," said Jim. The shower had passed and we sat on the wet seats of a pavement cafe, drinking ice-cold lager. Next, Jim decided that he really must have a tie - "'Don't want to let old Acy down" - and he took us on a tour of the local menswear specialists. But when Rosemary began to mutter about buying hats he declared that he was not going to stand for "any of that kind of nonsense". Nor was I.

The ceremony itself went off without a hitch. Acy seemed thrilled that we had even remembered to turn up, and he managed to restrain himself from whipping out a comb to tackle Nick's thatch. We picked our way through cabbage leaves and rotten fruit - vestiges of a street market held on the pavement that morning - and on entering the little registry office we were immediately rushed to the altar. Or rather, to a desk in an adjoining room. Rosemary stood to one side, looking rather aghast, but Jim had just been presented with my camera. We now found that his every movement was to be choreographed by the registrar, whose attention to lighting and camera angles was greater by far than his interest in the legal details.

Acy had agreed to act as best-man-come-translator, and so he stood beside us while the registrar rattled off his spiel. Then, when the gentleman paused and looked expectantly at us, we, in turn, looked to Acy.

"Say, yes," said Acy. We said, yes, each in turn.

After that it was indicated that we should swap rings, and then we were told to kiss. Then we had to kiss again, on the registrar's instructions, because Jim was seen to have neglected to snap this detail. And that was that.

At the end we both signed a piece of paper which, for all we know, may have been a hire-purchase agreement, or something worse. As we signed, I noticed that my career had been translated as "painter and decorator" whilst Nick was down as "officer in the merchant marine".

Jim took some more photos, of us all looking very pleased with ourselves, and then we piled into Acy's car and set off to celebrate.

"Take us to the best restaurant in town," Nick commanded gaily, safe in the assurance that Daddy would pay. The best restaurant, in Acy's estimation, was the Hilton Hotel, and here the five of us held a deluxe reception and put away a respectable quantity of steak and salmon and hearts of palm, washing it all down with champagne, whisky, and gin, and chasing it up with cake and chocolate mousse and liqueurs. When, finally, we were presented with the bill we were all surprised to discover that it came to only £30. Life in Brazil is cheap and full of fun. It was only two days later, when we looked at

the bill again, that we realised we had only paid for the bubbly. Acy
had paid for the rest!

6

THE RIVER OF LIFE

A journey on the Amazon.

Jim Dickin Schinas

For a few days more, while Jim and Rosemary were still aboard, we contented ourselves with explorations around Belem and made short voyages into the adjacent creeks, or furos.

Memories of this idle time are like snap-shots in my mind. In the old town we came upon a little fleet of "galleon" traders, stranded by the falling tide and squatting on the slimy mud. Amongst them, a gaggle of ugly, bare-necked vultures was picking through the garbage and orange peel which the river had dropped, and the picture seemed so incongruous that it has remained with me for all time. Vultures are not glamorous, even at the best of times, but always before when we had seen them the birds had been circling overhead, with blood-thirsty longing. Scavenging through rubbish on the foreshore surely ought to have been beneath their dignity.

Etched on another page of my memory is the image of a cobra, almost as fat as my thigh, coiled tightly around the branches in a palm tree. A rare sight it must have been, for the people who found the snake called us over to have a look. When one of the children threw a stone into the branches the reptile slithered around until it was completely hidden in the crown of the palm fronds - and ever since that day I have shuddered a little whenever I see anyone scampering up into a coconut tree.

Another slightly incongruous scene was the beach which we found an hour's journey from the town. A crowd of holidaymakers romped in the surf, with jet-skis and body-boards and windsurfers, suntan lotion and string-and-patch bikinis, ice creams and inflatable rings. A typical beach scene, in fact - but what made it seem so odd was the location. Here, there was no blue Atlantic, flecked with crisp white horses but only yellow-brown water and yellow-brown surf as the river lapped the shore.

Printed so vividly on my mind that I could paint the scene, is the picture of a young girl standing naked as she takes a bucket shower on the stern deck of a passing shed-boat. On another occasion I saw a kettle flung, on a length of string, from a tiny cabin window sliding by. In the next moment the kettle was hauled back in, by an anonymous brown arm - and we made a mental note to decline any invitations to tea which we might receive during our perambulation on the Amazon.

By now we were sufficiently recovered from our experiences in the river entrance to look forward to the long and winding journey ahead, but when Jim and Rosemary flew home we planned, for our first morning a-deux, a little self-indulgence. We would start the day with a long lie in, and follow it with a leisurely breakfast. Then, we told ourselves, we would stroll along the riverfront and take lunch in a riverside cafe. Then ... and then there was a sudden, violent bang, as if we had hit something. We had forgotten that this, the first true day of our honeymoon, was also the first anniversary of that chaotic beginning in El Ferrol.

Nick leapt from the bed to poke his head out of the companionway and I heard him say, "Where the hell are we?" I started up the ladder in alarm.

Life's disasters are often caused by nothing more weighty than the final straw on the camel's back, and this was a classic instance. Two days earlier, while we were exploring a nearby creek, one of the hoses on the engine water pump had fractured. The pump had continued to function, but instead of chucking the water out into the river it had poured it into the bilge, eventually flooding the engine. Without the engine we could not drive the electric anchor winch and so, having sailed back home to our habitual mooring place, we had dropped the light-weight, kedge anchor, on a length of rope. So was taken the first step down the slippery slope.

The next step concerned our batteries. Because there was little or no wind they had not received their usual charge from the Aerogen. This left us without lights and so, in honour of Nick's parents, we had run the lights off the battery reserved exclusively for starting the engine. This is a mortal sin, of course, and it was step two in our downhill slide.

As it happens, Nick had quickly sorted out the engine, but he had failed in his efforts to get the wet alternator going, so that we could not recharge the dead batteries that way. And the little electric generator, which was our emergency reserve, was found, in this time of crisis, to have bent a valve. Steps three and four. Fate, it seems, was conspiring against us. There we sat, inadequately moored and with no ability to start the engine. We were a disaster waiting to happen.

On the day in question there *was* some wind, and the wind was blowing contrary to the current and with roughly equal strength. As a result, *Maamari* had sailed round and around the little anchor like a bull prancing around a stake, until, at length, she managed to tear it out and break free. When Nick and I bobbed out of the cabin the runaway was galloping upriver through a stretch we had never seen before. The loud jolt which had alerted us was not the hook breaking out - there was no chain to rattle around and so the escape had been stealthily made - but the anchor had evidently fouled a pipe or cable, bringing the boat up with sufficient violence to snap the shackle which joined it to the rope.

So there we were, careering along on a four knot current, with no engine and with the sails snugly furled beneath their covers and beneath a big sun awning. There was only one thing to be done: we kicked the main anchor over the side and it brought us up just in time, in about three metres of water, a few metres more from a brick quay.

Now what? Even if the wind continued to blow it would be a couple of hours before the Aerogen had replenished the batteries sufficiently for us to start the engine. In the meantime, with the tide about to turn and fall, we would soon be on the putty. There was nothing for it but to sail.

"I'll get the awning off," I said, and I moved to do so, but -

"Don't bother," said the skipper. "We can do it with the genoa."

With a rope led aft to the sheet winches we eventually got the main anchor aweigh, and by the time we had managed it the tide had turned in our favour. Before the hook was even clear of the water we were off again, rushing madly back downriver through a china shop of shed-boats and fancy Brazilian yachts - I at the helm, Nick still sorting out the anchor and chain - with just a snatch of the genoa to give me steerage. All eyes in the yacht club were upon us. I felt a strong urge to dive below and hide in the loo.

The gap between the two yachts ahead of us was small - too small - and immediately beyond them stood the club's wooden jetty. I furled all but the last few inches of the sail but the current, together with the windage in the awning, were enough to keep us charging along. Which of the two yachts looked the less costly, I wondered, and which the more robust? Just when it seemed that we could not possibly avoid impaling ourselves on one or other Nick finally got the chain stowed. At once he gave the windlass a kick to send it all overboard again in an orderly style. I leant on the wheel and the bow answered... *so* slowly... before the anchor bit and, abruptly, the boat slewed around. The bull was once again tethered by the nose.

From the yacht club restaurant the stuffed shirts eyed us disdainfully, and we felt that the sooner we got away from this place the better.

The channel from Belem through to the Amazon is well marked, but for weeks now we had watched the local boats head away in a completely different direction, disappearing around a distant corner and off the edge of the chart. Curiosity got the better of common sense and we decided to follow suit.

After a couple of days spent fixing up the engine, and having bought armfuls of charts at the local naval base, we said farewell to Belem. As we slipped quietly upstream on the current the various individual buildings became lost in the one clump. Ahead of us was big yellow mail boat – just the sort of vessel that we had been waiting for, to guide us on this expedition - but as we tucked ourselves in behind him we did wonder whether he carried even half our draught.

The town was still in sight and the river a broad, open expanse when our pilot began to stick so close to the trees that we thought he must be trying to prune them. With the echo-sounder showing just one foot more than *Maamari* draws it made sense to pull out a bit, *away* from the shore. We did so ... and, even as we did, slithered gently to a halt.

A quick thrust astern with the engine soon brought us off the mud, but by now the mail boat was disappearing into the distance. We doubled back and scraped past the trees, as he had done, showering the deck in leaves and broken twigs. Then, with no one to show us the way, we went forward hesitantly, with one eye on the echo-sounder. So often taken for granted, that gadget's invention was a breakthrough of significance at least equal to satellite navigation. Lately, our echo-sounder had been behaving itself and we hoped that it would continue to do so and would not let us down as it had on the river Geba.

Our first night travelling the river was spent in Furo de Arroz, a channel between two quite large, densely forested islands. Our advance along the narrow creek seemed to part the still air above the river, just as our bow parted the water. As we touched it, the empty silence was all at once saturated with shrill churring. Surely the sound could not come from the riverbank? It was so loud and intense that it must come from the air only inches away. Or were the creatures who made the din somehow lodged inside my brain? The noise was so insistent and pervasive that I began to think that it really must come from inside my own head! It was *everywhere*, and it was so intense! Even after weeks on the Amazon we never saw the culprits, but we learnt that they were a large, dowdy, flying insect called a cicada.

As dusk settled over the forest the insect world joined together in a last piercing chorus and we pulled over to the side of the channel and set up camp for the night. This was to be the pattern each evening over the ensuing fortnight as we journeyed through the backstreets and into the Amazon's great highway. Soon the thick eiderdown of a moonless night was spread over the forest, and the strident song of the cicadas ended abruptly. Only one sound trespassed into the silence. It came from the impenetrable blackness on the far side of the river and it sounded, at first, like a man sawing. After he had sawn without cease for an hour we re-assessed the noise and made of it one lonesome toad, charmless but persistent in his courtship call. Perhaps he finally found a princess, or perhaps he gave up. At any rate, by midnight the silence was almost suffocating. Come dawn we would awaken with a start, as the first of the shed boats came along the furo with the sound of its engine ricocheting off the trees like machine-gun fire.

Maamari was a gypsy caravan roaming along the Amazon waterway. Each morning we hitched on the sails, shook the reins, and were off again; off down a narrow, tree-lined lane or along the invisible trail which led over the broad heath of a lake's expanse. As we passed their homes the Indians and the half-breed mestizos could only stare in uncomprehending astonishment. Even the people of the Bijagos had not been more surprised. Who were these odd looking foreigners, and what was this bizarre ship? Was it a trader, they asked us? No? Well then, it must be a fishing boat. Where had we come from, and why come here, into their little back street? Why these masts, so incredibly tall, made from metal instead of from wood? Between us were a linguistic gulf and an even greater cultural divide.

Beyond Furo do Arroz the river is broad but much of the seemingly open expanse hides sandbanks, and there are even a few rocks, so that the channel generally wends its way as if through a minefield. Which mariner, newly come from the sea, would think to squeeze behind the little island tucked close alongside Ilha Marajo, instead of favouring the calm sheet of water stretching away endlessly to the south? The little emblem for a wreck still resting on the bottom is sprinkled all over this section of the chart.

These days there can be no excuse, for the tiny path amongst the islands is well buoyed. We followed its unlikely course, with the wind pulling us gently along. On the left now was Santana, a classic Amazonian settlement having its origin in some native Amerindian village but owing its present form and size to a big sawmill. So far as we could see, the sawmill was derelict - and this, too, was typical of the villages we were to pass in the next couple of weeks. A time of prosperity had just passed.

Many of the houses at Santana were abandoned and half-ruinous. The paint had long since peeled from their planked walls and the timber stilts which supported their weight were worm-eaten and perilously wasted. Thatched roofs sagged. Chasing new jobs, the workers had moved to the city or had gone deeper into the forest, with the lumberjacks and hauliers. However, there were still a dozen homes where the window frames and the walls were brightly painted, and where the colourful plastic strips of door curtains flicked and fidgeted in the breeze. Here, sliding past us, was a Pentecostal church, looking just like my impression of a church built by the pioneer settlers in a new, raw North America - but it was dated, not 1860, but 1980. Here were galleon traders, tied to a robust tree trunk jetty. Here was a shop with a pile of beer crates outside the door...

"Beer?" said Nick. "They've got beer? Let's stop."

The aproned women who had watched us from their doorways now slipped within the sanctuary of their homes, as the odd-looking foreign vessel suddenly, and for no apparent reason, swung around to point its noise directly at their privacy. Why was it coming to Santana? The sails, so big and smooth as the boat slid by, were now a wild tangle of clattering canvas. Soon they fell towards the deck and a chain went rattling out over the sharp bow.

The little children were the first to allow curiosity to overcome their anxiety. After a short while we saw them tumble into their various canoes. They paddled towards us, but they were a quiet, uncommunicative crowd who just sat and stared. The youths watched and waited with their parents on the shore.

We rowed across. Our greeting went unanswered, but the little mob followed us into the adjacent shop and, in response to our behest, two bottles of the local ale were placed on the counter. Our attempts at conversation fell into a vacuum. Smiles were met with blank, uncomprehending stares. Our every move was studied; every shift of posture, every swig from the bottle. Two visitors from Mars could scarcely have been received with more astonishment.

As we left Santana a big, green container ship hove into sight and the kids, who seemed already to have got the buzz, went paddling out to meet it.

Without a boat you're going nowhere, in Amazonia, and the canoe is, for the river dwellers, the equivalent of a bicycle, or a donkey, or even just shanks' pony. If the children of the Swiss Alps are born skiing, these little ones are born into a boat. By three or four years of age they are paddling a diminutive replica of Daddy's canoe, and by five, they can handle the dug-out as well as he.

As they paddled out into the middle of the channel we watched the children and wondered what mischief they might be planning. Just as young boys on bicycles will catch hold of a lorry to cadge a free ride up a hill, so the kids on the river enjoy chasing after the galleon traders and shed boats and looping their painters onto the sternpost. Often one sees such vessels wriggling violently to and fro as they try to shake off two or three parasites. In this instance, however, the ship was far too tall. It was an ocean-going merchant man and its sides were sheer cliffs.

As the ship came thundering along the narrow channel a tremendous wave rolled off the bulbous bow. High up in the bridge the officers saw the children in their frail canoes - a handful of ants in the path of a juggernaut.

"Boom, boom," the horn sounded. "Boom, boom, boom!"

The captain must have been having kittens as the tots disappeared from his sight below the immense bow. The truly daring crossed his path but most of the youngsters could get their thrills just from being near to the monster and from surfing away on the great, curling bow wave.

As we moved on from Santana the hour of an important decision was upon us. The great island of Marajo was once joined to the mainland shore, but across the neck of this one time peninsula the river has hewn half a dozen tiny tracks, or "estreito"s. Which estreito to choose - this was the decision which now faced us. If we chose the shortest we would presumably have to share it with all the other traffic - including ocean going ships such as the one we had just seen. We had half a mind to take this route, simply for the fun of seeing a container ship pushing its way through the forest, but then it occurred to us that the ships would also have to push their way past us. We would get no peace, either by day or night. We therefore picked on a B road. After we passed the first and only town on our chosen estreito we were just about the only item of traffic on this back street - and certainly the only one from another world - and I am sure that this affected the way in which the "natives" received us.

Our passage through the Estreito Macacos was, in fact, the most interesting part of the journey around Marajo, and although it was by no means the most exciting from a navigational point of view it did hold a considerable challenge. We were determined to get through to the Amazon under sail, and since the river hereabouts is seldom more than 50 yards wide and the winds are light and the tide strong, this was no easy matter.

The spectacle of a boat zigzagging to and fro across the river was evidently the most ludicrous one that the river dwellers had lately beheld, and now the aproned women, with babes in their arms, called for their husbands and mothers-in-law and cousins to join them in the doorway. Solitary travellers strolling by in their canoes pretended not to notice us as we tacked to and fro, almost scraping the bushes on either side. For all our efforts, we failed to cover the ground any faster than they. When the town of Breves came into sight we stopped this silliness, aware that even if we tiptoed in under engine *Maamari* would still draw plenty of attention to herself.

We could not find anywhere to anchor off Breves; although the river was narrow the water was far too deep. Reluctantly we cast our eyes along the shore, over a throng of ferries and trading boats jostling each other about all along the waterfront. Even from this distance it was evident that the river is the world for the people of Breves – as, indeed, it is for all those who dwell along its banks. No one on the Amazon looks beyond the cradle of the river. Beyond the river are trees and the sea, and both are frontiers so vast that no river dweller would even think of trying to cross them. As we looked at the shutter-board buildings which made up the little town I thought how insulated her people were from the wide world. How would this lot receive their alien visitors?

It is a fact of the cruising life that one can anchor in safety off almost any town in the world - in doing so one retains a certain level of isolation - but to tie up on the quay is to take up residence. When one moors alongside, the door is open to every kind of lowlife, from the two-legged to the four-legged and even the six-legged variety. In some trepidation, therefore, we doubled back towards the riverfront, searching our eyes for a niche which might offer some protection from the thieves and rats and roaches of Breves.

At our approach the men who work the boats rushed to the rails and began clamouring for our company, but their enthusiasm only made us hesitate. Amongst the colourful wooden boats there was one black tug whose crew waved cheerfully and beckoned, but with less desperate eagerness, so that we sensed a more mature reception and anticipated a calmer night. In the first respect we were right: the crew of the tugboat were friendly without being overbearing. On the other hand, the night was not very restful for no sooner had we gone to bed than there came a sudden, loud thud from somewhere up for'ard. We hurried outside and found that the neighbours were already on deck.

"Just a little one," they said as, by the light of a torch, they showed us a massive tree stump. It had been borne down by the tide and had lodged between our bow and theirs. For the remainder of that night we sweated and fretted, concerned at the thought of the damage that such a "little one" might do if, when the tide turned, it struck our self-steering rudder. This was another, and unforeseen disadvantage of tying-up alongside.

There were few villages in the Estreito Macacos and after our experience at Santana we were, in any case, a little more reticent about stepping ashore. In Africa we had come to realise that arriving unannounced in a place at the back of beyond is effectively to trespass. It is not like turning up in a quaint English village, where the people live behind closed doors and within the demarcation made plain by walls or hedges. Walking around a West African village one has an acute sense of being inside the garden gate and intruding across the lawn. In Amazonia, if one wishes to step ashore there is not even the lawn, still less the street, since the homes cling to the very edge of the waterway. If there is any land at all it is behind the house and can only be reached via the tree-trunk jetty and the front door. For the rest, there is only the dense forest.

Although there were very few villages in the Estreito Macacos we were seldom beyond sight of one dwelling or the next, for the little wooden huts are strung out through the strait like beads along a necklace. As we trotted slowly by in our gypsy wagon, the children who lived in the houses ran nimbly down a palm-log plank or hopped down a ladder, and raced after us in their canoes. At night, when we sought to anchor well away from their doors and so avoid disrupting their privacy, the children or their fathers would seek us out, never arriving without a gift of coconuts or bananas. At the time when we made our journey we knew of no other yachts which had come this way. When we arrived in the city at the farther end of the strait we were told that we were lucky not to have been robbed, and when Sir Peter Blake travelled along the Amazon, only a few years later, his boat was attacked while it was at anchor and the celebrated yachtsman was shot dead.

I am often asked how we "got away with it". In answer I can only say that we felt perfectly safe at all times. Indeed, after the aggro we had met with in West Africa we felt that the Amazonian Indians compared very favourably. The majority of the people were too over-awed even to speak with us, and from the rest we received a shy welcome - and endless questions. For a long time our curiosity about the lives of these people was as great as theirs about us, but eventually we learnt that there are gardens hidden away in the forest.

Thus, the way of the Indians still echoes the self-sufficiency of their ancestors.

Journeying slowly through the mighty Amazon rainforest we began to see that it is a secret place, full of mystery and surprises. For us, one of the strangest discoveries was the echo which comes from the trees. If we anchored, the noisy insect world went to sleep and silence sat heavily upon us, but if one of us so much as dropped a spoon, or clapped our hands, then the forest would answer with the most incredible crashing clang, as if a hundred-weight of nails, or a lorry-load of stone, were being dropped from a great height onto a pile of steel-sheeting. Certainly, the echo seemed to be far louder than the original noise and when we first discovered this amazing acoustic feature Nick had to go aloft and peer out at the forest to see if he could find out what was making the din.

The most delightful of all the surprises waiting for us was the dolphins. The dolphins on the Amazon are pink. Often, as we lay in the cockpit in the evening, we would be startled by an explosive snort. One has to be quick to catch a glimpse of the culprit; usually there is nothing to be seen but a few ripples on the otherwise-glassy, brown surface. Another muffled shot breaks the stillness - but, again, it comes from behind and there is no trace of the perpetrator. If you have your wits about you or happen to be looking in the right place at the right time, even then you will be lucky to see more than a long, greyish snout and the top of its owner's head. "Bouto" is often mistaken for a crocodile - he does not even have a fin - but just occasionally the dolphin leaps, and on a couple of occasions we were granted a glimpse of his cosmetic-pink face and belly. The local Amerindian people believe that the creature is magical. Its tooth has tremendous power and can bring great fortune, if it is found, but to kill a dolphin is terribly unlucky. We considered ourselves blessed to have seen the animal at all: some Brazilian friends who travelled all the way from Manaus to Belem had not had one sighting and swore that the pink dolphins are mythical!

Just as we had slipped easily into the pace of life on the ocean wave, so, by now, we had settled into the rhythm of the Amazon river - and it was a lazy rhythm for the most part. With temperatures in the forties (115+° C) lazing about was a survival mechanism. The wind in the narrow channel which we followed seemed to be made of nothing more than the breath of the trees and the friction of the air on the water sliding by, so that we drifted along like a ghost, with our white sails outspread. Every morning the sun climbed up into the sky and blazed down on the world until the forest steamed. But every afternoon brought a respite. In the afternoon it would rain.

Sometimes the torrential shower which came to the Amazon each afternoon would drench us. On the day that we arrived on the river Para we had used it to fill our water-tanks and got 700 litres in under ten minutes! Sometimes the rainstorm passed away to the south, but even then it brought sweeter air and gave us a short respite between the smouldering heat of the day and the sweltering blanket of night. And always, after the storm had passed, the sky above the rainforest was striped with a rainbow.

On one occasion we left the mother ship and went wandering in the dinghy, only to get caught out by the anvil-headed cloud. It suddenly loomed up above the trees, dragging a grey veil, and we could not beat it back to the boat. Within a little while we were soaked to the skin and shivering, but the remedy was very simple - provided that one put from one's mind thoughts of crocodiles and piranhas and those weird parasites which are said to seek out some unmentionable orifice in which to set up camp. Sodden and cold, we stepped as we were into the yellow-brown river. It was warmer than a bath.

Although its arrival was as predictable as a commuter train, we were never quite ready for the afternoon rainstorm. Once, when we were anchored rather near the bank, it almost drove us ashore. A few days later we were drifting along with our white wings spread when I saw the cloud begin to peep above the trees. As ever, the heat had been building up all day so that now, while I sat and painted, sweat poured in rivulets down my naked back and my face. The metal palette was too hot to pick up, prompting memories of another day, in another world and another lifetime, when the paint had frozen into Jack Frost patterns while I tried to work.

We drifted carelessly onward while the monstrous cloud rose, towering and billowing, in the distance. After it had reached its full height, the head of the cloud gradually flattened and spread. Soon the sky astern of us was blue-black and the trees had taken on that fabulous hue which only comes in the minutes before a storm. By the time we realised that this one was going to hit us it was already upon us. I ran to shut the hatches and then drop the main;

Nick furled the genoa. Under mizzen alone *Maamari* sped over the river like a puck suddenly smacked by a hockey stick. The water was at once completely white with falling, bouncing raindrops and the banks, so very close on either side, vanished completely. It was too deep for us to anchor, and so for the next half hour we pottered along blindly under engine.

Later that same day, after the sun had dried our decks, we reached the end of the narrow Estreito do Macacos, and as we came out into the wide sheet of flat water beyond we realised, with some excitement, that we were now on the Amazon proper. The other estreitos also emerged into this same lake and looking over our shoulders we saw a big, red container ship appear from out of the trees. We were back on the main highway. The ship was probably bound for Santarem or Manaus, some way further up the river, but our next destination was Macapa, a town which lay a few days downstream.

In a little while we pulled over to the side of the river, in our usual way, but this time there were no houses in sight. We had not seen any houses for some hours and for the first time we had the river to ourselves.

Over the next couple of days we did see villages, but they were very small ones. Varying our style one evening we parked ourselves right in front of a sparse group of huts, and the next day we were invited into the home of one Hilario Tupinamba, direct descendant of cannibalistic Tupinamba indians. He was a mild mannered fellow, and his mother was terrified of my camera and crossed herself whenever I raised it to my eye. Together we spent a few hours struggling with the language barrier - at one time I asked Hilario to write his address in our visitors book, and we later discovered that he had, instead, listed all the Amazonian animals he could think of. Then we said our goodbyes and moved on. It had been an interesting experiment but we preferred solitude and, accordingly, found our own piece of the river for the following night.

Four o'clock in the morning is not the best time to be faced with an urgent intellectual problem, but it was at this hour that we were awoken, that same night, by a dull thud and a sound like a waterfall. We hurried on deck to discover a full-grown oil-palm tree straddled across the anchor chain. The current was running at five knots and it sluiced over and around the 50 foot long trunk just as it would tumble over a weir or pass through rapids.

It occurred to us that since the tree was not actually rubbing against the hull we might simply wait until the tide turned in a few hours time. But could the anchor and the rest of the gear stand the quite phenomenal extra drag? It seemed doubtful. The next, most obvious, solution was to upset the perfect equilibrium which the tree had somehow achieved, and tip it down one side or other of the yacht. Efforts with the boat hook proved in vain. The thin aluminium pole simply bowed and quavered, whereas the tree was quite unmoved.

In the end we launched the rubber dinghy and Nick climbed in. Armed with a machete and a panel-saw he set about dismembering the stout fronds each in turn, again with the intention of unbalancing the tree. From where I stood, in the pulpit, the possibilities for stabbing the dinghy or lopping off a leg looked dangerously high, but the objective was achieved. With the last of its branches reduced to stumps the palm tree finally swung to one side and slid away into the night. The Amazon must be a real laugh in the wet season when the debris of so many hundred thousand acres of freshly flooded land comes tumbling down to the sea.

The following day we pressed on to Macapa, a town which we imagined to occupy a similar situation to Belem, and which we had assumed would be equally ancient and quite as important. Macapa turned out to be rather a disappointment. From a distance it looked a bit like Bournemouth or Bognor, and on closer inspection it proved to be even less inspiring. We were hard put to see why the place exists at all. The greatest surprise was the fact that Macapa is not a port. Having made this discovery we remembered the advice given to us by Acy Marcos dos Santos and turned off up a narrow creek towards the town of Santana.

Santana was reminiscent of Breves. It was a town of wooden huts and warehouses fronting onto a bustling waterfront. With its unmade streets and scrolled writing on tall weatherboard shop fronts there was something rather wild-west about the place. In the golden light of evening we motored upstream in search of an anchorage. Selecting one was not easy. Off the town itself the water was 60 metres deep. A little further along, the settlement faded into a string of houses joined together by narrow jetties and here we found

13 metres. Rather than take our chances alongside, we decided to settle for that, but we had scarcely dropped the anchor before a battered old launch came rushing towards us. Sitting stiffly in the bow were three Brazilian naval officers one of whom hailed us in English. "This is not a good place to be," he said, with a faintly embarrassed smile.

"Why not?" The anchor winch was playing up - again - and the thought of winding up 40 metres of chain by hand was less than pleasing.

"Because of the people," the officer answered. A fair number of the people were already clinging onto the sides of our boat, from their canoes, and some had even invited themselves aboard. This was unusually forward behaviour, and not something of which we approved - but still, to us these folks seemed no more threatening than the man who had invited us in for breakfast a couple of days ago, or the two who had given us a fish that morning and flatly refused any payment.

The naval officer raised his eyes to heaven and smiled that embarrassed smile again. "This lot," he said, "will remove every single item from your deck before daybreak."

We were invited to turn back the way we had come and tie alongside two naval vessels which lay a mile or so downstream.

Ten years later, Sir Peter Blake was to moor his yacht in this same spot, off Santana, never to see the sun rise again. Since his death we have wondered what fate might have befallen us during the night had the navy not come to fetch us away. What would have happened if we had been boarded by men wearing motor-cycle helmets and clutching guns? At the time we thought that the Brazilian officer's warning was quite ridiculous, and we followed its advice only through a sense of obligation. Raising the hook was at least as tiresome as we had envisaged - it seemed to be lifting with it half the seabed - and by the time we had crawled back up to the naval base night had arrived. Our hosts were awaiting us.

I have a feeling that if the Brazilian military forces ever had to repel an invasion they might not fare terribly well. It is difficult to imagine such nice people loosing off mortars and grenades with calculated animosity. Perhaps the Superpowers could also teach the Brazilians a thing or two about stiff, unsmiling discipline. But when it comes to public relations the Brazilians are surely the world leaders. On our arrival at the base in Santana we were received, quite literally, with open arms. We were welcomed aboard the *Tenente Castello* and then taken to Macapa for dinner in the best restaurant. The young man who had come to fetch us from our anchorage proved to be the captain of ship, one Nilo Sergio Sülzer Brasil. Sülzer not only invited us into his home but also appointed himself our chauffeur, tour guide, and interpreter, and throughout our week long stay at Santana he was always available to answer our questions and meet our needs. The winch was fixed, our clothes were washed, charts were photocopied - and lest we had any worry about the safety of our yacht she was provided with a twenty-four hour guard.

Sülzer took us to ice-cream parlours, where we sampled a dozen different tropical sorbets. In the zoo he showed us a jaguar, trapped in a tiny cage, and a manatee imprisoned, like a goldfish, in a giant bowl. He took us to stand on the equator, and he took us out on the river in a leaky old dug-out canoe. In his garden we found two brightly coloured lizards over a foot long, and diminutive frogs that could climb up a window. Other frogs, as big as footballs, crept out of Sülzer's toilet at night, and a hairy, black spider, of a scarcely smaller size, came scuttling out from beneath the sofa. This was a side of life from which we were completely isolated on the boat, and we revelled in each new discovery. Our voyage along the river had been rather like a train journey, but whilst we acknowledged that we had missed much we were also rather relieved to know that the only creatures who could trouble us were the winged things.

Or were they? We were alongside now, and while I lay drowsing one night it suddenly occurred to me that we might pick up a rat. If there were rats aboard the Brazilian ships they might easily decide to switch their allegiance to us. In the morning I went on deck and to my horror found the most monstrous rat imaginable perched on the rail of the *Tenente Castello*. It was as big as a cat! Worse yet, there were two matelots feeding the animal! When Sülzer next came to visit, I told him of my fears and he fell about laughing. My rat was something called an agouti, and the sailors were fattening it for the pan.

On the 21st of May we took our leave of the Brazilian navy. "You came like birds," Sülzer wrote in our visitors book. "Please don't leave like them too." We promised to visit him again some day - and we will. Eighteen years down the road we are still in touch.

Since the equator was just around the corner, off Macapa, we thought that we may as well follow tradition and spend the night crossing it to and fro. There are actually not very many places where one can drop the anchor precisely on that magical line which divides north from south. Spinning the globe we counted twelve other possibilities but in some, such as Ecuador, the water is probably too deep, and in others the coast is exposed and unsafe. At Macapa it was an easy trick. At the command only of the river's ebb and flow, *Maamari* crossed the line four times in the space of 24 hours and each crossing was celebrated with a glass of bubbly. The next morning we stepped back into the northern hemisphere to stay for good - or at least for a few years - and continued on our way down the river.

Beyond Macapa the Amazon is so broad that one cannot see either shore, and it inspired in us feelings of reverence which the little winding straits could never arouse. Our friends from the naval base knew the river well, for it was their job to maintain the buoyage, and they had spoken in respectful tones of its might. The commander of the base had corrected our charts to show, here a sandbank newly arrived, or there a navigation mark gone missing. He had also indicated suitable anchorages and we now used these as way-points, hopping from one to the next.

The last bolthole in the Amazon is a small island called Curua, and it is here that the traveller makes his final camp and prepares for the assault on the river entrance. For us, the challenge ahead seemed truly to be the aquatic equivalent of scaling a great peak, and just as the cold, vengeful goddess of Everest might be thought to dwell amongst the clouds on the mountain's snow-capped summit, so the unforgiving deity who inhabits the Amazon lay in wait on the shoals through which we must now pass. We could imagine sailors of yore down on their knees before Nossa Senhora, their hands making the sign of the cross. And how many hundreds of lives have ended on the treacherous sandbanks? Surely, the Amazon is not to be messed with. Even the big ocean-going ships still wait for the green light of the tide's favour before they tackle the entrance.

It was the navy who recommended Curua Creek, and without the knowledge that they use the place we would definitely have passed it by. We arrived off the narrow entrance just as the sun was setting, and having been told to enter on a bearing of 290° we overstood it accordingly. In fact, by the time we had got the mainsail down the entrance was almost a mile upstream. Even after two months on the Amazon we had not got the measure of the current. Hoisting everything again, we motor-sailed back whence we had come at a painfully slow pace. The trees on the island right beside us ambled past, but night raced across from the east to meet us. Bats emerged to flick about the darkening sky and skimmers flew by with their bills in the water.

It was dusk when we regained the entrance to the creek, and it was low water. In the failing light we could see mud banks extending from either side across the tight opening. They overlapped to leave a narrow passage which ran almost parallel to the shore - and the passage itself was covered with swirling eddies. Hearts in mouths, we slipped between the mud banks. I stood on the bow to watch for any unseen danger, whilst Nick kept one eye glued to the echo-sounder. From "No Bottom" the depth came crashing down to seventeen metres, to six metres and then, when we were just within the creek, it fell to only two metres. Clearly, we thought, our friends do not bring *Tenente Castello* in here at low tide - but having said this, I must confess that it was the lowest tide of the year.

Inside the creek, we anchored straight away. Sülzer had told us that there was a radio beacon here, manned by four men, and two of them now appeared and sat on the end of a dilapidated jetty. They waited until we were nicely settled in before waving a torch and calling us over. Given our experience of Brazilian hospitality we expected that they might be going to invite us in for a beer - but, no, they only wanted to let us know that we should move further up the creek. We hurried back to the boat and moved it. A star pinned above the silhouette tree line was our marker while we checked that the anchor was holding.

With the racket of the engine finally stifled, night fell like a heavy cloak. The only noise was of tree frogs whistling shrilly to one another and ours was the only light. From the shore-station there issued not one note of music, nor even the flicker of a candle flame, and we now observed that the light in the mouth of the creek was dead. Before entering we had tried to call on the radio but no one had answered, and now we saw why. The station was without power. How remiss of us! This time it should have been we who made the invitation for a beer.

During the night *Maamari* pitched up and down on the swell coming into the creek, and we were glad to have moved away from our vulnerable position in the entrance. The next morning we were met at the end of the jetty by the four keepers of the beacon, but they proved all to have that annoying tendency to talk to a foreigner in monosyllables and sign language. It is a habit which afflicts many people, and it does nothing to aid communication. Eventually we managed to strike up some kind of rapport with one individual and he took us on a tour of their simple homestead. In his kitchen the man opened a fridge and pointed out packets of snake venom serum which, he told us, would be useless now that the power was off. Then he brought forth two small but deadly snakes, pickled in jars of formalin and, pointing at our flip-flops, wagged his finger. He and his colleagues wore wellington boots.

The tour complete, our guide called out to an old Amazonian man, who was paddling by in a tiny canoe, and we were invited to go for a ride. With the three of us aboard the little boat had precisely two inches of freeboard and so we novices sat perfectly still, for fear of a sudden dunking, while the old man toiled. Several houses, a newly built school and a sawmill drifted by before, after a mile or so, we came to a sizeable factory. Silent now, though not yet overgrown, the place had been a processing plant for hearts of palm - but now there were no palm trees left. It costs the lives of two trees just to fill one tin.

Poor old Ernisto, our canoeist, had now to carry his idle tourists back downstream against the flood. Beside the bank, beneath the overhanging branches, he paddled diligently and the canoe inched forward. Green parrots and bright red macaws screamed harshly to their mates as they crossed the river above our heads, and from somewhere in the distance came the endless whooping of a pack of howler monkeys. In the forest, Ernisto said, lived sloths and armadillos. There were uakari monkeys and marmosets, and even jaguars. Once again, we were not at all sure whether it was a bad or a good thing to have missed all these - and especially the last - but it would have been nice to glimpse an alligator lurking in the shallows. Ernisto insisted that there were no dolphins, pink or otherwise, around Curua and when we claimed to have seen one that very morning he told us that it could only have been that most fearsome of reptiles. We did not swim at Curua.

After he had shown us around the village our friend took us back to his house, which was the nearest one to the boat. From a palm log ramp on the river's edge a rickety jetty led across ground now flooded by the tide and towards a typical, white-painted, wooden hut. Beyond the door was a wall adorned, like others we had seen, with pictures of Roman Catholic saints; in this case the pictures had been placed diagonally in their frames and the whole lot arranged in the form of a diamond. A table occupied the better part of the living room and at its exact centre, on a neat, red and white check tablecloth, was placed a bowl of plastic roses. One wall of the room was taken up by a dresser covered in the usual Portuguese nick-nacks. A mosquito net covered the only window, but chinks of light showed between the painted, upright planking of the walls and we judged the chinks to be quite big enough to admit the evil, plague-bearing bug. The roof above our heads was made of corrugated iron at the front but of palm thatch on the less public, back half of the house.

Ernisto's wife greeted us with a warm smile and, while we studied our surroundings, served us coffee in her best china cups. After we had drunk our coffee she proudly showed us around the rest of her simple but well kept home. The kitchen, like others that we had seen, was open on one side. Its bare walls were hung with aluminium cooking pans. Beyond the kitchen was a veranda, and here we met a quite astonishing menagerie. A small dog lay curled up beside a sleepy cat. A fat mother hen flustered out of our way but left her offspring to peck hopefully at our feet. A tethered terrapin poked his head out of his shell and then retired again. One of two huge white rabbits fled for the security of her cage whilst the other set off down a series of planks leading away across the flooded ground.

Marooned on one of a haphazard patchwork of inter-connected wooden islands was a sugar-cane mangle. An outhouse perched on another. On a third we beheld the sorry spectacle of two sheep and a newborn lamb penned together in a space hardly bigger than our table.

Before we left her home Ernisto's wife gave us a big bowlful of bananas and made us promise to call again "next time". We walked back down the jetty to the canoe, and on the end of the jetty the old man proudly pointed out a shiny brass pump and a thin metal pipe leading back into the house.

"What a pity that the pump is not at the other end", I thought to myself, but certainly the system was one step up from a bucket, and Ernisto considered it to be quite splendid. I suppose that if the hand pump had been installed in the home, then I would probably have thought that it needed a wind pump. And perhaps, for when the wind failed, a little donkey engine... Ernisto had found the perfect level of technology for his situation and, like the other Amazonians we had met throughout our journey, he showed no desire for 'better things'. Men such as these are all too rare in a world now terribly strained and perverted from its proper order by whispers of "look what you're missing". In Amazonia, The American Dream had yet to rear its horrid head or spread its wicked lie.

We awoke the next morning to hear the sounds of the jungle curiously intermingled with those of the English countryside. Cicadas trilled and monkeys howled - and Ernisto's sheep bleated plaintively in answer to the strident call of a cockerel. Today was to be the big day - the day when we set forth to face the almighty power of the Amazon. In our minds it occupied the place of a trial by ordeal, and we could only hope that the river spirit would find us innocent.

The timing of our departure from Curua was a matter of the utmost importance, for this last refuge and the springboard for our final sally still lies twenty miles from the first channel buoy, and after the first buoy is reached there are then a further 12 miles of channel still to be covered. It was clear from our experience that we stood no chance of making up against the contrary current in the river's mouth and so, ideally, we needed to be at the start of this channel through the sandbar at the very moment when the tide turned in our favour. Unfortunately, if we left Curua with five or six knots to fight then we would not gain ground here, either. The perfect solution to this puzzle would have been to take one tide down to the entrance and then tie up to the first channel buoy while we awaited the next favourable tide, but this plan had to be dismissed on the grounds of its illegality and impracticability. The odds of some shipmaster reporting us, and of *Tenente Castello* coming more than a hundred miles downstream to arrest us were, indeed, pretty remote - but the chances of our managing to scramble aboard one of the vast iron cans without pranging the boat seemed equally slim. And anyway, that would have been cheating. We were all psyched up to face the Amazon on her own terms and sneaky dodges were out of the question.

As we left Curua I looked back along the creek and recalled the story told by Tristan Jones of a "pororoca" sweeping through the tree tops here. The pororoca is a tidal bore of legendary stature, but Ernisto had lived all his life in Curua and swore that he had never seen one. Certainly it seemed an unlikely event. Would anyone build houses and a radio station in a place which could suddenly be swept by a 60 foot wave? Ah, well - the old man told a good tale!

Outside the sheltered creek we found a good breeze blowing from the east and under full sail, with the engine thundering, we were able to make up quite well against the last of the flood. When the tide turned to ebb, a couple of hours later, we were galloping along like a stallion over the open plain. Above us the sky was an infinite expanse of blue whilst all around us the boundless sheet of orange-brown water was as flat as the prairie savannah. A trading galleon hove into sight and came bowling down towards us, the wind straining in the fat, round belly of her sail. A little palm-thatched sailing canoe tugged at a string in her wake. Two men surfing along on the little boat raised their straw hats and waved them to us joyfully, exulting in their own perfectly wonderful adventure and in ours. Have we ever enjoyed a more glorious sail? Certainly I cannot recall any.

At four o'clock we reached the first channel buoy and it shot past, straining vigorously at its cable. Between this mark and the next we timed our passage and discovered that we were making good 12 knots over the ground. Now we knew why it felt so good!

The wind was getting up, and so we dropped the main. Now began our race against time and the changing current as we tacked to and fro down the narrow, well-buoyed lane. In two hours we were through the most dangerous part of the shoals - but would we be able to stay clear when the tide turned?

Night fell and the last channel marker disappeared. The landfall buoy was somewhere up ahead - 64 miles ahead, to be exact. It was well beyond the range of our radar and so was the coast. How could a mariner know if the current was dragging him in or out of the river? With the benefit of our new Satnav (a wedding present from Nick's parents) we were able to see that although she was still making five knots through the water *Maamari* was actually proceeding back towards the treacherous bar at a rate of about one knot!

Would we be able to rediscover that tiny gap in the shoals, if we needed to? And how had anyone ever got through before the channel was buoyed? We certainly did not wish to attempt the feat. We could well see, now, why even the master of a powerful, modern ship prefers to enter the Amazon by way of the Rio Para - even though it means that he must wind his way through the estreitos - and we also understood why a port grew up at Belem rather than at Macapa. Even in leaving the river many a ship has been lost, and anyone who ever succeeded in entering by this way before the channel was buoyed must have had very influential friends on high. Peering out into the blackness which now enveloped our little world, we hoped that our own relationship with the lord of life would not be so sorely tested.

7

HURRICANE CAESAR

(In which is forecast a happy event)

Maamari pushed on, still hard on the wind but leaping and pounding now in the open sea. After so many weeks of flat-water sailing the transition was all a bit too much for my stomach. Fortunately the pull of the Amazon is not quite so strong as its push and goes on for only four hours instead of eight. Thus we were soon able to fight clear of the dangers which lay astern and at midnight, when the tide turned again in our favour, we could even turn off the faithful engine. With the tide under us our speed over the ground increased to nine knots and by daybreak we were 75 miles from the last buoy. At this point the water began to taste salty again but it remained green for several days more, and the tug of the mightiest river on Earth continued to affect our speed until we were 250 miles distant.

Cayenne was the next port which lay along our way, and so we made it our objective. Unfortunately, when we leafed through our charts we found that the only one we had of this region was a rather inadequate photocopy of something old enough to be in a museum. The shore all along this coast slides gently into the sea and its silt-laden rivers deposit their cargo just offshore, so creating a wide, shallow border. Just as a river will corkscrew across a meadow, perpetually carving a new bed for itself, so also, when it meets the ocean such a river continues to meander, forever scouring a new course and dropping its burden of silt in new patterns. There was every chance, therefore, that the soundings on our veteran chart were now completely inaccurate. So far as we could tell, Cayenne could only be approached at high water - and by now it probably goes without saying that we had nothing to tell us at what time that might be.

A short way to the south of Cayenne lies the commercial port of Degrad des Cannes, with its dredged, deep water channel. As the rocky islets off-lying the port came into view we tried to raise the authorities on the radio, and when they failed to come through we called "Any Station". From a ship within the port an English voice responded to our plea, and we learnt that high water was at 20.00 hours. As it was still only about ten in the morning this was rather a bore. For the next seven hours we reached to and fro in the sunshine. The current was fairly strong and the visibility was not great, so that the crucial matter of keeping track of our position was rather tedious.

After a time a small trawler came to wait in the mouth of the channel leading to Cayenne. To judge by its size it drew a little bit less than *Maamari*. At about six o'clock it began to edge up the channel and we quickly fell in behind. The journey was a fairly tense one, for the echo-sounder seldom showed more than 2.5 metres and for much of the time it slipped down to 1.8.

In the old, silted harbour at the head of the channel we could find nowhere deeper than 2.3 metres, but experiments with the lead line showed there was nothing much to fear from grounding at low tide. In fact, grounding is probably not the word to use. The bottom was difficult to find, since the lead and its line just went on down into several feet of soft, black ooze. Six or seven other yachts were already lying at anchor. They were nearer to the quay than we, in shallower water, and at low tide their keels simply sank into the mud and they sat on the lumpy, brown field. All but one of the yachts looked as if they had been there for a long while. We were back in the ex-pat scene.

The contrast between French Guyana and Amazonia was simply

stunning. When we went to clear-in to the country the officials frowned in puzzlement at our passports and said, "Why have you come to see us? You are citizens of the European Community. You do not need to clear into France."

And, really, we were in France. French Peugeots and Citroëns jammed the high street, and mulatto French women minced down the pavements in the latest Parisienne fashions. All manner of luxury goods and labour-saving utensils gleamed alluringly from behind big plate-glass shop fronts. The supermarkets overflowed with fresh goods flown in from the motherland, and in fast-food cafes with tables and floors as hygienic as an operating theatre there were spot-lit cabinets stuffed full of croissants and vol-au-vents. And - "ooh la la!" - the prices! On the Amazon we had been paying the equivalent of 15 pence for a beer, and here it cost over a pound.

"Have you come to work?" the other yotties asked. It was the only reason that they could think of to come here. The wages were evidently as high as the prices and it was for this reason that they endured a rotten climate, swarms of mosquitoes, a town with no soul, and one of the worst anchorages in the world. The only work available to unskilled vagabonds was in the construction business. Nick preferred to follow up his contacts in the Caribbean and get a job in the marine trade.

Just a few hours to the north of Cayenne lies the Salut archipelago - three tiny islands born of one seamount and brought to fame by the bestselling novel, *Papillon*. Papillon was a Parisian who, to use his own words, made a living out of opening other people's safes. Convicted not of this crime but of murder he was shipped over to French Guyana, and when he made a bid to regain his freedom he soon found himself in the maximum security prison 13 miles offshore.

The islands lay right in our path and so, naturally, we stopped to check them out. Islands of any sort are magnets to the traveller, and these ones were all the more interesting for the story attached to them. However, strolling around the largest of the three pin-prick dots we found it hard to re-live Papillon's narrative.

Above a forest of damp palm trees on the plateau summit of Île Royale stand the roofless ruins of an old prison; that much is true. And a red and white striped lighthouse hides behind the derelict prison hospital, its one bright eye raised just high enough to peep over the omnipresent foliage. The warder's houses are here, too, and the governor's house has become a hotel. But the pictures on the wall in the hotel bar-room are of huge tarpon caught in the nearby waters, and nothing speaks of Papillon and his extraordinary tale. We spent a day wandering aimlessly amongst the mouldering trees, and then we moved on.

"June soon," says the mantra for the Caribbean hurricane season, and June was already upon us. Just the previous year, while we were getting ready to leave England, Hurricane Hugo had ripped through the Caribbean devastating the land and destroying more than a hundred yachts. That we were willing, nevertheless, to risk encountering such a disaster is an indication of how badly we needed to find work. The cruising life is cheap - no rent or rates or taxes to pay, and no fuel bills; just our ship to maintain and our two mouths to feed - yet even that little must be found, somehow. The Caribbean was the place for us - but we did not intend to do any island hopping during those dangerous summer months. We meant to find a safe haven long *before* the hurricane season set in. We pressed on northwards, as quickly as the current could carry us. The weather was dreary and seeped into my mood.

On the 7th we sighted the island of Tobago. Since we did not have a chart we made one ourselves, from the directions in the Admiralty pilot, and this proved to be pretty accurate. (So it should have been, for the directions are really not much more than a verbal chart, but unravelling them is a bit like putting together a jigsaw.) We entered the port of Scarborough without encountering any difficulties and were directed to moor alongside a small wharf.

Tobago was Crusoe's isle - or so advised the title page of a booklet in one of Scarborough's tiny, waterfront bars. I knew it to be wrong, of course - Robinson Crusoe's isle is close by the Isla Juan Fernandez, far off the coast of Chile - but the booklet was only about 50 pence and I thought that it might provide an evening's entertainment. As it turned out I was completely wrong.

Within the first few pages the author of this quite capacious tract had provided his reader with irrefutable proof that Daniel Defoe based his story in the then quite newly discovered and unsettled island of Tobago. The proof is in the reading of the original work. Defoe describes the place whereupon the hero was washed up in explicit detail. It had "pleasant meadows and brooks", and woods where there grew cocoa and citrus trees. Neither of these is to be found growing in the Chilean isle. There were also sugar canes growing in abundance, and there were wild tobacco plants - tobacco being a Carib word and the probable origin of the name Tobago. Within sight of Crusoe's island there lay another, distant, mountainous shore, and whereas Trinidad and the mainland are to be seen from Tobago, the vista from the Pacific isle can be only of sea. Crusoe's domain was visited from time to time by cannibals - whereas the islands in the Juan Fernandez archipelago are too far offshore to have been frequented by natives from the mainland. More to the point, Defoe gives the co-ordinates for the position of his ill-fated vessel at the time when she was struck by the storm. He tells us that she was "carried westward" towards a "land of savages" and that the Captain was "standing on for Barbados." His mystery isle lay to the north of the Orinoco river - and to clinch it all he even has Crusoe declare that "the land which I perceived to the west and north-west was the great island of Trinidad." What more can one say? In mitigation it should be admitted that the isle known as Isla Robinson Crusoe was home to a real castaway, and that Defoe interviewed the man before penning his famous tale.

We could have stayed a long while in Tobago. The people were wonderfully friendly - they would stop us in the high street to shake our hands and thank us for coming! – and the place was wonderfully tranquil. Knowing how overcrowded the Caribbean has become in recent years we were surprised to find that there was not another yacht in the island, and nor did we meet any other tourists when we made an excursion on the tandem. On the debit side, the bay in which the town is based is subject to the most terrible swells - but we soon discovered several more restful and beautiful anchorages.

To the east, the snug little bight called Kings Bay cradled *Maamari* in a forest of damp palm trees. Here we were greeted by a young Rastafarian who swam out to the boat and climbed aboard via the anchor chain! Our initial alarm was soon quelled, and this same lad later turned up, in a boat, with two great sackfuls of mangoes, papayas, and green coconuts. He wanted no payment; he wanted only our gratitude and our company.

From Kings Bay we set off again to continue our journey around the island. Having tacked towards the most easterly part we weathered the rock known as Little Tobago, eased the sheets and went bowling down towards Man o' War Bay.

What a glorious sail that was! Boobies swung and soared over the waves like fighter planes, and *Maamari* danced and skipped and swayed over the white flecked, Oxford-blue sea. On our left stood the Tower of London – a rock which actually bears a passing resemblance to Marble Arch and none to the Tower – and beyond the rock lay the mother isle. A tropic bird came out from the distant cliffs to shriek a greeting and then tacked back across the sea to join his fellows on the white-stained arch. Above us, as we approached the bay, the frigate birds circled high in the sky like vultures.

Tucked away in the corner of Man o' War Bay we discovered the village of Charlottesville, with fishing boats drawn up on the beach in front of colourful wooden houses. Immediately north-east of the village and hidden from it by a small forested headland is a little niche called Pirates Bay, and it was here that we chose to drop the hook.

In the 18th century the Caribbean was quite over-run with buccaneers and it is not hard to imagine that the name of this place is based on more than romantic fancy. Tobago was one of the last isles to be successfully colonised, and I found it very easy to picture Pirates Bay as a nest for rum-swilling outlaws. All was perfect peace when we arrived, however. There were no buccaneers nor even any yachts; we had the place entirely to ourselves. I went overboard and swam round the boat which, in these limpid sapphire coloured waters, seemed to hover rather than float. I hung at the surface, looking down at the seabed, and was soon overcome by a curious sensation with a hint of vertigo about it.

That night the sun, a scarlet fireball, tumbled down through a smoke screen of smouldering cloud. Darkness then took swift hold of the land. The pretty hillside became a sinister, black hump raised against the star-splattered night sky - and then something truly magical occurred.

"Look! Look at the hill!" We were sitting, sipping sundowners when it happened, and both simultaneously uttered a hushed cry of wonderment. We were basking in the heady tranquillity of the tropical night, serenaded by the shrill chorus of countless tiny tree-frogs, when suddenly, as if in response to a cue, the hillside was lit with a thousand fairy lights! It was as if Oberon, king of the little people, had led his nymphs from their hiding places. Erratically the tiny beacons drifted over the black mound, flashing on and off all the while. Perhaps Puck was weaving spells in Pirates Bay - and we alone of mortals were there to see the fun.

Oh, yes, we could have stayed for a very long time in this heavenly place - but, as we reminded ourselves, our purpose in coming to the Caribbean was to look for work. Our stores were getting low, and until we put some money in the kitty we could not get on with our journey south towards the tip of South America.

Having just spent three years delivering yachts across the Atlantic and the Pacific for The Moorings, Nick reckoned that he had a toe in the door with that particular charter company. Indeed, after the last delivery trip the managing director had more or less promised us a position as skipper and hostess. Unfortunately, when we arrived at The Moorings new base in Grenada we found that the said gentleman had retired.

The man running the show in Grenada was also well known to Nick - he had been in Tonga when Nick took a boat out to that new base - but unfortunately he had no work to offer us. He introduced us to the resident duo, an all-American couple who called the company yacht "our boat" and who lavished upon it all their energy and every moment of their sparse spare time. Each day they polished the stanchions and scrubbed the already gleaming deck. When a new charter party arrived they greeted them like bosom buddies, even when the people concerned were as likeable as rottweilers that have rolled in manure. Upon reflection, we decided that we were probably not cut out for this kind of work.

Plan B was procreation. If we could not find work immediately then we might as well get away from the Caribbean islands and spend the hurricane season hiding out in Venezuela. If we started a baby now I would be five or six months pregnant when we came north again. While we waited to deliver the baby we could get a job delivering boats... and then, after the birth, it would be business as usual with baby in tow. That was the plan. Looking back on it all I can hardly believe that we could have been so naïve!

Leaving Grenada we made the overnight hop down to Los Testigos, a group of tiny islands belonging to Venezuela. Here, *Maamari* lay at anchor in a tranquil turquoise pool which is notched into the side of

Testigos Grande - and here, for the first time, I swam over a coral garden, feeling as bizarrely out of place as if I were floating in the air over beds of heather and lupins. Little zebra-striped fish grazed amongst the flowers like bees. Delicate orange and purple ferns swayed to and fro as though rocked by a gentle breeze. There were also round, yellow brain-corals, each the size of a small car, and these exuded a strangely animal presence and gave me the eerie sense of being watched.

On this, the leeward side of the island we discovered an enormous sand dune, and having scaled its steep, scarp face we found our way across to the wind-swept, wave-strewn north coast. The distinctive trails ploughed by a couple of big turtles were the only prints in the sand, and perhaps it was the sight of their 'nests' which turned our thoughts to similar matters. We retreated to the lofty sanctuary of the soft, white dunes.

The inhabitants of Los Testigos belong largely to one family. They make a living from the sea. If what they told us was true, a man can make enough from a day's fishing to last him through the year and so for the rest of the time the people live a life of ease. When a shoal of fish happened to pass by we saw the fishermen run to their boats, but most of their time was spent lazing beneath the palm trees in front of their tin-roofed huts. They had little use for surplus cash; without roads they were not cursed by the need for cars, and without electricity they were not prey to the devious directives pumped out on the television screen. There were no shops to tempt the appetite for possession, and there was none of the disparity of property ownership which sparks-off the rat race. When they wanted a crate of beer or another T-shirt, then someone "drove" off to the metropolis, a day-trip away on the isle of Margarita. Petrol was three pence a gallon and the massive outboards which we were to see throughout the country had been bought, at a fraction of their real cost, from the government.

Much can change over a period of ten or twenty years - especially to a village perched on the edge of a greater, consumer minded society - but when we passed through their islands, the folks of Los Testigos enjoyed a standard of living so low that it would have upset Oxfam, and a quality of life which went off the top of the scale. By now we were thoroughly convinced that the two do not go hand in hand.

Chon-Chon, the grandfather of all the Testigans, made his home not on either of the main islands in the group but on Testigos Pequena, a dot which the relentless sea has torn away from its mother isle. Having established that he was the "chief", we thought it only proper that we go and pay him our respects. During the course of our conversation we asked the old man if we could buy some fish, and he at once dispatched two teenaged grandsons to dive. Twenty minutes later the fellows were knocking on our hull. They had caught four lobsters for us and not a penny would they take in payment.

In the old days, Chon-Chon told us, it had taken seven hours to reach Isla Margarita. When we asked him how long it had taken to beat back again, against the wind and current, the old man groaned and raised his eyes to heaven. As much as seven days, he admitted. Nowadays, with two 65 horsepower outboards, Chon-Chon's sons and grandsons made the trip in an hour and a half, and the old man was proud of the feat. *Maamari*, with her sails, was an anachronism and he teased us about her lugubrious way.

Yachtsmen are normally allowed to remain only two days at Los Testigos, but through our friendship with Chon-Chon we were given permission to remain as long as we liked. A French couple, similarly favoured, decided to remain for the whole season but we felt that this was straining the old man's hospitality somewhat. After a couple of weeks we felt that we should be moving on. We wanted to see the mainland, and our next stepping stone along the way was Margarita.

Isla Margarita is famed as a duty-free port and heavenly holiday resort, but we found that the heavy-handed consumerism of the former has tainted what may once have been paradise. Nevertheless, it is a very popular venue amongst cruising folk and that summer it was busier than ever. Hurricane Hugo having laid waste the island of St Croix, wreaking havoc in many a supposed hurricane hole, American yachtsmen who had formerly maintained a fingers crossed approach to the hurricane season were now taking no chances. In the Margaritan harbours of Porlamar and Pampatar we found a great flotilla of craft from the U.S. Virgins. Oddly enough, this crowd seemed to have learnt very little else from the traumatic experience of the previous year. When the first cyclone of the season was forecast to pass just north of Isla Margarita the general response was to tidy up on deck and throw out a second anchor.

In a restaurant on the beach at Pampatar the local fishermen shook their heads solemnly. When Hugo stormed across the Virgin Islands, they told us, there had been no wind in Margarita - yet the hurricane had sent a tremendous swell down to the Venezuelan coast, driving several vessels ashore. History records the destruction of a fort which once stood on the Venezuelan mainland but which was destroyed by similar, monstrous waves.

The forecast was not for 120 knots but only for 60, and so we prepared for sea. In the event, Hurricane Arthur caused quite a bit of damage to Grenada but passed twenty miles north of Margarita. It sucked up every breath of wind and left the island utterly becalmed.

Leaving Margarita we headed for the adjacent small islands, and then we made our slow and casual way over to Peninsula Araya, where there are ancient salt pans. Salt is so cheap, nowadays, that we take it completely for granted, but that old adage, "worth his salt" once had meaning. Before the days of refrigeration, salt was absolutely vital as a preservative. The pans at Araya were so valuable that the Spanish, who colonised the place following hot on the heels of Columbus, were obliged to build a massive fort to guard the treasure from covetous Dutch entrepreneurs. In 1726 an earthquake shook the region and the fort fell down. The salt pans lasted longer - in fact, they are still in use and we were able to look down, from the ruined fort, over the modern workings.

On the Venezuelan mainland we caught up with the American clan, some of whom had chosen to spend their summer in Cumana. I suppose that if they hailed from Charlotte Amelie, in the U.S. Virgins, then this little fraternity were already inured to the steady roar of traffic running past a concrete marina and to the possibility of being knifed, in broad daylight, for the loose change in their pockets. Still, that satellite-city of the United States cannot be even half as awful as Cumana.

Cumana marina is a life-sized realisation of an architect's model, with landscaped banks and flower borders and a miniature shopping complex. Yet for once the artificial environment normally so repellent to our aesthetic sensibilities was a welcome sanctuary from the grim and sordid real life going on outside. Cumana city centre was only about half an hour's walk, but the route led along a busy highway - where some friends were held at gun point in the middle of the day - and through a shanty town where the refuse and sewage lay knee deep in the gutter. The stench can best be imagined. The town centre was not much more salubrious than the outskirts, and even the supermarket smelt of rotting food. For the most part, the yotties spent the long months huddled together within the protective walls of the marina, besieged by justifiable fears of violence and by their distaste for the world outside. Guards dressed in bullet-proof vests and mirrored sunglasses patrolled the concrete walls with Kalashnikov rifles.

If ever an award be offered for the most detestable city on earth then I shall be pleased to nominate Cumana. Mind you, my opinions are perhaps just a touch coloured. By the time we reached Cumana I was pregnant and beginning to feel the effects, so that the merest whiff of putrefying meat or the sight of rotting garbage had me throwing up.

The news that we were soon to be parents took the folks at home completely by surprise. My mother and father received the news in stunned silence. "Oh, what a shame!" said our friends. "You'll have to come home, now." What nobody seemed to realise was that the child had been planned before we even set out.

And what could be wrong with that idea? Babies have lived in mud huts and igloos and covered wagons - and on sailing ships, too. Nick and I had both been sailing since we were in carrycots. Why shouldn't our children grow up sailing, too? For us the issue was "no big deal" - but, as we shall see, that was largely because we knew nothing about babies. I had met one, once, and it had seemed to spend most of its time asleep.

Mothers-to-be come up with all sorts of daft names for the new life growing inside their own body, and how could it be otherwise? One cannot go around calling a baby "it", for nine months just in case He turns out to be She. We decided to name our embryo child for the next hurricane. Arthur and Bertha had been and gone, and out in the eastern Atlantic a new storm was being born. We followed its progress.

Before the force of the wind reaches 60 knots a revolving tropical depression is known only by a number, but at that point - like an African child who has survived its first week of life and is deemed to have come to stay - the storm is given a name. On the day that my pregnancy was confirmed tropical depression number three came of age and was duly christened Caesar. It was some months before anybody pointed out to us the possible implications of this name, for a child who has yet to find his way out of the womb, and by then our little Caesar was a great bulge in my belly and not to be stripped of his title.

Having left from England in such haste we had plenty to keep us quiet aboard *Maamari,* and we saw the weeks ahead as time in which to attend to the chores. Equipped with resin, fibreglass matting, and sheets of plywood, we fled from Cumana and crossed the Golfo Cariaco intent on finding a quiet, dry place where we could hole up for a few weeks. The mainland coast of the gulf receives regular afternoon downpours but the peninsula is a desert and was therefore the ideal spot for us to work on the leaky deck. Rumour has it that the place is now unsafe, and that the local fishermen will happily murder a yacht's crew to get their hands on her stores, but back in 1990 we encountered no troubles – nor even any fishermen.

Laguna Chica, the nearest notch in the rocky peninsula, was small, inhabited, and much frequented by other cruising yachts. Further along the coast at the head of Laguna Grande we found just the place we sought. Pocketed within the arid slopes of the soft, vulnerable mountains was a narrow blue lake; a secret place so hidden away that the world outside immediately seemed more distant than another millennium. A fringe of mangroves hid a broad, burnt-sienna valley, and had a brontosaurus lumbered across in the distance we would not have registered any surprise. On the contrary, a dinosaur would have seemed wholly in place. The appearance of a car would have been much more shocking for we had stepped back in time to the Jurassic.

Through half-closed eyes, a pair of pelicans flapping around the lagoon were pterodactyls, but the other creatures of the long ancient past had hidden themselves away and the valley and the tall hills were silent. Life lay in wait, patiently attending the moment when our backs were turned or our craft disappeared around the time barrier of that entrance between the rocks.

We spent a long time in Laguna Grande. By day we worked at our various tasks, and the sound of saw and hammer echoed off the hillside. In the evening we rowed ashore to set a net amongst the mangrove roots and to stroll in the valley of the dinosaurs. Sometimes at night, if we strained our ears, we would hear the wind tearing past in the gulf outside, but the secret lagoon was always silent and still.

One day we abandoned our chores and set off to explore. We fought a path through a dense forest of cacti and thorn bushes, and we struggled up the ruinous slope of the mountainside to win the view from the summit. We found ourselves standing on the spine of the Araya peninsula, able to look down at both Laguna Grande and the Caribbean Sea. The view reached for miles, but all that we could see were orange-brown crumbling hills, and the fossil shells at our feet were the only sign of life. In all that barren, waterless desert not one trace of human habitation did we glimpse, and the impression of having slipped into another age was further reinforced.

Down in the valley, in the antediluvian forest, not one note of bird song did we hear - but from somewhere close by came the sound of something much larger than ourselves lumbering about. I hurried my pace, and almost tripped over an insect fully five inches long. It was a huge locust with orange and yellow stripy legs. It stumbled up from beneath my feet on lurid green wings and then perched within the safe confines of a thorn bush; from there it regarded us with eyes which betrayed no fear. Equally unafraid was the beast tramping about in the bushes. It proved to be from a herd of long-horned, wild cattle and it chased us back to the boat.

After six weeks or so the barren landscape and heavy silence of Laguna Grande became oppressive. We grew sick of eating catfish and crabs, which were the only creatures stupid enough to overlook our net, and the final straw was a plague of flies. In one evening we slaughtered 140, but there were plenty remaining. After a quick trip back to Cumana, to stock up, we set sail for the island of Tortuga. We had fixed up the worst of the leaks in the deck, and we told ourselves that we could build a fridge and get to grips with the bathroom and one or two other things while we cruised.

By now morning sickness was the dominant feature of my existence and within a few hours of leaving port we came to realise that pregnancy and sailing do not go well together. I was sick constantly throughout the journey and arrived at our destination in a miserable state.

Again, I have read terrible tales of the things which nowadays go on in Tortuga and in the other Venezuelan islands. If the word on the grapevine is true this is certainly a no-go area – but in our time it was just a kind of no-man's land; ungoverned, perhaps, but certainly not lawless.

Isla Tortuga is as flat and low as could be, so that we did not sight it until we were almost upon it. It was late on a sunny Sunday, and as we entered the turquoise blue waters of the island's sheltered anchorage a Cessna aeroplane went running along amongst the scrub and roared into the air. Scarcely was it off the ground than we saw the plane bank into a steep turn - a turn so steep, in fact, that for a moment the aircraft was in knife-edge flight and fell through the air. The recovery to level flight was swiftly made, but still we were not too delighted when this same cowboy drove his machine low over the mast-head. On going ashore we discovered as many as five aircraft carcasses littered about near the sandy runway, one burnt, the others merely crumpled and broken. The aluminium bones of each were stripped bare of anything useful.

Nobody lives on Tortuga and apart from the turtles, who come here to breed, the only visitors to the island are nomadic fishermen, foreign yachtsmen, and a few "idle rich". The latter fly over from Caracas at the weekend, and we had just seen the last one off the premises, so to speak. For the next five days the rest of us had the island to ourselves.

The following Friday night it rained. It rained as, surely, it has never rained since Noah set sail in the ark; and when the first rich Venezuelan arrived, the next morning, his Cessna came down out of the skies and landed like a float-plane, throwing up sheets of spray. It came to a halt with water over the door-sill. A low-wing aircraft would probably have come to a halt on its back. Later arrivals, observing the stranded aircraft from on high, beat a hasty retreat.

Come Sunday night most of the water was gone from the airstrip, but there were places where it was still almost knee deep. The stranded aviator needed to be back in Caracas on the morrow. He taxied his plane carefully to the end of the strip and then went further on, into the rough grass. Then, with full flap and maximum throttle, he came chundering along towards us. The strip ended in a turquoise blue lagoon. At the moment when I would most certainly have aborted, our man pressed on... and he made it. Just. Looking at the tyre marks afterwards, we saw that the plane had limped up into the air only six yards from the water.

The rainstorm which had caused the Venezuelan pilot so much trouble was, of course, the fruit of the sultry doldrums, for the equatorial weather-belt had drifted north with the sun until it covered the southern edge of the Caribbean sea. Leaving Tortuga in the lightest of breezes we slipped around the western end of the island and as night descended were caught in another downpour. Dazzling strips of light tore a jagged path through the black sky as a million volts of electricity arced between sky and sea. Thunder crashed overhead. The wind sneaked round and round the compass, leading *Maamari* into a series of slow pirouettes. In the midst of the storm a huge owl appeared and landed on the mast-head where it perched like some Shakespearean portent of doom.

The next day, as we drew close to the mainland coast and the town of Puerto la Cruz, another squall loomed. It arrived with predictable vigour, bringing a westerly wind, but then it continued to blow hard for some hours. This was most unusual, for the Caribbean is a region of predictable easterlies. Just a few hours later this same squall, with its unexpected wind direction, was to cause thousands of pounds worth of damage in an island further to the west - but at the time we knew nothing of this.

Fifty yachts were anchored off the seaside resort of Puerto la Cruz, and whilst it would never win any accolade for its beauty or amenities the place was certainly several dozen steps up from Cumana. In those days the local police had not got into burglary - or at least, they had not begun breaking into the foreign yachts - and so the anchorage was fairly secure. At night the restaurant-lined promenade came alive with families taking the traditional Spanish evening stroll, or paseo, and whereas in Cumana we had feared to walk the streets in broad daylight, here we felt safe at any hour. Still, Puerto la Cruz was no more our kind of place than any other city and after having replenished our stores we moved on.

The Venezuelan island most famed amongst cruising folk is the atoll-archipelago of Los Roques, and it was for this place that we next embarked. To judge from the chart it would seem that Los Roques is formed of one massive volcano which has since slipped back down into the sea. All that remains is one ancient lava plug whose surrounding cinders have long since been worn away. The rest of the land at Los Roques is actually coral.

Coral is one of nature's weird wonders. The organisms responsible for building the various colourful forms are actually minute animals. They wear their skeletons on the outside and in multiplying they arrange themselves into plant-like shapes. Corals are fussy about such things as temperature and salinity. Light is important to them, and so they live only at relatively shallow depths. Typically, the colonies form around a tropical island newly arisen from the sea and create an off-lying ring around the mountain. In many instances the host island has collapsed, so that all that remains is the coral ring – or atoll. In the case of Los Roques, the volcano must have consisted of several peaks, and as the mountain sank these became islets. All that is now left is the series of small atolls which once surrounded these islets.

The windward edge of an atoll endures the tireless onslaught of the sea, but the waves which crash onto the reef and enter the lagoon must also, somehow, escape. A weakness in the far side of the circle is eventually breached and becomes the pass. On either side of the pass, and all along the leeward edge of the reef, the sea dumps pieces of dead coral which it has carried across from the windward shore; and in the course of time it grinds these calcareous, creature-made rocks until they become the fine, white sand of sunshine holiday brochures.

Navigating amongst coral requires great care, because even the colourful, plant-like forms of the living polyp-colonies are as hard as granite. Nick and his father had lost their first ocean-cruising yacht on a reef in Papua New Guinea, and all because they had broken the first rule of "coral seamanship". Eager to reach a safe haven before nightfall they had pressed on and were sailing into the light. With the sun high, or to one's back, coral is easily visible in the limpid water which it inhabits, and so the usual form is to put a man aloft in the cross-trees.

Los Roques is very popular with itinerant yotties, but because it consists of several mini atolls there are always enough anchorages to go round. We never had any trouble finding a private isle, all to ourselves - but there was always a little something which ruined our seclusion. A very little something. While we approached one particular island pass, with Nick perched on high to show the way, I suddenly found myself attacked by a plague of vampirous, black mosquitoes. To Nick's consternation and puzzlement I threw the boat around. "It's clear!" he cried, but all that was clear to me was that the mozzies had not had a decent meal in weeks. And as the little demons infested every anchorage, to a greater or lesser extent, we had soon had enough of Los Roques.

The most westerly of the Venezuelan islands is Las Aves, and having explored all the others we thought that we may as well complete the tour. The greater part of Las Aves is just an obstruction to navigation - a patchwork of reefs waiting a foot or two below the surface of the sea - and as the edge of a reef is not easily visible from windward we had to be very careful. Plenty of ships have been wrecked here, and quite a few yachts, too.

Even after we had found the place, and found the pass, we still had to tread carefully, for the lagoon within the atoll is choked with coral heads which have grown on the sunken land. We picked our way towards the one tiny piece of Las Aves which has managed to hold its head above the waves. One tiny crumb, it was - yet, with what astonishing vigour the world of earth and air had staked its claim here! This was no speck of sand and dust; it was entirely, triumphantly, *defiantly* overrun with trees. And tripping upon the heels of soil and seed, have come "Las Aves" - the birds. Frigate birds nest here, in their season, but at the time of our visit the crooked boughs of the mangroves which fringe the tiny forest were bent with the weight of young boobies. The sight of our dinghy slipping by beneath their nests seemed to cause the boobies no anxiety, but one lone flamingo took offence and went flapping away over the trees.

By the time we reached Las Aves the cyclone season was pretty much over and there was nothing to keep us from heading back up to the West Indies; but it would have been a shame to miss the chance of visiting the ABC's...

Aruba, Bonaire and Curacao are part of the Dutch Antillean group whose other members lie far away in the Windwards. A tour of all three islands would have been time consuming, but a visit to the nearest one seemed in order. Accordingly, we set course for Bonaire. We arrived, the following morning, to discover a low, flat isle. The only striking feature on its skyline was a row of white pyramids. Having failed to wrest Araya from the Spanish, the Dutch established their own salt pans on Bonaire; and, once again, the pans are still in production to this day.

Close by the salt pyramids we spotted a line of stone huts and, referring to our pilot book, we learnt that they were the one-time homes of the ancestors to the present-day islanders: African slave workers. It occurred to me, as I surveyed the drab, parched scene, that the life of a slave at the salt-pans must have been just as dire, if not worse than that of a plantation slave. Here there is not even the shade of a tree, or the sight of one, to give rest to a tired spirit.

As we slipped quietly down the side of the island, towards the town which was marked on our chart, we wondered what sort of place it would turn out to be. And what would the anchorage be like?

When an island rises sheer from the sea one expects to find trouble in anchoring, for the water will generally be very deep. By the same token, if the island is just a tedious plain then one assumes that anchoring will be easy. Logic says that beneath the sea the land will surely continue its slow descent and that in order to find sufficient depth a yacht will need to keep its distance from the shore.

The appearance of a chart can also be deceptive. The best ones not only give soundings but also show every contour of the land. When they do not, and terra firma is just a yellow-painted patch, then my subconscious mind creates within me the expectation of a flat island.

Bonaire defies all the usual rules. Having read in our old, dog-eared pilot book that the coast plunges down into a virtual abyss, I had come up with the mental image of an island with tall, perpendicular cliffs. With the land now spread before us, the pancake picture on the chart was, for once, confirmed. And now intuition came tiptoeing silently across our minds, and we found ourselves subconsciously reverting to the preconception of a slowly shelving bottom. Arriving off the little town of Kralendijk we discovered the error in our reckoning. The fact of the matter is that the ancient coral and sediment of the land do, indeed, slide gently into the sea - but then, after just 20 or 30 yards, the bottom goes crashing straight down into a void.

The prevailing wind in the anchorage was offshore - of course - but what if a squall should come by and the wind go into the west? We made a quick survey of the anchorage, motoring through with our eyes on the echo-sounder. It seemed that if we could manage to perch our anchor right on the very edge of the precipice then, if *Maamari* were to swing towards the shore, she would still be in six feet of water. It was touch and go. But, then again, westerly squalls are a rarity. We had seen none since that day, some weeks earlier, when we were off Puerto la Cruz.

The next problem was getting the hook to take hold, for no anchor, apart from a Fisherman, sets well in dead coral. Most sit on top of the thin veil of sand which buries that hard bed. The Fisherman anchor can find a crevice within the dead reef, and with its long, curved arm it is able to hold on tight. But our Fisherman weighs 80lbs, and it was stowed beneath cans of fuel and water in the lazarette. We put out the main anchor (a CQR). After the fourth try it held.

Maamari was now floating over the bottomless sea beyond the wall - it was too deep for our echo-sounder to pick up a reading - but the hook lay in only five metres. We put out 15 metres of chain and then added five metres more, for luck. Under the circumstances we would have done better to anchor with rope, for a moment's conjecture will show that in anchoring just on the edge of the wall we had *not* actually laid out a handsome weight of chain but instead had dangled it over into the chasm, where it increased the strain on the anchor. We did not take that moment for conjecture. Instead we hurried ashore for lunch.

After four months spent either in uninhabited isles or in side-stepping the filth and poverty of Venezuelan cities, the neat, clean, quiet village of Kralendijk came as a welcome relief. The frenzied pace of Latin American street life had been irksome, but here the mood of the people echoed that of their Dutch overlords. This is an uneventful place, in danger only of being termed boring.

Unfortunately, prices in Kralendijk are also the equal of those in Holland and so our lunch ashore became abbreviated to a quick pint. This was just as well, as it happens, for when we came back to *Maamari* we found that she had dragged the hook and was now a couple of boat lengths further to seaward. In breaking free and tumbling over the edge of the precipice the CQR had chanced to snag something in the living coral wall. Were it not for this, the boat would by now have disappeared over the horizon.

Nick unearthed the big Fisherman anchor and lugged it onto the foredeck. Then he put it together and lowered it over the side. We anchored again, and this time I dived to take a look at the hook and ensure that it was doing its job. While I was in the water I

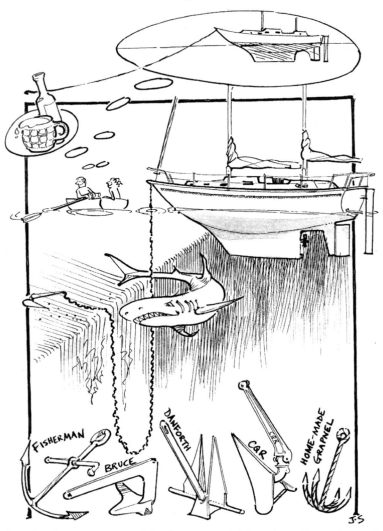

thought that I may as well look at our neighbour's tackle, and then I checked out every other yacht anchored on the narrow ledge. There were eight boats, all told, and apart from our own only two were properly anchored. One yacht was held by a Bruce, which had somehow managed to bury itself completely, and another was held by a home-made grapnel which was carefully deployed across a massive ground chain.

Warily, we ventured ashore again. It is always rather nerve-racking to leave all that you own dangling on the end of a chain and hook, and it was all the more so after our experience of that morning. This time we restricted our wanderings to the seafront, whence we could cast the occasional nervous glance at our pride and joy and could also keep an eye open for approaching squalls. We had already walked around the town and so we now explored in the other direction, and here we came at once upon a line of half a dozen yachts.

We had noticed the yachts from the anchorage and had wondered what they were doing, high and dry, at the side of the road. As we approached them we now saw that each one was badly damaged. Indeed, one was split in half from the deck all the way down to the keel! There could be no mistaking what had happened, but still we needed the sorry tale spelt out to us before we could believe the evidence spread out along that tranquil water front.

"It all began late one evening, just a few weeks ago." In answer to our puzzled enquiry the sailor clambered down a makeshift ladder set-up against the side of his battered yacht. He was an American; a sad and weary character in his late fifties. Four months earlier he had put his business into the hands of an agent so that he and his wife could take a two year sabbatical, but now they had discovered that the life of a live-aboard is not all sunshine and sandy beaches.

When the man told us the date of his misadventure I realised that it was the same one on which we had been sailing from Isla Tortuga to Puerto la Cruz. So far as we were concerned, the squall which had met us as we approached the mainland coast had been nothing more than a mild inconvenience. Meanwhile, in the crowded anchorage off the town fifty yachts had swung at the end of their tethers, and perhaps, in painting that arc on the water, a handful had come up against their neighbours. Topsides may have been scuffed, perhaps, and a few harsh words may have been passed from one yotty to another.

By the time the line squall reached Bonaire it was evening and most of the yachtsmen were just sitting down to dinner in one of the water-front bars. Our man was having dinner aboard. He had seen the squall approaching and, in his own words, was taking no chances. When the wind struck, 13 pretty sailing boats swung through half a circle and 12 found the beach. Even the careful fellow who was our witness had left it too late for his salvation. With the wind and sea pinning the yacht to the beach it was impossible to power out under engine. So it was that 12 yachts were soon lying on their beam ends in the surf. In time, a big road crane arrived and, each in turn, the stricken vessels were lifted up unto the road.

"It was me that called for the bloody crane," our friend claimed, huffily, "but the bastards started from the other end and left my boat until last."

Of the twelve casualties, six were said to be complete write-offs.

Needless to say, our confidence in the anchorage was now reduced to zero, and the following morning saw us hoisting the sails and slipping away down the coast of Bonaire. The weather was perfect. Little, wispy clouds straggled across an eggshell-blue sky and a steady force four leant on the stern and sent *Maamari* bowling along.

In the north, the island's desert plain was lifted into a jumble of low peaks and the shore rose from the sea in a wave-chewed cliff. There are lizards six-foot long living on this parched wasteland. Seen on the skyline they could be mistaken for something even bigger, and in the not too distant past explorers came here to look for "the last of the dinosaurs". Yes, dinosaurs again. Why dinosaurs should be associated with deserts I cannot say. Children's textbooks show them wading nonchalantly through pond-weed, or crashing about in a damp and steamy forest, but there is something about the atmosphere of the empty desert which inspires thoughts of a past age surviving secretly into the present.

Off the north-western tip of Bonaire we sighted a little fishing boat. It was drifting on the lazy current while two tiny figures tended lines at bow and stern. In all that broad, blue expanse of ocean it was the only other boat. I aimed to pass within hailing distance, and greet the fishermen with a friendly wave, and so I pointed *Maamari* to leave them close to starboard. The wind was now meeting us on the beam, and with her sails billowing and the sea scarcely rougher than a lake, *Maamari* soon ate up the mile which separated us and bore down towards the little open boat. The tiny stick-men became black

Antilleans, swinging baited lines around their heads and then letting them fly out and fall.

In the last few hundred yards I changed my mind. I decided that by leaving the boat to port, rather than starboard, I could save us a little bit of ground. The distance was insignificant and the change broke all the rules of holding a steady course and making clear one's intention, but the other fellow was not underway, so what did it matter? I headed up - just a touch - and our bow swung across from its earlier course onto my new intended heading. Immediately, the old man sitting in the stern of the fishing boat let go his line and made a grab for the motor. With two pulls he had started the outboard. The boat leapt forwards into our path.... and then the motor died.

Now I made another duff decision. At this point I should have headed-up further but, mindful of the fact that the fisherman might suddenly re-start his motor, I turned the wheel sharply back to port, intending to bring *Maamari* back off the wind. In the same instant Nick threw himself across the cockpit and let go the mizzen halyard - but it was too late! With all that weight of wind in the sail, and with the mizzen carefully arranged to hold her bow up to weather, *Maamari* was a freight train running along iron rails. As I tried to force her to jump the rails and slew to port, the force on the wheel was too much and the steering cables broke - again. The wheel spun freely in my hands. The fishing boat disappeared from our sight below the bow, and with a cry of horror Nick and I both dived for the genoa winch and let the sail fly free. The runaway train spun into the wind and came skidding to a halt, brushing gently alongside the little open boat.

What the two fisherman thought of us can best be imagined. I picture them with their friends in the bar that night, with a yarn to tell of the incompetent foreign yotties who had the whole sea to choose from but who still managed to run down the only other boat. "Come straight for us, they did, from over the horizon, like they was intent on sending us to the bottom!"

Lying the full length of the clinker boat was a shark, not long dead, and there were a couple of other biggish fish. All in all, it seemed that the men had been having an eventful morning. Their fury the two old fellows spent in abusing each other, in the local creole, and the only words they addressed to us were ones of profuse apology! Either the folks of Bonaire are sweeter than any others on earth or else, in their youth, this ancient pair had been required to bow and scrape before the white man in a manner which I had formerly thought belonged to the last century.

By now I was more than four months pregnant and no longer suffering daily bouts of morning sickness, but it was clear from our recent island-hopping adventures that for the journey ahead I could still expect to be suffering mal de mer. St Lucia was our destination, and since it lies roughly 500 miles upwind from Bonaire we reckoned that the trip would take about six days. If I were to be sick five or six times each day, as our experience implied, then clearly Caesar and I would arrive considerably the worse for wear. The only solution would be for me to spend the entire journey lying on my back - and so that is what I did. Nick sailed the boat virtually single-handed, and I took my watches reclining on a cushion in the cockpit. From this position I was eminently able to study the sails, and now and then I raised my head to look at the compass or scan the horizon for ships.

Had we been making this trip sometime between January and April then we could have expected a steady force four to five north-easterly, but it was still November and in the absence of the tradewinds, with the doldrums still hanging about nearby, the best we could hope for was a light south-easterly. Unfortunately, we got, instead, the worst we could have expected, barring a laggard hurricane. We got a zephyr breeze right on the nose.

As a rule it does not bother us at all if a voyage takes longer than had been reckoned, but bearing in mind my condition we wanted this journey over and done with. At the present rate, with the current ferrying us gently along, our best ETA was about a month - and it was on Nicaragua.

Reluctantly, we started the engine. For two days we put up with its infernal racket and fretted about the damage it was doing to the environment and then, on the third day, we heard a tremendous clunk and a clatter and the boat once again ceased in its forward motion. The drive-plate had broken. For sometime I had suggested that, at certain revs, the engine produced an ominous rattle, but obedient to his philosophy of leaving alone that which still works, Nick had ignored the symptom. There were, after all, plenty of other tasks to occupy his time. At this stage the deck was still less than half done and progress in the bathroom had stopped just after I gutted it of all but the loo.

The entire journey to St Lucia took ten days, of which the last two were spent drifting in circles just off the island. The part of me which thinks I am a ship's boy on an Elizabethan brig began to fear that we would be stuck out here forever, while "all the boards did shrink", and we felt a great deal of empathy with the sailors of the ancient past. Specifically, we felt that we could now begin to understand the feelings of the crew of the 18th century warship – one of Anson's round the world fleet - which spent weeks drifting about in sight of Isla Juan Fernandez while most of the men died of scurvy. The remedy to their ailment grew on the shore within their gaze. So near and yet so far.

Finally, one of the fierce drafts which tumbles down from St Lucia's peaks came rushing out across the water to take us under its wing.

St Lucia we found to be not much to our liking, and so we were not too disappointed when casual enquiries after work produced no leads. On, then. Perhaps we would have more luck in St Martin or in the Virgin Islands - but they were a long way away. We decided to break the journey at Antigua.

English Harbour seemed unusually crowded, we thought, as the cliffs peeled away to reveal the secret hurricane hole. The engine was still in a state of disrepair and so it was under full sail that we pinched through the narrow entrance, almost scraping our keel on the rocks below Fort Berkley. Even after we had safely gained the sanctuary of the harbour there was no time to breathe a sigh of relief; rather the reverse; we were immediately in amongst the throng. There was not even space for us to round up and drop the main and so, with hearts in mouths, we bore away in a great arc, all the while praying that the steering cables would this time hold up to the strain. Nick had his hand on the anchor and I was poised by the mizzen halyard, ready to drop the sail and help *Maamari* bear away in haste. Thus, once more a bull in a china shop, we charged through the crowded anchorage, through a fleet which we now could see was made up of the world's finest charter yachts, brought together here for "Agent's Week". Happily, our dramatic arrival and our gallop amongst them were mistaken for panache, so that the liveried crews grinned and applauded us as we passed.

Just when it seemed that there was no place for us - and that we should have to plough straight on, around the quay and into the mangroves at the head of the creek - just then, we stumbled upon a patch with enough swinging room for a 44 ft yacht, and with the shout, "Now!" Nick kicked the anchor overboard. I let go the genoa and *Maamari* spun up into the wind, instantly obedient to the hook.

A splendid arrival it appeared to be - and one is tempted to suggest that such a demonstration of seemingly first-class seamanship tends often to border closely on timber-shattering disaster. This time we got away with it. Moreover, purely by chance, we had dropped anchor in the prime spot, just off the little shipyard and only a few yards further from the quay. It seemed like a good place to spend a week or two, and a week or two was all we planned on spending in Antigua. We ended up staying two years.

8

BABY ON BOARD

(In which we welcome two new crew-members
and put them through their paces)

"Do you need a mechanic?" Clad in a misshapen T-shirt and tattered shorts, and with his hair sticking out of the back of his head like a Mohican's comb, Nick was, as usual, the very picture of sartorial inelegance. The manager of Antigua Slipway was a little man, with a tidy coiffure, and he was neatly dressed in a pink polo shirt, stylish white shorts, and designer sunglasses. He was sitting behind his desk, thumbing through a pile of bills.

"Do you need a mechanic?" Nick asked, diffidently. We had no expectation of finding work in Antigua, but as we were anchored just off the boatyard there seemed no harm in asking.

At Nick's enquiry the man in the pink shirt flew up like a jack on whom the lid has been lifted. "Mechanic? Stay there! Stay right there!" He shot out of the door.

With him, when he returned, was the chief of the engineering shop, a tall, olive-skinned mulatto who was introduced as Carl.

"You're a mechanic?" said Carl, and he eyed Nick incredulously, as if he were someone who had just appeared from a hole in the sky. "God, I'm pleased to see you. Can you start today?"

Antigua is a very special island, not least because it is beautiful and has a beautiful climate, but also because of the place which it occupies in the history of England. Were it not for Antigua, England might never have gained control of the Caribbean; might never have subsequently grown rich through the success of the sugar industry; might never have been able to finance the Industrial Revolution; might never, thereafter, have had the ability to build up an empire larger than any other that the world has ever seen.

Having laid claim to Antigua, England was able to subsequently get her hands on almost every other island in the Caribbean, and the reason for this was very simple: without a hurricane-proof harbour the 18th century navies dare not remain in this part of the world during the summer months. Having acquired the only decent hurricane hole, the English were able to stay on, and send out expeditions to the other isles, when everyone else had gone home.

Having set up camp on this island the Admiralty then equipped it with all the shore-side facilities necessary to refit and repair His Majesty's fleet, for without modern paints and modern antifouling wooden ships need to be slipped, or careened, and cleaned and repaired every year. When the navy eventually moved out of the place, in the late 19th century, these facilities were simply abandoned. So it was that many, many years later, in the 1950s, an English family sailed into English Harbour and discovered a silent ghost town of derelict barracks and rotting wooden capstans, on a quay overgrown with long grass. The Nicholsons had been on their way to Australia but, like so many others since, they became ensnared in the charms of Antigua. They stayed for good.

Besides beginning the restoration of the 18th century naval dockyard, the Nicholsons also recognised the harbour's enormous potential for charter yachts. It was scenic, it was unused - and if it had proved a safe refuge to the British warships of old then why should not the seafarers of this age also find shelter here, even from hurricanes? From the seed of a small beginning, Nicholson's charter yacht agency grew, until Antigua and the old harbour became the axis of the Caribbean luxury charter yacht scene.

From the old stone shed where the chippies once worked with adze and chisel comes now the sound of an electric saw. In another workshop, where the smith might once have forged cranse-irons and cringles, Carl Mitchell and his minions labour by the light of the welder's blue torch, enveloped in the scent of diesel. Until the early 1990's, when a new marina was built on Antigua's western shore, Antigua Slipway held a virtual monopoly on servicing and refurbishing the world's finest charter yachts during their Caribbean season; and their plunder and pillage of this fleet was merciless.

A biggish boat, by the standards of our home waters, in English Harbour *Maamari* was a little runt, dwarfed by the mega-yachts and sometimes even by their tenders. In English Harbour even an 80 ft Swan is nothing to turn the head.

The motor ship *Stefaren* looms above Berkley Point, and its bow appears from behind the ancient fort. Slowly and carefully the monster edges its 189 feet of gleaming fibreglass and chrome amongst the moored craft, now and then sending out a 20 ft RIB to nudge a path through the flotilla. And *Stefaren* was not the biggest. With our sight jaded by familiarity we soon grew accustomed to seeing a couple of 200 ft "stinkpots" on the quay. 120 ft Jongerts, with a price tag of around twelve million dollars, slipped in and out unnoticed. *Endeavour* and *Velsheda* shrank, and huge gin palaces growling with the harnessed might of more than 2,000 horses seemed as nothing more than Ford Escort boy racers - a comparison which acquaintance with their skippers tended to reinforce.

The super-yacht scene positively reeks of money, and when the armada returned from the Mediterranean in November, then the good folks of English Harbour lined up to lighten them of their loot. Oh, yes - there are pirates, still, in the Caribbean!

A lick of varnish, laid on by the local rastas? That'll cost yer ten dollars an hour, me hearties. A fiddle for the cooker? You can have it tomorrow, but it'll be hand-made and it'll set you back around $200.

One day a skipper arrived, with the owner's blank cheque, and ordered a simple, stainless-steel socket for his gang plank. It took the lads in the engineering shop all day to sculpt the item from a solid bar, and with it the yard presented a bill for $400. The skipper didn't bat an eye-lid. On the contrary; he was proud of the expense.

A week on the slip and a coat of the finest paint? "Pieces of eight! Pieces of eight!" Yet who could have looked the gift-horse in the mouth when the skippers were so eager to unburden themselves of the owners' booty?

Nick has worked with motors since he was about 12 years old and likes nothing better than to be up to his elbows in crank-case oil. His efforts in the engineering shop were soon appreciated by all, and from our point of view too it was the ideal set up. The anchorage was secure, the grocery shop was close at hand, the pay was good - and although the cost of living was proportionate to the scale of the wages, our expenses could be limited to the food we ate and the rest could be put away in the piggy-bank. That, at least, was the theory.

If we had to stop and earn some money then this was certainly an idyllic way. Each morning at two minutes to seven Nick would set off in the dinghy to be at work on the hour. My days were spent in painting pictures, for sale to the wealthy charter guests, or in attending to the usual household chores.

Every day the sun poured down incessantly from a cobalt-blue sky ornamented by a sprinkling of cuddly, white clouds. A host of pale-yellow butterflies danced across the rippled water, looking like thousands of rose petals stripped from the bushes by a boisterous gale and now blown along on the caress of the soft breeze. From the cactus-covered hills above and behind us came the sound of young goats calling to their mothers. Charter yachts came and went. Dinghies dashed hither and thither, leaving trails of foam.

Cruising folk, too, began to appear. A few we knew from our tour of Venezuela; others arrived from across the pond, some by themselves and some as part of the annual ARC race flotilla. The tradewinds were as yet still unreliable, as these voyagers had discovered - most had run out of fuel on the way, and a couple of boats had called up passing ships to beg for a can of water - but it is the fashion nowadays to be in the Caribbean for Christmas.

By now I was more than five months pregnant and beginning to worry about hospital provisions in the island of Antigua. The first option was the general hospital. Its main advantage was that its services were free, but as we stepped within the portals of this melancholy institution, with its prehistoric beds and an aura of the Victorian age, I could feel myself recoiling. Peeping apprehensively into the maternity ward we were confronted by a nurse who eyed Nick as a pit-bull terrier eyes an intending visitor to his master's house. "Men," she barked in answer to our enquiry, "are not admitted into the delivery room."

The only other alternative was a private clinic, run by two American-trained obstetricians, and so it was here that we enrolled.

Now that this matter was settled, our next requirement was for a car. Without a car we were dependent on the Reggae bus - and the journey into town aboard this ruinous Bedford van was an adventure in itself, and not one that we wished often to repeat.

With the benefit of experience gained in Africa, we would aim to sit right at the back of any commercial vehicle, for this was the place we considered to be the least hazardous; if the bus hits a wall, the guys at the back are more likely to survive than the ones riding near the front window. But when we clambered to the back of the brightly-painted Reggae bus we found that the speakers were positioned in a row beneath this seat, and the upholstered bench throbbed to the thud of the bass drum.

Like the drivers in Africa, the man who chauffeured the reggae bus was disinclined to move off until every seat was taken - including a row of folding chairs which occupied the centre aisle - and so we waited, numbed by the oppressive volume of the music into a kind of hypnotic trance; our senses were withdrawn like the horns of a snail into his shell.

The driver revved the engine and let his machine roll to and fro, like a horse pawing the ground, on a little incline in the road. A fat, old woman in a colourful straw hat waddled out from the dockyard, where she had been selling T-shirts, and heaved herself and her bulging bags aboard. Flopping into the nearest seat she sprawled inelegantly, and then she turned to strike up what seemed to be an argument with a thin, droopy-eyed man on the other side of the bus. Above the noise of the music the conversation was scarcely audible, but even those words which reached us were incoherent. English is the first and only language in Antigua, but the local dialect is utterly foreign; one has to have been born and bred here to understand it.

Suddenly the bus lurched forward, and we were off. Not content with the already unbearable level of noise, the driver turned up the volume of the reggae music until the beat pounded inside my heart and womb. It soon became apparent that our lives were in the hands of a maniac. The man seemed only to know of stop or go, and the bus thundered along, crashing through the pot holes which are the dominant feature of Antiguan roads, and lurching around the corners.

As we hurtled through the villages the driver played a little ditty on his musical horn, and goats and children and chickens all dived for cover; they knew that tune. At each curve in the road the melody was reinforced by a deafening blast on the air-horns, and we swung around on the outside of the bend.

Nick and I clung to each other. Since we were at the back of the bus I reasoned that we ought probably to survive the inevitable head-on collision, but we were in danger of being thrown out of the open window. Our fellow passengers, although they had given up trying to converse, seemed completely blasé about our journey. As we smashed past the overhanging branches of a tree, on the wrong side of the road, I peered forward to catch a glimpse of our pilot. To be fair the man was somewhat preoccupied. As I watched, he made a lunge for the schoolgirl seated two rows back and across the aisle, and was firmly repulsed. He evidently had little time to be looking out of the front window.

Rattling along through the pot holes, the bus struggled to reach the top of a small hill. Then, just as we began to roll down the opposite side, a herd of cattle set off across the road ahead. The bus driver pumped the brakes, achieving very little, and then crashed down through the gears. As we hurtled toward the cows he hammered on his air-horns and the animals glanced up. On seeing the bus tearing down towards them they stopped altogether. We skidded to a halt amongst them, with one wheel up on the verge.

No one stirred. Expressions of alarm and dismay are anathema to the West African and the West Indian psyche, and besides that, there was nothing to get excited about; this kind of thing happened every day.

If we were to avoid enduring this ordeal each week then we must have some other means of transport - or else we must remain cosseted within the self-contained community at English Harbour.

For many of the itinerant yotties, their view of the island was necessarily restricted to this ex-pat enclave, but we were determined to remain outside that clique and involve ourselves with the native scene. The first obstacle in this ambition was to actually acquire the car.

Like everything else imported into Antigua, cars are subject to an extortionate duty. In fact, the tax is more than 100% of the vehicle's estimated value, regardless of whether the car be new or old. As a result, even second-hand cars command a very high price. Happily, the Antiguan road test was anything but stringent; all the cars on the island were tested in the same week, and so there was no time for the authorities to do more than glance at a couple of features on each vehicle. Thus any machine that could be persuaded to hold together and get us from A to B would answer the need.

We ended up with "Wangy", a 1976 Nissan Sunny which ought long ago to have been given new life in the form of tin cans, but which, at 400 quid, cost more than any other vehicle either of us had ever owned. On the only occasion when we had to put the car through its paces for the law we received word in advance of which two features were subject to inspection that year. One was the tyres - and we had four, one at each corner, and so met that requirement. The other was the hand brake, and although the hand break lever was not actually connected to anything its mere presence satisfied the officers. Had we been required to test the horn it would probably have sufficed to lean out of the window and say, "Beep, beep."

When we were not using "Wangy" he sat in the lane outside the boatyard, and the mongooses climbed in through the holes in the body-work and did unspeakable things on the back seat. Once, while we were driving at night, a tarantula ran across the windscreen. On another occasion a bright green lizard darted across my lap and ran out through the open window and onto the bonnet. On reaching the front of the bonnet he posed in the exact centre - head forward, tail stuck out and up behind - looking quite as splendid as the statuette on a Rolls Royce.

Our increased mobility gave us a new vision of Antigua, for we could now explore its every intricate corner. Up muddy, unpaved roads we would struggle; up to the old fort, high on Monk's Hill, where once the early British settlers used to hide from the Carib Indians and the French. We would go down to the rainforest, where the slave runaways once found shelter, and on out to Darkwood Beach. We went to the museum and learnt about the brutality of slavery and the sour cost of sugar; we went to John Ffryes Beach, where the ruined, rubble walls of an old windmill whispered nothing more than gentle rumours of the wickedness cloaked in the past. From Boggy Peak we looked out and saw Montserrat and the pyramid-shaped rock of Redonda. In the east we found an islet joined to the mother isle by a floating bridge.

During the two years of our stay in Antigua we got to know the island about as well as the locals know it, finding favourite beaches which could only be reached on foot, and favourite night-spots where the "pepper-pot and fungi" were "hot" and the calypso music played until dawn. But in our ambition of getting involved with the people we were constantly and deliberately thwarted. Even Nick's workmates gave him the cold shoulder when we met in public, for it appears that Antiguans are embarrassed to be seen associating with a white man. Only one of our many acquaintances ever invited us into his home. For all that, I became increasingly interested in the West Indian people and in their history, and I began to plan a little detour into their motherland. Nothing too time consuming, of course - for we still had our sights set on Patagonia and Cape Horn - but it seemed to me that we might just as well break the journey south with a visit to Ghana and the Ivory Coast...

Time was moving on and every passing day added a few more ounces to my waistline, so that by the middle of March I could scarcely haul myself aboard *Maamari*. On the 9th of April, Caesar passed the date which our highly trained and expensive carers had determined for his arrival, and so they decided to intervene. We were given six days grace before, on April 16th, I was summoned to the clinic. Caesar's birth was to be induced.

As we made our way across the island and towards St John's I felt strangely apathetic. The excitement and apprehension that I had always envisaged were absent, and instead there was only a vacuum. I felt cheated. Everything had been taken out of my control.

"It feels like Christmas morning," said Nick, as we reached the clinic, but all I felt was an impending sense of doom.

I was ushered into my cell and the duty nurse chained me to the bed with a drip. Within a minute the oxytocin fed insidiously into my bloodstream had taken control and, at its bidding, my womb was induced to make its first contraction. "This is it, Caesar. They're going to drag you out of your cosy home."

The idea, as it was explained to me, was to get the contractions coming at between four and five minute intervals, but every nurse and doctor coming to peer at me in this early stage was apt to turn up the wick until, within an hour of my arrival, the contractions were coming at two minute intervals. Since they lasted about a minute, this did not give much time for relaxation. Man, in his usual desperate haste, could not be bothered to do the thing at nature's pace.

"You are only one centimetre dilated," said the doctor, in an accusatory manner. He had just broken my waters and let them gush all over the bed. "At this rate," he said "We will be delivering the baby at eight o'clock tonight."

Well, in that case it would be by the knife! The idea that I might survive the pain for another ten hours was utterly inconceivable - but fortunately the learned man was mistaken. At three o'clock the baby began his descent into the great wide world and within half an hour he was amongst us, and we were parents.

Our little son yawned and stretched his arms, as if to say, "My! It's good to be out of there." Then he began to smack his lips in anticipation of the first meal. For the next three and a quarter years that activity, of sucking at his mother's breast, was to be Caesar's one, singular fixation.

The sun in its orbit passed overhead Antigua, and as it journeyed north towards the Tropic of Cancer so the steady tradewind began to fade. The hurricane season was drawing nigh again, and the charter yachts began to make tracks for the Mediterranean. We had decided to stay put. We did not have to worry unduly about the weather, for the safety of the harbour had been proven many times over the centuries.

With the charter yachts gone the old dockyard was like a ghost town. We had the harbour almost entirely to ourselves and could easily picture it as the Nicholsons found it, forty years earlier. The boatyard was completely empty.

The little, shabby town of St John's was quieter too, but although the northern summer is the low season for tourism in

Antigua, it is her people's favourite time. December 25th may be the most important day of the year for sun-seeking ex-pats, but for the Antiguan populace Christmas is a triviality and the first Monday in August is the highlight of the calendar.

The first Monday in August is known as Jouvé Morning (from the French, jour-ouvert, or opening day) and it was at the dawning of this day, more than 160 years ago, that the grand-parents and great-grand-parents of the present "sons of the soil" of Antigua were officially liberated from slavery. Jouvé was originally observed by giving thanks to God, but such details are now completely overshadowed by revelry in the street.

In memory of the dawn emancipation the fun officially begins at four-thirty, and by eight in the morning the streets of St John's are thronged. Half a dozen tractors prowl the grid-plan town, each one towing a large trailer decked out with two dozen "pan men" and two dozen carefully tuned oil drums. The steel drums rattle and hum to the rhythm of a calypso smash-hit. Beethoven and the William Tell overture are strictly for the white tourists; today the orchestra is tapping out the latest hits of the island's number one pop group, The Burning Flames.

As for the "Flames" - they have been playing all night at the Lion's Club, and they look as if they could do with a nap. Their faces are long – but that is just their manner. They never smile; that wouldn't be cool. Nor is yawning an option.

Tired they may be, but the adrenaline is still running high for the Flames and they are still in control. They are going to keep on playing, on the back of their flat bed truck, until their fans wilt away – and that will not be for many, many hours.

> "I want to rub your belly,
> Line-up on your boompsy,
> Bend you over with ease,
> Ram you nice and steady..."

The Burning Flames' lyrics are anything but subtle - but then, subtlety has never been a feature of West Indian song. The band are as professional as The Rolling Stones and there is a not dissimilar edge of menace to their lewd wit. In the Caribbean, no one else can hold a candle to their popularity.

Behind the trailer, an ancient old granny dances along the street, thrusting her hips forward and swaying to the music in true African style. A line of youths is "wining-up", stacked, each right behind the next boy or girl - their legs splayed, their backs arched - in exaggerated imitation of the traditional, solo posture. Some of the girls raise their arms aloft. Some of the boys dare to put their hands on their girlfriends' thighs. After a while someone collapses onto the fellow behind, and the whole line crumbles amidst shouts of laughter. The kids melt into the crowd or go rushing off to look for another friend or another band.

These days, the focal point of the emancipation party is a colourful carnival. Tacked onto the celebrations quite recently, and with the purely commercial motive of extending the holiday season, it has taken over and become the highlight of the show. On the Monday afternoon there is a formal parade, with men walking on stilts, as their ancestors walked for their own cultural celebrations, and with "mass" - or masquerading - troupes in fancy-dress. The day after Jouvé is called Las-Lap (last lap), and for this occasion the bands lead the liveried carnival troupes along the highroad and into the cricket stadium, where they will be judged.

In the side street where we waited for the Las-Lap procession young girls were fidgeting with their turquoise ballet tights, or rearranging the tinsel on a tiny sibling's head-dress. There were men dressed as Roman gladiators but sporting mirrored Raybans and swigging cans of coke. A fat, mulatto lady twitched her enormous, orange-stockinged bum in time to the music.

The music thundered, like the roar of a jet plane's engines, from two dozen speakers stacked on the back of a passing flat-bed truck:

> "...Tie your hen, 'cos me cock leg-o',
> Tie your mare, 'cos me stallion leg-o'..."

Although we were by no means in the front line of the crowd thronging the street, we cringed from the quite terrifying volume of the noise, and I pressed my hands to Caesar's little ears. Behind the lorry marched a troupe of women, each clad in an identical uniform of black tights and star-spangled red satin tunics. In their hands they held silver wands, and there were satin-covered wings on their backs.

Another troupe was dressed as bats, and claimed to represent The Future Of The World. According to the banner carried by its leader, another showed the horror of war; its members wore camouflage leotards and sprayed the crowd with water-pistols. The allegories were tenuous, but the costumes were fabulous. What did it have to do with emancipation from slavery? Nothing at all, but we reckoned that this was all to the better. Their former status is something of an obsession amongst Antiguans - to hear them talk one could be forgiven for thinking that slavery was abolished only last week - and so it seemed to us that their ability to forget all about the thing they were celebrating was a very healthy sign. They were partying for partying's sake, and we admired them for what they had created.

By now we had been in Antigua for almost a year and the pennies were slowly trickling into our bank account, but hanging on to them was turning out to be more of a problem than we had anticipated. We needed a new genoa - we could shred the old one with our hands - but that item alone would set us back £1,000. Then there was the stays'l - it was also pretty ropey - and then, perhaps we ought really to replace some of our frayed and faded running rigging. The list went on.

Whereas, alone, we two had been willing to take the responsibility for our own lives, we had now to think of Caesar. The nesting instinct which afflicts females and brings about the dissolution of many a partnership between boat and man was in my case diverted towards making our seaworthy vessel even more secure. Besides the essential net around the guard rail I wanted extra life buoys, and the life-raft must be seen to be a going concern. I wanted more flares, and a water-activated danbuoy, and at the top of my wish list was an Emergency Position Indicating Radio Beacon, or EPIRB.

Nick needed no convincing of the benefits of an EPIRB - friends owed their lives to such a device - but we already *had* an EPIRB.

"Ah, yes, but it isn't a four-zero-six." It could communicate only with an aeroplane passing overhead, and not with satellites. Suppose that, in the time of some unspeakable disaster, we chanced to be somewhere far from any air route. The thing that I wanted was a state of the art device and it cost over a thousand dollars.

Nick ground his teeth and gave in, thankful at least that I had not demanded a nice little cottage in the country.

And then there were more mundane expenses. Modern vessels need very little maintenance compared to those 18th century galleons, but they do still need to be antifouled. That meant slipping - and while the boat was out of the water we might as well sort out the steering. For years Nick had been itching to play about with the rudder, moving it to a site of greater advantage directly below the transom. Naturally, this was not the work of a moment; it entailed building a new rudder and fitting a strongly reinforced skeg. The steering cables would need to be longer and, while we were about it, they ought to have a bigger quadrant which would lighten the load on the gear. If ever we were going to do the work now was the obvious time, and so we bit the bullet and arranged to have the yacht slipped in the empty boatyard.

Many came to see the work in hand. "It won't make a scrap of difference," said the local surveyor - a man of some renown, locally - but although his condemnatory advice was a crushing blow, Nick pressed on, pursuing his own intuition and understanding.

Proof came, of course, when the boat was relaunched, and the learned naval architect was shown to be very much mistaken. No longer had we any need to hover by the mizzen halyard, dragging the sail up and down to get *Maamari* on and off the wind, and never again did we have any trouble with the steering cables. The boat now handled beautifully.

The outcome of all this expenditure was that after a year of hard graft our funds were scarcely more abundant than when we had arrived. Nick signed on for a second year with Antigua Slipway - and while we were about it we decided that we might as well take the opportunity to make a play-mate for Caesar.

Xoë was known throughout the nine long months of pregnancy by this and no other name, and even while we drove towards town, after a whole day of contractions, we were still trying to come up with a name for a boy. The uncertainty about who it is that dwells within, is one of the strangest things about pregnancy.

"Go straight to the clinic," said the good doctor - the same who had delivered Caesar. Instead we went to the beach, and as each new contraction gripped me I ground tight circles round and around in the sand. Caesar was still nursing, and whenever things seemed to be slowing up I invited him on to my lap. Excitement of the nipples is said to be a powerful stimulant towards uterine contraction, and I can certainly confirm that fact. Soon we were trotting back up the road to the clinic, and within an hour Xoë was pushing her way out to meet us.

Our firstborn was still just 19 months old and he watched the drama of his sister's arrival without the least hint of surprise. Only one thing puzzled Caesar. As his Daddy brought him forward for a closer look he pointed at the baby and said, "Willy gone! Willy gone!" - which is baby speak for vive la différence.

Xoë was around three months old when we first began to leave Antigua. After more than two years at anchor in the dockyard the break was best made gently, for although we were itching to be on our way we had also grown passionately fond of the island. We decided that our first move towards departure should be a shakedown sail. Since we knew from hard won experience that sailing and pregnancy are sorry companions *Maamari* had sat idle for the past twelve months, and during that time rust and other forms of corrosion might easily have corrupted some of her apparel. A quick spin outside the harbour would give us the chance to identify any such problems.

Rather than head out on a quiet afternoon, as commonsense suggested that we should, we decided instead to enter the weekly Antigua Yacht Club race. And in a gay and extremely stupid fit of enthusiasm we invited eight friends to join us for the event.

In order to protect our claim to the patch of harbour we had occupied during the past months we decided to leave the anchor in situ, marking and buoying it with the dinghy. The Avon was duly fastened to the gear, the remainder of the chain was lowered aboard, and I made ready to cast off. Nick turned the key to fire up the engine - and the engine answered with a feeble whine. A perfunctory investigation revealed that one or other of us had flicked the wrong switch, so that our cabin lights drained not only the domestic battery but also the one reserved explicitly for awakening the beast. "No problem," Nick told our guests. "We'll leave the harbour under sail."

The main and genoa were duly hoisted and then, with all eyes in the dockyard upon us, we cast off the anchor. Having backed the mizzen, to encourage the bow to pay-off away from the shore, we quickly began to unfurl the genoa.

All was proceeding according to plan. Once again, we were providing a marvellous example of seamanship. Caesar was below-decks, playing. Xoë was asleep in her hammock. The men were on the foredeck, noisily trimming the genoa... but the bow continued to pay off.

"Bring her up a bit! Hey, mind that boat!"

The chap on the helm already had the wheel hard to port but everybody had their own piece of advice to shout in the next few seconds, so that it was some time before any of us heard his reply and even longer before I noticed that one of our younger visitors - an eleven year old boy - was on the aft deck, pointing at the dinghy. In leaving the mooring we had somehow managed to sail over the painter and it was now wrapped around the self-steering rudder, tethering us by the back leg, so to speak. Meanwhile, the sails attempted to drag us down to the harbour mouth. In compromise, we were brought up ignominiously alongside *Stormy Weather*.

As for the race itself - we were five minutes late to the starting line and on the first tack discovered that the starboard genoa winch was seized. All in all we acquitted ourselves extremely badly - but it was quite a good party, and Caesar and Xoë seemed scarcely to notice that we had left the calm sanctuary of the harbour.

This lack of concern on the part of the children was yet more noticeable on our second foray abroad - and in this case we went, quite literally, abroad, to the neighbouring isle of Guadeloupe.

That Xoë showed no interest in the adventure was not surprising, although we were glad to find that, unlike Caesar, she suffered no mal de mer. What was much more remarkable was the little fellow's blasé attitude. The last time we put to sea Caesar had been ten months old. During a week-long cruise of St Kitts and Nevis he had puked repeatedly and had also made clear his dislike of having the familiar cabin floor tipped through an angle of 30°. Now, however, Caesar behaved as if we went sailing every day, making no complaint or comment about the adventure.

By contrast *Maamari*, and in particular her engine, were quite ill-prepared and inclined to misbehave, so that we returned to the harbour with clouds of acrid black smoke issuing from the cabin.

"Your toast's on fire," our friends quipped as we rounded up to drop the hook.

One other thing that we had to do before we quit Antigua was to dispose of Wangy. By now the old banger could scarcely make it into town and was little safer than the Reggae bus, but it still had a resale value. Before we sold it we wanted to make one last journey - a farewell pilgrimage to all our favourite places around the island - and so, one typically sunny Saturday morning we set off on what was to be a highly memorable valedictory trip.

Our first stop was the old church in Falmouth, the foundation stone of the British colony. Wangy was parked just outside the gate and we wandered into the parched churchyard. The bare, dry earth within the walled enclosure was covered all over with bare, humped graves, and each brown mound was decorated with a bunch of bright hibiscus or a sorry bouquet of faded, plastic chrysanthemums tied with a tattered pink ribbon. At our approach, a family of goats who had been feasting on these offerings took fright and scattered across the uneven ground.

We had taken only a dozen paces before we grew aware of someone shouting, and we turned around to find an angry youth following us up the path. In his hand the man held a broken bottle. He had smashed the bottle just a moment earlier, and it transpired that he had already used the weapon to slash one of the car's front tyres. Now the young hooligan spewed forth a torrent of abuse, most of which we found wholly incomprehensible since it was spoken in the local dialect. The gist of the problem seemed to be the colour of our skin.

We retreated quietly to the car and put Caesar and Xoë inside. Meanwhile our assailant continued to brandish his piece of glass and announced his intention of killing them both. Killings, in Antigua, are all too frequent for a nation of only 70,000 souls - they seem to happen on a weekly basis - but they seldom involve tourists or expatriates. For myself, I felt no fear in the heat of the moment; rather, there was an air of unreality. Nick suffered no such disbelief and was for driving away at once, and at speed.
"Don't be silly," I said. "That would damage the tyre!"

The youth disappeared down the lane opposite, continuing, as he walked away, to hurl his cannonades of abuse. Nick once changed a wheel with a lion watching and can do it very quickly. As he set about the task, I noticed a young woman beckoning to me from a crack in the doorway of a nearby house.

"Psst! Pssst!" A pale, spectacled face peeped around the door, and then a long, white arm reached out, and a curled finger hooked the air. Somewhat puzzled, I crossed the road.

Huddled inside a pretty wooden house set in a garden of rambling bougainvillaea and hibiscus were four young American women, and I could tell at a glance that they were members of the Peace Corp. On the wall of the cosy sitting-room a framed picture, painted in the style of an embroidery sampler, said, "OK, so it's *not* home sweet home. Let's adjust."

If ever an organisation could be guaranteed to alienate local people against the white, Western world then it would have to be this one, with its well-meaning, we-know-best purveyors of the All American Dream; with its unwitting, uncomprehending meddlers, who are sent out to carry the gospel of consumerism to all corners of the world. Throughout the six months of their stay, the four girls had lived in terror of "Bambi." They begged us to report his doings to the police and said, "Now they'll lock him away!"

We doubted it.

That evening, and not without certain misgivings, we did as the girls had asked. The policemen on duty in the station all laughed heartily.

"Dat Bambi! Him allus makin' trouble wid' de white man." They were not the least bit interested in our damaged tyre - but by this time neither were we.

Our tour had been only half complete when the car had begun to shudder and shake, the front part of the vehicle twitching to one side while the cab wobbled to the other. We pulled over. A quick inspection inside the bonnet revealed that the front cross-member had broken, so separating the engine, the front wheels and the steering from the rest of the car. Only the gear-box kept us moving along the road together.

The children and I rode home in the bus, but Nick managed to drive Wangy round to the scrap-yard, where he was finally laid to rest. Even in this state of terminal decay the car was worth £200.

Many repairs and a few days after our trip to Guadeloupe, it was time to say a last good-bye to English Harbour and to the many friends we had made during our stay.

"See you on your next time around," said the ones who had swallowed the anchor.

"See you in New Zealand," others called.

We were on our way again - at last! - but although we had looked forward to this day, the leaving was still quite a wrench.

"We'll come back," we said to ourselves. "The kids will grow up in their native land."

But in a while the dream faded. In Africa we were to find yet more beautiful places, whose open-hearted, welcoming people made for an odious comparison with the fun-loving but often embittered folk of Antigua.

But why were we heading back to Africa? Were our hearts no longer set on rounding the southern tip of the American continent? Indeed they were - Cape Horn and the Beagle channel were once more our objective - but, as ever, we were obliged to obey the rules and follow the winds and currents. It *is* possible, if one's craft is sufficiently weatherly, to travel down the northern coast of Brazil, but those who have made the trip describe it as an exercise in head-banging. Not for us such masochism. We would go with the flow; we would cross back over to Europe and then turn towards the south again.

Winter was giving way to spring, and the time was almost ripe for us to be off across the pond - but there was still plenty for us to see on this side of the ocean and so we pottered along, in our usual manner, hopping from one gem to the next in the Leeward Island chain.

Our first stop was Barbuda. Her Antiguan suzerains call Barbuda their little sister, but the place actually bears no family resemblance to the busy, bubbly, bossy, governing isle, and nor do the people of either land tend to mix. Barbuda is flat and barren and her inhabitants all live in the hamlet of Codrington. Codrington is the kind of place where people stop and pee in the street when they feel the urge, regardless of who is coming. In fact, they might even greet their friend, "Good morning", whilst still engaged in the deed.

On our arrival in Barbuda, we went in search of the immigration officer. He was not at the police station, nor at the grass-strip airport. Eventually we were directed to find him in his own, humble abode, where he sat in his underpants with a beer in his hand. The curtains had been drawn, to darken the room, and images of a cop with a gun flickered from a small-screen, black and white

TV. The formalities were soon completed and we were thenceforth free to explore the island.

Barbuda is all about beaches. One long, thin strip of silvery-white sand entwines itself around the whole convoluted coastline. At Coco Point, on the island's southern tip, a hotel of long-standing and high repute nestled in a grove of palms. Notices on the sand made pretence of a territorial claim to about a mile of beach, and a line of orange buoys sought to persuade those who would anchor within the bight of that same terrain that the water, too, was privately owned. Yachtsmen, no matter how well-heeled they may be, were not welcome at Coco Point.

On the other hand, "yotties" might enter barefoot into the high-tech, designer portals of the adjacent K-Club. This hotel prided itself on being one of the ten most expensive in the Caribbean - and to be honest, it had little else of which to boast. The accommodation was a line of charmless chalets whose new and sparsely planted gardens would, for a long time thence, fail to bring any refreshment to eyes burnt-out with the glare of the sand. Behind the hotel was a golf course - or at any rate, it was labelled as such. I am not familiar with the game, but I must say that I have always been under the impression that the sand is supposed to be in the bunkers only, and that the green of a golf course should be just that.

Still, for one who asks only to bask in the sun and float in water the colour of a swimming pool, the K-club has it all. We got these things for free - these, and more besides - since, aboard *Maamari*, we could choose either the turquoise waters of Coco Bay, or else could anchor in splendid solitude off Codrington Lagoon or Spanish Point. From this last place, trails lead off across the sandy heath and onto a stunning, weather-blown, windward beach.

On its leeward side the island shore is adorned with a thin line of tiny, pastel-pink shells, but on the ravaged eastern side the tide-line was made up almost entirely of glass bottles, light bulbs, fishing floats, and buoys, most of which had been carried 3,000 miles across the sea from Europe. Without a doubt, the people who were the first colonists of the Caribbean surely knew of the existence of another civilisation, over the eastern horizon, long before 1492.

Sad to say, mention of Barbuda would be incomplete without

reference to the events which took place in the anchorage off Codrington Lagoon less than a year after our stay. When it was found that four yachtsmen had been brutally murdered in these calm, pacific waters the local population raised a hue and cry. How dare the evil hell-hounds of Antigua spread their demonic debauchery to sully the little sister's reputation? There was talk of drugs, for in recent weeks parcels of cocaine had been found floating about in the reef-strewn passage between the two isles. Had the yachtsmen seen something that they should not have seen? The papers even hinted at government involvement. Then again, perhaps the yacht had been pursued from Antigua by youths who knew that $8,000 had just been withdrawn from a bank by the skipper. The truth, when it was discovered, took everyone by surprise.

Scotland Yard was called in to investigate the crime which, because it involved white tourists, had hit the headlines the world over. Within days of their arrival the British police arrested four young Barbudians. Three of them were later found guilty and two were eventually sentenced to hang. Since the safe had not been tampered with and even the victims' jewellery remained on their bodies, robbery was clearly not the motive. Neither had the killers any personal grudge against the ones whom they tortured and shot; it seems that they had never even met them before. It would appear that the murderers were simply doing their bit to make up for the wrongs of the past.

According to the local newspaper, all three men were unemployed, and so they probably spent their time watching American movies on the television. To paraphrase the editor, the youths had been educated, in the usual modern manner, to fill situations which did not exist within their world. They were therefore not fitted for the life and lot to which they had been born.

To train a whole nation of children to scorn agricultural work and seek after a place on the ladder of worldly gain is worse than ludicrous. And yet the whole world is now being taught the same inappropriate trade of clerk and consumer. As for Barbuda, long will its limpid waters be crimson stained - but we had no premonition of such things. We spent happy days building castles in the pristine sand - and then we moved on.

The little French island of St Barts was only another gentle hop up the Leeward Island ladder; a hop achieved by the light of one short, tropical day. Again, as we sailed the children showed no concern over the rollicking waves or the unusual inclination of our home. Caesar made no fuss on finding himself newly restrained in a harness, and Xoë slept soundly in a little home-made hammock slung from the deck-head.

Many a splendid beach garnishes the scalloped shore of St Barts, which is truly a prize diamond in the jewel-studded lapis-lazuli of the Caribbean. In Anse Columbier, which is one of the loveliest, Caesar celebrated his second birthday - and then we travelled on again.

Too close for comfort to St Barts is St Maarten, an island which Nick and I had visited twice before. We like it a little less each time we find ourselves here. One yachtsman of our acquaintance was murdered in the little town; two others, in two separate incidents, were beaten and raped. We had come exclusively because we needed to buy food for the crossing, and this was the cheapest place. In the hyper-market in Phillipsburg we stocked up as quickly as we could, and the next morning we set sail for the adjacent isle of Anguilla.

At midday the wind fell away, leaving us becalmed. Our destination was as yet an uninteresting, brownish-green smudge, and it looked as if we might be out here for a long while. To pass the time, I brought out a packet of alphabet flashcards acquired the previous day. A short while after his sister was born, Caesar had demonstrated what seemed to be a spontaneous knowledge of the alphabet - a knowledge which I had since bolstered by pinning letters in prominent places around the cabin. Beneath a large D there was a picture of a dinghy; A was for an anchor; G was for a gin bottle... The new cards were rather less relevant to our lifestyle, but Caesar regarded them with interest. R was for rainbow, S was for sun, T was for... "Potty," said the student, with a confident smile.
I looked at the card. It showed a stripey tiger sitting on a small, round circus podium.
"T is for potty," Caesar repeated happily. "Tiger on a potty."

As evening drew nigh, Nick and I each watched the other from the corner of an eye, neither wanting to be the one who gave in to temptation. In the end it was I who spoke the words which broke the unwritten taboo: "Let's motor," I said.
Nick put up a pretence of preferring to spend the night "a painted

ship upon a painted ocean", but I was tired and wanted to spend the night sleeping. We started the engine, and by midnight we were anchoring off Roadtown. As it turned out, there was not the slightest breath of wind for the next five days.

Caesar seemed to have taken to the water like the proverbial duck. Sailing was in his blood, we decided. Often, while we were in harbour, he played make-believe sailing games.

"Look out, Xoë!" he would cry, as he hauled on the genoa sheet. "Caesar tacking! Mind your fingers!"

Sand, sun, and splashing in the surf were also pursuits much favoured by the little fellow, and he was never happier than when ambling about on a beach. Off Anguilla's northern shore lies Sandy Island, a tiny, uninhabited place whose name says it all. Here we spent many an enjoyable hour - it was plain that Caesar loved the place - but when, at length, we dragged him away and he voiced his displeasure with the wandering life, we assumed that this would be a very temporary set-back. How wrong we were.

Up until now most of our recent sailing had been done by day, whereas what lay ahead was a week-long passage up to the Turks and Caicos Islands. The difference might not have mattered if we had only had the sense and common decency to explain it to the ship's boy. As it was, when we failed to reach terra firma after the expected interval our bright and cheerful child became withdrawn and sulky. And then, to add insult to his injuries, on the second morning at sea he was sick.

For the next 24 hours Caesar could keep nothing down - not even the merest sip of water or rehydration fluid. Then, on the second day of his ordeal, I hit upon the idea of feeding the lad my own milk, in little gulps. This was a child who had lived at his mother's breast, refusing all other food, until he was over a year old, and who still nursed with unabashed enthusiasm alongside little Xoë. What was often an inconvenience and always a physical burden now turned out to be the perfect remedy for Caesar's distress: he had no trouble in keeping my milk down and soon recovered his energy. Unfortunately, the same could not be said for his joi de vivre.

On our third day at sea our little lad announced, "Caesar not like sailing", and he gathered up his bucket and spade. "Going ashore" he said resolutely.

Alas, there was nothing but water all around us and so the poor chap had to be content with building a pretend castle on the carpet, which was no fun at all.

When, after seven days, we finally sighted the island of Grand Turk, Caesar steadfastly refused to come on deck. It was as if he had given up all hope of ever seeing land again. However, on hearing the anchor go out, he was up the ladder in an instant. The sight of a beach close by sent him below decks again - but only to fetch his bucket and spade.

The Caribbean is a curious mixture of the colourful and the drab, the vibrant and the dormant. Tourism and western attention have encouraged and favoured certain isles, whilst others have remained quietly in the background. Antigua, for example, receives so many visitors that on certain days of the week, when the big cruise ships are in port, 10% of the people on the island are tourists. Of course, tourism means jobs, and more money for the man on the street - and money changing hands invariably makes for a faster pace of life. By contrast, those islands yet to be exploited for tourism are quiet, slow, sleepy places. Anguilla is one: a slice of the English countryside incongruously sited beside the hyper, aggressive, wannabe island of St Maarten. Anguilla's only port is an unremarkable beach, and the capital "town" consists of a small, modern shopping arcade stuck in the middle of ploughed fields. But if Anguilla was sleepy, Grand Turk was comatose. The only thing of any interest here was a small museum of marine history, run by a likeable young American. He was thrilled to have some customers and gave us a personal tour.

Unlike the Windward and Leeward isles, the Turks and Caicos were never covered in plantations of sugar - their climate and soil are not suitable for agriculture - but still the islands had their part to play in the commerce of that era. Slaves have to be fed; very little, to be sure, but enough to keep them alive. Maize, and cod caught on the Grand Banks were the usual provision, and while their brethren to the south toiled in the cane fields, the people of these low, flat islands were put to work producing the salt with which the cod were preserved.

Salt is no longer in production in Grand Turk. So far as we could see there was *nothing* in production on the island. There was nothing happening at all, and so we decided to take a look at one of the neighbouring islands. With us went four merry lads, with a transistor radio, who wanted to travel from the stagnant capital isle to their still more sleepy home, known as Salt.

> "Don't like 'em black; don't like 'em white.
> Grand Turk woman, she all right.
> Twixt sugar and salt is something sweet.
> Grand Turk woman; really neat..."

The radio throbbed to the calypso beat and the four mulatto lads, who were sitting on our coach roof, twitched their shoulders and tapped their toes. After an hour or so, when we were still only half way across the divide, their dancing ground to a halt and their laughter came a little less readily. We had warned them that on this sultry day the going would be slow - but, of course, they were all astounded to see just *how* slowly a sailing boat goes. In answer to their questions about the engine - Didn't we have one? Why didn't we use it? - we spoke of pollution and global warming. Our companions nodded agreeably and then looked at us askance, in the manner of fellow passengers humouring the nutter aboard a bus. When we eventually arrived they pointed out a tiny detached mole – a free-standing wall set up to protect a landing place – and while we anchored outside the wall they swam ashore in great haste, leaving before the hook was even set.

Salt is so named for rather obvious reasons: half of the island is covered in salt pans. The other half is covered in scrub. The only settlement is a small line of small cottages close to the beach. These must formerly have housed the people who worked at the salterns. One rather larger house, at the seaward end of the line, presumably housed the manager. An American gentleman had recently converted this larger house into a rustic hotel, and since the hotel was also the island's only pub - and an ice-cream shop to boot - it had become the focal point for all who lived on Salt.

   We reserved a table - or rather a meal – at the hotel, and then we spent the afternoon walking along the maze of tiny walls which divide the pans of saline water one from the next. That morning it had rained heavily, and we had watched a waterspout build over the sea and then fall apart. With signs like this written in the sky one did not need a calendar to know that the hurricane season was nigh.

In the afternoon the sky remained grey, so that evening slipped stealthily upon us. At its coming the wind rose, but it was only as we ambled back towards the anchorage that we saw its full strength, and it was only now that we realised that the weather had also nipped around the nearby headland to leave the beach - and *Maamari* - exposed to the full force of the waves. There was no time even to run to the hotel and cancel our dinner date; we needed to get out, *fast*.

That morning the sea had been as flat as a mill pond, so that we had not bothered to bring the children's lifejackets ashore; the idea had not even occurred to us. Now there were waves breaking between the little detached mole and the shore - and the wind was still getting up. If we waited while Nick rowed out to the boat and fetched the lifejackets then the situation might become completely untenable; by then it would be dark and the seas would be invisible. In great trepidation, we set off, and in the interval between two rolling waves we slipped out from behind the wall.

Maamari was bucking and plunging like a frightened horse, and it was hard for me to board her. Nick handed up the children, neither of whom had picked up the least sense of danger. Xoë was soon ensconced in her hammock, slung high up in the saloon, whilst Caesar opted for his chair, firmly lashed in the cockpit. *Maamari* thrashed back up towards Grand Turk, but the children both slept soundly, uncaring of the demented howl of the rigging or the crash of the sea, or even of the change in attitude each time we tacked through the wind.

Our slow passage north through the Caribbean had given us all a chance to get our sea-legs, and our two infant crew were shaping up well. Babies were certainly a lot more work than I had realised, but it seemed that they could adjust quickly to a new way of life. It seemed that the doom-mongers were wrong, and that our little family could live just as happily afloat as ashore.

9

OILSKINS AND NAPPIES

On the joys of cruising and crossing an ocean, en famille.

Jru Dickin Schinas

The man on the radio spoke of armed robbery and car theft, crimes which are unusual on a small island. The second would have been virtually impossible in a close-knit society such as Antigua's. Could this place really be so different, we asked ourselves?

Intent upon seeing as much as we could of the Caribbean before we crossed back to Europe, we had sailed north from the Turks and Caicos to the Bahamas. Before our arrival we had formed a very definite picture of these islands. We had envisaged sport fishing boats and sun-bathers, night-clubs vibrant with the thud of pop music, and boutiques and beach-bars propped up on the sand. The reality, as we quickly discovered, was very different. From where we sat, in *Maamari's* cockpit, the Bahamas were islands forgotten by time and by the rest of the world. Mile after mile of untarnished sand fringed their tree covered forms. When we ventured ashore we had trouble in finding even a bar or a grocery shop; sometimes we could not find even a single house. In spite of this, in our brief tour of the Outer Bahamas we never quite managed to adjust our expectations - we were always expecting that the *next* island would be the "happening" one - and for this failure I am sure that the local radio station was at least in part to blame.

Was it really to this same archipelago that the air-headed caricatures referred, in their phoney American accents? Could it really be that just over the horizon more than a hundred thousand people were clinging to the sides of an island only half the size of Antigua, and chasing each other around in stolen cars?

Bowling down the 25 mile long coast of Mayaguana we saw not the least trace of man, and as we lay at anchor off the northern shore we felt as if the place were ours alone. That, at any rate, was how we felt until the helicopter turned up. It was a big white chopper with a red band around it emblazoned with the letters USCG. It hovered just above and a little to port, sending down whirlwinds which darted away across the flattened water. I came into the cockpit with the children in my arms and Caesar, at my bidding, waved solemnly. Eventually, a black man sitting in the doorway responded with a cursory gesture of his arm. We were tiptoeing close to Uncle Sam's front door, and Big Brother was going to keep an eye on us now.

Just a day's sail to the north of Mayaguana, at the tiny uninhabited island of Plana Cays, we anchored in water of a stunning, electric blue, such as I have never seen before or since. No palette could echo its hue, and even when the sun declined to shine the sea remained almost fluorescently vivid. On the morrow we planned to sail to Samana Cay and so settle, in our own minds at least, the mystery of Columbus's first Caribbean landfall - for Samana had recently been proposed as the most likely candidate.

Columbus swore, even to his dying day, that the islands which we call the West Indies were *The* Indies - the Spice Islands upon which no European had yet set eyes. He insisted that Cuba was Japan, and he even managed to convince himself that the northern coast of Venezuela was that of an island. Because he believed himself to have travelled to the other side of the globe he was greatly derided by the academics of his time, and he is often still derided now. He found a New World, but he found it by accident, and having found it he failed to recognise it for what it was. In the year of the 500th anniversary of his achievement one West Indian scholar referred to Columbus as "that failed navigator."

Whether we call the man a genius or a fool, one thing is for sure: the description which Columbus left of his journey amongst the Bahamas is distinctly difficult to follow. The log is a jigsaw puzzle of misshapen pieces. We wanted to see Samana for ourselves and make our own decision as to whether this island was Columbus's landfall - the most significant landfall of all time - but the gods intervened and we woke fitfully in the early hours of the morning to find *Maamari* pitching up and down and rolling violently. Once again, the wind had risen and crept around the corner to run amuck in our anchorage. Once again we had to get out fast.

While Nick got the anchor aboard, I took the helm, and Caesar was left below with instructions to entertain the baby. From where I stood, in the wind and the lashing rain, I could see him offering her toy after toy until finally there were none left, and they both burst into tears!

Looking at the chart we could see no place in the Outer Bahamas which offers shelter from a tropical, cyclonic gale such as the one which we were now facing. Samana Cay was out of the question; even at the best of times its anchorage would be dodgy. The sea was the safest place to be and so, throughout the day and during the following night, we ambled northwards, with San Salvador now our destination.

As the new day dawned and the wind slowly subsided we sailed into a roadstead anchorage off what we took to be the island's main town. In the aftermath of the gale it was an unpleasantly rolly spot, and through the binoculars we could see that a tug and a fishing boat had been washed ashore in the night. There was no safe place for us to land with Caesar and Xoë, and so Nick ventured alone unto the beach and went in search of the immigration authorities - for we had yet to clear into the country. He returned with the news that the 'town' consisted of just ten or twenty houses, and he handed me back my shopping list. There was no shop on the island. Codrington, capital of far away Barbuda, began to seem like a city.

San Salvador used to be called Watlings Island until the authorities decided that *this* was the one which Columbus found first and named so. At the risk of swimming against the tide of modern opinion I, too, give this place my vote. No, I cannot make the story fit when the *Santa Maria* sails on from here to the next place in the trail, but I am quite certain that this was the island which Columbus described in his log, and I do not see how anyone who has visited the place *from the sea* could be in any doubt about the matter.

Columbus tells us that he anchored off an island which was fairly large and very flat, with many trees and several bodies of water. This description fits San Salvador to a tee, especially in the last detail. He then sailed to the north-north-east and found that "the entire island is surrounded by a large reef. Between the reef and the island it remained deep," and having found a narrow break in the reef he went within, to where "the sea moves no more than water in a well." This is a marvellous description of the vast, tranquil, pavonian-blue lagoon which we found, that afternoon, when we sailed to the northern end of the island. Although the sea outside was still heaving, the water in here was as calm as a swimming pool. We had to pick our way carefully for, as Columbus says, "there are a few shoal spots, to be sure." He reckoned that this huge natural harbour was "large enough to hold all the ships of Christendom." Certainly it would hold several hundred vessels of the sort that were familiar to 15th century Europeans.

As we entered the lagoon I saw what seemed to be a little island - and indeed there are a couple of islands - but this one, as Columbus noted, "looked like an island even though it is not." We sailed closer and I was thrilled to see that the discoverer's words rang true. It was almost like seeing the fulfilment of a prophecy. The neck of land was so thin and low that, as the man also said, "It could be cut through and made into an island in two days." On the island he proposed to build a fort.

Standing here, where the history of the world changed course, one cannot help but feel moved and awed. This place was the very one where the great explorer made that one small step, more dramatic and much more far reaching in its consequence than that "giant leap" on the moon.

But after Columbus leaves San Salvador everything goes wrong. The subsequent bearings and distances, from one island to the next in his chain, do not add up - not without a large measure of interpretative juggling. If one starts at Samana Cay the mathematics is a little bit tidier, but still by no means perfect - and Samana Cay, as it is portrayed on the chart, fits no aspect of the description. There is no harbour or lagoon - indeed, this island is described in the pilot books as having a somewhat dangerous anchorage - and there are no lakes of fresh water; the convert to this theory has to believe in lakes of water left by a recent rainstorm. Samana is uninhabited, and if I ever get there I mean to try to discover if there is any fresh water at all, for as we know, Columbus met many people and saw many villages at his San Salvador. These he would obviously not have discovered on an island with no agua vita.

At one time, L-shaped Cat Island was also a candidate for The Landfall. Arriving there from San Salvador we found an old plaque, on the quiet shore, which boldly and unequivocally makes the claim - but that claim seemed to us to be entirely without basis; the island did not fit even one single aspect of the navigator's description. Already we had seen a similar plaque in Grand Turk, which made the same vain pronouncement for that isle.

Does it really matter which island it was that Columbus first stumbled upon? Not really – but when one has read his log and is travelling amongst these islands the mystery becomes as enthralling as a whodunnit. Eventually, however, it becomes frustrating, because there is no solution. San Salvador is certainly the island described by Columbus as his first landfall, but the course he sets us from there leads to nowhere. No matter how one plays the game, the facts do not fit the story; the numbers in Columbus' log do not add up. In the end one is forced to admit that the scathing West Indian scholar may have a point.

Again, we were surprised to discover that there is no village and only one small, ill-stocked shop on Cat Island, and this despite the fact that it is a green and fertile place, measuring some forty miles from north to south and a further 15 miles along the lower leg. Clearly, very few people live on Cat - but do they all make and grow everything that they could ever possibly need? How is it, we asked ourselves, that the Outer Bahamas have remained so sparsely settled whilst the sugar isles, to the south, are really very densely populated?

And all the while, if we tuned in the radio, it jabbered on about traffic jams and nite-clubs. It occurred to us that the shores of the United States were only just over the horizon. Perhaps the beckoning characters of Disney Land have lured away the populace.

The Cat Islanders cannot seriously pretend that their home is Columbus' hallowed landfall, but they do have one claim to fame: of all the many hundred Bahamian isles and islets, theirs is the highest. At its loftiest Cat Island is just 206 feet tall. A radio mast, or the spire of my home-town cathedral would both dwarf it, and we had seen trees in Africa which were almost as big.

Atop the diminutive hill someone confident of his sense of humour has gone to the trouble of building a church and a monastery to the same scale, and this creation is far more remarkable than the dull topographical feature. In England the buildings would be called a folly, and seeing them brought to mind tales of eccentric Georgian gentlemen who had elaborate towers and tombs erected on the rolling South Downs, apparently without concern for the cost.

"What's that building?" we asked the few islanders who happened to pass by on the road above the beach. They all told us that it was The Hermitage, but none could tell us much more. Estimates of its antiquity varied from, "Very old" to, "It was there when I was born." This last remark was made by a teenager. On strolling up the hill we found that the sundial in front of the Hermitage is engraved with the date 1642 - but it is held onto its pedestal with Phillips screws.

Finally we came across someone who claimed to have met the architect of the Hermitage, and who described him as a very small man, "with a very small beard", who had grown tired of worshipping Mammon in America and turned instead to God. If the convert really lived the life of a recluse, in this private hermitage, then he must certainly have been very, very small. Either that, or he must soon have acquired a stoop, for the doors were all sized so as to be suitable for a two year old. The chapel - a wonderful replica of the real thing - was quite the nicest wendy-house that Caesar could ever have wished for.

The Hermitage also has a tower, shaped as we used to draw space rockets when I was very little, but its most interesting feature is a series of Roman Catholic "stations of the cross". These ritual prayer stations begin, some way down the hill, with a painting of Pilate condemning Jesus. The next five or six stations consist of icons and statuettes which are placed beside the path leading to the chapel. One shows Our Saviour carrying the cross, and the next shows Simon of Cyrene taking over.

In front of the chapel we find a large alabaster sculpture of Jesus crucified, and then we come upon his family and followers carrying the dead man into a tomb. The final station is a life-sized model of the tomb, with the round stone of its entrance rolled away. And, in true and proper recollection of the traditional form, the penultimate scene is the sealed tomb. In this case it is sealed for good reason. Besides being the eleventh station of the cross, this tomb is the burial site of the said architect and builder.

Now, was this a pious man, I ask myself? To me he sounds just exactly like the self-indulgent, millionaire of old. Such eccentric characters are regrettably thin on the ground.

It was just as well that we had stocked up for our crossing in St Maartens, for in the Bahamas, as the reader will have gathered, we found no place to provision. Now we were ready for the off. Time was marching past and although hurricanes hardly happen in June we had, of course, already seen the first of the season's tropical depressions.

After our unhappy voyage from Anguilla up to Grand Turk, we were more than a little apprehensive about the adventure ahead. It might take us a month to reach the Azores. In an effort to explain the score to our infant son I produced a little book entitled, "Caesar and Xoë go sailing." In it, we said goodbye to Antigua and the tale was told of all that had happened over the past few weeks. There were sketches of the coastguard helicopter and of the Hermitage. There was one of Caesar bobbing about in the blue-green sea beside the beach, and another of us playing in the sand. Then we set off from Cat Island into a wide, blue yonder. There were pages and pages of empty sea and doodles of dolphins before, at long last, *Maamari* reached the end of the book and another shore. The production was an instant success and, several years on, was still very popular. More to the point, it also achieved its objective; Caesar took the crossing of the Atlantic in his stride.

According to accepted wisdom, if one wants to cross the ocean travelling eastwards from the Caribbean one must sail north to find the wind. Yachtsmen who ignore the circulation of the ocean winds and who set off on a bee-line route for the Azores will wander into the Horse latitudes and into the infamous Sargasso Sea. Having already travelled to a latitude of 24° N, we reckoned that we must have reached the top left hand corner of the Azores high, and we assumed that on leaving Cat Island we would at once encounter a good south-easterly. Instead we were met by a mere zephyr breeze, and a northerly one at that. This light headwind was to be our lot for the next three weeks, seldom being pushed to one side and then only by the still, empty air of the centre of the high.

It was a dull beginning to our adventure - but, on the whole, that was no bad thing. While the boat idled along we could sit out in the cockpit. The children could play in a paddling pool which I wedged on the floor between the seats and filled from the sea. Xoë was content to spend time in her chair when it was in the cockpit, and Caesar passed the hours with pretend fishing and even resumed his sailing games. Most of his play was conducted sotto-voce, but every now and then he would peer into the compass knowledgeably and say, "39.2". At other times he would remark complacently, and to no one in particular, "We're going the wrong way."

During the first three weeks of our crossing there was just one exception to the calms and light headwinds, and that came on our fourth day out. On that day we picked up a decent breeze from the north. It was on that day, too, that we received visitors.

When the long, low sliver of Cat Island slipped away into the blue-grey haze astern, Nick and I had stepped easily into our offshore routine. Basically, he does nights and I do days. Thus, I can only confess that I was entirely to blame for what happened that afternoon while we were, at last, trotting along quite nicely. Nick was awake, as it happens, but he was down below whereas I had settled myself comfortably in the cockpit. The sprayhood was up, and so was our makeshift bimini, and I had chosen to sit on the leeward side. As a result, since the boat was well heeled, my view of our surroundings was limited to a small strip of sky - but this was of no import, because I was keeping a proper look out. Every ten minutes, or thereabouts, I stood up and poked my head through the small gap twixt sprayhood and bimini, and I scanned the horizon all around. In the respite I simply sat. Xoë was on my lap, playing at the breast. I was dreaming – dreaming idly of nothing in particular - and into my daydream, and into the narrow strip of sky between the windward cockpit coaming and the bimini, sailed the radar scanner and bridge-top aerials of a small ship or a big motor yacht. I saw them as they might be seen in a marina, if the boat was almost alongside...

"*What....!*" I came crashing out of my daydream.

Nick and Caesar were both startled by my cry. "What's happened?"

"A ship! Oh, Christ! Look! A bloody great ship! And it's almost run us down!" But then I saw that it was not a great ship. It was a white patrol vessel with a gun on the foredeck, and a shield and the old familiar letters painted on the bridge. "Oh, it's *those* bastards. Quick! Turn on the radio."

We turned on the radio telephone just in time to hear the captain of the ship calling our name: "*"Maamari, Maamari,* this is the U.S. Coastguard."

They had studied us at Mayaguana and once, in the night, we had heard their chopper flying, unlit, between our anchored vessel and the adjacent shore. Now they had stormed upon us from over the horizon, and they wanted to come aboard.

Did they have the right? No, but they had the might.

At first we were inclined to tell the U.S. Coastguard where to go – but then, upon reflection, we thought that this could be quite a laugh. And it was.

We were instructed to hold our course and speed while the coastguard vessel launched her boat - and by the time they had managed this task, the ship was but a grey speck, almost two miles astern. Our first glimpse of the RIB came when it was about half a mile away, and even then we only spotted it amongst the blue-grey waves because it had become entirely airborne.

At length the inflatable boat arrived and we saw that it contained no fewer than ten men, all wearing crash hats and sopping wet waterproofs and not one of them wearing a smile. Now they had to get from the boat to our deck. Given that both boats were travelling at five knots, this was a little bit tricky – but it was nowhere near as difficult as these fellows made it seem. It would have been a lot easier had they chosen to board on the leeward side, where our deck was currently at about the same level as their tanks; but the advice which we gave fell on deaf ears. In fact, as we were shortly to discover, the USCG seemed quite incapable of hearing or understanding anything that we said.

With a bit of assistance from Nick, five men eventually managed to scramble up the weather side of the boat and get aboard. Had we chosen to steer an erratic course, and to make things really difficult, none of them would have stood a chance. Having finally gained their objective the men stood in the cockpit looking ill at ease – and in the case of one, just plain ill.

"First we will make an inspection below decks," their commanding officer said.

"Oh, no you won't," said we. "Not unless you first take off those wet oilskins and those clumping great boots."

"Oh. Well, in that case, we'll skip the inspection."

We asked about the guns which each man wore at his waist. "Do they work when they're wet?" (They were very wet.)

"Uh? Er...I don't know." The commander looked vaguely perturbed.

"How often do you board a yacht?" we wondered. To judge by the ineptitude recently demonstrated it was obviously not a daily occurrence.

"All the time," the commander answered, vaguely. He was becoming rather irritable. He was the one who was supposed to be asking the questions. No, he did not want a nice cup of tea.

In the end they all went away again – after I had made them write their names in our visitors book – and we were left none the wiser as to their purpose. Their actions seemed to serve no function, besides that of demonstrating just how high-handed the U.S. authorities can be. The manner of their sudden, sneaky arrival seemed to demonstrate a desire to intimidate other seafarers - even those who are well beyond the limit of any territorial waters. From our guests we learnt that the USCG patrol an area extending from Canada down to Venezuela and reaching 1,000 miles out into the Atlantic. This explains why, on two other occasions, Nick has been startled in the same way, by small ships which appeared out of nowhere. On the second occasion the vessel appeared alongside at night and was completely unlit. It shone a dazzling spotlight on *Maamari's* deck. In each case the ship failed to respond to a polite enquiry on channel 16. The reader, even if he has never crossed an ocean, will surely be able to imagine the fear invoked by such a strange, and wholly illegal visitation.

In search of the wind we went further north, until we were almost at the latitude of Bermuda. We had not planned on going anywhere near to that island but eventually passed within fifty miles. Not one, not two, but seven tropic birds came out to greet us, and for three consecutive days we saw them at ten o'clock each morning, chasing each other - three pairs and one straggler - in wide circles around the boat. Perhaps they flew out each day from the island.

Bermuda looked fragile and fascinating on the chart, which we now unearthed. We would have stopped were it not for the fact that, by now, the hurricane season really was nigh. Where, oh where, was the wind? We limped and lolloped onward. The skies were overcast and so the nights were a thick blanket, without the trace of a seam twixt the inky ocean and the firmament above. On nights such as these I am filled with fear and loathing and do my watch under duress. One night, at about ten o'clock, I peeped my head out of the cabin, like a mouse surveying the scene from its hole, and was alarmed to see an odd, yellow shape, hovering just above what I took to be the position of the horizon.

"What the...?" We were in the Bermuda Triangle! The realisation set my heart pounding. Then I saw that the strange shape was actually the gibbous moon ascending behind a hedge of woolly cloud, which had smudged and altered both her colour and her form. The next night, at eleven, the same trick caught me out just as surely.

On about the 20th day out I sighted a sail, far away on the horizon, and over the course of the afternoon it drew closer and closer. As evening came upon us it seemed prudent to call up the other fellow and ask him what course he was steering and whether he planned to show any lights. One of us certainly must show our lights, or else we were likely to run into trouble in the night. The yacht turned out to be a French one, and her skipper told us that he would be continuing north, in search of the wind. Nick, on the other hand, felt that if we went any further to the north we would probably end up with a surfeit of wind and so, accordingly, the French yacht crossed our path just after dark.

The next day we picked up a decent breeze and *Maamari* kicked up her heels. We were away - but not for long. We were all below decks when we heard a mighty crash. Nick thought that the mast had come down and I said we had hit something. We rushed on deck to find that the clew of the genoa, together with the roller-furling drum, was careering about wildly, eight feet above the deck. The bottlescrew which secured and tensioned the forestay had snapped.

Our first task was to tame the beast, which we did by pulling it close with the roller-furling pennant. Then, when the dancing, jigging drum was near enough to catch, we put a stronger rope around it and winched it back into place on the deck. After that we got the genoa down quickly. With the drum lashed it could not turn, and so we could not furl the sail in the usual way.

When everything was safely secured I went below to reassure the children, who were somewhat troubled by their mother's long absence from the cabin, and Nick was left to make good the damage. Before we could hoist the sail again he had to go aloft, because the violence of the breakage had also damaged the halyard block. Normally happy to be 50 feet up in the air, the captain returned from this particular expedition looking somewhat the worse for wear. It is one thing to go aloft when the boat is alongside but quite another when it is pitching and rolling like billy-oh.

Within a day or two the wind had arrived with a vengeance, and we were soon thrashing through the sea with a force seven to eight on the starboard quarter. Even before the wind filled in, the journey had been anything but relaxing, for I had found that the task of entertaining two very small children whilst at the same time sailing the boat and cooking and navigating was an arduous one. And I have to say it: the pessimists who had said that parent-hood would force us to give up sailing were almost proved right.

Even when the weather was calm, occupying Xoë had proved to be a tedious, all-consuming task. A baby is amused by all the usual mundane activities of everyday life - hanging out the washing, making the beds, a walk in the park, a trip to the supermarket - all these things are of interest to a baby, and she only craves to be allowed to join in. But letting the children join in with the chores was virtually impossible at sea.

Navigation and babies do not mix, yet Xoë resented the time which I spent standing at the chart table. If I left her and went on deck with the sextant she screamed in such a way that I simply *had* to respond. I don't think that the similarity between an infant's cries and the cheeping of a baby bird is sufficiently understood. Like a mother bird, I was *helpless* to resist that plaintive cry. I was therefore obliged to leave the navigation entirely to Nick.

Nick was proving to be the ideal skipper for a family boat. He needs very little sleep. He can get by on four or five hours which he will happily take in short doses. We could count on our baby bird to sleep soundly during the early part of the night, and so this was when Nick got his longest nap. Even when the wind was up, and the boat moving so violently that the stretchers on her hammock banged on the deck-head, still Xoë would sleep on. On one occasion I put her to sleep in my bunk instead, and when I looked in on her, a couple of hours later, she was rolling to and fro like a pencil on the chart table - yet still she was out for the count!

While the baby was safely out of the way I had time for myself - or rather, for the boat - and Nick was free to stand down. Alas, the respites did not last long; feeding and caring for a baby are very tiring, and by midnight I would be yawning my head off. As often as not, Xoë woke at this time anyway and demanded a top-up, so that the skipper would be obliged to resume his duties. He got the rest of his kip in the morning while I managed both the babies and the boat.

No, this trip was not to be compared with the restful crossing that we had made in the days BC (Before Caesar). This trip was the hardest thing that I have ever done in my life. I think that if I had the choice of one or other, then, for an easy life, I would far rather sail single-handed in the Ostar than cross the ocean two-up but with a baby and a toddler in tow.

When the wind came up, our spirits lifted - but so did the cabin floor. The galley was on the windward side, so that now if I wanted to make bread, with the "help" of the children, they had to be lashed into their seats and their seats had to be lashed to the worktop. This did not leave much space for the actual industry.

With the wind came the rain, and lashings of spray too, so that the nappies which I was accustomed to spread all along the guard rail now had to hang around our heads, in the saloon. And still they failed to get very much drier. The air was thick with spume and drizzle which cut the visibility drastically. By rights, we should now have been on deck all the time but in our present situation this was quite impossible. I kept to a strict regime of five minute look-outs, and so got plenty of exercise traipsing up and down the ladder. Even so, on one occasion I went on deck to discover the sinister, grey outline of a ship just aft of the beam. He had just passed us. According to the radar, he was only a quarter of a mile away. Had he altered course on our account, I wondered? Had he even *seen* the little yacht, with its sails and its hull the colour of the breaking waves? After this experience I turned on the radar every half hour -

any more would have flattened the batteries - but it was still not enough, and I knew it.

In spite of the weather Xoë loved to be outside and insisted, loudly, on going with me every time I put a foot on the ladder. When the weather was not too grim I sometimes took her along. The leaping waves and the wind-blown spray brought a huge smile to her face, and her greatest delight was to peep out over the dodger. A little bit of salt spume on her cheeks caused Xoë no dismay. She would have been happy to stay on deck, and she whined when I took her below, but with the boat leaping through the waves and leaning at such a steep angle I found it hard to hang onto both the baby and the ship. Caesar, meantime, had no interest in the ocean. He passed his time building ships out of Lego bricks and doing alphabet jigsaws on the sloping, heaving table.

When, finally, we reached the Azores, neither Caesar nor Xoë showed any pleasure or surprise at sighting land again. It is true that the vague shapes on the horizon were initially rather obscure, but in the course of a few hours the place grew to fill the view. Still, to judge from the children's demeanour it appeared that the fertile, green island of Faial was quite invisible to them. Even while we entered the harbour at Horta they both remained seemingly oblivious. It was most odd. Caesar actually had to be ordered on deck to see his new surroundings - and this despite the fact that, after thirty full days at sea in the company of their little ones, his parents were skipping with glee.

Despite the fact that the harbour is ample and well protected by a seawall, yachts are no longer permitted to anchor at Horta and so we were obliged to use the marina.

Nick had been to Horta before and spoke enthusiastically about Cafe Peter Sport. Caesar's only interest was in having an ice-cream - something of which he had read in a book. Baby Xoë had been settled into her sling before we disembarked, and as we climbed the steps which lead up from the marina she was preparing to go to sleep. And then a car drove by.

Xoë struggled to sit up. Another car flashed past, and she followed its progress until another one went by in the opposite direction. To and fro her little head spun, and her eyes were open wide in astonishment. A visitor from outer space could not have been more surprised.

When we went into the bar, Xoë saw that there were other people all around - and she laughed with glee. She had been six months old when we left the Bahamas. At sea, her whole world had consisted of the tiny islet of our cabin, bouncing about in the leaping waves, and the entire world population had been four. Nothing more existed for her; all else had been forgotten.

Now that she had rediscovered the world, Xoë would be sorry to leave it all behind again, and when we sailed from the Azores, two weeks later, she made plain her discontent.

In Horta marina the mood was one of celebration. Most of the other folks had also come from the Caribbean, and although the Azores lie 900 miles from the European continent and everybody's true destination, there is the feeling that if you have got this far then you have made it. We were pleased to note that the French yachtsmen whom we had met in mid-Atlantic arrived two days after us. Nick was right: they got too much wind.

Of course, yachtsmen were not the first to fall on Faial island with such enthusiasm. Even Columbus, on that first Atlantic perambulation, returned to Terra Cognita via the Azores - although it would seem from his log that just a few days earlier he had thought his ship to be in the same latitude as Casablanca and Madeira.

The first explorer came this way because this is the way that the winds and currents carried him, and in his wake came the entrepreneurs – the men who could see the financial opportunities represented by the New World - and then came the slave traders, scoring their golden triangle around the pond. Next came the whalers. Before the bloody slaughter was finally banned, the whaling ships had landed countless thousands of tonnes of blubber in the Azores, and with them the bones and the teeth of the beasts. In Cafe Peter Sport, Horta's favourite watering hole, there is a marvellous museum of whaling memorabilia and of sperm whale's teeth. Each tooth is engraved with the scene of its former owner's capture, or with a portrait of some old, leathery salt.

Apart from these tooth marks in the bar the ancient mariners left little trace of the time they spent in the Azores, but not so the seafarers of today. No one seems to know who it was who started the tradition, but scarcely a yachtsman visits Horta these days without making his mark on the wall; or on the pavement, or on the quay - indeed, these days, a budding Leonardo is hard-put to find an empty space whereon to display his talent, and the peeling paint of earlier works of art is prey to land-hungry usurpers.

It all began on the outer wall of the harbour. In those days there was no marina and yachts could anchor, free of charge, in the space which had once been full of whalers and which had more recently provided a landing strip for transatlantic sea-planes. Nowadays it is only the crew of the fishing trawlers and other 'big boats' who paint their pictures on the outer wall, but for anyone interested in the history of the art form, this is the place to look. Unfortunately, Interlux and odds and sods of anti-foul do not last forever on an unprimed, often sea-swept, stone wall, and the earliest images that we could find came from the late nineteen-seventies.

It is around the marina that the tradition of the paintings has really taken off. The works produced here are no mere daubings, and neither is there any place or space for uncouth graffiti. Leaving the yacht's emblem or portrait on the sea wall is a task which can occupy the artistic members of the crew throughout much of their stay in Horta, and amongst the countless, colourful pictures there are some genuine masterpieces. At least one local photographer keeps an ongoing record of the finer work. Besides being an attractive decoration, the murals are a fascinating visitors book. Anyone who is anyone has left their mark in Horta. Interspersed with the famous names are images of ordinary cruising boats, and one of the chief pleasures whilst strolling about the quayside, and side stepping the wet paint of new creations, is to look for your chums.

"Look! Here's *Moogooloo*! We met them in Antigua. I wonder what's become of them now."

But why does everybody *want* to paint their picture on the wall? Is it mere egotism? A story has arisen which provides a more poetic answer. They say that ill-luck will befall anyone who fails to make his mark, but that good fortune is assured for as long as a painting remains on the wall.

For as long as a picture is still legible the artist's right of occupation is respected, but select sites on the wall are much sought after; once the bare, grey concrete clouds six octas of the masterpiece then the tenancy is up for grabs. Nick was pleased to find that the lettering he had painted some five years earlier was still intact. We touched it up and added the new date and a little picture of *Maamari* sailing in the company of dolphins.

Dolphins we saw in abundance when we left the Azores. Once again, there was no wind and their reflections skipped along beneath the lovely creatures as they leapt. We saw 200 or more arrange themselves into a line and then go racing away, side by side. Xoë was entranced, especially by the dolphins which came to our bow. She sat on my lap, watching them swim under the water and then come up to breathe, and one could see that she wanted to know more. To encounter the natural wonders of the world for the first time through one's own eyes – without having heard descriptions or looked at photographs – must be especially wonderful. Caesar had already been educated. He knew that these things were fishy animals. He squealed with delight, as the dolphins jumped, and said, "Eat 'em!"

There were whales, too. Whales which only a short time ago would have been hunted and harpooned for their flesh and oil, but which nowadays are pursued only by boat-loads of tourists armed with cameras. In the orange light of evening a great tail waved in the air, in the classic manner, flicking droplets of liquid fire. Closer to the boat, the knife-like, black fin of an orca cut through the glassy sea, and on the next day we saw the unmistakable square head and brown back of a sperm whale.

Far away, in our wake, the island of Faial was the greatest whale of them all - a vague shape on the horizon, glimpsed briefly and never to be identified with conviction. Shrouded regally in a great cloak of pink-tinged white cloud, the adjacent island of Pico looked magnificent, but upon reflection we realised that this was a grey day for the residents. Islands always look better from seaward.

Now we were heading for Vilamoura, which lies about a week or ten days from Horta. Our purpose was to find a safe place to leave *Maamari* while we took the kids to England and introduced them to family and friends.

Against a trickle of ships on their way to the Americas we moved towards the mainland. Off Cape St Vincent we crossed the oil tanker lane, and then we crossed the great highway which ferries the bulk produce of the world to Northern Europe, and carries

Northern Europe's refined goods to the world. At one time we had eight ships in sight and twenty on the radar.

Throughout the night the Iberian coast was shrouded in a thin mist which hid the light on the great cape, but even before the sun rose to burn through the veil the land made its presence known; the scent of unseen trees and flowers wafted across the water. Gone, when the day dawned, were the shearwaters which had followed the yacht for the past week. We wondered if they would find their way back to the islands all alone. Or perhaps they would hitch a ride behind one of the passing ships. On the other hand, perhaps they did not care whether they went back to the Azores. I pictured them already heading aimlessly for Cape Horn.

The day was absolutely calm. Under other circumstances we would have been patiently pragmatic, but this was not an interlude for introspection on the ocean's vast, vacant plain, and nor was it the close of an idyllic journey. This was the finish to a marathon. When it seemed that we would otherwise not be home and dry by nightfall, we started the engine.

Maamari sliced a path through the brine. The sun, in opposition, marched briskly across the sky heading westward. We were lolling in the cockpit, munching sandwiches, when there was a sudden, small, clunk - and a nut and severed-bolt fell from the sky and hit the seat just beside Caesar. They hit it hard enough to gouge out quite a chip in the paint work.

Instinctively, we all looked up to see if there was a plane far above us in the blue, but there was none; and, besides that, the nut and bolt were very familiar to behold. Something must be amiss at the mast-head, but if that was the case why hadn't one of the stays come down? If this was the bolt which held the forestay then, by rights, the roller-furler and the sail should by now be trailing behind us in the sea.

We had to wait until we were in the marina before the mystery could be resolved. Then, when Nick went aloft again, he found that the bolt holding up the forestay had, indeed, sheared. The remnant was still lodged in its place, precariously doing the work of the whole. After the stay failed at the lower end (while we were off Bermuda) Nick had made a visual inspection of all the rigging, but the fracture in the bolt had evidently been concealed within the forks of the rigging terminal. It was ironic that the damage should have come to light when the sail was stowed and the fitting no longer under strain, and it was a mercy that the whole caboodle had not gone overboard while we were crashing along on our way from Bermuda. Our guardian angels had evidently been working overtime again.

But we had yet to discover all this. As the sun, on its descent to the horizon, sank instead into a murky bed of cloud, we reached Vilamoura and joined a column of power-boats and jet-skis straggling home after a Sunday afternoon's entertainment.

We had done it. We were here. We were home and dry. With toddler and baby for crew we had brought ourselves back across the Atlantic. But could we - should we - continue our travels in this way?

10

FROM SANTA CRUZ TO SÃO NICOLAU

(Christmas in the Canaries : Calamity in the Cape Verdes)

In the entrance to Vilamoura marina we were beckoned alongside by a man in uniform. Nick was directed to go straight to the port captain's office. In the meantime Caesar took a much needed stroll on the jetty and Xoë did her best to shuffle along behind, on her belly.

So here we were, I thought to myself, at the end of one adventure and the beginning of another. In a few weeks time we would be heading south again, on the first leg of our journey to the Magellan strait and the Chilean canals - but first we must make the overland trek across the continent to England. It would be many years before we were again within easy reach of the motherland, and family and friends still unacquainted with the new crew-members were eagerly awaiting us.

Time ticked by and the children soon grew bored. We waited and we waited. Something had gone wrong, I knew, for it does not take an hour to fill in a couple of forms. When Nick finally reappeared his face confirmed my fears: he wore a glum expression. "You won't believe this, but..."

"What?"

"They've got a new law. They say we have to pay VAT."

"What!"

"Yes, I know - it's unbelievable - but they showed me the forms and it's the same all over Europe. Anyone whose boat wasn't here on the 31st December 1991 has to pay VAT at 17% - again - when they bring it back."

It must have taken almost half an hour for Nick to convince me of the truth of this outrageous and illogical demand for a tax already paid. How could it possibly be believed? If this had been Africa we would have sworn that it was some corrupt official's attempt at bribery, but the printed papers seemed to prove the point. This scandalous and immoral piece of law was on the statute books of the European community.

"Well, we're not bloody paying," said I, my anger boiling over.

"We have a choice," said Nick. "We can either stay and pay - or stay and fight it - or else we have to get out now, within the hour. But if we go, we have to get right out of Europe."

And go where?

Go south; go on down to Africa.

It was too much. To have our whole scheme overturned, on someone else's silly whim, was simply... too much! We had just crossed an ocean. Our provisions and water were running low. We were tired; the boat was tired - at this stage, having only just arrived, we had not even had a chance to investigate the mystery of the bolt from the blue. Nor were we ready, from a psychological point of view, to suddenly cast off the well-laid plan and spend another couple of weeks out on the ocean. To have done so would have been the height of folly.

"The bastards. We're trapped."

We would have to stay. But we would fight.

The next few days and weeks passed in a whirlwind of activity and at a pace which, although it may be usual for the Western world, was far too hectic for us. The morning after our arrival in Vilamoura, *Maamari* was craned out of the water and the very next one found us boarding a bus. Of the journey across Europe I need say nothing, except that a would-be toddler does not take kindly to being restrained, for hours, on her mother's lap.

After an absence of three years, we were at first bowled-over by the sheer abundance and variety of produce to be had in our native land; the supermarkets, with row upon row crammed full of fabulous goodies; each high-street shop an Aladdin's cave overflowing with loot. Very soon, however, we saw through the glitz to the reality beyond - to the obvious madness of a system which calls for ever escalating industrial growth and ever escalating consumerism; to the addiction which everyone around us seemed to have for things new; to the perpetual race to be the biggest, fattest rat. Our contempt for Consumer Society and for those who direct the machine increased.

At the end of it all we set off back towards the Algarve in a bargain basement Ford Cortina Estate which was stuffed to the roof, and beyond the roof, with our own new purchases - most of them made at car-boot sales and jumbles. Every conceivable space inside the car had been filled with books and food and clothes and chandlery, until we found ourselves obliged to abandon this dictionary or that jar of Marmite through the lack of any more cracks and crevices wherein to wedge the stuff. The weight was such that we had just two inches clearance between the tail of the exhaust pipe and the road.

Caesar endured the long voyage across Europe with admirable stoicism, but Xoë had soon had enough of sitting idly in her car seat, so that we were all very thankful to arrive back in Vilamoura. By now the poor old banger was also feeling fatigued. The metal of the roof had stretched so much that with the load on top removed it went "whoop, whoop, wobble, wobble," as we drove along the road, and the strain on the body had been such that only the driver's door could now be opened. The tail of the exhaust had fallen off when it had met the steel ramp onto the car ferry. Regardless of all this, we got our money back, selling the vehicle to one of the many expatriate Brits of the region.

The matter of the VAT had now to be addressed - or else, the authorities had made clear, we would not be given clearance to leave Portugal. Fortunately we had by now found a loophole, or a means to avoid the curse, but could we persuade the port captain to believe us exempt? We had learnt what this man had not revealed; namely, that non-residents, such as ourselves, who are just passing through Europe are *not* liable to pay any duty. (And even had we been returning to resettle in Europe, we could still have brought in our possessions tax free.) It took an hour of argument and several phone calls and faxes between ourselves and the tax office in England before the authorities in Vilamoura very grudgingly agreed to let us go. Since then we have heard similar tales, often of greater woe, from yachtsmen who have visited Vilamoura from abroad.

Presumably our first, instinctive guess was right: someone is on the make.

Marinas are the suburban estates of the aquatic world. We left Vilamoura as soon as we could. Just a little to the east lies Faro, with its estuary of tidal creeks and rythes, and its cold, grey mud. To folk who grew up pottering about in Chichester harbour it was a home from home.

Amongst the few boats anchored off the town of Faro was another with a family living aboard and, as luck would have it, their child was a boy only a little bit younger than Caesar. At long last he had a playmate. Xoë was still only ten months old but could already climb onto the saloon seats and had started to walk, with the result that I had my hands full. The small matter of sailing offshore with these two in tow had yet to be properly addressed.

"Never again!" I had declared when we reached Vilamoura, but the memory of that long haul across the Atlantic had since faded, until I began to believe that it had not really been so bad. Nick even seemed to think that it had been fun, which encouraged me to feel that I was making a fuss about nothing. Besides that, what were the options? Certainly, Nick was not about to be tied to a life ashore, and nor had I any desire, myself, to settle down. Settling down did not feature anywhere on our agenda. Still, I was discomfited.

"We'll just have to play it by ear," said Nick. "Madeira is only a short hop - less than a week - and then the Canary Islands are only a couple of days to the south. The Cape Verdes are about another week or so from the Canaries..."

"And then there's a dirty great ocean crossing in our path," I said gloomily.

"We'll just have to see how we go," Nick said again. "We know that we can manage the short passages quite happily, and it's not as if we were setting off to cross the pond again tomorrow. You know how it goes; a month here, a month or two there. I'd like to take a better look at the Cape Verde islands; you want to visit Ghana. We're not in any hurry, are we? By the time we set off for South America, Xoë will be bigger. It will make all the difference. You've seen how Caesar looks after himself." And that was certainly true; Caesar was as laid back and steady as his dad and needed very little attention from me.

In the meantime, Nick kept himself busy with the endless task of maintaining *Maamari*. First item on his list was the removal and repair of the engine mounts, for in recently servicing the beast he had noticed that they were all broken and needed welding.

Now, what do you do when you need a welder? You go to the chap, just across town, whose workshop you have passed every now and then, or else you ask a mate. Things like this are no problem when one is on one's own turf, but when you do not know the lie of the land and can scarcely cope with the language, then trying to find someone to fix up a bit of broken boat is always an infuriating pastime. After two days of following false leads around Faro, Nick came to the conclusion that there were no welders here. He had asked in a garage, and then gone on to a factory. Helpful souls had sent him to a re-spray shop and even to an address which turned out to be that of a chemist. Foot-sore and frustrated, he was ready to think about making up engine mounts in wood. And then, who should come paddling towards us but the neighbourhood singlehander.

Every anchorage has a singlehander -- a man, or sometimes a woman, eager to sail and see the world but who finds himself out there on his own. There *are* singlehanders who sail alone by choice, but most singlehanders are lonely souls, forever desirous of company. The singlehander is someone whom others regard warily, until he has proven himself to be suffering neither from melancholia or verbal diarrhoea. The singlehander of Faro suffered from both these ailments and was also a perfect fool. Why, only the previous day I had seen him rowing frantically against the ebb tide - and getting nowhere at all - whereas had he gone just three yards to the right, and from the centre to the side of the channel, he would have found slack water. The very same evening the man had got into his dinghy and cast-off before *then* turning back to pick up his oars... If our friends had not heard him yelling, as he slid past in the dark, he would have been half way to Madeira before dawn. *(Any resemblance between the singlehander and anyone living or dead is wholly coincidental, etc, etc.)* Only the singlehander's most persistent knocking brought us reluctantly on deck, and frankly when the man told us that he had found a welder only a stone's throw from the anchorage, we did not believe a word.

The welder was supposed to be in the old town, and this seemed most unlikely. Old towns, in my mind, were quaint quarters filled with antique tenements. Heavy industry had no place in the old towns of my acquaintance. Still, we had nothing to lose except another hour, and so we passed within the old town, entering beneath a grand, stone archway topped with a disorderly thatch of straw. (This was the stately residence of tall, red-legged, storks who have nested here for generations and whom we had seen walking on the mud at low tide.) At length we came upon a small scrap-yard - a feature so equally out of place amongst the old buildings that our hopes began to rise. This would obviously be a good place to begin asking anew, and so we picked our way through the piles of debris, looking for someone who might be able help. The only man in sight deliberately ignored us. He got into a little excavator with a hydraulic grab; he started it up and... Hey presto! People popped up, like frightened rabbits, from all over the dump.

The first one whom we collared greeted our enquiry with a shrug. The next fellow to hand was elderly and stooped and looked, from his glazed expression and sagging jaw, as if he might recently have received the benefit of electric shock therapy. Either that, we decided, or else he was a dangerous half-wit. He lumbered towards us carrying two bent and twisted chairs. It looked like a hopeless case but, ever optimistic, Nick lunged into his rehearsed recital.

The old man lifted his tousled grey head. It was many days since he had bothered to shave and many more since he had washed or changed his clothes. Groping uncertainly for the words he said, "I...er...I...speak English."

What a remarkable stroke of good fortune! There are not many Portuguese who speak English.

"Where's the welder?" Nick asked.

Not so good. The man frowned at the ground.

"Blacksmith?" I suggested, helpfully.

Now he looked up. "I'm most frightfully sorry," he said, in a true-blue Etonian accent. "I haven't a clue. I'm a poet, you see?" He turned to the man whom we had tackled first and asked, "Est ce qu'il'ya un..." but at this point, realising that he did not know the French for welder, the poet stopped short and stooped down to enact a charade of welding, with the broken chairs. A small audience gathered.

"Welder," said Nick, in Portuguese.

"La," said the first man, pointing over the scrap-yard wall.

Beyond the wall we were greeted by two large mongrels and by a one-eyed monster who made the poet look quite respectable. The grisly appearance of this new man did, however, suggest that we were on the right track and, sure enough, he guided us into a semi-derelict barn where his son was hard at work - without goggles - grinding a chunk of iron. The problem having been made plain, largely by the presentation of the self-explanatory broken engine mounts, the younger man got to work at once - without goggles. He did use a mask while he was actually welding the metal, but one could imagine that he had learnt the hard way about the pain and inconvenience of arc-eye.

"Don't look," we told Caesar. "The blue flame will damage your eyes."

We stepped outside but, even so, Caesar held his hands tightly over his eyes. Having noticed the old cyclops he had evidently put two and two together...

From Faro we sailed to Porto Santo, the smaller of the two Madeiran isles, and on the way we had an interesting and enlightening near-incident with an oil tanker. Nick, who was on watch, had for sometime been studying the approaching lights. We were hard on the wind and to have got out of the way of the ship would have meant tacking. And then, of course, we would have needed to tack back again. Tacking is a tedious activity in the dark of night and, after all, power is supposed to give way to sail. Nick turned on the radio and spoke into the silence.

"Ship on my port quarter, this is the yacht on your starboard bow." It was not the ideal way of identifying the two parties - in a place as busy as the English Channel it would have been worse than useless - but for a mid-ocean encounter it ought to do, Nick thought.

There was no immediate response but then, just as he was about to key the microphone again, a Scottish voice burst into the cabin. "Vessel calling *Gulf Carrier*, come in please." *(This was not the ship's real name.)*

"Hello," said Nick. "I take it you know I'm here."

Another long pause and then, "Where are you?"

"I'm down here, about a mile ahead of you, and we're converging. I was just wondering... I'm hard on the wind, you see, and I don't really want to have to rush around the deck in the dark, and besides that it would wake the children. Would you mind altering course, just slightly?"

There was another brief silence and then came the telling rejoinder, "Is that your light?"

"Well, I guess so." Nick could imagine the man peering out, with his nose pressed against the glass. Or perhaps he had needed to go out onto the bridge-wing. For him our little world far below his bow was just a sparkle on the shimmering path that the moon had spread across the sea. "I am sorry to put you to this trouble," Nick continued, "but if you wouldn't mind altering by just five degrees, or so."

"Is that all right now?"

Nick poked his head outside. The oil tanker, for such it could now be seen to be, had turned about 90° away from its original course. Nick hurried below again to say, "That's fine. Thank you very, very much," but there was no further comment or remark from the man in the ship, and when he went outside again, immediately afterwards, Nick saw that it had already resumed its proper heading. It passed about a quarter of a mile astern.

At dawn the Madeiran islands could be seen peeping over the far horizon, but as the sun rose their pale, blue-grey shapes merged with the sky and were gone. The wind, which had been quite strong, now fell away to the merest breath. We ambled along at a lazy pace. At one point Nick thought that he heard a leak bubbling away and cried, "Listen! What do you hear?"

I listened and heard the sound - a high pitched whistling, or squealing.

"Dolphins!" I answered, and sure enough, when we hurried on deck, we found a school of spotted dolphins surfing in the swells just off our port quarter. They surged forward in a ragged line and then went back for more. Once again Xoë was enraptured.

The next morning we reached Porto Santo and sailed into the newly built harbour. While we were anchoring Caesar said, "Oh, look! A butterfly."

We looked... and saw a hang-glider.

What a curious wonder-filled world the toddler inhabits. Did Caesar think that the hang-glider was much nearer and very much smaller, or did he imagine that there were butterflies big enough to carry off a man?

The Madeiran islands had just been swept by a storm which we ourselves had witnessed from the sanctuary of Vilamoura marina. Folks in Porto Santo said that the marina in the capital isle had been utterly destroyed. The dry "barrancos", or canyons, had become raging torrents, and cars and children were supposed to have been washed down them and out to sea. Yachts had dragged and been sunk, we were told. The truth, we discovered when we sailed across, was not quite so terrible - no yachts had been sunk - but a lot of damage had been done and up in the rain washed mountains a number of lives had been lost.

Down by the sea, some of the survivors were so shaken that they were fearful of sailing on, but the citizens of the town of Funchal had put the past behind them and were getting on with life. The season of good cheer and tinsel and shopping sprees was upon us. At night, Funchal twinkled with a radiance to rival the heavens. The street-lights along the promenade were bedecked with an intricate necklace of lights, like jewels, and the trees lined up along the seafront were so smothered in gaudy red, green, and yellow bulbs that they seemed like the trees in Aladdin's underground garden, bearing rubies, emeralds, and topaz for their fruit. Finest of all the decorations was a squadron of huge caravels which made their way along the outer wall. Their sails were outlined in strings of white lights and carried the familiar red, Maltese cross. Their hulls were planked with tawny orange lights, and the sea which swirled below them was almost as beautiful in colour as the tropical deep. The show was not for the benefit of the local folk but for the people arriving daily on an endless stream of cruise ships. While we were leaving, the *QE II* sailed in.

We were now bound for the island of La Palma, in the Canaries. As we were clearing the harbour wall I looked back at Madeira and saw that it was smothered all over in two-tone flecks, the white houses with their orange roofs almost blotting out the verdure of the gigantic hillside. The valley just above the sprawling town held a pocket of eerie, yellow light, which intrigued me.

Maamari romped away on a rising breeze and when next I looked back, the radiant glow had been surmounted by a misty, red band. Five minutes later, the red and yellow topped a hazy greenish glow. One by one, as we sailed on, the colours of the rainbow appeared like a multi-layered smog above the town, and then, by way of a finale, the surreal radiance rose up out of the valley and spread itself in a crescent over the island.

By now we had discovered that there was a lot more wind out in the ocean than we had imagined, but it was on the quarter and *Maamari* was loving it. Plaything of Aeolus and Oceanus, she came to life at their command. The waves were leaping and rolling and crashing; rushing under the stern to hurl us onward. The vitality of a greater spirit washed through my own being; God in all things. I stayed in the cockpit until dusk - when the children demanded Mummy's company - and thereby escaped feeling seasick.

This glorious sleigh-ride carried us to our destination in double quick time: we reached Santa Cruz de La Palma in just 36 hours, which was exactly half our estimate for the journey. After a tour of the port turned up no suitable alternative, we squeezed our way into the tiny fishing harbour and were received with broad grins and arms opened wide to catch our lines. It is difficult to imagine English fishermen welcoming a yacht - still less a foreign yacht - with such warmth.

When our two little-ones emerged from the cabin they were greeted like long-lost grandchildren, and soon they were borne down with gifts of biscuits and oranges and chocolate. The port captain was also thrilled with the latest arrivals to his small domain and in particular with Caesar, whom he kept patting and kissing. Small blond children are very good for P.R.

La Palma is billed as the one Canarian Isle not over-run with English lager-louts and German nudists; the only one of the seven where life still flows to the rhythm of the ageless past. This, which turns out to be more or less true, is for a very simple reason; lager-louts and nudists like to spend their holiday prostate in the sand, and although there is quite a bit of sand around La Palma, it is all volcanic in origin. Even Caesar was put off by a seaside strand darker in colour than tarmac. When the urge to run about and build sand-pies overcame his first apprehension, our boy got to work in the usual way and Xoë mucked in - muck being the most fitting word. Within minutes the children and their clothes were soot black. It was impossible for their mother not to think of them as being covered in filth, although, in reality, La Palma's black sand brushes off just like the ordinary white stuff. I have since been told that the beaches in

Tenerife and Gran Canaria were originally made of black sand, too. The pristine sand which the holiday makers love had to be imported from the Sahara.

Wherever it is possible, as we travel, we like to see beyond the seashore and the port. To this end, while we were in Santa Cruz we hired a Fiat Panda and set out to explore the isle. The road which we followed was coiled like a snake on the mountainside, and as we tacked to and fro in an unrelenting series of tight, hairpin bends Caesar and I were soon feeling distinctly queasy as. Frequent stops were made in the cold pine forest, but Caesar, poor lad, had soon spilt his breakfast.

At the top of the mountain we finally broke free of the trees, and from the edge of the world's largest crater (or so they say) we looked out and saw the snow capped peak of Tenerife floating on a calm sea of cloud. There was no snow on La Palma's summit, but we found beautiful, transparent icicles more than a foot long, which hung down from the rocks beside the road. To pick one seemed as great a sacrilege as to cut an orchid, but pick one I did, as a present for the children. Both winced at its touch and Caesar cried, "No, I don't like it!"

After lunching in a restaurant near to the summit, we set off down the other side of the mountain. This journey was even steeper, and the hairpin bends even tighter. Having only just been filled full of goat stew and chocolate cake, poor Caesar succumbed again, planting the whole lot on the nicely upholstered car seat.

At last we came to the bottom - or rather, to a cliff edge still a thousand feet or so above the sea. Above us, villages clung to the terraced slope and vines rambled up the giant steps. Prickly-pear cacti grew by the side of the road. Here and there, small barrancos dived down headlong to the waterside, and eventually we came upon an over-sized specimen. Indeed, La Palma's most striking feature is not the crater itself but this truly massive barranco, or ravine, which issues from the crater's broken rim and comes crashing through the grey rock of the island tearing a great jagged scar. Dry though it be now, a canyon spells water - not enough, for much of the year, and far too much at other times - but water still. In time of flood a ravine can be deadly, but in a land where the rainfall cannot be taken for granted this is the only safe place to plant your food.

The sides of the great, tumbling ravine in La Palma are too nearly sheer to be called slopes, yet man, in his ingenuity, has caused them to be cut into terraces. Rank upon rank they ascended either wall and there was something almost military about their orderliness. Nor did the pipes plunging hundreds of feet down the slope seem like the work of the peasantry; this was a Big Business enterprise. Each terrace bore a regiment of banana trees - but they were shabby specimens, not to be compared with the lush ones growing like weeds in Antigua. Here, the cold catabatic winds hurtle down the mountainside ravaging all that lies before them, and the broad waxy banana palm leaves are shredded until they resemble the fronds of a coconut palm.

Far below, at the water's edge, we found a small seaside town, and here we watched the waves cast their frilly white lace upon the iridescent black sand; a stunning combination. Then we headed back home via a tunnel cut through the backbone ridge of the mountain. For some days now our side of the island had been overcast, whereas this other face was basking in the sun. As we ascended to the ridge we saw that the top was buried beneath a mantle of cloud, and that the cloud had begun to roll rapidly down the slope towards us - yet it never arrived nor even gained another few feet; it was in perpetual descent, but its progress was that of a man walking down an up-coming escalator. We watched the rolling cloud in awe, for it was a quite astonishing and beautiful marvel. In Santa Cruz de La Palma, pride of place in the religious hierarchy goes to an effigy of Nuestra Señora de las Nieves - Our Lady of the Snows. Could it be that the snow referred to is not the smattering which sometimes tops the island summit, but this wondrous, snow-like manifestation?

Christmas was coming and I dressed the ship overall in garlands of glittering tinsel hung with bunches of ripe balloons and baubles. Nick's father flew out to join us. Caesar had heard that Father Christmas was on his way, and since Jim arrived bearing gifts naturally assumed that this must be the famous man.

No one celebrates Christmas as the British do, and so every Christmas spent in foreign parts must necessarily be something of a disappointment. We made the best of things, and bought a leg of smoked ham instead of a turkey. The poinsettia, with its seasonal red blossoms, holds some kind of local significance at this time of year, and so one served us in place of the usual tree.

Jim follows the Roman Catholic faith, but even he was not aware that in Roman Catholic countries Christmas Eve is the big day. When he could not quite work up the enthusiasm to walk into town for midnight-mass he decided to go, instead, on the morrow. But on the morning of the 25th the church was locked. Party over. The shops were open and the people of La Palma were all back at work.

We left La Palma on the first day of the new year, 1994, and by nightfall the island was no more than a cluster of dim lights and a bleary yellow beacon flashing astern. Tenerife cast a loom on the clouds of the eastern horizon and feeble blurs of light up ahead betrayed La Gomera and El Hierro. We were on our way south once more, once more bound for Cape Verde. Jim sailed with us and, as Nick foretold, was a splendid addition to the crew having a liking for the long watch between midnight and six in the morning. Moreover, Jim pretended to enjoy doing the washing up and claimed the task for his own. Better yet, he was willing to read 'The Naughty Sheep' and 'Tell the time with Thomas' three times each, every morning and evening. This was a magnificent contribution to the harmony of the home, for Caesar was now beginning to read and wanted plenty of repetition to aid him in this ability, whilst Xoë, even before she was a year old, had shown herself to be an avid bookworm. On our crossing to the Azores she just loved to tear paperbacks to pieces, but now her greatest pleasure was in being read-to.

By January the tradewinds have regained a firm grip on the tropical belt of the North Atlantic, and our ride south was a rollicking one. The sun shone; the blue sea glittered; the clouds sailed past on the horizon. And with Jim to share the chores, Nick and I began to recapture some of the harmony of the old days - of days and nights passing unnumbered while time lost all meaning. Even so, there were occasional small incidents which made some of the days more special than others:

"3rd January. *This morning, while he was rinsing Xoë's nappies, Nick emptied a bucket of water over a pilot whale... She was hanging about near the Endeavour Seamount. We watched her until she fell so far astern that the waves hid her.*" (Excerpt from the ship's log book.)

On the 7th, towards evening, we began to search the horizon for land. We saw the sun set behind the islands of São Nicolau and São Vicente and then they disappeared, as they had done on our last visit, into the black void.

That night a decent-sized flying fish flew into the cabin through the open hatch, almost landing in the frying pan.

"So where is it now?" I asked Nick when he told me the tale. "I suppose you've scoffed it already."

"I threw it back."

"What! Are you mad, or something? After all the effort we go to, dragging lures around, you go giving back the freebies!"

"Well, one flying fish isn't much use on its own."

There was some truth in this, but later that morning, at anchor off Mindelo, we found five of the first fish's brethren lying stiffly on the deck. One each for breakfast.

Mindelo was just as we remembered it. The seafront buildings, like a film set; the concrete replica of the Torre Belem; the orange brown hill known as Monte Verde forming a backdrop to the scene. But, wait - one thing was different: snapping in the ever present breeze, above the town hall, was a flag quite unlike our red, green and yellow courtesy ensign. From its earlier, socialist path the young nation had taken a sharp swerve to the right. The new government had lowered the nation's African colours and hoisted an entirely new flag; a flag with a circle of ten yellow stars superimposed upon red, white, and blue cloth. The format was so obviously European that it could be seen as nothing more nor less than a public announcement of the way in which the islands had broken their tie with the continent. The rumour on the street was that Cape Verde would like to join the EC, please. "This is not Africa," a doctor told us proudly.

For most of the yachtsmen who come to Cape Verde, the islands are no more than a stepping-stone on the way to Brazil or the Caribbean. They put into Mindelo for a few days, and then they press on across the Atlantic. Our visit four years earlier had also been short, but even from that taster we knew that the archipelago had much more to offer. This time we planned to spend several weeks in the islands and really do them properly. As we shall see, this plan fell apart when matters were taken out of our hands.

But before we go any further, let's just get one thing straight: the Cape Verde islands have been misnamed. It was the Portuguese who first found them, cast out far away from the African continent. So far as anyone knows they had never been seen by man - whether black, white, or brown - before Antonio de Noli stumbled upon the northern rim of the archipelago.

Back then, in 1460, Portugal was the superpower of Europe, and in terms of world domination the Arabs were their only rival. The Arabs had access to the gold of some distant, unknown place, and they also controlled the highways to trade with the Indies. Bent on discovering the source of the gold and also of finding a sea route to the Indies (thereby enabling them to tip-toe around the edge of the Arabian empire) the Portuguese went creeping down the west coast of the African continent. The rumour was that if they went far enough they would be able to get round into the Indian Ocean. Even so, the explorers went forward very cautiously. Each summer's exploration took them to fresh pastures.

But pastures is perhaps not the best word to use, for the land which the explorers found was a barren one, inhospitable to man. When, after ten years of seasonal exploration, they reached the edge of a savannah, its comparative verdure was noted with relief. Cabo Verde (Green Cape) - now Cap Vert - marked the beginning of the end of that waterless wasteland to the north.

The islands which Antonio de Noli found, a few years later, happen to lie directly off Cabo Verde, and cartographers named them accordingly. Since that time many have followed behind Noli expecting to discover a lush and - well, yes - a *verdant* archipelago - but the mediaeval map makers have misled us all. In truth, the Cape Verde islands are nothing more nor less than a far flung outpost of the great Sahel desert.

How to survive in this parched land? This - survival - has been man's one objective and preoccupation since first he found himself in these isles back in the 15th century. Tuaregs with camels might have felt at home here, but for Portuguese fishermen, and for people accustomed to life in the luxuriant forests of the Guinea Coast, the contrast must have come as a terrible shock.

To tell the truth, the descendants of the peasant Portuguese and African slaves dumped here 500 years ago have, even now, *not* discovered a means to dwell in harmony with their land. Until post-independence governments linked them to the world network of foreign aid, death from drought and starvation was a spectre looming large for every man, woman, and child in Cape Verde. Every fifty years or so, a super-drought would wipe out up to a third of the population. In this place, so seemingly forsaken by God, even desert cacti and lizards are seldom seen, and despite the artificial prop of outside assistance things are still pretty tough.

The surprising upshot of this struggle against the odds is a people who are the unexpected flower in an impossibly hostile terrain. In the squalid shanty town which has grown up around Mindelo, the children were filthy and bedraggled and covered in sores. The hill-dwellers hoeing the rubble around their stunted maize were hollow-cheeked and boney and suffered from protein deficiency. Yet both of these - and all of their compatriots - were happy souls, trusting and friendly. They seemed to us to have an inner peace that only comes to people who are satisfied with the life they lead.

To those who glimpse Cape Verde only as they dash through, Mindelo it is an ugly place, with little to offer. But can a man really judge the flavour of a meal by standing outside the restaurant, sniffing? This book in its entirety would not contain space enough to describe all the wonders of the Cape Verde archipelago and its people - meek-minded, gentle, welcoming, and, above all, death-defyingly proud of their bizarre land.

Of all the islands which go together to make up Cape Verde, São Vicente is the one whose gaze seems most to rest on Europe. Many of the folks who live here have family in Holland or Portugal (there are colonies of expatriate Cabo Verdians spread all around the globe) and it may be for this reason that the ones who remain wish to hustle the nation forward into the bright new future which they see in the Western lifestyle. Then again, it could be the constant reminder of another world, far away from the barren rock, for Mindelo was founded exclusively for the purpose of doing business with outsiders. In the beginning it was a coaling station for transatlantic steam-ships. Now, as the nation's number two port, it sees the bulk of the one-way trade from the north.

Regardless of the Mindelense desire to adopt and be adopted by all that is European, the place still lagged well behind, and in a quaintly picturesque way. Fishermen's wives strolled barefoot through the cobbled streets with their babies lashed to their backs and huge bowls of tuna balanced on their heads. The shiniest black and green taxis rattling through town dated from 1959, and some of the lorries looked exactly like the Dinky toys that my big brother used to play with.

As for the tugs which we saw hauling fuel out to visiting ships, in the manner of the old colliers, two of these were wonderful antiques, still driven by steam! The ugly skeins of black smoke which they dragged to and fro across the bay were strikingly at variance with the latest, high-technology, wind-driven generators standing in a line in the valley beyond.

Amongst yachtsmen, Mindelo is best known for its wind. The channel between São Vicente and the adjacent island of Santo Antão is a classic, walk-in, sail-in demonstration of the famous Bernoulli effect, which the reader will remember from his school-day physics lessons. A handy force five flows into the top and comes out of the far end transformed into a furious banshee. In the meantime, fierce gusts tear down from the brown hills above Mindelo like depraved demons, and the foreshore all around the bay is decorated with the rusting remains of tugs and ships whose anchoring gear was not heavy enough.

"Must be the windiest spot on earth," Jim grumbled as we fought our way to the beach under oars; but he was wrong. That honour goes to São Pedro, a fishing village on the south side of the island. Here, the wind which has already picked up speed in the channel gathers further momentum in a low, straight valley. The people of São Pedro walk with a permanent 30° incline and swear that it never blows less than a gale in their bay throughout the whole of January, February and March. Speed sailors call it the best wind in the world and records have been set here.

Just across the way from São Vicente, yet often scarcely to be seen through the grime carried on the wind, is the massive rock of Santo Antão. For me this is quite the most interesting and astonishing of the Cape Verde islands. This is the one that the local folks call green - but since its public, western face is utterly brown, and naked even of soil, the casual visitor must assume that the name is applied in jest.

There is only one village on the eastern side of Santo Antão, and its sole purpose is to serve the ferry, winding and unwinding a fragile thread between the two isles. Since there is no natural harbour on the rugged, wave chewed coast, the little port – Porto Novo – depends for its existence on a short stone wall which was constructed by the independence government. Before the wall was built, in the 1980s, this place was no more tenable than any other on this side of the island, and the ferry had to journey thirty-odd miles around to the opposite shore.

Happily, we found that there was just enough space for *Maamari* to anchor behind the wall at Porto Novo. Leaving Jim in charge of the ship, we went ashore to reconnoitre the place and soon found ourselves accompanied by dozens of ragged but happy children, for whom the sight of two white toddlers was evidently a novelty. A travelling circus, complete with a dancing bear, could scarcely have attracted more attention.

When the ferry arrived, early the next day, we took advantage of the buses which turned up to meet it and embarked on a journey over the island - and over is certainly the word. Santo Antão is a mountain 6,000 feet high and the only way to reach its other side is to climb over it. This is a journey to remember for the rest of your life. If Alexander Humboldt left it off his list of the world's seven greatest natural wonders then it can only be because he did not pass this way.

One hesitates to apply the term ugly to an entirely natural landscape, but the windward face of Santo Antão is as bare and rubble-strewn as if it had recently been bulldozed. Its only saving grace is its truly awesome stature. Like an ant, our bus ascended. Up and up climbed the hand-crafted, cobbled road, clambering steadfastly over and around dry ravines; patiently, pragmatically, meandering like a stream.

At long last - with the ferry port now just a scribble at the foot of the orange-brown mountain - we drew close to the backbone summit of Santo Antão. Although the landscape here seemed to change little, we suddenly found ourselves passing amongst stone-built terraces which curved and wriggled around the mountain like the contours drawn on a map.

"But surely," we said to ourselves, "this land could not support life?" The brown strips supported by the terraces were empty of anything but a fine, powdery dust. We saw tiny cottages, built of the same rock which lay all around them, but not one tree, nor bush, nor blade of grass could we see. It seemed that in the past this place must have been a little bit less arid. Now, the farmsteads had been destroyed by drought. They were obviously abandoned; no one could have convinced us otherwise, for seeing is believing and we saw a dead land. We had to wait until summer to see these hopeless acres tenanted and green – and to see them then was to witness a miracle.

Arriving at the mountain top, the road was swallowed up by a bank of cloud, and as we entered the cloud the scene changed swiftly - we might have turned a page in a book, or flicked to another channel on the television. Forgotten was the parched wasteland - could it really be only a few yards behind us? - and now the road wound its way through a grey-green forest of dank, dripping, feathery pine trees. But if this change was remarkable, what lay ahead was just out of this world.

As the wardrobe is to Narnia, in the tales told by C.S. Lewis, so the cloud hiding the top of Santo Antão is actually the gateway to a fantasia beyond. When the blindfold was raised we had been taken into a magic land of plummeting canyons and grey peaks jagged as a shark's teeth. The majesty of the scene defied description. Our road crept down a narrow pinnacle between two immense, dry ravines, and tiny thatched-cottages clung to every ridge.

And, yes - this side of the island was green. By no means could it be called lush, but it is a farmed land. Every conceivable, possible slope in those ancient "ribeiras", or dry river valleys, has been terraced and made to bear food. And in the right season - directly after the sparse rain falls - one can find streams and even waterfalls in the secret gardens of Santo Antão's lost world.

For the backpacker Santo Antão is a paradise - provided that he comes bearing his own house on his back, and with sufficient food and a cooking stove and, above all, with plenty of water. One might imagine that things would be easier for the visiting yachtsman, but he has his own problem; namely, the want of a decent anchorage. As we were to learn at a later date, even Porto Novo can become an open, lee shore. The south of the island is sheltered from the tradewind, and so we decided that it was worthy of further investigation. The chart showed no roads penetrating this grimly rugged region, but we noted that there was a settlement called Tarrafal perching in precarious isolation on the edge of the coast.

We made ready to leave Porto Novo, and no sooner were the sails hoisted and the anchor weighed than the gale hurtling down the alley between Santo Antão and São Vicente snatched up *Maamari* as if she were a piece of paper and sent us bowling along the coast. At the helm, I was a charioteer once more. The waves streaming out ahead of us were horses in reign, and the god of the sea himself cannot have had a finer team.

Surging onward in this frenzy of wind and water, *Maamari* soon made the southern tip of the island and opened the Ribeira do Tarrafal. Then, just as we came within sight of the houses, our full-bodied gale went phut... and that was that. Less than a boat's length astern the sea still leapt and danced and tried, once more, to snatch at our heels - but to no avail. The wind, in its careless rampage of delight, had spat us out. We sat on the glassy mill-pond of a gigantic wind shadow. Ironic though it seemed, to say the least, there was nothing for it but to motor the last half mile to the village.

As for Tarrafal - its anchorage proved not quite so suitable as we had imagined. Or rather, the anchorage was fine, but getting ashore was almost impossible. In trying, we were all flung out of the dinghy and ended up wearing it on our heads.

When the time came to leave the island, conditions were just the same. Because there was no wind in the lee of the great mountain we motored along, with the mizzen and genoa set. A few puffs reached out towards us. Up ahead we could see the waves breaking as if on the edge of a hidden reef. When we were within a couple of boats lengths of the seething sea, Nick and I began hastily to furl the genoa whilst Jim, whose eyesight and hearing are not quite so good as they once were, protested loudly in puzzlement.

"What's going on? We need more sail, not less. How about getting the main up?"

In the next instant *Maamari* was flung onto her beam ends with water lapping over into the cockpit.

It says quite a lot for the safety and seaworthiness of the yacht that Caesar, who was playing on the cockpit floor, stayed calm and reasonably dry throughout. Xoë was sound asleep behind a lee-cloth and remained so in spite of the sudden, radical angle of heel.

São Pedro, on São Vicente's southern shore, was now the object of our desires. From Tarrafal to this next village the distance is only 18 miles, but São Pedro is seven miles up wind - the nautical equivalent of scaling a sheer cliff.

"We're wasting our time," said Jim, who had assumed the helm. Each wave crashing into the bow delivered bucketfuls and bathfuls of cold water up, and over, and onto his head, yet this septuagenarian seafarer had no mind to hand over to Nick or me.

Now, the gale which had once been our playmate was an enemy to be fought against. Left in the hands of the self-steering gear *Maamari* would only have limped to and fro. She needed our help to steal each inch of the way as we clawed onward, upward, towards our goal.

"Let's forget it," Jim said. We had just tacked through 150°. The frothy trail tailing off the port quarter told of the leeway we were making, and to this could be added the disadvantage of a two knot current, pushing at us as it tore through the bottleneck channel between the islands. "Let's forget it. Okay? Let's go to the next one."

The next one was São Nicolau, still further up wind. In an effort to console Jim, I took bearings which showed that *Maamari* was actually making up - but only at the rate of one knot. We eventually arrived at São Pedro at about midnight, having taken more than 16 hours to cover 18 miles.

With easy access to the little town of Mindelo, São Pedro is a more modern version of Tarrafal. Whereas that village had been built of tiny stone houses and was somehow reminiscent of the ruins, which

I once saw, of a bronze-age village, the houses in São Pedro were mostly built of home-made concrete bricks. In Tarrafal the only source of fuel had been sugar-cane trash and wood scavenged from the shore, whereas here in São Pedro everyone was cooking on gas. However, the principal difference between the two villages lay in their climate, the one being set in a that perpetual wind shadow and the other, as has been mentioned, beset by a perpetual gale.

Caesar and Xoë were, as ever, a fantastic hit in the wind-swept fishing village. A hoard of children waiting for us on the beach grabbed Caesar before the dinghy had even touched the sand and made off with him on their shoulders. The poor lad had no idea what was happening and whimpered in terror until we rescued him. Xoë resisted all the arms out-reached to cuddle her and ran off, yelling "Nur! Nur!" The little ragamuffin gang went in hot pursuit, dogging her every footstep, her every tottering twist and turn; oohing and aahing in unison as she tripped and almost fell on the rubble slope. Now and then Xoë glanced up, as if to see what all the fuss was about, but she never seemed to realise that she was the great attraction.

All day and all night the wind howled through the valley of São Pedro. The noise was exhausting - one felt assaulted, and withdrew into an inner shell. Going on deck we were physically assailed by the sand scoured from the valley and blasted across the bay.

An open fishing boat came by, with her crew of a dozen men all wearing balaclavas improvised from T-shirts. They waved and whistled and grinned, keeping up their enthusiastic greeting until it was answered not once but twice, and with equal gusto. They threw us four or five huge flying-fish, fully 18 inches long and with a 20 inch wingspan. In return, Nick tossed out a packet of cigarettes, bought duty-free in the Canary Islands, and there were shouts of applause. Two more fish, exactly like the first, were promptly landed on our deck, by way of change.

On the following day a man swam out and presented us with another fish, which he had just caught. Diving under the boat, he next appeared with an octopus. A moment later he was waving a moray eel on the end of his spear gun.

"No, no!" I cried in alarm. I did not want a moray eel, with its mouth full of needle sharp teeth, wriggling about on our deck.

In an instant our visitor was climbing aboard, and demanding the use of a sharp knife. In the twinkling of an eye he had killed, gutted, and cleaned the eel and the fish, and had turned the poor old octopus inside out. The next thing he needed was a cooking stove; the request was made by signs as much as with words, and no sooner had I waved a hand towards the galley than the fellow was down there, cooking our lunch. He declined to stay and eat, but hopped back overboard and was never seen by us again.

We left São Pedro bound for São Nicolau, the next inhabited island in the necklace chain. Out in the open water the wind was blowing about force five or six, and the sun shone out of a cloudless and seemingly clear, clean sky. Still, the headlands of São Vicente faded fast and we ran about taking bearings before they vanished all together. The satnav, given to us by Jim as a wedding present, had long ago given up aiding our navigation, its last effort having been to place us in the Panama Canal when we had been somewhere off La Palma.

Stalwart as ever, Jim took the first trick. Nick prepared lunch whilst Caesar and Xoë took it in turns to fall asleep in my arms. In the distance, eight miles or so to the north, the uninhabited island of Santa Luzia was a vague outline traced on the sky. It was to be many months before we got to know it any better. Next in the line was a rock called Ilheu Branco.

Branco emerged from the mire as a neat, white triangle, and an hour must have passed before the pale, cloud-like outline of the island took form around this shape. The huge triangle is made of sand which the wind carries all the way from the Sahara and then drops in the lee of the rock.

This was another magical islet - a last, over-looked fragment of the lost city of Atlantis, or the abode of an unknown, forgotten god; it throbbed with the vitality of a living thing. It was a sacred Dreamtime shrine - the equal of Australia's Ayers Rock - and although it was far away in the distance I felt it watching us as we passed.

Ilheu Branco is small but magnificent. Its cliffs rise from the sea to meet in a backbone ridge. In the late afternoon light the rock was tinged green, and the sand had a rose-pink hue. Once again, it was to be many months before we came closer and anchored off the islet but even then, when our feet had desecrated the sand, Ilheu Branco still retained a mystical aura.

Next came Ilheu Raso, the third uninhabited island, and had I checked the dictionary beforehand I would not have been peering through the gloom, searching for a sharp, jagged, *razor*-shape. Raso means flat, level or *razed*. On first and even on later acquaintance this was the island which aroused in us the least interest. It slid past, into the shade of dusk, and as night fell we strained our eyes to see São Nicolau.

But São Nicolau lurked in the mire of darkness. It refused to show itself. An hour or two after night had fallen a vivid yellow loom appeared and grew, behind a great, towering cloud - a cloud which, until that moment, had been hidden from our eyes in the blackness. The moon was rising. As its loom grew brighter, so the cloud's edge began to seem as sharp and solid as rock; and so it was, of course. When the brilliant Phoebe herself was finally hoisted aloft in all her radiance, then we saw São Nicolau painted in silhouette against a Prussian-blue sky. Far below the moon a chain of twinkling lights danced and dipped, and finally rested above the sea. And at precisely the moment when this, our destination, appeared on the horizon, the wind once again disappeared as if at the throw of a switch. Again, the village lying in the wind-shadow is called Tarrafal, so that it is tempting to assume that this might be the creole word for such a phenomenon. However, there is also, in the archipelago, a third village which has the same name but which does not share the same meteorological attribute.

In fact, the wind-shadow at Tarrafal do São Nicolau is not so sure as the one at Santo Antão. For three days *Maamari* sat at anchor above a perfect image of herself. But on the fourth we awoke to the sound of a wild wind screaming through the rigging, and we went on deck to find great gusts whipping up sheets of spray and driving them far out across the sea. Dry gullies in the massive rock of São Nicolau were the chinks in her armour.

Rowing ashore in these conditions was completely out of the question. Although the fetch was very short there was sufficient chop in the harbour to sink a couple of the little open-boats. However, it was not the spray nor the wavelets, but the sheer force of the wind which made journeying ashore quite impossible. Every now and then the dinghy leapt into the air and performed barrel rolls at the end of her painter. Even with only Nick and Jim aboard, it could never have been worked to windward, or even made to hold its ground; it would have been blown out to sea.

The severance of our tie with the land would ordinarily have been of no concern, but looming large on our horizon now was the issue of Jim's flight back to England. Jim was scheduled to leave us in five days time, from the international airport in the island of Sal - and although Sal is adjacent to São Nicolau he was becoming distinctly jittery about our chances of getting there on time.

What was the wind doing beyond the microcosm of Tarrafal? Was it blowing a hooley in the world outside, too? If it *was* blowing, would we stand any chance of making up and reaching the more windward isle? Jim pointed to our past performance. He wanted to get ashore and book himself a passage on the inter-island ferry.

To cut short a long story, Jim finally got ashore the next day, and on finding that the once-weekly ferry was headed in the opposite direction, he booked himself onto an inter-island flight. The wind had by now died down, but still he preferred to sit, for two days, and wait for the more reliable means of transport. The two days passed, and on Thursday afternoon we waved Jim adieu - and then we rushed quickly back to the boat and made sail. We had a point to prove!

"3rd February. *17.30 Weighed anchor. Bowled along the south-western coast of São Nicolau, on a beam reach, but the wind gradually came round onto the nose. The course to steer is 100°, but we are only able to get 120°. Standing on until daybreak.*"

"4th February. *09.00. Took sunsights, which put us about 15 miles off the south-western tip of Ilha Boa Vista, about 35 miles to leeward of our destination. We have 1¾ knots of current to contend with. Wind strength, force 5 to 6. We are unable to carry the main. Genoa reefed. We tacked through 100°...*"

On our last tack we had been proceeding almost parallel to the swell, and since our new tack put us almost bows on to the seas I expected them to stop us dead. Happily, I was wrong. *Maamari* rose to meet each wave and continued on her way at about five knots, only occasionally missing her footing and tumbling, with a juddering slam, into a solid wall of water. Perched behind the sprayhood, watching our progress, I would duck quickly below the cover when *Maamari* was wrong-footed, there to cringe – but also to congratulate myself on my fleet-footed agility. The wave-top, in the same instant, would fly along the length of the boat and dump half a ton of water on the frail hood above my head.

When it had seen enough of my smug arrogance, the sea waited until I popped my head back up above the sprayhood, and then it promptly slapped me in the face with a second great bucketful, thrown directly after a first.

In the course of the day we took half a dozen sun-sights, for with islands hiding all around us in the harmattan murk, it was important to know the exact whereabouts of the vessel. At 21.00 hours we calculated that we were 25 miles off the village of Palmeira, which was our destination, and an hour later we sighted a row of white lights which, as it transpired, were at the airport. We switched on the radar and found that the coast was 16 miles away.

It was a lovely night. I renewed old friendships with two dozen stars and was just observing the rise of the southern cross, for the first time in many months, when a flash on the horizon far astern caught my attention. A thunderstorm. But it was a long way away; I could not even hear its rumble. Still, I began to wonder what it would be like to be struck by lightning. The cockpit would not be a good place to be, I decided

The clock began to chime. It was midnight; time to wake Nick for his watch. At that very moment there was an almighty crash from aloft, and another bang as something hit the deck, and with thoughts of lightning still wafting through my mind I almost jumped down the hatch.

Nick leapt out of bed in the instant that I yelled his name. Whatever had hit the deck had hit it right above his head, and now he could hear the sound of wood splintering. I snatched up a torch and shone it aloft.

"Oh, Jesus!" The mast was curved like an archer's ready bow. "Let's get the sail in!" So saying I thrust the winch handle at my sleepy partner and eased the genoa sheet.

Even with the sail furled the mast still slumped to one side, and it was pumping horribly. Nick was for going aloft to put a line around the hounds, but I was appalled at the idea and begged him not to.

"I have to," he answered, "or else we'll lose the lot."

"You must be joking! If you seriously think that it's going to go over the side then you can't possibly think about climbing it!"

The issue was shelved for a moment while Nick went below to check on the mast strut - the support which takes the load of a deck-stepped mast down through the cabin and onto the keel. He came back with the news that the two deck beams at either end of the box-shaped strut were cracked, and that the deck itself was split along the leeward edge of the tabernacle. The whole lot was still moving and creaking.

We started the engine - partly to get us to the shore, but also to stop the dreadful rolling which had begun when we furled the genoa; rolling could only put further strain on the mast. Nick went below again to hunt in the rope-locker for a light line. I stood at the helm, my imagination running wild. Suppose the deck and the mast strut gave way? Then the mast would surely topple down, heel first, into the cabin, and from there it would go straight on down, through the hull. I shouted to Nick, above the noise of the engine, telling him to get the lifejackets ready.

The lifejackets conveniently laid on the pilot berth, to assuage my fears, Nick emerged from the cabin with a line in his hand. One end was weighted with a nasty-looking lump of iron. The target was cross-wind, but on the third try Nick managed to lob the rope and its projectile over the spreaders. With this line we could now get a rope around the mast and stay it, to stop it from pumping. Our delight was short lived, however, because the weight promptly led the line round and around the mast and then tangled itself through one of the mast-steps.

Nick fetched another line and had another try, but after twenty or thirty goes he gave up. I waited for him to say, "Just six steps and it would be done", and I wondered whether to agree, or to point out that it might be the last straw. Before the matter could be brought to a head, Nick received sudden inspiration: we would take the main halyard and wrap it round the upper half of the mast - in the manner lately demonstrated by the thrown line - before then taking the tail of the rope to the genoa winch and tightening it in hard.

Nick was about to go for'ard and implement the scheme when who should appear at the foot of the companion ladder but one small, sobbing, shaking little girl. Never before had Xoë's cries gone unanswered. On this occasion they had gone completely unheard, because of the noise of the engine.

Now what should I do? At this juncture I could not possibly go below - I was needed on the helm - but I was loathe to bring the baby outside. Out here she would be an inconvenience to me and a danger to herself, most especially if the mast fell down. The only alternative was to stick her back in the aft cabin and lock the door. Left alone, and uncomprehending, the tiny child would clearly not go back to bed. On the contrary, I guessed that she would cry and cry. She might even cry so much that she threw up, and then she might choke.

Nick opted for the line of least resistance and bundled Xoë into her coat, her lifejacket, and her harness. I plonked her on my hip where, to my surprise, she sat quietly, although with a puzzled look on her face. Even the spray breaking over us never once caused her to whimper, but every now and then she looked at me with an odd little expression, as if to say, "Why are we out here in the dark, Mummy?"

Nick's jury-stay was very effective. It immediately took most of the curve out of the mast and stopped the deck below from moving. We plodded onward. It was five in the morning when we finally reached the harbour of Palmeira - exactly the hour at which Jim's flight was due to leave; in fact, we saw it leave. We had proved our point; given just a little bit more time – and certainly, given the three days which were originally available – we could easily have got Jim to Sal on time. But, looking back on it all, I wonder if he might have received some kind of premonition of disaster.

11

DESERT ISLANDS

In which we continue our tour of the Cape Verde archipelago.

Jill Dickin Schinas

After the rugged grandeur of Santo Antão and São Nicolau, Sal comes as a great disappointment. It is as barren as a building site and it is also virtually flat. Only a few mounds relieve the monotony of the rubble-strewn plain, and even these bear an unfortunate resemblance to industrial slag heaps. But if it was not the most wonderfully scenic place to be holed up for weeks while we sorted out our problems, Sal at least had one advantage over the other islands: it had the best connections with the outside world. In this time of crisis, with the need for wood and resin and fibreglass - and perhaps even for a new mast - this was of the utmost importance.

The first job was to get the pole down, and this was done the very next morning with the aid of the small hydraulic derrick on a resident dive boat. In fact, *Polar's* derrick was so small that it could not lift the mast at all - although this did not become plain until Nick had already undone all of the rigging screws. Then we found that the crane was already at its maximum reach. The only thing to do was to bang on the heel of the mast with a sledgehammer, and so tilt the load.

To our great relief we found that the mast itself was undamaged, but there was still plenty of work to be done to the deck. Until we got down to business it appeared that the accident had been caused by the failure of a bolt which passed through the mast, securing all four lower shrouds; the starboard lowers and their tang were the item which had fallen to the deck with a crash. However, when Nick began to measure things up and make the repairs it soon became apparent that there was a more fundamental and serious cause to our grief. The chap who built the boat, some 25 years earlier, had managed to put the compression strut an inch off to port. Meanwhile, the tabernacle had been placed an inch off to starboard. An inch here or there may not sound like much to get upset about, but in fact a two inch discrepancy is something quite considerable when you are dealing with a compression strut only four inches wide and a mast which weighs perhaps three-hundred-weight but which is only six inches wide. The centre of the mast had been perched on the very edge of the strut which bore its weight.

For 25 years, throughout storms and steep seas, the bulkhead below the mast's after-edge had borne the greater part of the burden, and when the crunch came it was the bulkhead which saved the day and the mast - and our bacon. If the precarious set-up had failed during the storm off Casablanca, or while we were thrashing along on our way to the Azores, then *Maamari* would probably not have reached port.

While we busied ourselves with the task of putting right the wrongs inherent in the yacht's construction, one question was uppermost in our minds: how would this business affect our plans of reaching Patagonia in time for Christmas? February was the month which seemed to us to be the most favourable for venturing south to Cape Horn - February is the August of the southern high latitudes - and we had set our hearts on being down there *next* February.

What could be the problem with that, you may ask? Surely it could not take us 9 months to make all ship-shape again? Ah, but there was a catch; another little spanner in the works. I had come up with one more little diversion from the true path. Ever since our time in Antigua, the lands whence the West Indians were brought had held for me a great fascination, and the more I read of the culture and beliefs of the people living in this corner of the African continent, the more interested I became. I wanted to see for myself the Asantes, with whom the Antiguans claim kinship, and I wanted to visit the coast where the old sailing ships once anchored and took on board their ill-fated, human cargo.

All the same, with nine months to play with there was surely time to make the necessary repairs and *then* visit Africa? Ah, but, with Caesar and Xoë in our crew, we did not want to visit mainland Africa during the rainy season, when the risk of malaria would be so greatly increased. And the rainy season arrives in West Africa in May. If we rushed through our repairs, then we might just get finished by the middle of March, but this would give us only a few weeks on the Dark Continent. And we reckoned that we needed three months to "do" it properly. Either we had to drop the idea of a West African tour, or detour - a thing which would have disappointed me greatly - or else...

"Or else we'll just have to hang out here for a few months," Nick said, calmly. "No point in rushing, anyway. That's not what this life is all about. That's what we came to sea to get away from; one of the things, anyway..." and so he rambled on.

To shelve, for *another* year, our dreams of getting to Patagonia - that was frustrating. However, as it turned out, this largely-self-imposed delay was of considerable benefit to us: by the time we left the islands the children were that little bit older and could amuse themselves while we sailed. And, as it turned out, our confinement in Cape Verde was actually the silver lining to the cloud of our misfortune.

So, then - to the work in hand! The decision made, we knuckled down to the business of making *Maamari* ship-shape. Not content with merely mending the damage, we resolved to make everything in the area of the mast very much stronger. We would double up the deck beams and replace the old, plywood compression-strut box with some hefty, four inch by two inch timbers. We also decided that rather than just patch up the damaged area of deck we would saw out the section all around. Our plan was to replace this with a broad plank of ironwood, which would help to spread the load - but where could we get hold of ironwood, or any other kind of hardwood, in a country where trees are a novelty? Even to get straight and true chunks of pine for the compression-strut was proving difficult, and as for marine plywood and marine adhesive, they were unheard of. The local folk were building boats out of packing crates and using white-glue and nails in the making.

To get hold of enough fibreglass and resin for the deck repair we went begging around the lobster boats and amongst the folk who hired out windsurfers on Sal's sandy southern shore. Everybody was tremendously helpful and generous, but resin quickly goes off when kept at tropical temperatures and so each fellow had only enough to cope with the minor emergencies of daily life. We were scrounging sticky plasters from every first-aid kit in town to make one giant bandage for intensive care.

The capital of Sal is a one horse village called Espargos. It did not exist until the 1980s, for up until that time Sal was home only to a few hundred fishermen and a few salt makers, all of whom lived on the coast. By the time of our visit the population had risen to six or seven thousand, and the increase was due entirely to the construction of the international airport. Neither of the principal islands has sufficient flat land to permit the creation of runways half a mile long, but Sal was eminently suitable.

Clearly, the airport was the new town's sole raison d'être – but we were surprised to find that it had also contributed materially to the foundation of Espargos: on the edge of the village there stood a shanty town consisting of brightly painted tin shacks, each of which was made from several avgas drums. The drums had been rolled out to make flat sheets, and then nailed onto a wooden framework.

For us, the chief merit in Espargos was its bank - neither in Santo Antão nor in São Nicolau had we been able to get hold of cash with a credit card - and since fibreglass and such things do not come cheap we were often to be found in the long, snaking queue for the single till. One day, while we were waiting in the queue, the chap next to us said, "Hello" - and this was not the least bit unusual, except that he said it in English.

In the space of a few minutes the gentleman had discovered our purpose in Sal, and without further ado he said, "Come! My car is outside."

He took us to see his father's carpentry shop, hidden away amongst lines of concrete cottages. Then he said, "Leave it to me. I will get your piece of hardwood." He also said that he would find some wood from which Nick could laminate the extra beams.

Weeks passed. Nothing happened. We gave up on Manuel and renewed our own line of enquiry, but with no result. Then, one day, there was Manuel waving to us from the shore. He had got our piece of wood: it had been especially imported, all the way from

Chile! His carpenters had now shaped it, and the beams were ready, too.

We went to fetch the wood. And the bill?

"I will give you that another day."

Days passed. Weeks passed. The invoice never came. We went to see Manuel and he suggested that we all go out for lunch. The waiter never brought the bill, because Manuel had spoken to him, beforehand, in the local Creole.

In short, Manuel never did let us pay him for his time and trouble or even for the net cost of the wood and its shipping. "My friends," he said, "I cannot charge you. You are guests in my country and if you are in need, then it is my duty to help you on your way." The best we could think of to do in return was to give Manuel one of my paintings, as a memento.

All work and no play makes for a dull life, but our time in Sal was enlivened by many adventures. There was always something going on in the port. We got to know the procession of little ships which trot round the islands and soon we thought of them as friends; they developed anthropomorphic qualities. The "toy" tug-boat was a particular favourite, especially with Caesar. One morning it fell to us to arouse the port when we saw that this vessel had broken its mooring and was blowing down onto the rocks.

When the work got on top of us and we felt like a change of scene, then we would head for the old salt pans, hidden inside a crater on the far side of the island. The salt pans were rather special, because they could only be reached through a tunnel in the crater's rim. This was another of Caesar's favourites. The great pan shimmered in the sun, and as he ran about it looked as if he were playing on a snowfield. On his third birthday we picnicked here - by special request. That was the day we got the hire car stuck in the sand... Yes, there was always something happening.

Back in the port there were daily excitements. Printed in my mind, as if it were captured by a camera, is an image of the Tonka-toy road crane tumbling off the quay into the water. It had been trying to lift a motor boat. It fell and landed with its jib across the boat, on the bottom of the harbour. I remember my cry of alarm and my quavering lip as I called to Nick and the children. The driver! Did the driver get out? Yes, there he was swimming away. Our relief turned to rather ghoulish interest and then swiftly changed to annoyance and dismay. It was with this little crane that we had hoped to re-step the main mast. Now, instead, we must go knocking amongst the ferries and cargo boats on the quay.

The crane on the aft deck of the inter-island ferry, *Barlovento*, seemed amply strong for the task of raising our mast and it looked to be quite tall enough. With an army of yotties, recruited from the only other two boats in port, we went alongside - or to be more exact, we were driven there by the wind, so breaking two stanchions. There is a lot to be said for a two man crew, with eyes in the back of their heads, over an uncoordinated rabble who all have their attention on tying one bowline.

With the yacht secured alongside, the monstrous bionic arm leaned over and lifted *Maamari's* mast from the deck. Up, up, and... not up enough. With its arm extended over our yacht, the crane could not lift the mast high enough. It could only lift the mast higher by inclining the jib towards the vertical and, of course, this took the mast-head off to one side, towards the ship.

"Right!" cried Nick, with the ingenuity borne of frequent such adventures; there is no better training ground than the life at sea for lateral thinking and bodge-manship. "Right. Let's have some of your passengers down here on the side deck."

One by one they descended until, with 15 or 20 people lining *Maamari's* port deck, she was heeled to precisely the right angle. "Stay there," Nick commanded them, with a melange of Portuguese and gesture, and while they stayed he rammed the mast-foot into the tabernacle and we hurried around fastening the bottle-screws. There were a couple of extra bottlescrews nowadays - we had fitted a pair of stays between the upper and lower spreaders - and just to be even further on the safe side there was also a set of runners.

We had planned to do all kinds of other things to the boat while we were in Sal, but now that *Maamari* was seaworthy again we were in a hurry to move on. The bathroom, still unfinished, could wait until another day. We could paint the new beams and our new, super-strong mast-strut while we sailed. And one day we really would get round to replacing the "temporary" fresh water foot pump with a new pressure-switch and motor.

Near enough to Sal to be often visible from the southern shore is its partner and neighbour, the island of Boa Vista. For a long time the delicate image on the skyline had beckoned and now, at last, we could spread our sails again and continue our explorations.

Boa Vista is all about sand. It marches across the island in drifts, and lies, glacier-like, on the mountain slopes. Pristine white beaches encircle the austere, grey-brown rock of the interior and where the rock gives way, in its place there are wind-carved dunes.

At Sal Rei, the capital of Boa Vista, we discovered a sleepy village with one general store selling everything from tins of tuna to toilet bowls. There was also a small market selling over-priced (and over-aged) vegetables which had been shipped in from the other islands. These were pretty much the only commercial ventures, and yet a spacious plaza and a handful of ruined mansions hinted at a more noble and successful past. The name itself betrays the story of Sal Rei's one-time importance: the island was the "Salt King".

As we have seen, salt was once an item of tremendous value. Much of the lower coastline around Boa Vista was divided into saltpans, and a fort was built to guard the vital industry against attacks by pirates and by foreign powers. Now, almost every trace of this historic past has disappeared. The pans lie buried beneath a thick blanket of white sand - that same sand which looks so pretty on the beaches. The sand is said to have come on the ocean currents all the way from the Sahara.

In the winter the entire Cape Verde archipelago suffers from "bruma-seca", or dry fog - a fine, brown dust which cuts the visibility to less than two miles, and which dirties everything it touches. Throughout our stay in the Cape Verdes the windward edge of our rigging was permanently coated in a thick layer of the brown muck. Tedious as it is, the bruma-seca dumped here by the African winds presents no real problems nowadays. It used to cause shipwrecks - one of the last British full-rigged sailing ships was lost on Boa Vista, in 1929 - but modern ships have radar enabling them to see through the murk, and engines to help them escape from deadly lee shores.

The bruma-seca has never been a problem for the locals. The white sand is another matter. Like an invading plague it creeps over Boa Vista, devouring farmland and engulfing whole villages. At one time the town of Sal Rei had to be dug out on a daily basis! One suspects that the sand, more than anything else, is responsible for the fact that, although it is one of the bigger islands, Boa Vista's population at the time of our visit (1994) numbered only 3,000.

Most of these people lived in the town and made their living on the sea, either by fishing or by diving for lobsters.

Even without the additional problem of the sand, existence was never an easy matter for the farmers who inhabit Boa Vista's oppressively spartan interior. In Cape Verde there is nowhere any living off the fat of the land - the land is skin and bone, if it is not just bare bone - but the Bubistan lifestyle seemed to us to be especially severe. For their water these people had to walk to a well which might be more than a mile away, and all the long morning we would see the women and their daughters going back and forth bearing great jars or jerrycans on their heads, in true African style. Next they went to scavenge for wood, perhaps with a scrawny donkey to help them carry the load. Wood is even scarcer, in the Cape Verdes, than water. The main source is the acacia trees, grown expressly for the purpose.

The men fetched wood too, and we saw them get fodder for their pigs from the same scruffy little trees. They would also go down to their dry, naked fields in the parched ribeira (or dry river valley) and try to keep alive a few stalks of maize or some beans. Further up the ribeira, and creeping nearer with every winter's wind, was the deadly glacier of sand which would someday come trampling over all.

The Bubistan were never remotely aggressive or even unfriendly towards us, and they were certainly not the sort who would steal from a visitor, but they were notably less welcoming, less out-going, and less joyful than their fellows on the other isles — possibly because their lives were almost too hard to bear.

With a draught of almost six feet, *Maamari* could get nowhere near the town of Sal Rei. Instead we headed south, around the off-lying island of the same name, and sailed into a vast, blue-green bay, its shore one unbroken arc of untrodden sand. Behind the beach were dunes so big that we at first mistook them for cliffs. The biggest and best were as much as 60 feet high, with faces almost too sheer to climb. The children - and, more especially, their mother and father - had a marvellous time blundering down in a kind of avalanche of sand. In fact, to be truthful, the dunes were so steep and tall that the children preferred to keep their distance while their parents frolicked. My only previous experience of dunes had been in a conservation area, with the words, 'Keep Off', writ large, and so I grabbed the chance to run amuck. There was nobody to chide me. In fact, there was nobody at all for miles.

There cannot be very many places in the world where one can have six and a half miles of fabulous ivory-coloured sand, acres of dunes, and a turquoise bay - not to mention, also, an uninhabited offshore island - solely and exclusively to oneself; yet for weeks on end this fabulous bay was ours alone. There were no other yotties, and the Bubistans took this paradise utterly for granted - or perhaps they were too busy elsewhere, eking out their meagre livings. Our few visitors were curious fishermen, in lateen-rigged craft, who sometimes brought us lobsters or grog. Only the green turtles, arriving en masse to lay their eggs, showed any interest at all in the beach.

We wondered how it could be that Boa Vista had been entirely overlooked by the tourism industry. Surely, here was a pearl lying waiting to be picked up! The simple answer is that the socialist government had been wary of allowing foreign investment in the islands. With the coming of the new, pro-European, pro-Capitalist government this all changed. 14 years later, when we revisited our island paradise, we found that it had been "discovered". The town had been spruced up and hotels were sprouting up on the pristine beach. Within twenty years Boa Vista will look like Gran Canaria.

And will the people rejoice? Seemingly not. There can be absolutely no doubt that they are now better off, both financially and from the point of view of their health; they now eat a Western diet, with sufficient protein (and too much sugar), and they now wear nice clean T-shirts. Their fishing boats are now propelled not by lateen sails but by outboard motors. They no longer need to scrape a living from the land; they can earn one catering to the whims or needs of their guests. Nevertheless, a great many of the people are not thrilled with the developments taking place in their country – they are experiencing all the usual social problems associated with the arrival, amongst them, of hordes of "rich and indolent" people (tourists), and hordes of "heathen" immigrants (West African labourers). Ultimately the proof is in the voting, and in their last general election the people chose to return the old socialist government – albeit with a very narrow margin.

Ever since we arrived in Cape Verde it had been blowing hard. It blew less hard as winter moved towards summer, but still it was windy by most people's standards and the faithful Aerogen, spinning round at the top of the mast, pumped out so much power that we could just about turn our fridge into a freezer. Some days we had to unplug the device for fear that it would otherwise boil the batteries. So it went on, all throughout March, April and May - and then, one morning, we woke up to find that the wind had gone.

The bay - our vast bay – had often been so rough that we could not get ashore. In the first two months of the year it is sometimes so rough that one cannot even enter. Yet this morning the bay was a great, shiny mirror. The rocks which wait in its mouth to catch the unwary were today not betrayed by even a ripple. A Portuguese man of war floated by with an escort of stripey fish; dolphins slashed a path with their fins, heaved themselves up, and then sank back down into their perfect reflections and into the deep.

We had been warned about this. We had been told that when the wind failed there would be no more until November. It was not true, as it turned out, but in the intervening months the winds were fickle and generally light, and as often as not they came from the south. True to sod's law of the sea, they came from the south while we were heading south to Ilha Maio.

Sunshine and a glassy sea; a herd of pilot whales moving with the casual gait of cattle; a tropic whale surging by with single-minded purpose - these are the mementoes of that lazy beat against the light breeze. We were carried southwards chiefly through the effort of the current.

The word was, Maio is as dull as Sal - and it certainly looks to be even duller. I never got the chance to say for sure; swells rolling in onto the little quay from the south made it quite impossible to think of landing with the children, and so only Nick got ashore.

Next stop, Praia, on Ilha Santiago. This was a place which we knew from our previous visit. It was rather busier now than before; indeed, it had become quite the little city. Traffic hurtled around at high speed on the loop road which runs across the top of the old, fortified plateau and circles down onto the plain behind it - but it was only a self-generating hyperactivity. The same could be said for the entire Western system, I suppose. Here it was, laid out in a kind of miniature parody.

Praia is the capital of Santiago island and the national capital of the Republic of Cape Verde, but it has not always held this position. The first founders of the colony settled some miles further to the west, in the mouth of a dry ribeira. This was the place which they considered to be "the least unpromising", to quote contemporary records. Here they built fine houses, a church, a cathedral, and a great, inaccessible hill top fort.

Perhaps the settlers should have built the fort lower down, on the little headland which overlooks the ribeira. At any rate, it proved inadequate in defending the fledgling city from Sir Francis Drake, and after the place had been sacked by pirates for a second time the capital was moved down the road. As a port, too, Cidade Velha - or the "Old Town" - is lacking in one important amenity. The snug little cove is guarded by a chain of off-lying rocks, but it is *so* snug and *so* small that there was not even space for *Maamari*. We were obliged to anchor outside, in the open sea.

Like the beaches of La Palma, the sands at Cidade Velha are of volcanic origin, but in this instance they are dark brown, rather than black, and they not only look filthy, they *are* filthy. Lean and lithe, the local children romped in the sand, their dark skins - in various shades from a Piz Buin tan through to plain chocolate - all to some degree camouflaging the grime with which they were plastered. By contrast, our two little rascals wore a pattern of muddy blotches. Their T-shirts were soon indelibly marked.

As ever, our arrival in this village had caused quite a stir. By now one might have supposed that Caesar would have grown accustomed to the throng which always assembled on the beach to greet us, but although he was very happy to play with the local children on a one to one basis, to be surrounded by a score of half-naked boys jabbering excitedly in a foreign tongue was quite an ordeal. On this occasion the welcoming committee reassembled to give us a good send off. Like pall bearers, eight or ten of them carried the dinghy on their shoulders to the surf. Half a dozen more hung onto its sides while we embarked through the waves, and these had to be sweetly but forcibly removed. Then there was the problem of turning the oars while the kids swarmed around us like fish in a feeding frenzy. Again, gentle force was the only way. Still grinning broadly, the boys fell back to join their fellows, and the whole shoal, totalling about forty kids, pursued us half way back to *Maamari*.

Fogo is next after Santiago in the Cape Verde island chain. Fogo is completely round - a cone rising from the sea - so that the swell gets right around it and even sails into the little port which lies close to the town of São Felipe. There being no possibility of anchoring outside in the open sea, we tucked *Maamari* in behind the port's stubby wall. Having dropped the hook we then also ran out a very long stern line to the shore. This was necessary in order to keep the boat out of the way of the little cargo ships or the ferries, any of which might turn up at any moment.

The top of the cone, and the island's summit, is Fogo's principle attraction, and it was this that we were bent on seeing. However, on the morning after our arrival we awoke to find the cargo ship, *Arquipelago,* anchored just astern of us. While we were still at breakfast she began to unload a Transit van, using her derrick - and, realising that there was some good entertainment in the offing, we decided that the cone could wait.

The first motorcar reached Cape Verde not so very long after their invention, but although its arrival caused a stir it was not an event with great repercussions. It is only very recently that the mini-bus has taken over from the donkey as the chief form of transport in the islands.

Of course, the first car was one of those wonderful old things with running-boards. It had been ordered by a rich land owner in Santo Antão, and it had to be craned from the ship to a lighter, and then lifted from the lighter onto a tiny quay. Why anyone should have gone to all this effort and expense is beyond me; there was nowhere to drive the thing, anyway! In those days there was no road over the island of Santo Antão.

Times have changed. In Cape Verde, as throughout the world, cars are characterless tin cans. However, some things remain the same. Anchored in the tiny port of São Felipe, we watched as the Transit van was hoisted from the coaster *Arquipelago.* For a few seconds the van hung precariously in the air over the small, shabby ship, and then it was lowered, none too gently but without mishap, onto a raft.

The raft was made of oil drums, lashed together in two layers, and with the vehicle aboard it adopted a rakish tilt. Next the stevedores paddled, indian style, with their oars and - surely but slowly – they ferried their cargo towards the quay. Getting the van up onto the quay was even more of a game, with the swells rolling in. The quayside crane had to make a grab for its would-be cargo at precisely the right moment. Then it was back out to the coaster for another, and another... six Transit vans all told. And none of the vehicles was lost or even damaged.

However, with that load both literally and metaphorically lifted, the driver of the ship's derrick let down his hair. Baskets of bananas and bunches of reinforcing rod went twirling through the air with complete abandon. One load of timber was handled with such murderous ineptitude that a boatful of dockers had to jump out of the way, and out of their lighter, into the sea. At one stage, the derrick somehow got free and turned a wild pirouette, while all aboard the ship went running for cover. And I think I can leave it to the reader to imagine what happened to the cargo of glass panes. Glass is quite rare in Cape Verde, and we now saw why.

Fogo, "The Fire", used to be called São Felipe until its settlers learnt that they were sitting on a live volcano. 9,000 feet above the sea, peeping out over a collar of cloud, the great caldera at the summit of the cone is cold now, but its floor is carpeted in cinders. The mountain had blown its top back in 1976, sending out great showers of rock and lava fountains. Lava gushed down the slopes to the sea and the knobbly, black, petrified rivers whose trail tell the story run perilously close to the town of São Felipe. Fortunately, the prevailing winds carried the smoke and gas and falling ash in a different direction, out over the empty sea.

The journey by bush-taxi up Fogo's slope was expensive and slow. 9,000 feet is a quite a distance when the road has to wriggle its way to and fro, tacking up the steep slope. Until the arrival of the taxi the people who lived in the villages scattered on the mountainside must have been very isolated; trotting down to the seaside for the day might be a possibility, but trotting back up again before nightfall would not. Even now, the cost of the journey must ensure that they seldom visit the folks living below.

As we climbed higher the sky got greyer, until eventually we were ascending through a cloud. Then, after a time, we emerged from the cloud – but we were still far from our destination. The rock strewn slope continued on up - and so we continued too.

Finally, after a couple of hours, we arrived at the top, and through a breach in the most splendid, sheer walls - walls almost

1,500 feet high - we entered into the crater. Inside this place there was no wind; a curious calm and silence hung in the air. There was no view either; the mountain, the sea, the clouds, and all the world outside had disappeared from our sight. We had entered into an impossibly vast courtyard, lying within massive castle walls; a giant's lair, high up above the clouds, which ought surely to have been accessible only via a magic beanstalk.

Shielded from the eyes of the world below, but dominating the plain like some kind of fantastic ziggurat, was a gigantic, black cone. It glistened in the sunlight. It was said to be 800 feet high, but its slopes were forever trickling down onto the floor below. Ancient man would almost certainly have made it into a sacred shrine.

Remarkable as the cone was, for us the most astonishing thing about the crater was the villages which had arisen, phoenix like, from the black cinders. And to see apple trees, orange trees, guavas, and beans sprouting from a soil whose resemblance was to road chippings - this was quite extraordinary. In this strange secret world, up above the clouds, we saw vineyards basking in the sun.

Some children, more ragged even than the usual examples, emerged shyly from their houses and then came forward as a little gang. For 50 escudos they offered us a black stone, bubbly as the froth on a chocolate mousse, but with one flat and shiny face.
"It comes from the top of the cone."
I handed over some loose change - about 20 escudos - whereupon the kids stooped down and produced a couple more pieces from the ground.
"20 escudos, 20 escudos," they chirruped.

As usual, Caesar and Xoë were the centre of attention. Someone produced an extremely fat baby, as Cape Verdian babies typically are, being exclusively breastfed. This one was at the crawling stage but weighed quite a bit more than Xoë - which did not stop our infant from claiming the other baby as her very own. She cried when I would not let her bring it home.

I took Caesar aside to give him his first geology lesson, telling him how the mountain had come into being. He listened, and then his lip quavered: "I want to go back to *Maamari*."
"Why ever...?"
"I'm afraid." He was afraid that the volcano might go bang again at any minute.

Mother and father laughed. "Don't worry," we said. "It won't go up today."

And, of course, it didn't.

It went up a couple of months later, and the black cone and the villages in the caldera were all wiped out.

Ten miles away, on the island of Brava, the people ought to have had some premonition of what was about to befall their neighbour. The fishermen living in Furna - a pocket-sized, sunken and flooded crater - told us that the ground kept shaking under their feet. But it was apparently nothing to worry about: "We all know that our volcano is extinct."

Three quarters of the population of Brava live in Boston, New England, which is just as well since, were they all to come home at once it would be standing room only on the little islet. Brava is slightly taller than Snowdon - something which we ought to have borne in mind when we set out to climb it - but in its longest axis the island measures little more than five miles. With the desert dust-bowl of Furna on its eastern shore and a verdant valley running with water on its west, the island surely possesses the maximum diversity in the minimum of space.

It was in Furna that we met Olaf, a young man of 23 years. He knew everyone on Brava. He knew the names and credentials of each man and woman in the village-sized capital of Nova-Sintra, which sits in the cloud on top of the mountain. He knew all the fishermen in the village of Furna - although now that he was training to be a school teacher he thought himself somewhat better than they.

Olaf walked with us up the twisting, turning, cobbled road to the mountain top. We marvelled, first at the view, and then at the baobab trees in the mist swirling across the summit. There were hedges of hibiscus, and rubber plants 60 feet high lined the main street. But there were no shops, and the town consisted of a post office, a bank, and a bar, all seemingly built since independence. Set amongst the three facilities was a plaza boasting formal gardens, and at the centre of these flower beds a bunch of ornate pipes, ensnared in cobwebs, sprouted from an encircling, parched pond. These fountains are a feature of every capital town in the Cape Verdes. Perhaps they reflect some ambition of the independence government: "We will bring you water in the desert."

Olaf was flattered by the praise which we heaped on his native isle - we had seen them all now, and this one was the prettiest of the lot - but the young fellow did not share our delight. Flowers and trees were all very well, but the people needed jobs.

"The new government is a liar. They promised us jobs. We need factories everywhere - they should build factories in Furna and in Nova-Sintra. We need factories where thousands of people can have jobs."

There were no beggars in the island of Brava and we saw no one with a lean and hungry look. The peasant farmers ate well enough on fruit and beans and vegetables. The peasant fishermen ate fish and lobster and imported rice. Certainly, so far as we could see, there was little trade between the two communities; there appeared to be no surplus to trade. It was true, therefore, that all was not perfect in Brava. The material needs and wants which could not be met by the work of the Bravense inhabitants themselves were being met by their relations in the States; indeed, contributions from ex-patriot relatives were said, at the time, to provide one third of the nation's overall 'product'. Still, it was clear that factories were not the answer.

We tried to explain the facts of real life to our young friend. "The trouble is, Olaf, you don't have any raw materials here in Brava - nor in any of the other islands for that matter."

"Well then, the government must import the raw materials!"

Would the Cape Verdian people want to labour for such a pittance that foreign capitalists will find it worth importing the raw means, so as to then export the finished goods from factories in these islands? I do not believe that they would. Goods imported to the island are very expensive, and in order to be able to afford the things they want - the CD players and pressure cookers and trendy clothes - the people would need to be earning good money.

And then one must consider the change which factory employment would inevitably bring to Cape Verdian society. Factories for a thousand slave workers in cloud-topped Brava! But we could not persuade Olaf of our viewpoint. As the saying goes, you don't know what you've got until you've lost it.

We had heard much of the Cape Verdian émigrés, forced to leave a drought-stricken land or else die of famine. Nowadays, with the promise of perpetual foreign food-aid, there are no such fears - yet still the young people leave their native land. Today's exiles go because their education has taught them to despise the adverse struggle of their father's lifestyle and to seek after a higher standard of living.

Before we met Olaf, I used to think it was a shame that the young people left their country. Now I thought the matter through again and decided that it was better, if they hankered for the American dream, that they went chasing it far, far away from this precious refuge. It would surely be better for the state of the world if all those people who desire running water, television, cars, washing machines, and fast food cafes went to live in the places where they already to be found, rather than introducing them to the few untarnished corners which remain.

Of course, what Olaf had overlooked was the Cape Verde islands' potential as a tourist destination. It is not factories but tourism which will bring wealth to the nation and drag it up, out of the era of subsistence farming with African hoes; out of the era of fishing with one line from a boat little bigger than a yacht's tender; out of the era of crushing sugar canes for grog with a donkey-driven mill.

"Tourism will provide jobs and money for the people, and in ten years time none of these antique things will be seen here anymore," we said. "They will be history."

"It cannot happen to soon," said he.

Now our tour of the Cape Verde archipelago was complete. We had now seen each jewel in the necklace - Santo Antão as different from Boa Vista as emeralds are from agate; Brava a little diamond; Sal, a pebble amongst bijouterie... We had even visited the uninhabited islands and islets. Now we knew that each one had something to offer. We knew them well enough to know that we had just scraped the surface.

But the seasons were processing around the sun, chasing time ever onward, and soon we must move on too. The doldrums were still hovering round about, but their lord, the sun, had gone south again - already he had reached the equator - and soon the retinue of thunder clouds and squalls would follow after him. Then, the rainy season on the continent would be over, and we could begin our journey to Ghana.

Up until this time most of the Cape Verde islands had lain

untouched by even a drop of rain, while on the horizon - right there, beside the parched wastelands - the callous seasonal squalls poured their precious life into the ocean.

Santiago was the only island which had seen any rain. It had been blessed by a day-long down-pour. One would have expected the people to greet this little deluge with peals of pious praise and dancing in the street, but in fact it had only produced grumbles. "Not enough," said the peasant farmers. And it was *not* enough. How could a few hours of rain be anything like enough to quench the thirsty ground and refresh muddy water holes? It was not enough by any means - but at least it was something. Would the other isles be passed over, as often in other years they have been passed over, sometimes for ten years and more at a stretch?

When we got back to São Vicente, the Monte Verde was still brown - but that was nothing to be wondered at; it was impossible to conceive of that mountain behind the town ever being any other colour. That name was surely given in jest.

Then, for three days, the "green mountain" was buried in cloud. Meanwhile, another huge cloud enveloped the whole of Santo Antão. After three days, the clouds both lifted... and, lo! The orange-brown rock of Monte Verde was covered in a delicate green veil! Meanwhile, there were green shoots sprouting in the dust of those seemingly abandoned farmsteads atop Santo Antão, and on the far side of the island the secret world was running with streams and waterfalls.

Ah, but the *crime* of it all! You would imagine that in a place like this, where rain is so very obviously the fountain of life, the people would have found ways and means of trapping and collecting every last drop, so that none of it should go to waste. The post-independence government did build a few dams and reservoirs – but they did not build enough, and the people themselves seem to lack the initiative to do anything of this sort. As a result, countless hundreds of thousands of gallons of precious water now spilled off the old mountain, carrying away with them the still more valuable soil. We visited Santo Antão just after the rain, and while we stood by the gushing streams and bemoaned the terrible waste of water, the locals played in it without regret!

Our eyes were now fastened on the continent, for we planned to spend Christmas in Dakar, but Christmas was weeks away – and, besides that, before we could leave Cape Verde we had a new problem to resolve. A few weeks back, whilst we were taking some fishermen for a little jolly, the old Swan mainsail had split in two. The cloth was as rotten as the proverbial pear.

The thought of trying to get a new sail made and flown out to this remote spot was really rather daunting, but there was nothing else for it. We scoured the world, from the cut-price lofts of China to the big names of the British cruising scene. We even followed up a couple of Portuguese leads. But in the end the best price and the quote for the quickest turnaround came from Arun Sails, sailmakers from our own stomping ground, back home. Within ten days our new mainsail was threaded onto the boom - and within a couple of weeks in the ambient atmosphere it was looking quite part of the scene.

There was no longer any reason for us to be kicking about Cape Verde and we planned to leave... soon. We worked our way westward again, but lazily. The more we saw of the islands, the more we realised that we had seen very little. We promised ourselves just one more visit to this place or that.

For Xoë's second birthday we decided to go back to Boa Vista and to the off-lying island of Sal Rei. With its toy-town fort and with the light-house keeper's long-abandoned, coral-brick cottage for a "wendy-house", this place was a playground paradise for the children. On the day in question Caesar woke with the sun and went bouncing over the family bed, with the result that, very soon, the rest of us were dragged from the land of slumber. "It's Xoë's birthday," he cried, with as much jubilation as if it had been his own.

"Is it my birthday cake?" asked Xoë. Neither of them liked cake, but they had quickly latched onto its ritual significance. The greetings cards, too, were greatly cherished. Presents were a lesser issue.

Caesar helped Xoë to tear off the paper from her presents. One was a large box. Xoë peered inside and saw a baby. Her eyes lit up. "I want to hug it!" she cried. Desperately she scrabbled at the lid. "My baby," she said proudly, when it was safely in her chubby arms. This one is mine and nobody can take him away.

I had been expecting a girl and had dresses lined up but, no, apparently it was a boy. He was called Eddie, for the last flesh and blood specimen that Xoë had encountered. She undressed him, dressed him, and undressed him. She gave him bread and carried him everywhere, by the head, in a passionate embrace. She lifted her shirt and fed him, and then she put him to bed. Then she got him up again. "Needs more milk."

None of the other presents got a look in, but eventually Xoë noticed that Caesar was having fun with a jigsaw. "I'm going to play now," she said, "and my baby doesn't want to." With that, she hurled Eddie affectionately to the ground.

Well, we did not reach Dakar in time for Christmas. We spent it with some villagers in São Nicolau. In a stone hut with an earthen floor we dined upon goat and spaghetti and cachupa - the local staple dish, of boiled maize. Then there was a further delay while we waited for the sugar harvest to begin, for we wanted see, again, the cattle-driven mills crushing canes to make molasses and grog. Then there were friends whom we must visit once more, and bid adieu... The longer the traveller stays in one place, the harder it is for him to move on.

The 300 mile trip from Sal to Dakar was the worst we have ever made, not on account of the weather but because we were all ill. After so long in port, or island hopping, it was only to be expected that Caesar and I would suffer, but when Xoë was also sick we knew that something was amiss. She had never previously been upset by the motion of the boat. The following day Nick joined us in the sickbay - with vomiting, diarrhoea and a high temperature - and we realised that some kind of food poisoning was to blame for our misery. Nick could not remember being sick since a time, in India, when he had had dysentery. Certainly, he had never once been laid low in all the time that we had been together.

We struggled by. Nick's main need was for sleep and mine only to be prone. Caesar, who was the illest of us all, could care little about anything but Xoë soon recovered sufficiently to become very demanding, and to the need to look after the ship were added her requirements. By the time we reached Dakar the whole crew were on their feet again, but nobody was ever more pleased to be able to drop anchor.

The Muslim festival of Ramadan had begun the day before we arrived and as the sun set, and a pale pink haze washed over the sky, from across the calm water there came the sound of Arabic chanting mingled with the hee-haw horns of passing trains. Somehow, the two together reminded me of wolves howling at dusk as a train passed through a snowy valley - a memory from Canada, of all places! Cape Verde, too, was far away; another world, another life. Already we were being absorbed into the exciting world of the Afro-Muslim city.

12

CROOKS AND CROCKS

(Senegal, The Gambia and Guinea Bissau)

J·H·Dickin Schinas

Our chief recollections of Dakar were of the club which denied us any water for our tanks and of my grandmother's silverware. To this day it remains, I suppose, in a little pile amongst the weed on the seabed. On our last visit I had carelessly tipped it over the side with the washing-up water and had baulked at the thought of poking about in the long waving grass below. Who knew what lived there? I recalled reading that this kind of vegetation is the favourite haunt of deadly sea snakes. Now, on our return, I remembered the pile of cutlery. The stench of seaweed rotting on the beach and the sight of sewage trickling down through the mire wiped away any fresh ideas of diving for the treasure.

We went ashore the morning after our arrival, on the day known in Muslim circles as the 3rd of Ramadan. We walked the length of a rickety jetty which carried us over the rotting weed and onto the soft, dry sand beyond. Above the beach towered tall cypress trees in whose branches the wind whistled softly. Xoë looked up at the dark, dancing fronds. "What are those?" she asked.

She was not looking for the botanical classification. The only trees of her acquaintance were shrubby acacias bent over before the perpetual gale.

In the streets beyond the beach, more surprises awaited the children. They stood and watched the traffic hurtling by on the road; the horses trotting briskly ahead of two-wheeled carts; the same old, battered, blue and yellow buses that Nick and I had seen four years earlier, still racing by in convoys. And then there were the people; the men in their turbans, the women in gaudy silk gowns embroidered with golden thread.

In Cape Verde a man or woman thought herself well-dressed if she wore a clean T-shirt. T-shirts, in one state of cleanliness or another, were also our daily garb. Not to be out done, or to encourage the youth of Dakar to believe that we found Western fashion superior and more desirable, we decided to go to town and find something more suitable.

"Salaam alaikum." Our greeting was awkward and clumsy.

"Malaikum salaam." The response flowed as one mumbled word from the tailor's tongue.

El Hadj Amadou Ndoye worked elbow to elbow with others in a cupboard-sized workshop at the side of the main street. Examples of his handiwork hung around him on the walls. The tailor pulled us within his lair, to shake off the pickpockets - pickpockets so gauche that even we had identified them. Like a pack of hyenas waiting for the opportune moment to attack, these young men now paced about in the road outside.

"A robe for Madame and the little girl. A chemise and pantalons for Monsieur and his son." The sheik measured us, and then sent us around the corner to choose and buy the cloth.

Young men with hour-glass-shaped, talking drums were quite literally drumming-up trade in the haberdashery stores by the Marcheé Sandaga. The traffic hurried by on the busy street. The crowd hurried by on the pavement. The drummer tapped out a hurried rhythm. In the store, the Libyan proprietor hurriedly cut three yards of blue silk and two of green, for the "toubabs" - the whites. Everything in Dakar is done in a hurry, but often with great panache.

We gave the tailor the cloth and came back the next day to collect the finished garments. Nick tucked his away in a locker, but the rest of us wore ours regularly and to great effect. People were invariably pleased to see that we were trying to look like them. They took it as a compliment. Our appearance was often greeted with applause, which is the local gesture of approval. However, some months later we saw ourselves wearing our Afro-Muslim apparel in the pages of the Daily Express, in a picture entitled, "The family relax aboard their yacht." Of that more mention will be made...

We also acquired one other souvenir while we were in Dakar. A proper tourist item, this one - it was a carved wooden statuette which actually came originally from Cote d'Ivoire and which was supposed to represent a female ancestor. On the whole we doubted whether the sales pitch which the man gave us contained the least shred of truth, but we liked the little figure and we wanted it for a purpose. The deck-head aboard *Maamari* was supported, in the region of the companion way, by two posts. One of these led directly from the cabin floor; the other stood on top of the fridge. This second post was a hideous thing which appeared to have come from a balustrade and I had always said that I would like to replace it. The Cote d'Ivorean statue was exactly the right height to fill the gap, and so we bought her and carried her aboard. She needed a name, and so we called her Nan, which means Mother in one of the several Cote d'Ivorean languages. Nan looked rather severe and cross, but she did her job well and was soon an established member of the crew.

Should we go to The Gambia? - this was now the question. The Gambia is a river - nothing more - and it intrudes into the state of Senegal like a dagger. Presumably the British, when they held the place, saw it as nothing more than a trading station for slaves and other commodities; they left it to the French to claim and conquer the vast interior all around.

We were keen to take a look at the curious enclave and compare the two countries - but there was a catch. Just a couple of months earlier the long-time president of The Gambia, Jawara, had fled before a little gang of junior army officers; the usual story. Now the coup had turned bloody, with the new man bumping-off the leaders of an opposing army faction as they lay in their suburban beds. Shots rang out in the street where the hotels also stood. The tourists fled to the airport and got out.

As a result of the outrage Britain had imposed some kind of sanctions and The Gambia was out of the Commonwealth on its ear, or so it was said. The impression that Europe sought to give to would-be visitors to the little republic was that the new, illegally established government would retaliate against all this by victimising expatriates and tourists. But the word on the bush telegraph was that The Gambia was down on its knees and begging the tourists to return. After all, a great many of the country's leading lights are deeply, financially involved in the business. We decided to follow the local advice.

The passage from Dakar to The Gambia takes about 24 hours, the winds being very feeble on this stretch of coast. Remembering our previous night-time experience in these waters we decided to break the journey in two and, accordingly, we spent a few days on the river Saloum. Even so – even with the benefit of this stepping stone - by the time we reached the channel which leads towards the entrance to the river Gambia it was dark, and we had trouble finding the buoys which mark the way. At 22.00 hours we finally anchored off Half-die point, where, many years before, half the population of the British town of Bathurst had died of yellow fever.

Yes, here we were, in the white man's grave where "there's one comes out, for forty goes in." We had not seen any mosquitoes, but since the first evening of our arrival off Dakar it had become a ritual to put in the screens before dusk. In the matter of malaria, prevention is decidedly better than the cure, but since the prophylactics themselves are known to be dangerous we were not using them. Thus it was absolutely essential that the children should not receive even one bite.

Bathurst, bastion of the British Empire, has been renamed Banjul since independence. Now, as then, it is an insalubrious dump. The old town of sad, grey buildings is sited on an island surrounded by swamps, so that the suburbs have had to grow up elsewhere. Pursuing the advice given to us years before by another yachtsman, we followed a silver thread of water spun through the mangrove swamp and soon came to the low road bridge which unites Banjul with the mainland. On either side of the road, close by the bridge, soldiers dressed in combat clothes were squatting beside automatic rifles.

"It wasn't meant to be," explained an English expatriate, speaking of the coup. "The lads had a complaint to make about their pay, but Jawara saw them coming and feared the worst; so he fled. He took himself off to a U.S. warship which just *happened* to be here. The lads found the front door open and the throne empty, so they helped themselves."

Our new friend was Steve Jones, The Gambia's lone resident yachtsman and the author of a local cruising guide which, at that time, was still a work in progress. He worked for a medical laboratory and was more concerned about malaria and other exotic ills than he was about any interference from any government. It transpired that the new president had once worked at the lab, too, as a trainee technician. "Not a particularly bright fellow," said Steve. So far as he was concerned, the yanks had stage managed the whole show, encouraging the old uncooperative president to believe his life to be in danger and replacing him with a more malleable substitute.

The traveller must weigh for himself the words of advice to be got from the grapevine. Some stories need to be taken with a whole handful of salt, but some do not arouse such scepticism. Our visit to The Gambia had been made in defiance of official British government recommendations; we did not believe that any danger existed here - and we were right. On the other hand, the news that the infamous terrorists of the Casamance Separatist Movement were still on the rampage did cause us considerable concern, the more so when we heard that they had set up camp in Guinea Bissau, which was now our destination.

With evident contempt for the sovereignty of the neighbouring republic, Senegal had retaliated against the guerrillas by air bombing the Guinean village of Cabo Rosa, where they were thought to reside. Two weeks later, heading from The Gambia to the Rio Cacheu, we found ourselves becalmed just off this very place. For once we did not feel the least inclined to answer curiosity and go ashore to explore. We did not even use the cabin lights that evening, still les an anchor light; we just dropped the hook quietly and went to bed, and in the morning we got underway again as soon as the wind allowed.

Of all the places that we had visited on our travels so far, Guinea Bissau was the one which interested us most. We felt that our brief foray into the islands had not done them justice and we also wanted to explore a little of the mainland, by way of the country's rivers.

Like the Rio Geba, just to the south, the entrance to the Rio Cacheu is a nightmare to behold on the chart. When you get there you start to feel that the nightmare is coming true. There are no buoys and there seems to be no very obvious and uncluttered path through the shoals which surround the entrance to the main channel. The channel itself is marked only by the shoals on either side. According to our ancient Admiralty pilot, published in 1968, this main channel has "not been used since 1873." Presumably such traffic as there is takes the southerly channel, by which we were later to depart.

Having considered the chaos of the channel entrance, as displayed on the chart, we noticed that it would be possible to take a short cut from our anchorage off Cabo Rosa. Accordingly, we headed off along the coast, inside the rocks and sand-bars, with the intention of popping into the cannel at the last minute through a breach in the shoals which lined its either side. However, once we were embarked it became plain that the course for the pass put the wind dead on the stern. Just for a change it was blowing about force five so that this produced an unpleasant motion, with *Maamari* rolling her gunwhales under and with the sails pumping away, filling and backing, and the booms straining at their preventers and torturing the rig. Abandoning the plan, we brought the bow up and made for the tangled mess at the channel's proper entrance. Did we but know it, the angels were directing our path.

As we moved out from it the coast disappeared into the haze, and we thanked heaven for the invention of the echo-sounder. With the aid of this electronic eye we groped from one charted shoal to another. In the days before it was surveyed and charted, this river-mouth must have claimed a fair few ships and lives. I would not mind betting that the last ship to use the channel, in 1873, was one which came to grief on the sandbanks.

After we came into the channel things became very much easier, for since it was low water the reefs were a seething mass of white foam, marking the way as clearly as lamp posts along the edge of a motorway. I quaked at the sight of them. We reached the break in the shoal, exactly where we had planned to pass, and - heavens above! - we were shocked to find it occupied by the aluminium mast of a sunken yacht! The yacht had obviously struck the reef and bounced off into deeper water, where it sank. If we had continued in our intention and come that way, I doubt whether we would have had the courage to pass the wreck close by - and we would have had to almost touch it to negotiate the pass.

That sight - of one of our own kind wrecked - is amongst the most disturbing and ominous that the yachtsman might behold. The image haunted us over the weeks to come and returned to trouble me whenever we closed a rocky or reef strewn coast. There, but for the grace of God...

That night and the next we spent anchored off a village not dissimilar to the ones we had seen before in the Bijagos islands - a village of mud-built houses and half-naked men and women. Guinea Bissau is chiefly a nation of heathen peoples - by which I mean no insult, but only that they are neither Muslims nor Christians. Instead, the various tribes follow their own ancestral religions. At this village, on the banks of the Cacheu, the shrines to long-dead fathers, or spirits, or gods were numerous. With only signs and gestures for a language, we were unable to learn much about them.

It would have contented us to go crawling up the creeks and rivers of Guinea Bissau without ever getting involved with any aspect of the metropolis - but, as ever, we had to go and clear in. Could we do the necessary in Cacheu, a few miles up the river? Steve Jones, guru of sailing on the Senegambian-Guinean coast, had assured us that it was perfectly possible, and so we pressed on.

Cacheu is decidedly not a metropolis. Perhaps it once was, when the peanut barges called, or when it was the terminal for the ferry across the river. Then, it stood on the main drag from Senegal through to Bissau. Now, the ferry and the highway have gone north and Cacheu finds itself a ghost town in a forgotten back-water. The hotels and guest houses which once served the traveller are empty and overgrown with weeds. The ostentatiously broad high street is crumbling away. Close by the shore we found some big, modern buildings of the office type, but they too were empty and echoing. All that remained of the settlement was a quiet village of typical mud-built houses hidden in the shade of the trees. In a tiny toy-town Portuguese fort overlooking the river we discovered a bizarre collection of gargantuan bronze statues which lay propped on their sides, gesticulating at one another.

At low water, getting from a boat to the riverbank in Cacheu is a rather muddy experience. Having managed it, we went straight to the police station to commence our dutiful tour of homage and supplication.

The village policeman greeted us warmly. He seemed pleased to have something to do. Unfortunately, since overseas arrivals are a rarity he had mislaid the stamp; it must be at his house. We were told to leave the passports with him and call back in half an hour.

One does not like to part with one's passport, but there seemed little alternative - and, besides that, there seemed to be nothing to fear. In Cape Verde the authorities like to try to hang onto the visitor's passport for the duration of his stay. What was half an hour compared with that?

We wandered back down the empty high-street to the river and stood looking at the boats. Besides our own vessel there were a handful of dug-out canoes and two other 'ocean-going' craft. One of these was a small fishing boat which had sunk beside the little town quay. Whether because this was a Muslim village or through an innate West African attitude, no one seemed inclined to attempt its recovery. Perhaps they all felt that these things happen according to the will of Allah. Or perhaps they had not heard of road cranes, or lift bags; perhaps neither of these things existed in Guinea Bissau.

The only other sea-going boat was a pirogue which had come down from Senegal with a cargo of plain, white cloth. We met the customs officer, who was counting the bales into a truck. No, he did not need to visit *Maamari*. He smiled and shook our hands warmly. He offered to change our Senegalese francs into pesos and gave us a rate which, as it turned out, was better than the banks in the capital town. Then came a messenger. He told us that our passports were now ready. The port captain had them and he was awaiting us in his office.

The port captain met us in a dingy little reception area with a grimey floor and grimey walls, but he took us behind the reception desk and away from other ears, into a back room. We smelt a rat.

The man sat himself down but left us standing. He had not smiled yet. He showed us a book full of lists of charges which seemed to relate to commercial traffic. He totted up some figures on a piece of paper and then calmly said, "The total is $130 (U.S.)."

This was where we made our mistake. We hit the roof. We should have played it cool and smiled. Better still, we might have apologised - never mind for what. Finally, we marched out without having paid - but without our passports, of course. We had threatened to contact the British Consul in Bissau, but we already knew, from our previous acquaintance of this person, that he was not likely to do anything to aid a tourist. We considered faking an American accent and contacting the U.S. Ambassador. He was said to be much more worthwhile.

That afternoon the port captain took Nick aside and reduced his demand to $60 (U.S.). Nick was for paying, but I was outraged. Before, we had wondered if the charges might actually be legal, but now it was evident that this was just the usual bid at blackmail. A principle was at stake - and besides that, we had to think of others who might come behind. We would not part with one penny.

Still later that same day we met a young man called Sanboudjan who, when we told him of our woes, cried out in dismay. The port captain was his uncle, he said. Belying the theory that blood is so thick as to forbid any other alliance, Sanboudjan vowed to see the matter resolved in our favour. What is more, he acted purely out of the desire for righteousness - good Muslim that he was - and he did not ask for any remuneration, in kind or in cash, for acting as our agent.

It took four days, but in the end Sanboudjan was successful. We had to apologise to the port captain and shake his hand respectfully - as did everyone in the village, in acknowledgement of his power and wealth - and we had to generally make believe that we thought this corrupt crook a jolly decent chap, but in return for this humiliating charade our passports were returned and we were able to proceed on our way. Sanboudjan, who is a baker, benefited from our gratitude by the donation of a very large sack of flour.

Free to move on, we left the river Cacheu and set course for the most northerly out-lying Bijagos island. Besides sharks (of the aquatic kind) and besides many crocodiles, there are also supposed to be a handful of hippos in the Bijagos, and this is one of the places where they are said to live.

We found our way through the reef which guards the northern end of the island and then we set about choosing a place to drop the hook. Since the waves were breaking over the reef there was no very good site; the whole area was beset by metre high swells. To compensate, we laid out some extra scope (extra chain) and an extra long snubbing line. Then we fitted our mosquito screens and settled down to eat supper.

Half way through the meal there was a loud crash and the whole boat juddered.

"What the devil...? Nick, we've been hit!"

"'Can't have been," he replied nonchalantly, still chewing on his grub. "It was just the chain snatching. I'll have to give her a longer snubbing line."

Two minutes later there was another crash.

"Nick, I can't believe that that's just the anchor chain snatching! It feels like..."

"It's the anchor chain. Stop fussing. I'll go and sort it out in a minute."

I took the kids into the aft cabin, and while I was getting them ready for bed there came another loud crash - and this time I felt the hull beneath my feet receive the blow.

"Nick!" I shot through the cabin and out into the cockpit. "Nick! We've hit a rock! We *have*!"

"I know. 'Saw the echo sounder." He was already rushing for'ard. "Start the engine, while I weigh anchor."

The next few minutes were very tense ones. The night was as black as pitch, but as soon as the anchor was clear of the ground I motored away from the unlit lee shore and towards the unlit reef, only stopping when I felt that we must be well clear of that underwater obstruction. While we worked, we both imagined that the boat must be sinking under our feet. Surely you cannot slam a fibre glass shell down onto a reef without it breaking?

As soon as the boat was safely anchored again we both jumped below into the cabin and started tearing up the floorboards – but there was no hole; there was no water in the bilge. And when I dived on the boat, some months later, when we were back in the clear waters of the Atlantic, I found that there was not a mark to tell of this adventure; I could not even detect which part of the boat had been hammering the rock.

On the following morning, rowing ashore to the beach at low water, we passed by the rock. It is not on the chart, but it is there alright; large, black, and unbelievably knobbly. Seeing it gave me the shudders, and the inauspicious portrait of that aluminium mast protruding from the water hovered before my eyes. In this place, where mire hid the secrets of the seabed, we really must be more cautious.

Having searched unsuccessfully for hippos, we wandered inland to take a peek at the local village, Anipoco. This time there were no adolescent boys to plague us, and nor were there any men in residence. Presumably, they were all working in their paddy fields or harvesting the oil palm nuts. We spent a happy afternoon in the company of the women-folk, many of whom were very fat, and all of whom were very jolly. Theirs seems to be a strictly ordered and very sexist society, but nevertheless, one which is quite egalitarian. The women build the houses, making the mud bricks and putting them together, assembling the roofing struts without any help from their menfolk, and laying on the grass thatch. Indeed, the men are not even allowed to cut the grass for the thatch; for a man to have anything to do with this job is totally taboo. The women, meanwhile, may not enter the rice fields and they may not climb the palm trees. The village is the women's domain; the men are responsible for providing food.

When a girl reaches adolescence she is scarified, a strange pattern of cross-stitches being carved into her belly. The men, on the other hand, are not circumcised and prepared for marriage until they are in their twenties. (We have yet to encounter a Bijagos male between the ages of 15 and 30. Either they live an entirely separate existence – a thing which is by no means unknown in West African societies - or else they spend their whole day in the fields and in the trees.)

When a girl is ready to marry, her suitors woo her with rice. He who has the most rice wins – although, one suspects that physique and character also play their part. If what we were told is true, the couple move into their own abode, and the chosen male has one year in which to get his girl pregnant. If he fails, she gets to keep the rice, and he moves back to his mother's place. The girl then chooses a new husband!

With no common language we had difficulty communicating with the Bijagos women – there were all sorts of questions that I wanted to ask: I wanted to know all about the tatty statuette which stood outside a shrine at the entrance to the village; I wanted to know whether these people carved wooden masks; I wanted to know about their beliefs and rituals – but these subtleties were well beyond the scope of sign language. Eventually we managed to make the women understand that we would like to buy some rice. Actually, we had no need of any rice, but we wanted to establish a proper trading relationship – we did not want to hand out charitable offerings, because charitable offerings are almost always a negative contribution to a stable society – and we assumed that since rice was the staple it must be readily available.

The mud-built village was liberally sprinkled with little phone-box-sized granaries, but the idea of selling even a couple of pounds of rice was met by a firm "No" and lots of head shaking. We might as well have walked into an English village and suggested to the people that since they had plenty of money they might like to swap it for butter beans. In the end we traded Nick's T-shirt for two grass skirts. It was clear that the women reckoned that they had done very well out of us; they couldn't see why anybody who owned a pair of shorts would ever want a grass skirt.

Leaving Anipoco, and its reclusive hippos we moved over to the mainland side of the Geba channel and anchored for the night off a large island barely separated from the coast. The next morning we awoke to the sound of drumming and curiosity led us to investigate. Walking through the forest we came upon several mud-built homesteads which were completely different from anything we had seen elsewhere; the buildings formed an irregular, lopsided circle around a large courtyard. There was no space between them – they formed a continuous wall in which there were no doors nor even any windows - and the only access to any of them was via a mud-built archway in one corner of the compound. This set-up could only be interpreted as defensive - and as we drew nearer to the place whence the drumming issued, I began to worry that these people might be hostile. We had been rather hoping that the drumming might be associated with some sort of festival, but it now occurred to me that it might be associated with a secret rite. What might be the consequence if we were to suddenly blunder into a sacred, magic ceremony?

Since nobody had so far discovered our presence on the island I plucked up the courage to peep into one of the compounds. I had hoped that no one would notice me, but within the courtyard a group of women and girls was at work. Fortunately, they greeted the sudden intrusion of a timid white face with laughter and smiles, and we were beckoned within. Although they were surprised to see us the people were not utterly astounded, and they did not mob us as the Bijagos islanders tended to do. Using sign language, we asked them about the drumming and we learnt that somebody had died. Not wishing to intrude upon anyone's grief, we returned to the boat.

We went on up the river estuary to the town of Bissau, which was rumoured to be really jumping now. It was not; indeed, it had gone still further to seed since our last visit. The supermarket had shut down, together with several of the hotels and the bar which was once the centre of the social scene. The taxis were still driving around with no windscreens and their doors tied on with string. The beer factory had shut down, having run out of bottles. The post office had run out of stamps. There were piles of garbage standing waist high at the side of the main street.

The infrastructure of the Western lifestyle was collapsing - we reckoned that if we came back in ten years time we would find Bissau a ghost town - but life was flowing along, undaunted. The people had never abandoned the old ways, and nature would soon swarm over this ridiculous aberration and reclaim the land.

Although all else may have been lacking or unserviceable, the miracle of satellite communications had arrived in Guinea Bissau. On our previous visit one had needed to book an international phone call eight days in advance - not something which people like Nick and me can really cope with - but now, by means of a fax, and at considerable expense, we were able to get word of our whereabouts to the folks back home. In return came the news that Nick's brother, Johnnie, was on his way out to meet us.

A hail from the adjacent shore disturbed our breakfast preparations. Through the glasses we could see that the figure waving was a white man.

"Good Lord! He's grown a pony tail."

Gone was the style-conscious youth whom we had left behind. Nick's baby brother had turned into a worldly-wise backpacker. His presence, and his rucksack, filled the cabin. Xoë hid under the table but Caesar sized up the new arrival and, having formed a somewhat optimistic impression, went to fetch a few favourite books. For the next half hour Uncle Johnnie listened to "Postman Pat on Ice" and "Pig Gets Stuck", before thirst overcame him and we all went ashore for a pint.

Johnnie came for "a couple of weeks" and ended up staying for six months, during which time he received a crash course - or baptism by fire - in the matter of living in a confined space with two typically excitable and rowdy under-fives. We like to think that it set him up for his future role, as the father of two even more rowdy youngsters.

With our crew now augmented by another ableseaman, we set off to explore a little more of the Rio Geba and her tributaries. First we traversed the river, following after the ferries which we had observed criss-crossing it every day. These ferries are nothing more than large dug-out canoes and their chief propulsion comes from the tide, but they also carry sack-cloth sails raised on poles. We had watched the ferrymen strike their sails as their unseaworthy craft heeled to a sudden squall. They were always very over-laden and we wondered how often one of them sinks on the ten mile crossing. Our old, rotten mainsail was still aboard, taking up space, and so we gave it to the master of the shabbiest ferry. He was thrilled to bits – but thereafter the other ferrymen all hated us. As I have said before, charity is rarely a positive thing.

Making our way carefully downstream, through the shoals, we next visited the old, mouldering capital of Bolama. Bolama was once claimed by the British as their own capital - of Sierra Leone! In the abandoned town, trees forced the roofs from typically splendid, colonial piles, and the crumbling walls, and ornamented facades, and balcony balustrades were overcome by black mould.

The high branches of the mango trees were hung not only with fruit but with hundreds of shrieking fruit-bats. Men sat beneath them, on the ground, weaving long narrow strips of cloth on the usual West African loom. In their hands, the shuttle carrying the weft flew to and fro. The far end of the warp was fastened to a convenient tree and they raised and lowered the threads, to create the pattern, by moving pedals with their feet.

Behind Ilha Bolama, the Rio Buba winds its way into the land. We followed its course, riding upstream on the tide and anchoring when it turned to ebb. Bottle-nosed dolphins cruised about near the boat, doubtless feeding with the aid of their sonar, for nothing could be seen by eye in the murky river. Humpback dolphins showed us the ill-shaped hunch which has earned them their name. We had hoped to catch a glimpse of a manatee or a hippo, but the creatures were elusive. Johnnie saw a big shark leap into the air - an odd sight at anytime, and all the more strange on a narrow river.

Someone once said that it is better to journey than to arrive, and on the whole, I agree. Nowhere was this better illustrated than on our happy dawdle up the Rio Buba. We had read that there was a container port, newly built, at the head of the river, but this idea - always ludicrous - began to seem increasingly unlikely. Outside of Bissau, we had never met any other vessels on the Rio Geba, and certainly no ship could have navigated the Buba. As we approached the head of the river we became quite excited about what we might find. A silly foreign aid development, perhaps - or another stone-age village?

As it turned out, although it was high water there was not sufficient depth for *Maamari* to reach the head of the creek. We anchored and got into the dinghy. Of course, there was no port, and soon our disappointment was complete: there was a village, but roads linked it to the 20th century. The people wore T-shirts and travelled by bus, and their mud houses had tin roofs exactly like the ones in Bissau. We trudged back down the river, and made our way out to the Bijagos islands.

The chief excitement in the Bijagos is in finding one's way amongst the islands, for the tide makes a fine art of navigation here. It does not always flow in the direction in which one expects it to flow.

We would have liked to visit the outer islands, beyond whose western edge the sea is uncharted. Along the seaward extreme of the bare, white patch on our chart were written the words, "Within these limits patches of rocks, shoals and rollers render all approach dangerous." We felt that we stood a good chance, here, of meeting people who may not have seen white men - or at any rate, not for some years - but it seemed from the chart that we might have difficulty in getting close enough to the islands to get ashore.

We visited some of the more accessible islands and discovered that the villages here were all much of a muchness. The people all wanted our T-shirts. In one we found a mud hut of the usual sort, topped with solar panels and a TV aerial! We could not imagine who could possibly live there – and we could not believe that images of coca-cola, American cops, and Western life as a whole would have anything but a very negative effect on a stone age people. For the Bijagos islanders, TV would be a Pandora's box, stuffing them full of insatiable desires.

"The echo-sounder has stopped working." Johnnie pronounced the words with absolute nonchalance, as if it were of no concern at all. Just the day before, and in spite of the fact that the gadget had still been tapping-out the numbers, we had run the boat aground whilst tacking down a narrow channel. In penance we had spent the night at a ridiculous angle on a mud bank. So, how - without the aid even of the magic eye - were we supposed to find the unmarked channel which led through another expanse of obfuscated ooze, just ahead of us? And why should this have happened just here and now, as it had happened, just so, on our last visit? Do the Bijagos have a jinx over depth-sounders, or is this merely the appropriate reward for one who detests the marvels of modern technology?

Fractured by estuaries which, in the long course of time, have nibbled paths right through it, the one island of Orango is now a compact archipelago consisting of Ilhas Meneque, Orangosinho, Canogo and Imbone. Low as the other Bijagos, they sat on the horizon, so near and yet so far away. Between the islands and ourselves lay that broad belt of hidden shoals.

There was nothing for it but to adopt the method of the ancients. We anchored *Maamari*. Taking up the lead-line, a bamboo sounding rod, and a compass we embarked into the rubber dinghy. And soon we had given up lamenting the untimely demise of our late, electronic friend and had discovered a pleasure in the art of swinging the lead and lustily singing out the depths. We were dare-devil, swaggering, jolly jack-tars, months from the sanctuary of European ports, searching out the way towards some (unspecified) shore, hitherto unseen by white men. Columbus, Captain Cook... Livingstone? In the wake of men such as these we sailed. Having plotted the channel we returned to the mothership, created a chart, and sailed in with a great feeling of satisfaction.

Safe within the Orangosinho canal, we dropped the hook beside the mangrove thickets which lined the shores. In a rare fit of energetic enthusiasm we launched the number three dinghy. Number one was the rubber dinghy. Number two was *Dumpling*, the beautiful little, wooden sailing dinghy which my brother and I used to fight in and over when I was a mere eight years old. Third in the pecking order was a newcomer, an inflatable, Tinker Traveller sailing dinghy given to us while we were in England. Although that was getting on for two years ago it had never yet been commissioned.

The project took a little longer than we could have wished, but that was largely because the spars, as we now discovered, came from a completely different species. Still, the thing went, even in the lightest breath of wind, which was the only one available. Caesar and Xoë took it in turns to steer an erratic course, before the sun set and we all returned to take refuge behind the mosquito screens.

The Tinker came into its own a few days later. Whereas *Dumpling* could only accommodate two or, at best, three of us - and then only in a very cramped fashion - the inflatable sailing dinghy was sufficiently big and stable that the whole crew could pile in. Leaving *Maamari* anchored in the deep water at the mouth of a creek, we set off on a journey of exploration through uncharted waters, still hoping to encounter the elusive hippos.

For what seemed like mile upon mile we drifted along, following twists and turns as devious as the tubing in a euphonium. From the flimsy top-most branches of the encroaching mangrove, a sacred-ibis with a hefty, black, sickle-shaped beak watched our passing with wary suspicion. Herons were perched in a like manner, seeming as idiotically out of place and scale as would an elephant balanced on a wire. The liquid warbling of the curlew was almost constant in the still air as, in ones or twos, the birds flew by. Black and white kingfishers dived from the tree tops and darted away upstream. Tiny, turquoise-blue kingfishers kept their distance, moving in little spurts - an iridescent blur above the river - from one low branch to another, up the convoluted creek. Palm-nut vultures, plovers, ducks, and many more that I could not name - they were all here and appeared to consider our intrusion to be an outrageous wonder.

Nor were the birds alone. Creeping through the twined and tortured branches of the mangrove was a pack of monkeys who eyed us with nothing less than astonishment. To be sure they may occasionally have seen men before, but this was quite possibly their first sight of five fair-haired specimens floating along beneath a pair of yellow and white striped sails.

"Was that a fish?" Nick peered down into the turbid water below the Tinker's stern.

Johnnie had seen it too. "It was big."

It was gone now.

"Maybe it was a hippo," suggested Caesar.

The monkeys were still moving quietly through the trees. If they had been men they would have carried spears, or bows and arrows. They had a human attitude, of curiosity mingled with alarm. One could hear them murmuring to each other and believe that one understood their words and thoughts:

"What do they want?"

"Hush!"

"Why have they come here?"

"Do you think they've seen us?"

Something floating close to the boat caught my attention. A gnarled snout. A pair of yellow eyes met mine and the green head sank instantly and with scarcely a ripple. "Crocodile!"

"Where?"

"It's gone."

"Are you sure?"

"Yes, of course I'm sure. It was there, less than an oar's length away. God, you should have seen the look in its eyes? Not curiosity, more like..." I shuddered.

"How big was it?" the others wanted to know. "As big as the dinghy?"

"Bigger, I should think, but it's gone."

Heaven knows what would have happened if we had actually come across the hippos. I have since heard that they can be quite irritable. In fact, I have seen a film of hippos attacking and sinking a hard dinghy. Little did we realise how vulnerable we were, in our pneumatic raft.

Beneath an empty blue sky a confectionery-pink cloud arose and twisted, as if at the whim of a puff of wind. Hundreds, perhaps thousands - the flamingos were so many in number that we could not even begin to count them. Broad wings, the colour of tinned salmon; armpits of coral red. And what tremendous strength these awkward birds must have, to be able to hold their heads out before them and keep their legs trailing high as they fly.

We had returned to the mothership and to the main Orangosinho channel. Towards the southern end of this great creek the scouring tides have left great sheets of mud and sand on whose empty acres the flamingos flock at low water. Besides these tidal mud-flats, the river has also given birth to a couple of islets, one of which is sufficiently large to have been colonised by man. Yet this was something different from the rest. The houses which we saw clumped together beneath the inevitable oil-palm trees were not of the type usual to the Bijagos.

We worked our way as close as we could to the island and then dropped anchor. We were about a quarter of a mile distant from the village and from the white beach where we planned to make our landing. This anchorage seemed to be safe, but after our recent experience with the rock we were taking no chances and Nick launched the Tinker again, with the idea of sounding around the yacht.

"I want to come."

"Me! Me! Me, too!"

As ever, Caesar and Xoë clamoured to be allowed to join the expedition. Johnnie volunteered to go along too, provided that he was entrusted with the task of swinging the lead and not lumbered, as he saw it, with the chore of rowing. Meanwhile, I went below to get on with the usual household duties.

Nick cast-off from *Maamari* and the Tinker was at once caught on the tide and carried down, away from the yacht and away from the island. The captain dug in the oars. Not without a degree of foresight had Johnnie declined this recreation! The Tinker Traveller is a heavy boat and our champion oarsman was hard put even to regain the lost ground. He decided to launch the Avon instead.

As soon as it was within reach, Johnnie snatched hold of the railing at *Maamari's* stern and looped the dinghy painter around a cleat. Nick clambered out and went to launch the Avon which was still lying, half inflated, atop the hard dinghy. Safely tethered now, the

Tinker fell astern but was quickly brought up short and sharp.

"I want to get out," said Xoë. Johnnie and Caesar sat quietly and patiently while the skipper puffed air into the valves of the Avon. An assortment of pumps had long since rusted or otherwise fallen apart, but Nick missed them little. With a dozen lungfuls of air he filled the flaccid tank and gave it form.

"I want to get out." Xoë began to scramble along the orange canvas of the Tinker's foredeck. With his head buried in the other dinghy, Nick was oblivious to her progress. A few more puffs and the boat would be rigid.

"Xoë!" As soon as I heard Nick's scream I knew what had happened. Incredible though it may seem, I felt no sense of urgency. I assumed that Xoë had slipped from the dinghy, as indeed she had, and I supposed that her father would have grabbed her in the next instant even as he screamed. After all, it was not the first time that one of the children had tumbled out of the dinghy. I hurried on deck, ready to give motherly reassurance to the wet waif.

I arrived to find that Xoë, far from being safe and sound, was at least a boat's length astern of *Maamari*. In the second that it took to stride from the companion way to the rail I took in the whole scene. I saw Nick on the point of jumping, or perhaps of climbing back into the Tinker. In his panic he seemed unsure which course of action to follow. I had taught Nick to swim, but we both knew that he lacked stamina; in our practice sessions his efforts to rescue me had resembled attempted murder. As for Johnnie, I afterwards learnt that he cannot swim a stroke.

"I'll go." Still I was all calmness and control. Xoë was a coral-pink T-shirt floating away. Her belly scarcely broke the surface. Her back was arched and her head hung down. Without a pause in my passage I stepped over the rail and into the air and was swimming hard and fast. No problem; I could catch her easily. In my mind there was no thought of crocodiles and sharks, but instead I recalled that this was just how Caesar had floated when he once slipped out of the dinghy. Little children float with the buoyancy bag of their belly uppermost and the heavy head hanging down.

On that previous occasion I had been able to grab the child in an instant. How long had Xoë been under the water? How many seconds had passed? Now I was with her. The arms and legs were waving about. I felt no fear; she was alive, I could see it.

My arm was around her, her head broke the surface, cheeks and eyes both bulging fit to burst. She saw me. She took an almighty gasp and then she gave just one little whimper.

"It's okay, Xoë, I've got you now."

She was in a state of shock.

I turned onto my back and held Xoë as high out of the water as I could. A job well done; it was easy. I struck out for the mother-ship, kicking hard with my heels - thrust, thrust, thrust... There, we should be just about home. 'Don't want to slam my head into the transom. I turned, expecting to find myself only a few feet from *Maamari*, but discovered instead that we were as much as 50 yards away.

The current! In the heat of the moment I had forgotten about the current which, after all, was the cause of our present woe. Were it not for the current, now running at about three or four knots, Xoë would never have been swept away from the dinghy. Johnnie would simply have reached out an arm and pulled her to safety. Like a fool I had spent all my energy with a quick sprint intended to take us home, and now I had none left.

"I can't make up!" I shouted. Why were they all dithering about on the back of the yacht? Were they going to sit there and watch us drown? Had my calm entry to the water and my over-confidence fooled them, too? Alone I could have floated idly, and so recovered my breath, but I had to hold Xoë out of the water. All thought of making up had now vanished from my mind; I struggled even to tread water and keep my head up. Didn't they understand? Couldn't they see? I looked about me. Could I stay afloat and hold Xoë high until the current carried us to that mud flat, a mile downstream?

If only I could catch my breath! We're drowning, you idiots, can't you see? The shock of my predicament sent a rage sweeping through me.

"GET HERE!" The words were yelled with absolute fury. The outburst seemed to give me a new spurt of energy and so I shouted again. "GET HERE, you..." The river washed the last words out of my mouth.

At last the rubber dinghy was upon us. Nick scooped Xoë out of my arms and I hung on, gulping down great lungfuls of air, until I found the strength to haul myself aboard.

There were many lessons to be learnt from this misadventure. Some would say that the most obvious one is that the children should have been wearing lifejackets. They did used to wear lifejackets in the dinghy if there seemed to be any likelihood of an upset, but it would not be possible, nor to my mind desirable, to keep a child permanently imprisoned in great chunks of foam, from the age of crawling until the age when she is swimming proficiently. Certainly it would not have been possible in this situation, with temperatures in the nineties. Heat exhaustion and sores would have been the result.

And why did Nick dally for so long before coming to the rescue? He was reluctant to rescue us with the Tinker because, as he already knew, it would not be possible to make up again. Thus he had to launch the faithful rubber dinghy over the rail and then ship the oars and untie the bowline. He did not recognise that I was in serious difficulty until I hollered. He ought to have lobbed-out at least one of the life-buoys kept for this very purpose. In short, he ought to have treated this incident much as if it were a MOB drill at sea.

After we had all recovered from the excitement of Xoë's unscheduled dip we abandoned our flotilla of dinghies and hitched a ride ashore on a passing pirogue. The presence of such a craft was, in itself, sufficient evidence that the village which sat on the island was not the usual Bijagos community. From the infrequency with which they are to be seen on the water it would appear that the river is, to some extent, taboo to the Bijagos. Besides that, their skill in the field of boat building has not gone beyond hollowing out a log. No, this boat was very obviously from Senegal.

Having landed us on the beach, the captain of the pirogue got down with us from the great prow and took us on a tour of the village – or rather, the encampment, as he called it. Although it appeared to be a fairly temporary thing – the houses being nothing more than tents made of interwoven palm fronds – we learnt that it had been in existence for twenty years. About a year after our visit the place was attacked by the Casamance Separatist bandits and the inhabitants were all robbed and killed... but no hint of this approaching disaster was felt on this tranquil evening.

All was peace amongst the inhabitants of the little island, and this despite the fact that they were of several different nations, speaking various different lingos. Very few of the men were natives of Guinea Bissau. Some hailed from Senegal but most were from Guinea Conakry or Sierra Leone. Some were dressed in T-shirts and jeans; some wore the long Muslim gown. All were fishermen who spent the day on the Rio Geba or in the sea just beyond the Orangosinho Canal. They were happy to catch any kind of fish – whatever they hooked, they would land – but really they had come to the Bijagos to hunt for sharks. Fish would feed them and keep their outboard motors running, but sharks would make them rich. Unfortunately, the only parts of the shark which are edible are the fins – after death, the rest of the flesh quickly becomes polluted with urine – so that this industry entails a terrible wastage.

The shark fins were ferried straightaway to Guinea Conakry, thence to be despatched to China, but the rest of the catch remained with the men. In the afternoon when they returned to the camp their womenfolk were presented with the fish, which they smoked in thatch-built tents or in the open, over smouldering fires.

As for these women, some came with their men from Conakry but most were gathered along the way. Some were Bijagos women, recognisable by the pattern of scars on their stomachs, but we noticed that none of them wore the traditional grass skirt.

"If you take a Bijagos woman she will do whatever you want," remarked a Sierra Leonese fisherman. "They have a rich culture but they have nothing else, and so they feel inferior. They give up their customs very eagerly."

In our travels we had been careful to tread gently, in order not to disrupt the Bijagos culture with charity or to sew the seeds of envy amongst the people by indiscriminate giving. Now we realised that the little influence we might exert, be it good or be it bad, meant simply nothing beside the influence of the fishermen.

In the Bijagos village closest to the fishing encampment, no one smiled. Whereas in other Bijagos villages the women tended to be exuberant, with laughter and chatter filling the air, here they sat listlessly or worked in an apathetic trance, their expressions like those of someone heavily drugged. Their grass skirts were sordid; their children were coated in grime.

The young men of the village wore nice new shorts and new T-shirts, evidently given in payment for chickens and eggs and oil. Still, in the whole of this Bijagos village, the only man with a smile on his face was one who had a transistor radio and the batteries to make it work.

According to the fishermen, who travelled regularly between the Bijagos and Conakry, we could easily get out of the southern end of the Orangosinho channel - but our chart suggested no such likelihood. We explained that whereas their own boats drew as little as 18 inches, beneath ours their hung a lump of lead and steel six foot long. This information usually provokes gasps and incredulity and, at length, the question, "Why?" - but the Conakrense fishermen only said, "No problem."

We embarked along the proposed passage with all the doubts of Thomas, who had to put his hand into the Lord's wounded side to believe, and like Thomas we believed only when we found the hole - a little rift in the sand banks which garland the mouth of the channel. We popped out through the hole, once more into the deep, blue sea.

Ahead lay Conakry, capital of the state of Guinea and a place of which we knew nothing at all. (Why is it, you may ask, that we go blundering into foreign parts without having done our homework? Well, I suppose it is because we like to arrive without any preconceptions and discover places for ourselves.)

We worked our way south and east, once more into charted waters. As ever, the fishing lures were streaming out astern and late in the afternoon we heard the retaining hook on one of the lines spring shut as someone gave a sharp tug on the business end.
"Fish!"
We all sprung into action. Nick had the line in his hand even before the whole coil was paid out, but the sharks were quicker still. Hanging onto the hook we found just half a fish, with its eyes open wide in shock.

The next day, while I was tipping some scraps over the side, I seemed to see the culprit. It was a shark about a yard long which darted out from beneath the boat to gobble down my offering. Johnnie and I at once embarked on an intensive campaign of seduction, using all manner of bait and lures. We quickly discovered that there was not just one shark - there were four lurking in the shade beneath our hull. Each time we tossed out a line they would nip over and have a quick sniff, but none of them was the least deceived. The sharks of our imagining were dumb machines who would go for anything that hit the sea. What made these ones so damnably fussy?

"A spear gun is what we need," said Johnnie, but our spear-gun was hopelessly rusted and the rubber firing mechanism perished.

The wind died altogether, leaving *Maamari* to drift on a glassy plain. Just over the rim of the sea was a green and brown land of savannah and scrub. Houses, lorries, buses, crowds... Somewhere just over the horizon there were fishing boats and birds - but here there was only our lily-pad island, borne on the gentle yet mighty current and attended by her sinister cortege.

"Clip me on." Caesar stood on the top step of the ladder. He knew better than to set foot outside without first ensuring that the umbilical tether of his harness was joined to the mother-ship, but today he seemed unusually keen. Her recent experience notwithstanding, Xoë still regarded her harness with distaste and even as I slipped her arms through the webbing loops she began to whine.

"Come on now, Xoë. You don't want to go swimming again, do you?"

"You mustn't fall in here, Xoë," her brother added. "If you fall in here the sharks will eat you."

Our escort had grown tired of skulking beneath the torpid boat, but rather than abandon her they began to cruise about in circles. They swam close beside the hull, only inches below the still surface of the ocean, and with the advantage of such perfect viewing conditions we were now able to see that theirs was a case of mistaken identity. They were not sharks. They had soft, spined fins and tails. Their mouths were not on the underside but on the front, and whereas the shark breathes through an open grill, our companions had the conventional gill-covering. On making this discovery we gave up trying to tempt the fish onto our table and began to look on them as we looked on the dolphins, as fellow travellers come to honour us with their attendance.

Now, into our world there came a dark mote - a tiny speck on the far away horizon. With the help of the binoculars I could see that it was a pirogue. *Maamari* was two tall, white triangles above two more painted on the sea. They spotted her. The speck became a dot and then a long, grey boat animated with a dozen figures. Soon we could hear the whine of the outboard and our hearts beat a little faster. Alone on the empty ocean a little sailing boat is as vulnerable as a pretty flower begging to be picked. Here we were, two men, one woman, and two babies. Over the sea came twelve strong men who might take a fancy to the treasure trove.

Arms aloft in greeting, the fishermen approached. Smiles flashed from dark faces - but there were some amongst them who only stood dumbly and stared. With a thud the boat came alongside and half a dozen pairs of hands grabbed the guardrails. The usual request for water. The usual questions: where had we come from, and where were we going. The usual absence of any fenders and the thump of their battered hull against ours.

Fishing is like playing ping-pong or eating peanuts. Once the line is in your hand the action becomes compulsive, and even while their boat was at rest one of the men kept tossing out his line. The bait was a whole herring, silver and slippery. It spun around the man's head in a circle and then flew out across the sea.

Thirsts and curiosity both quenched, our visitors let go of *Maamari*. The helmsman tugged at the chord on the motor... and then there was a shout, and his companions gathered around the fisherman. One helped him to haul in the heavy line, and a moment later the big, brown fish was dragged to the surface, and someone leant over to club him. Our fish; our friend. Only a few hours earlier we would have been more than glad to land him ourselves, but now we felt sad to see his end. The fish's family took fright at once and deserted us, never to be seen again.

On April 16th we celebrated Caesar's fourth birthday. It happened to be Easter Sunday, too, but we could pay only lip-service to that festival. Our children had yet to discover chocolate eggs (or any other kind of chocolate, for that matter) and what they did not know they could not miss.

The wind was very light and it was dead on the stern. Egged on by Johnnie - who is really a racing man - we got out the spinnaker, which had only once before seen the light of day. We knew that the land was only just over the horizon and Johnnie evidently felt that we should press on towards it as fast as we could. Unfortunately, by the time everything was ready the wind had gone round, and so the sail collapsed and got torn on the stays'l halyard block.

We ambled onwards and that afternoon we sighted the Îles de Los, and beyond them the tower blocks of Guinea Conakry. With so much to celebrate I delved about in the booze locker. We had run out of beer the day before, but a thorough search turned up a bottle of bubbly left over from Christmas.

Conakry, capital of the Republic of Guinea, is decidedly not top of the list of places to which I long to return. Indeed, it ranks right down at the bottom, next to Cumana (Venezuela), as the one liked least in all our travels.

Believing that we would do well to avoid the big commercial port, we headed for the old harbour where the pirogue fishing boats and ferries come and go. We anchored right outside the tiny shallow bight which is their domain - and a lawless domain it was soon seen to be.

Intuitive doubts and misgivings already suggested that the rest of us should stay aboard while Nick went ashore to investigate and perform the necessary entrance formalities. From the cockpit, Johnnie and I watched with some concern as even before the dinghy touched the shore it was surrounded by a mob. This was no welcoming party. The men literally fought for the privilege of guarding the dinghy, laying about each other with their fists. Two others, purporting to be officials, flashed some kind of identity card at Nick and gave him a Ministry of Transport form to fill out. A fee was named. Nick needed to change some money. Together with the two men, he got into a taxi and was whisked away towards the centre of town.

When they reached the bank, Nick found that there was no need to get out of the car. As soon as it stopped it was surrounded, just as the dinghy had been, and the transaction took place through a half-open window.

Back at the beach, the man who had won the contest for custodianship of the dinghy did not simply hold out his hand but made a demand - for the equivalent of ten pounds! He had been at his task for all of half an hour. Nick offered the equivalent of 50 pence - a day's wage for a docker in these parts and the sum which a São Vicentian "boat boy" expects for safe-guarding the dinghy for a whole day. The crowd growled. Voices were raised in anger. After some heated negotiations the two officials who had adopted Nick persuaded both parties to settle on two pounds. Then they told Nick to get out straight away and take *Maamari* round into the commercial port. Otherwise, come morning time, we would be lucky if we still had the bare hull and our lives.

Besides *Maamari*, there were two other yachts anchored in the commercial port. One belonged to an Australian who owned a gold mine. The other was home to a Belgian who had lived in Conakry for the last ten years and hated the place with all his heart. "What in heaven's name brought you here?"

In ten years the man had seen just two other visiting yachts. The last one had been Spanish, and her crew had been arrested before they even set foot ashore. After they had been missing for a week the expatriate yachtsman had grown worried about their fate and had gone with a friend to investigate the matter. He found that the Spaniards were languishing in prison, although their only crime was in having dared to arrive in the country – not to step ashore, but simply to arrive – without visas. By greasing the appropriate palms the ex-pats were able to secure the yachtsmen's immediate release, "But, of course, by then their boat had been completely gutted."

Our new friend asked whether we had appointed a watchman. We told him that the job had gone to one Ousmane, a young man with the physique of a pitbull terrier and a visage and temperament to match. Ousmane had taken us to meet the military police and there signed a declaration whereby he accepted complete responsibility for protecting our vessel. Naturally, we placed absolutely no value on this document, and when he heard the story the Belgian snorted. His own boat had been broken into four times. On the last occasion the thief had tried to sink it. "Now he is behind bars, at least for a short time."

"Ah! So, they caught him," we noted with surprise.

"*They*! Pah! *I* caught him," the answer came. "It was not hard. I knew him well. He was the one that I had been paying all the while to look after the bloody boat."

No sooner was *Maamari* snugly berthed than we were beleaguered by a whole stream of people waving identity cards and "official" pieces of paper. It was soon obvious that all of these, and besides them the two who had helped Nick on that very first day, were no more than hoaxers. In the immigration office we were told with uncommon openness that there are no charges due to anyone arriving in Guinea

- but still the men who were to stamp our passports wanted $30 (U.S.)

"What for?"

"For us," they replied, in evident surprise. "Ten dollars each. It's not so much." You're white so you must be rich.

They did not get the full $30 but it was evident from the outset that the blue stamp was not going to budge towards our passports until the men got some kind of remuneration.

In Guinea Bissau corruption is a few blemishes on the skin of an apple. It affects very few. But in Guinea Conakry bribery is an everyday watchword, for the fruit is rotten to the core. It is said that the lines drawn on the map of Africa are arbitrary ones, made by Europeans. So they once were - the Mandingo, the Fula, these and other tribes are to be encountered on either side of the boundary bisecting the two Guineas - but although they may be said to be seedlings of the one tree, the two countries have grown up in a different soil and have evolved towards a different temperament - the one branch bearing beautiful blossoms, the other thorns - according to the influence of their socio-political fertiliser.

Guinea Conakry was the one place, in all our travels, where we had to pay a bribe to clear in; the one place where people wanted to charge me for taking photos; the one place where we feared to walk the streets at night. But still Guinea Conakry was not the place where we were mugged or robbed. Despite the dire warnings from our ex-pat friend, we got away unscathed.

13

FISH AND SHIPS - WITH CHICKEN

In which we count our eggs before they are laid.

"Please, Monsieur, we would like to buy some chickens."

In a quiet corner of the Marcheé Niger, in Conakry, ten or a dozen large wire and bamboo coops were perched one on top of the other. In some there were chickens. In one there were several fat guinea fowl. In the smallest and highest, in the darkest recess, was a sad and silent African-grey parrot. In front of the cages sat five elderly gentlemen dressed in long robes. They lounged about on the ground in a loose semicircle, drinking endless cups of strong, sweet tea.

From time to time, throughout our travels in West Africa, we had bought a chicken in the market and taken it home to eat. Now we had a different and much more ambitious scheme in mind. If Captain Cook kept chickens on deck then why shouldn't we? Fresh eggs would be ours every morning throughout the long journey across the Atlantic.

"Please, Monsieur, we want some chickens, and we want the kind of chickens that lay eggs." Nick addressed his polite entreaty to the eldest, the nearest, and the most beautifully attired of the little gathering. With a side-long glance at his fellows, the man got to his feet and smoothed an untidy ripple in the crisp, white satin of his gold-embroidered bou-bou. The loose folds of cloth were hitched onto his shoulders to liberate a skinny arm, and then he opened the trap door in the top of the nearest cage, shoved the arm inside and hauled out a thin, scrawny, white-feathered specimen. We peered at it.

"Alors." Since we did not immediately nod our heads in satisfaction, the man shoved the unfortunate bird headfirst back into the cage and grabbed another. "Bon?"

"Will it lay eggs?"

"Of course it will not. Not unless you have a cock." He opened the door in the roof of a second cage and brought out an example of a cock, wild-eyed with ferocity and fright.

"No, I would rather have two hens," I said. We were not trying to breed chickens; we wanted eggs only.

Monsieur raised his eyebrows and made an aside to his friends, who still sat nearby. The men convulsed into giggles. A crowd began to gather. "To make babies you will need a mummy and a daddy," the merchant said, holding one in either hand, rather as a teacher might when instructing a class of five year-olds. The onlookers sniggered.

"Non," I was becoming a little doubtful now, but I stuck to my guns, "We do not want babies. We want only eggs."

More raised eyebrows, and another much louder aside. The onlookers laughed openly and we found ourselves the fall guys in a comic routine for a growing audience.

"Regard," said Monsieur, revelling in the attention, and he plonked

the cock on top of the hen. Then he pointed at our children and said, in some local lingo, "Where do you think they came from?" Applause, and a roar of approving laughter.

We gave up. We bought the sorry-looking cockerel and five unhappy hens for his harem. Nick came to the conclusion that the merchant must surely know what he was talking about and when the cock expired, only hours after joining the company, I looked forward to my vindication. Sadly, it was not to be.

The day we left Conakry, the rainy season arrived. There was no warning; the sluice gates of heaven were just opened wide and it all poured down upon us. With the rain came an invasion of mosquitoes, the first mosquitoes that we had seen since our arrival in Africa. Trousers and long-sleeved shirts were now the order of the day for Caesar and Xoë. Yes, by this time we should have been on our way across the pond - we were supposed to get out before the arrival of the rainy season and the mozzies - but that was only the plan. Reality is always rather different, for us.

Not a breath of wind stirred the surface of the water, so that we had to motor to get out of the port, but once we were clear of the harbour walls the current intervened, and we were carried slowly but surely southward. Given that, in these parts and in this season, we could expect little or no help from the wind, we now faced quite a slow and lengthy journey around the corner to Côte d'Ivoire. Moreover, we were going to add on a few extra miles because, in view of the civil wars ongoing in both Sierra Leone and Liberia, we wanted to give the whole area a fifty mile offing.

We were still drifting along in the shadow of the city's mouldering, grey, concrete tower blocks when a fishing boat came paddling across the slippery, shiny, grey sea; paddling from the far horizon towards us, and towards Conakry.

"Three days! Ah, mon Dieu!" The fishermen grabbed hold of our gunwale in the accustomed manner and asked, simultaneously, for petrol, water, food, cigarettes, and our new chickens.

"Three days we have been at sea. Three days without food or water," their self-appointed spokesman lied.

The fishing pirogues of this coast often go to sea for three days. Plainly, this lot had run out of petrol, but now the end of their journey was in sight. Another ten or fifteen minutes paddling and they would be amongst their friends and enemies on the beach.

Besides that, we did not have any petrol; *Maamari*'s engine runs on diesel. While I went below to fetch mugs and a jug of water Nick began to explain.

"We do not have petrol. Our boat travels with the wind." Bearing in mind our present situation, this ought to have been utterly plain to see.

"And we cannot give you very much water," Nick continued, intending to explain that, whereas they would be able, very shortly, to bathe and shower with abandon if they so desired, our supply might have to last us a month and so was strictly rationed. Alas, he was not given the chance to get beyond that first, short phrase, for at once the fishermen began to shake their fists and shout abuse. In their excitement they all let go of the yacht at once, and they were then helped on their way by a shove from Nick and Johnnie. We watched uneasily as they fell astern with fists still clenched in threatened rage, and we were glad to see another pirogue take them in tow and lead them home.

"28th April. *This morning Hybrid Broiler died.*"

Thus far our venture into poultry farming had not gone very well. Fearing that an epidemic might be sweeping through the run we gave three of our remaining stock the freedom of the deck and set the fourth aside for supper. But who would despatch her? Accustomed to having our food killed by proxy, we all recoiled squeamishly from the task in hand. "I'll sharpen the knife, if you like," said Nick.

What an absurd place we have reached, in this modern society, where man is content to eat meat factory-farmed in the most obscene style, and yet cannot bring himself to shed a drop of blood by his own hand, for his own supper. I resolved to take the bull by its horns and the bird by her legs. The Muslims spread-eagle the chicken on its back, holding it down with their feet, and then slice off its head. They are not allowed to throttle the animal; their laws insist that the blood must flow. As this was the only kind of killing that I had ever witnessed, it was the only example that I had to follow.

The bird gazed up at me in wide-eyed horror, and for a moment I felt inclined to be merciful. But with one firm stroke of the razor's edge the horrible deed was done. Blood spurted everywhere, and the legs pumped up and down. Evidently the rumour is true: headless chickens can still run.

Caesar skipped about in delight - he would gladly have performed the execution, it seemed. Nick and Johnnie hid in the cabin until the blood was all washed away and the bird as bald and empty as the supermarket specimens. Ironically, Caesar and I are now both vegetarians, whilst Nick and his brother continue in the sinful way.

"29th April. *Spectacular thunder storm last night. In the evening the flashes frightened the children down the stairs, although they were still 20 or 30 miles away.*"

That night, the children and I were awoken rudely when *Maamari* suddenly lurched onto her beam. The sails were flogging and above their noise we could hear heavy rain. A flash illuminated the cabin. The thunder clap followed in the next instant.

I hurried to shut all the windows and the forehatch. Nick and Johnnie were both in the cockpit, soaked to the skin, wearing nothing but T-shirts and their under-pants. There were shouts from one to the other. More flashes. The terrible sound of thunder tearing the sky in two.

I felt the load in the rigging lighten as the genoa was furled, and then, as Nick dropped the main and tamed it, we were upright again. *Maamari* relaxed – but the squall and the storm went on unabated and brilliant flashes burst through the blackness. On the foredeck, the chickens stood around preening their feathers like silly women fussing about their hair-dos while around them the house burns down.

Many times in the past few weeks we had been warned about "tornadoes", as the locals call them. These squalls creep through the bland, grey sky to strike without warning, and since they can blow at 50 knots they are quite capable of felling the mast of a yacht which is dressed to make the most of catspaws.

Soon the wind moved away, but the electrical storm continued all night. *Maamari* was at the centre of a spider's web of jagged, white threads. The night flickered like a dazzling, million volt strobe light, and where the lightning struck, the sea hissed. I swear we heard it hiss!

When the thunder is right overhead it does not just boom and crash, it splits the sky with a sound like a gigantic piece of cloth being ripped. And the noise, and the thunder seemed to be falling directly onto us.

"How can it miss us?" I asked myself "with our enticing, 50 foot, metal pole the only thing so presumptuous as to rise up above the sea."

Nick spent the following afternoon running a heavy-duty, two centimetre diameter, copper welding cable from the heel of the mast down to the engine. The idea was that, if we were struck, the propeller shaft would carry away the current. I was all for the arrangement, but still it seemed utterly pointless. How could this piece of wire be expected to carry the kind of energy that we had seen last night? No, if we did not get hit while we were at the very centre of the most amazing storm I have ever seen in my life, then we were surely immune. Something was obviously shielding us - but whether it was a divine being or a scientific principle, I cannot say.

For days at a time the sun hid himself behind a grey veil and we had to rely on dead reckoning to feel our way south. Nothing that we did was of very much consequence anyway while we sat embedded in the doldrums. When squalls came to harry us, we hitched a ride southward, if we could. Otherwise, the current did all the work.

Besides the thunder and lightning, which were always around, this journey will be remembered for the dolphins who came to visit us each evening and sometimes in the mornings. Most were lithe and lovely spotted-dolphins, which we aboard *Maamari* call badgers. (Their spots are generally obscure, but they have a bright, white nose, and a broad white stripe along their dark faces.) There were also bottle-nosed dolphins, who behaved like others we have seen in the Atlantic, and not like the coastal dwelling members of their species. Whereas the pelagic members of this species like to ride at our bow, the coastal bottle-nosed dolphins pay us no heed. Pelagic bottle-nosed dolphins are patterned differently, too, having a pale, mottled saddle on their backs.

Sometimes at night the perpetual blackness in which we were engulfed would very suddenly be patterned by sparkling, corkscrew trails of phosphorescence, and we would hear excited squeaking.

"Dolphins!" the watch-keeper would cry.

Invisible dolphins! The heart skipped a beat and seemed on the point of bursting for want of a way to express its joy. Invisible dolphins, darting and diving - hither, thither - and all the while trailing trains of ephemeral glitter, like the ones drawn across the night sky by a firework.

One morning Caesar and Xoë parked themselves in the corner of the cockpit, in the shade of the sprayhood, and set about reading one of Caesar's birthday acquisitions - a Ladybird "Read it yourself" edition of *The Pied Piper of Hamelin*. Taking it in turns, they each tackled a page of the book at a time. I sat close by the children, scribbling away in a notebook. Nick was below decks, sleeping. Johnnie emerged from the cabin with a beer in one hand and in the other a length of rubber inner-tube and the somewhat rusty remnant of an ancient spear gun. I raised my eyebrows in enquiry.

"'Have to do something about all these fish," Johnnie explained, with a coy half-smile.

Ever since we got clear of Conakry *Maamari* had been escorted by an assortment of fish, both large and small, none of whom showed any interest whatsoever in our blatantly seductive lures. For two long days we had been tantalised by a great, juicy dorado, fully five feet long, who was often to be seen flashing close by the hull or leaping in an arc across the bow. Our mouths watered every time we glimpsed him, but we could almost hear him laughing at us. Most faithful amongst our followers was a band of fish which, we decided, were called rainbow-runners. They were shaped roughly like tuna and had a long streak of yellow painted the length of their silver flanks.

"A couple of those would do nicely," I suggested.

Johnnie went below again to fetch a whetstone. An age was spent in putting a point on the rust-encrusted spear. As much time again was devoted to rigging up the rubber catapult.

"Are they still there?" he asked, when he was through.

Hours had passed. The kids had finished reading and had gone below to play with their Lego. But the fish were still in attendance.

Johnnie stood by the guardrail on the windward quarter. He pointed his weapon at the water. Ah, but what angel of doom sent the fish swimming there, just below the hunter, at just this very moment? To be sure, this fish is a gift given to us by the sea!

"Twang", went the big rubber band. In the next instant I heard a little splash and, "Got him."

"What!" I dropped my note book and leapt to my feet.

Johnnie smiled triumphantly but seemed almost as astonished as I.

He held out the short, steel spear. Impaled on the end was a "rainbow-runner" two feet long.

"Oh, no!" Johnnie's face clouded over, and he looked a little bit sheepish. "The rubber's gone."

The perished rubber catapult had broken and gone over the side. So began and ended the career of a small time harpooner.

On the 5th May, just after dawn, we passed through another rain squall. Beyond it lay the next, and rather than turn away we thought that we might court it, and so find some useful wind. This, Nick told us, was how the Indonesian dhows cross the balmy South China Sea. Unfortunately, the wind beneath this particular cloud was from the south-east - our intended heading - and it was no mere squall. It blew a good force nine for an hour or two and continued to blow strongly all day and into the night. On the following day we were able to get a sunsight, which put us seventy miles offshore. The wind had fallen light again - force one to two - and there seemed to be very little current out here, away from the coast. There was quite a bit of shipping going to and fro along our route, so that we had to keep a strict and efficient lookout.

It was on this day that we ate the last chicken, the other two having died of the same mysterious disease which smote Hybrid Broiler and the cock.

"7th May. *Still no wind. We sit on an oily, grey sea, with grey skies all around and over our heads.*"

To the north, a continuous series of water-spouts formed and fell apart. The sun peered through his grey veil for just long enough to let us take some more sunsights, and we found that over the past 24 hours we had made good thirty miles. This was progress, indeed. For each of the three previous days we had made good only five miles.

The next morning I was woken in the early hours by the sound of voices raised in excitement. A squall coming, perhaps? Would I be needed on deck? Or could it be... Yes! There was a loud thud and then I smelt the unmistakable ozone scent of a fish freshly landed. In the next instant came the frenzied thudding of his muscular tail and flank on the cockpit floor.

Later that same morning, although we were knee deep in tuna, I could not resist having a go at the "rainbow-runners" which were still following faithfully below the keel. We liked to think of these fish as our larder, and just as long as we left them there they stayed nice and fresh - but I was afraid that they might go off in other ways; they might all be chased away by a shark. A fish in the hand is worth two under the keel.

I chummed the water with scraps of leathery, silver tuna skin. The "rainbow-runners" sniffed them contemptuously, but within seconds we were at the centre of a shoal of grey and white parrot fish whose presence had hitherto gone unperceived. The hand-line was already prepared, with a sliver of skin on each of two small, steel hooks. When I lobbed the gear overboard, the fish pounced like famished piranhas, and two were instantly hooked. "Success!" But it was a short lived moment of glory, because two plump parrot fish were too much for the line - or perhaps just too much for my slow wits - and in the same instant, they and the line were gone.

I went back to the business of harvesting that which we already had. The tuna weighed in at 28lbs, so that after I had set aside some for sushi and put a couple of pounds into a marinade there was still plenty left to salt and dry, and some to stew and bottle.

Caesar had watched with interest while the fish was filleted, and now he wanted one of the big, round eyes.

"Boiled, fried, or raw?" I wondered. I seem to recall reading that a fish's eyeball is a wonderful source of nutrition, but there are probably not many people who could fancy sucking a fish eye the size of a giant gobstopper. Nor was Caesar such a one. He put the item lovingly into a little pail and carried it around with him all day. At one stage the pet eyeball was found to be missing, having somehow absconded from the bucket, and we had to organise a search party. It was eventually found gazing up at us from the carpeted floor of the aft cabin.

"10th May. *I was sitting in the cockpit this morning, reading to Caesar, when I sighted a ship on the horizon abeam. Over the course of the next few minutes it grew closer and it grew bigger. Soon I could see that it was a huge oil tanker and that its bluff, blunt bow was pointing straight at us. We were more or less becalmed.*"

"Nick, I think you'd better come and have a look at this."

Nick took one quick look at the big ship and then hopped below again and turned on the radio. "Oil tanker on my starboard beam.

This is the yacht on your bow."

A voice with a French accent wafted into the cabin. "Do not 'av fear, leetle sailing boat. I am coming to 'av a look at you."

Yikes! "Not too close, please," we replied.

The ship was so big that even though it actually passed a quarter of a mile away, it looked to be very much closer. A vast wall of water was pushed along ahead of the towering black cliff of its bow. A lone figure on the bridge-wing betrayed the true enormity of the titan. He was a pin man, too far distant to have any identity; too tiny to be found at all without the binoculars. After having found and studied the man I saw that he, in turn, was peering back at me.

The radio crackled into life again. "Sailing boat, this is *Anitra*. Tell me, please. 'Ow old is your leetle boy?"

We told him, and bade Caesar wave. A moment later the great, black oil tanker answered the greeting with two deep, throaty blasts on the horn.

By now we seemed to have slipped south of the shipping lane which traces the bulge of Africa. The *Anitra* was coming up from Angola and would shave the corner of that route, but the traffic whose highway we had been sharing was already heading east - or so we guessed. A little bit of work with the sextant confirmed the fact, and we altered course to close the coast.

The wind continued light and the thunder still rumbled around in the distance, the lightning bouncing about from cloud to cloud. The dolphins still paid us their daily visit, and the fishing also remained good.

A couple of days after our encounter with the tanker, Nick spotted another big dorado. I sharpened the hooks and threw out the lures. Half an hour later the holding peg clicked as the line was torn from its grasp.

What a beautiful fish! She tore away as fast as I could pay out the line and then, when she got to the end, she leapt in the air and stood on her tail on the water. However, when we finally got the fish alongside we found that her mate was following her. This disturbed me rather. Most kinds of fish breed en masse and I had not realised that dorado were any different. The boys saw the situation in a different light and were for hooking the bull, too, but I persuaded them that one big fish was enough to be going on with.

More salting and bottling ensued, and that night we dined upon fresh, white dorado steaks poached in butter and white wine.

An hour or two after catching the fish we sighted the tops of tall silk cotton trees which were peeping over the edge of the world from a distance of more than twenty miles. They were so far away that they were grey in colour, and at first I swore that we were looking at a far away mountain range.

The next morning we made a more satisfactory landfall, on the telecommunications tower at São Pedro, and by afternoon we were off the entrance to that port. We had to motor in, or else be content to know the place by nothing more than its outline, as there was no wind and the current was carrying us past at about two knots.

Inside a tiny river-mouth we discovered a little port filled with logs and logging ships. Côte d'Ivoire was selling off her last few sticks of timber and helping the pirates to get their hands on the stuff upstream, in Guinea Conakry. Meanwhile, in the shadow of the big ships, dug-out canoes sailed by.

The harbour master welcomed us alongside with a smile and a handshake. The immigration officer would be pleased to see us at a mutually convenient time. Stay as long as you like; no charge. And no one pestering us for handouts regarding the safety of our dinghy or the yacht. From that world to this, the trip had taken 17 days.

The intricacies of chicken physiology remained unproven, but we reckoned that the abundance of fishy protein had more than made up for the lack of eggs. Ahead were such culinary delights as smoked prawns, and foo-foo, and garden snails as big as conch. Ahead lay visits to a rain-sodden market, where we must squelch our way through ankle deep orange mud, as gooey as clay, and barter for vegetables whose identity, nutritional value, and method of cooking were a mystery to the chef — but in the meantime we could take a breather. Ahead lay aggro of all sorts, amongst people whose language and culture were a puzzle — but in the meantime, we were in a civilised place, amongst people who prided themselves on their French connections and manners.

Pint-sized bottles of ice cold beer in our hands, we sat on the ample, hardwood veranda of an empty sport-fishing club. We had found this place purely by chance, on our ramblings. It was hidden amongst coconut palms and travellers trees, and whilst its entrance faced over the placid lagoon, the balcony overlooked the wave-swept beach. Huge blue and orange lizards stalked one another across the hefty mahogany planks, and brightly coloured birds flitted amongst the trees. A quiet pint in an old, ex-pat refuge; it was a sweet but short interruption in the mad safari. Soon we were moving on again, heading east along the old Slave Coast towards Ghana.

The Atlantic coast of West Africa is a place of calm, pacific waters. Its beaches slide gently into the sea and are lapped by little wavelets. The shore which faces the Bight of Benin is quite another story, and my over-riding memory of our passage along this coast is of the thunderous roar of mighty waves rolling and crashing onto a never ending, palm-lined beach.

Where the ivory-coloured sands are accessible, the coast is popular with surfers - and, each year the undertow exacts its toll. Also in peril are the fishermen who, although they avoid the wilder spots, must still launch through the surf and waves which invade every nook. Just as the Senegambia is known for its broad-planked pirogues, so here too there is a local type. Scarcely more seaworthy than the latter, it consists of a hollowed-out tree given a little bit more freeboard by the addition of bulwarks. Like the pirogues, these dug-outs are available in assorted sizes, from the one-man craft to a vessel hewn from a mighty tree of hundreds, or perhaps even a thousand years. The big canoes are capable of carrying twelve men to sea, although not in what I would call safety.

Every morning, from Sunday to Saturday, the brightly painted canoes put out to sea - although, strictly speaking, according to ancient custom, Monday is sacred to the local god of the ocean. On that day, according to the old beliefs, no one may venture out. Casting aside pagan scruples such as these, the good Christians of the old Gold Coast and the Ivory Coast flock to sea like gulls each morning, and in the early afternoon they come streaming back again.

Having observed this pattern, it somehow did not occur to us that the fisherfolk might also spend the hours of darkness abroad on the ocean. If we had realised this, then we would not have set out from São Pedro just as night was descending over all.

The first we knew of impending disaster was a faint cry which came from out of the blackness. A distant cry, without reason; a cry without even source. Then, in the next moment, we felt the boat slow and stop. We had run into a snare. Muffled shouts wafted over the water, and very soon we fell down upon the unlit fishing boat which was tied to the weather end of the net.

There followed a great deal of pointless and belligerent shouting from the captain. So far as he was concerned, a mightier beast than the intended ones had blundered into his trap, and now he had a tiger by the tail. By the light of the yellow moon and the stars we saw the glint of a long knife blade. To set us free they cut the net - but then they wanted compensation.

Next, a long argument between men who could speak neither French nor English and we, who had no word at all of Beté or Djioula. Besides the inability to agree upon a price, at the centre of the problem was our lack of the local ceefas and their captain's reluctance to accept the gringo's dollars, or his word about the rate.

An hour passed. We were falling down towards the shore. *Maamari* rolled in the light swell and the canoe thudded against her hull. Time and time and again we bid her crew to stand off, but always, within a couple of minutes, the canoe would be cuddling-up to our battered boat again. One of the fishermen had come aboard to cut the net, but I was keeping the others at bay with a boat-hook, held like a centurion guardsman's spear. In the inky black of the night they were not going to chance a swim.

We were few, and they were many, and their boat could go quite a bit faster than ours, but in the end it was we who issued the ultimatum: "Take what we offer and get off our boat, or else you're coming with us to Sassandra."

The captain blustered still, but his mate took the money and ran; or rather, he jumped – back into his own boat. We cast off their line and, while the two were arguing and trying to start their engine, we disappeared back into the cover of the night.

It would seem that the fishermen of this coast simply set their nets on the surface and then settle down to sleep until dawn. The engines of an approaching boat will presumably wake them and spur them into shining a light, or shouting, but they are not prepared for the silent arrival of a sailing boat. For the next eight or ten hours we picked our way amongst them with all the care and concern of people padding through a mine field.

The little fishing village of Sassandra was our next port of call, and we arrived there the following day. Half a hundred painted canoes lined the beach, and we took ourselves ashore and wandered amongst them. The fishermen paid us no mind while we were on the beach, but they were very curious about our boat. One lot of visitors tried to sell us a turtle, and I suppose we should rightly have bought the poor thing and set it free.

The next day we set off for Grand Lahou, and we arrived there after night had fallen and groped blindly towards the anchorage mentioned in our dear old pilot book. This place was once a slaving station - one of the many - and so it is evident that ships must anciently have anchored here, yet we passed a most uncomfortable night. At times we were rolling with such vigour that the side decks were almost awash. The light of day revealed no more suitable place where to lie, but only showed us the rolling swell and a yellow beach trimmed with fluffy foam. The distant growl of thunder mingled with the steady roar of the surf. The waves crashing onto the sand were a good eight feet tall, and breaking seas filled the entrance to the adjacent river mouth.

In amongst a sparse line of coconut palms on the beach we saw the derelict shells of old colonial buildings, and we wondered how it was that this place, or any other along this coast, could ever have been used as a slaving station. Getting the cargo out through the surf, to the ships off-lying, must have been a nail-biting experience for all concerned.

We continued our journey eastwards, drifting along on the current. On the other side of the shore which we now followed there lay a huge lagoon. Before we arrived at Grand Lahou, and saw the conditions there, we had entertained vague notions of entering the lagoon at that end, but now we pressed on towards the Canal Vridi. In 1951 this short, man-made cut gave sudden communication between Abidjan and the world beyond, with the result that an insignificant village of mud and stick became a port, and the de facto capital of Cote d'Ivoire.

The night was passed with the loom and the flickering flare of an oil rig on our horizon – first ahead, and then abeam, and finally astern of us. The new day dawned, as grey and sultry as every other of the past week. Soon we came within sight of a disparate flotilla of ships which lay off the Canal Vridi, but the best part of the day had passed before we were amongst them.

Last in the line of vessels was a small, red supply-ship, quite unknown to us, but as we drifted along its length we seemed to hear a cry: "Nick! Hey, Nick!"

A figure clad in a baseball cap and a boiler suit was rushing up and down on the aft deck, waving his arms and shouting. Having secured our attention, the man ran up into the bridge. Nick jumped below to turn on the radio, and at once a familiar voice burst in to the cabin. "Nick? I know your boat. It is Manuel here. You remember me?"

How could we forget? It was our good Samaritan, the one who had helped us so much in our time of need in the Cape Verde islands. To make friends and then move on is a sad part of the cruising life, but one to which the traveller becomes inured. Even so, to renew acquaintance for auld lang syne is amongst the greatest pleasures.

Abidjan, as we soon discovered, is a city vastly different form that other great ex- French metropolis, Dakar. The one bustles with life - African life - and is a living collage of turbaned heads and vultures in the gutter, of car horns and clip-clopping horses' hooves, of pickpockets, drums, mosques, high-rise banks, and buses, and of long silk robes sweeping by in a swirl of brown dust. The other – this great show piece of Afro-Gallic style and civility – is a characterless place of tall, ugly, ultra-modern skyscrapers parked on a plateau block. Below, and scattered all around, are seedy suburbs – together with a posh one for the extremely rich - and straggling all the way over to the canal is a very extensive port. And although the upper crust of this society like to boast of their sentimental affiliation with Paris, the truth is that the city has more in common with Lagos; a fact borne out by the figures for violent crime.

We threaded our way through the ships and past the high plateau, eventually choosing for our anchorage a little bight on the far side of town. There were half a dozen small yachts here, and an ex-pat yacht club, so that the prospects looked good. As it turned out, however, the management of the club were a stuffy lot and forbade us to use their jetty - in fact, they threatened to cast the dinghy adrift if we did! - but we found another place to land, and a nice old man to look after the dinghy, and on the whole we felt that the place was reasonably secure. What happened next therefore came as a surprise - but not a great one.

The cabin porthole was painted a soft pink by the pale dawn; but why was I awake at this hour? I had heard the rattle of the guard-rail above my head.

"Nick! Nick!" I hissed, as I shook him roughly. He would not believe me, but he would get up anyway, just for a quiet life. "Nick, there's someone on deck! I just heard somebody climbing aboard."

Was he really coming aboard, or had I heard the thief departing? We shall never know. Nick blundered outside, a little cautiously to be sure, but noisily enough to give the intruder a chance to run away. Who wants to disturb a man who may be carrying a knife or a gun?

In the obscure light of the dawn Nick could just make out the smudged silhouette of a canoe carrying two people. It was paddling swiftly away from the boat.

"Nothing's gone," he said, after a quick investigation.

Across the water came the cries of a muezzin as he performed the day's first adhaan, or call to prayer: "Allahu akbar! Allahu akbar! ... Ash-hadu anla ilaha illAllaah! ... Salaat! Salaat! Salaat! Salaat!" Prayer! Prayer! Prayer! Prayer!

Followers of a different faith, we snuggled down for another half an hour.

"I was wrong," said Nick. He had just launched the dinghy from the aft deck and now came back below with the bad news. "They got one of the gas bottles, and two empty jerrycans, and another small one full of diesel."

My flip-flops and the boat hook were missing too, but they had been lying on the deck just beside our window.

"It would have been virtually impossible for anyone to have taken the jerrycans and the gas bottle from *under* the dinghy," Nick said. "Besides, I'm sure I would have seen them in the canoe."

We decided that I must have been woken by the sound of the boat hook rubbing against the guard-rail, and that the other things must have disappeared in the day time, while we were all ashore.

We were pleased to note that the thief had also stolen a large black dustbin bag, full of rubbish. Less amusing was the discovery that the genoa sheet had been cut on one side, at the clew. Besides the fact that this would be difficult and costly to replace, there was a feeling of outrage. The theft of the gas bottle and the cans was an act of opportunism by one who presumably had no other means of income, but this other deed was vandalism.

In 15 years of cruising, this was the first occasion that anything ever went missing from *Maamari's* decks, whether by day or by night.

We were now within an ace of reaching the land which was our objective: the land of the Asante, the land of gold, and of the black gold of African lives. The reader will recall that it was my curiosity about the ancestral home of the people of the West Indies which had led us to make this giant detour into the Bight of Benin, and it was here that we would find that home.

Beneath a low, grey sky we were swept towards the east. Ever present in our ears were the rumble of thunder and the roar of waves, the one almost indistinguishable from the other. Over the invisible line we travelled, and into Ghana.

The coast here was just as ravaged as ever. We passed the first fort - Fort Apollonia - and once again we asked ourselves how it could ever have been possible to conduct any kind of trade along this shore. Beyond Fort Apollonia the beach was hemmed by a broad, white band which stretched for mile upon mile ahead of us on our left hand side. Waves rolled, and rolled, and rolled... rolled for almost a minute - and then crashed down to join the surf already writhing on the sand. Behind the wet sand the view was blocked by a dense, dank, unremitting forest of coconut palms, planted on behalf of foreign industry and Western needs.

As the grey day merged with night we identified Axim, in the distance, and before the darkness obscured everything we saw the little off-lying island where our chart showed a bisector light. Amazingly, the lighthouse was working, and so we obeyed the instruction of its illumination and were able to work our way around an invisible off-lying reef and into the safe water beyond.

Axim is another old colonial slaving station but, again, when we awoke in the morning we marvelled that this could ever have been. So far as we could see there was nowhere safe to land. Then the first of three or four score of canoes came by, and we saw that in each sandy indentation of the greater cove there lay strings of canoes. For an hour the boats droned past us, like a migrant colony of bees, and then in the afternoon they droned back again. We watched them landing through the surf and wondered if we would ever get ashore.

"It's all right, Caesar. Come on! It's perfectly safe." My voice was as reassuring as I could make it, but Caesar peered over the guardrail to where I sat, on a pile of wet fishing nets, and a wail of dismay issued from his quavering lips.

Nick was firmer and more forceful than me. "Don't make a fool of yourself," he said, as he handed our snivelling four year old son down into the waiting canoe. One of the fisherman reached up to receive his small passenger, but the rest were preoccupied with trying to prevent their boat from smashing itself to pieces on ours. The two vessels were rolling wildly in the surge which swept the bay.

Caesar and Xoë were both wearing lifejackets, but that only added to their sense of danger, and to be honest I shared their apprehension about the journey head. On the previous day Nick had managed to get ashore in the dinghy but had returned saying that it was much too dangerous for the rest of us.

"It is only like this in June," said the ferryman, as Nick and Johnnie bundled Xoë aboard and then scrambled down behind her. "For the rest of the year there is no problem here."

It was the 4th of June and, as we already knew, the coast had been rough for several weeks. Still, the swell sweeping into this particular bay was apparently something out of the ordinary. This morning some of the fisherman had been bottling-out and turning back to the beach, rather than take their chances with the combers which worked their way around the little island and over the maze of inner reefs.

As we set off for the shore, Caesar's screams grew wilder and Xoë joined in. There was ample justification for their fears. Though I tried to calm and quieten the children, I too was tense with anticipation of imminent disaster. The hollowed log would have seemed inadequate on a boating pool. Out here on the sea it rolled horribly, stirring my semiconscious memory with reminders of the death-rolls of a sailing dinghy on the point of capsize. I told myself that it was actually perfectly safe. It must be: these fishermen did it all the time. Later - further along the coast - we saw a dug-out just like this one turn upside down in the surf.

Three brothers were amongst the inevitable crowd who met us on the beach - one short, two tall and skinny as sapling trees. The short man was some kind of a step brother, but the other two were by the "same mother, same father," as they told us. We were to hear this qualification applied time and again in Ghana.

The brothers said that they had been dispatched by the "chief" - whom we did not encounter (and in whom we did not really believe) - to take us on a tour of the town. They showed us the old colonial buildings in the small, muddy streets, and they showed us the little mud built-homes in a suburb to the west. Along to the east lay another suburb - a village built entirely of stout bamboo poles which had been cut from the forest nearby. And lining the beach in front of the mud houses and the bamboo houses were the boats; boats with names like *In God we Trust* and *When One Door Opens Another One Closes*. Such sentiment and philosophy, and garbled sayings are also displayed on the shop-fronts throughout Ghana. Somewhat more ambiguous was the legend, *God is my She*, which was painted along the length of one craft.

"Did he run out of space?" Nick wondered.

Close by the beach, we saw half-built canoes still black from the fires wherewith they had been disembowelled, and by the side of a red, miry road lay giants newly slain after a prayer of apology and their dedication to the sea.

The brothers then took us to view another tree. This huge, ancient specimen was still standing, and it is hoped that it always will be, for it is a god. Sheltering in its shadow was a faith healing church where women in white praised Jesus as Lord.

From the religious quarter of the town we were taken to see a mill, where another group of women, each one holding her own little parcel, queued to have grains of maize ground into flour. The mill was belt driven and the rackety-rattle of its ancient petrol-driven engine shattered the peace round about. Still, who would not prefer this irritation to the monotony of hours of endless graft done daily with a quern? The three brothers were very proud of the mill.

Next we saw the dome-shaped, mud-built bread ovens - very like the ones we had seen elsewhere in this land - and then we had a guided tour of the open-air factory where coconuts eventually become coconut oil.

All the while, as we wandered around the town, we were attended by a retinue of children for whom our white faces were as intriguing as the Pied Piper's music. Little boys led even littler boys by the hand, and girls as young as six carried their infant siblings insecurely lashed on their backs. Every time I lifted the camera a dozen woolly heads peeped into the frame and as many bright grins shone from the dark faces. Inattentive to our request that the children be left alone, the three brothers tried, time and again, to shoo them away with switches - as if they were a plague of flies - but the youngsters were equally unobservant of the command to be gone, and they were very much more able to dodge than their elders were to aim.

On we wandered, then, like a carnival troupe processing along the streets. We saw men making fish traps out of withies. We saw the round ovens where the herrings were smoked. We were shown all the different kinds of fishing net, piled by the side of the boats. Oh, we saw *everything* that there was to see in this little place - but the highlight of the entire tour, so far as our hosts were concerned, was a visit to the old, mouldering fort - Fort St Anthony - whose foundation was the origin of the colonial settlement of Axim. Surely, that was what we had come to see?

Faced with solid evidence of the misdemeanours of the motherland one is apt to feel some kind of guilt, however illogical the sentiment may be. Am I to blame if Englishmen living in an age long ago made money by buying and selling other people? The cousins and brothers of those same Englishmen were probably sending my ancestors down a mineshaft, or demolishing their hovels to make way for a crop of sheep.

It was interesting to see that the Ghanaians accompanying us appeared to feel absolutely no guilt for the actions of *their* kinsfolk - perhaps their direct ancestors - by whose greed the slaves were sold overseas. On the contrary, we, the white men, were the only party to have sinned; we must carry the can all alone. Our hosts took delight in shocking us with all the horrors that the baddies had devised: "This is where the slaves were made to grind corn," and "This is where the slaves were made to fetch water." Rather ordinary chores, I felt, which mocked the genuine ordeal.

And, in this case, "we" were acquitted. The British did not manage to get their sticky fingers on Axim until 1872. By that time, slavery had been abolished and timber was the only trade. In Africa, the crime of stealing trees and destroying forests has yet to be recognised.

Eastward, ho. After two nights within the cradle of a bay rocked by wild, drunken seas we were not keen to endure a third alike. It was better to be lulled on the open ocean, we decided, even though it meant that we must take it in turns to sleep. Having been ferried back out to our boat by some friendly fishermen, we weighed anchor and embarked.

Of course, setting off in the evening also meant that we would once again be tripping along blindly, for we left beneath the lour of a sad sky whose low cloud concealed the setting sun and then hid the world from the gaze of the moon.

As ever, I took the first watch – and watch I did, most earnestly and anxiously. My eyes and ears strained to catch the least suggestion of trouble ahead. If we ran down a dug-out it would surely sink, and if we sailed into another net... then we would tangle ourselves in yet more trouble. My eyes drilled holes into the thick, stygian gloom – but I saw nothing; the opaque night hid all.

No sight, no sound, still less a silhouette, emerged through this imitation of primordial chaos. Yet, for all my vigilance, we were ensnared twice - we could feel the boat slow down and we saw the webs glowing in the water below our keel. We were on the ball now, and we swiftly cut ourselves free.

What must the fishermen have thought when they awoke to the feel of their nets being so mightily tugged by an invisible monster? They and we, both little bands of frightened creatures abroad on a night meet only for lost souls.

What stores did we carry, and how long would they last us? Where was the paperwork showing that our vessel was certified free of rats? These and a shower of other questions rained down on us as we welcomed aboard the officious clerks and agents of our next port of call, Takoradi. In a tone no less weighty, the harridan who represented the Ghanaian immigration authorities ordered that our children be dressed. I dressed them. And Xoë promptly tore her clothes off again.

The hour of arrival in a foreign land is a moment of truth, and always an anxious one. For yachtsmen there is no steel turngate, but there is an invisible barrier to be got across. We are on trial here. Will they like us and let us stay, without causing us too much ado, or have they the power to say, "Go, and never darken the door again."

Are our visas all in order? Our intentions, are they valid? Only twice or three times in many years of travelling has *Maamari*

ever been turned away, but still we quail. This time might be the
fourth.

     After our experiences in Cacheu and in Guinea Conakry we
knew not what to expect. What would be the end of this thorough
grilling? Had we stores too much, or not enough? Of course we had
no certificate proving that the yacht carried no rats!

What! No certificate? Didn't we know that this was essential? What
about our yellow fever certificates?

These we had, but it was the first time that anyone had ever asked to
see them, and I had a lot of trouble finding them.

     Where had we come from? What was our cargo? No cargo!
Well, whatever next? If we had no cargo then why had we come?

Tourists! But... in a boat? That stumped them. There was no
provision for tourism in their imagining.

     And then, as if at some unspoken cue, the officials dropped
their excessive formality. The clouds rolled away and the sun shone
down.

"You see," the customs officer said confidentially to the
immigration authority, "the white people do this kind of thing for
pleasure."

     Yes, what odd specimens of life we white people are. All the
while, as we travelled along the coast of West Africa the people who
met us had puzzled over our purpose. Now this gentleman had hit
the nail on the head. People living a settled lifestyle, on the lands that
their forefathers knew, understand no pleasure in travelling without
end or aim.

     But now, suddenly, we were personae gratae: "Welcome to
Ghana! Enjoy your stay." The officials now wanted to find us a
special berth, with a special guard to keep watch over the boat,
although the port itself is already as well guarded as a prison. As
unsure about their rat status as the vermin controller was about ours,
we persuaded them instead to let us lie at anchor in the middle of
the port.

     It was in Takoradi that we were first faced with the remarkable
continuity of temperament which exists between the Ghanaians and
their brothers and sisters over the sea. When Antiguan friends had
told us that they were really Africans, we had laughed. In all but their
colour they were as unlike the folks of Senegal and Guinea as we.
And was it any wonder, we asked? After a people has spent so many

generations living under a very different regime how could it be expected that they would share the manner of their forebears? Now, however, the words were thrown back at us.

The ancestral culture and religion of the slave-Africans was forbidden to them, and so their descendants are like trees which have no roots. Also, the chip on their shoulder makes them more than usually inclined towards aggression, especially where the white man is concerned. Yet in other respects the behaviour of the West Indian people, their mannerisms, and their attitudes, are quite uncannily like those of the people whom we met in Ghana.

Even the conduct of the officials whom we first encountered rang true. They had put up negative barriers, and then they had torn them down. The order that I dress the children suddenly reminded me of the bossy behaviour of Antiguan matriarchs, who will stop a stranger in the street and tell her that her baby is too hot, or too cold, or wants to feed. How many times, in Antigua, had I been told not to carry Caesar on my hip? Here, again, I was stopped by women wanting to tie Xoë onto my back. Nothing of this kind had happened in Cape Verde or Guinea - but then, why should it? Does a Spaniard behave like a Scot?

A part of our enterprise had reached its objective. I had wanted to find the land whence the Antiguan people came, and it was plain that this was, for many, their ancestral origin.

The port of Takoradi was so secure that we risked leaving *Maamari* alone and journeyed inland to Kumasi, capital of Asanteland. A decrepit diesel engine, with not a speck of paint on its body, dragged our equally ancient, rusty train through hour after hour of dank forest. The monotonous view was enlivened every few miles by the sight of an engine or a carriage lying, wheels uppermost, at the side of the track. Since the sight of these carcasses was not encouraging we decided that it would be better to travel back to the coast over night.

We returned to find the boat sitting exactly as we had left her, on the glassy, oil-stained water. Outside the wall the sea was the same - a great expanse of greasy greyness. We set off anyway, despite the dreary, melancholic sky and the lack of wind.

As day merged with night we reached Sekundi, and Nick and Johnnie decided that we should anchor here. I pointed out that Sekundi was a naval port and that, in Africa, one ought to give such institutions a wide berth, but they, in turn, pointed out that it was getting darker and damper by the minute. They had finally had enough of playing dare amongst the unlit fishing canoes.

We started the engine and turned, not into the port itself but into the lee formed behind its retaining wall. In a rattle of rusty chain, the hook disappeared into the grey-green deep - but scarcely was it over the side than we were struck by a sudden "tornado" which had crept up on us under cover of the low cloud. We were neither underway nor yet anchored - for the hook had not had time to bite - and directly behind us was the rocky harbour wall.

There was no time for Nick to get the anchor up again. With one eye on the wall, Johnnie opened the throttle wide and motored flat out. For some time now the engine had been giving us problems. We had even had to enter Takoradi under sail, much to the puzzlement of a patrol boat sent to escort us in. Unable to make the entrance, we had needed to put in a couple of tacks.

Now the engine boiled and bubbled. I poured water into its bowels, but to no avail; clouds of acrid black smoke filled the cabin. I abandoned my assistant stoker's cap in favour of my motherly duty, hurriedly waking the children and dragging them out into the fresh air. Their displeasure can surely be imagined.

Meanwhile, on the foredeck, Nick wrestled with the anchors. He had dragged the Fisherman along from the lazarette and now threw it over the side, but in the wind and rain and the descending darkness, with the bow plunging in and out of the waves which had suddenly arisen, he set it badly. It fouled the chain of the first anchor, so making matters even worse. If the engine quit now, we were on the wall.

And then, suddenly, all around us there were tubby fishing boats, quite unlike the usual canoes. They had burst from the shelter of the nearby shore as if with the aim of coming to our assistance. Friendly faces smiled, and arms were raised in greeting - but why did the men not take the line which Nick was frantically waving?

The message was evidently not getting through to the local guys - their arrival was purely coincidental - but on high our prayers were heard: the anchors finally bit and held; the wind eased from its initial 40 or 50 knot assault; and in an hour or less the squall had passed away to the west. We were left to sort ourselves out and then to settle down for the night.

The next day dawned as calm as the first, with rain in the air and the sea once more as smooth as satin. The engine refused to have anything to do with us, and while we tried to persuade it to start the battery was slowly drained of life. A few bare-wood canoes trickled by.

"Go away," somebody shouted as he paddled along. We were soon to understand why.

We sat about, twiddling our thumbs anxiously, while the little Honda generator charged the battery. Nick fretted over the engine, but this was not the place to take it apart. I cast occasional glances in the direction of the port, whose bleak wall stood so close beside us. Sure enough, after we had sat here for half a day some very observant look-out spotted our presence... and a big, grey inflatable dinghy came out.

"What are you doing here?" The young man in charge of the four or five soldiers was angry and nervous, and he held in his hands a very big semiautomatic rifle.

"Don't bring that aboard," said Nick, as the fellow hoisted himself onto our deck.

"Don't you tell me what to do!" came the angry retort. Right on cue, the radio on the soldier's belt began to cackle. In an altogether different tone he answered it and was told, "Don't carry your gun aboard the enemy boat."

"Yes, Sir." Now the boy became a little less surly, and even a little embarrassed. "Where have you come from?" he demanded to know. We gave him the answer which we knew would work best: "We are tourists."

He considered this, and then asked what he had been told to discover: "Are you on a hostile mission?"

We managed not to laugh.

Nick was taken off to visit a higher authority. The minutes ticked by and turned into hours. Two hours passed, and we began to wonder whether our captain and provider had been locked away. Then the grey dinghy hove into view and, with great relief, we noted that Nick was aboard.

Only one thing more troubled the commanding officer, who had now become quite matey and had left behind his gun. He looked around our cabin and then said to his erstwhile captive, "Are you a Christian?"

"Oh, yes," replied Nick, thereby avoiding a long and tedious discussion.

"Is your wife a Christian?" came the next interrogative.

"Yes, of course."

The soldier frowned. He pointed at Nan, our carved wooden statuette, who was still holding up the deck-head. "So," he said, "you are a Christian and your wife is a Christian. It is your brother who worships this, yes?"

BE THE CURRENT AGAINST US

In which the tide of our fortunes takes a contrary turn.

St George's castle sits on a low, rocky plinth, thinly veiled by a single line of slender coconut trees. The sea breaking on the rock flecks the massive white-washed walls with spray and spume.

This is the oldest of all the forts and the place which marks the beginning of the white man's interference in Africa. The Cape Verdean settlement now called Cidade Velha has the distinction of being the first European settlement in the tropics, but it was really not much more than a service station for the industry which soon arose on the coast of the Dark Continent. When they reached *this* place, on the coast of modern-day Ghana, the Portuguese finally found one of the things that they had been seeking for all those years.

Until this time the Arab nation, with their domination of the desert, had enjoyed a complete monopoly over trade with West

Africa, but with their discovery of this place the Portuguese opened the back door for the Christian world. To be sure, no one led the explorers hand in hand to Asanteland - the source, unknown even to the Arabs, of their wealth - but they did make contact with people who knew the way; and that was enough. So far as the cartographers of the fifteenth century were concerned the Portuguese had discovered "El Mina" - The Mine; or to be more precise, The Gold Mine.

Well, that is one version of the story. Another, more prosaic account says that El Mina is just a corruption of Al Mina, which is Arabic for "the port". As *Maamari* rolled and dipped in the waves, and lulled her crew to sleep, we could not help thinking that "port" was something of a grandiose title for this open roadstead. Once again, we had arrived after nightfall, so that it was not until the following day that we were able to take a look at the place to which we had brought ourselves.

We awoke to cries of, "Hombre!" and a tapping on the hull. It was just after six, and the local fishermen were already about in their frail one man canoes. They had an officious way of asking us where we had come from and what we were up to: "Excuse me! Hello? I'd just like to ask you a few questions..." And as one inquisitor left, another arrived.

Meanwhile, from over the horizon came the first of an almost endless stream of the larger dug-outs, driven by an outboard motor mounted on a wooden bracket on the starboard side of the hull. To judge by the number of canoes which came past us during the next hour or two, they must have formed the most horrible snare, lying offshore in the dark depths of the night. The drone of their engines was like a moped grand prix.

As for the thing which we had come to see - the castle - now that we lit eyes on it, we found that this magnificent structure far surpassed our expectations. It was the biggest ancient castle that we had ever seen and it looked as if it would have been utterly impenetrable.

Back in 1482, when St George's castle was built, the Portuguese were no more than alien tenants of the local chief, one Caramanca. They probably felt a need to protect themselves against the natives, in case they turned nasty, but their main preoccupation was in protecting themselves from Arab retaliation and from rival

Europeans. The story of The Gold Coast is one of continual feuding between the Portuguese, the Dutch, the Scandinavians, and the British, all of whom were frantically eager to get their hands on the loot. So it was that a castle was necessary, its walls of immense stature, its moat broad and deep. And what a gift from God Almighty was this purpose-made plinth of rock, making the place quite unassailable from the sea! Better yet, running directly behind the castle there is a river - a perfect secondary moat! Could nature have designed a finer redoubt?

Well, yes. Unfortunately, the Portuguese seem to have overlooked a hill which, in turn, overlooks the castle. In 1637 the Dutch used it to finally capture St George's. Subsequently, the victors built here a small but solid fort - Fort St Jago - whose sole purpose was to stand guard over the first mighty edifice.

Naturally, we wanted to take a closer look at this set up - but, as usual, the landing looked tricky. A low, rock-built wall trains the little river as it emerges from behind the castle. Coincidentally, the wall also provides the beach beyond it with a certain amount of shelter from breaking seas, but we noticed that the nastiest looking waves occurred just off the end of the wall. Rather than risk overturning the dinghy, we hitched a ride in a passing canoe.

It was low water, and behind the wall the river was so narrow and shallow that our canoe touched both the bottom and the rocks. We passed below St George's castle and beneath the bridge which now leads across the river to the town. Here our curiosity concerning the fishing fleet was answered, for we had been wondering how it was that so many hundreds of boats could disappear behind the sea wall. Did they go a long way up river, we wondered, or was there a proper port within? The answer was that the boats had just nipped into the mouth of the river, and here we found them lying gunwhale to gunwhale on the sand. Their brightly painted hulls formed a colourful mosaic along the edge of the muddy, orange-brown streets and the orange-brown mud houses of the town.

From the walls of the castle we looked down upon the scene. On the one side of the river stands the sprawling tin-roofed town which has grown out of Caramaca's trading station, and on the other - here, beneath our feet - the first European inroad into the business. The Portuguese wanted gold. Old Caramanca could get his hands on plenty of gold, but he also offered another commodity: men.

Slavery was an integral part of the West African social system, and the Arabs had been taking advantage of it for hundreds of years. I would imagine that the upper crust of Portuguese society had already seen some of these black slaves in and around the palaces of their Moorish overlords.

The first slaves to arrive in Portugal from El Mina were surely no more than a rich man's curio, but after the discovery of new lands on the far side of the Atlantic their value as cheap labour was almost immediately apparent. Before long, his customers wanted all the "black gold" that Caramanca and his successors could procure.

Cape Coast, Mori, Anomabu... our journey along the coast of Ghana was a pilgrimage from one fort to the next, as we sought and found the tangible last link between West Africa and the West Indies, and saw for ourselves the very brick and stone of the several thresholds whereby the reluctant émigrés were led from the old world to the new.

Where we could not comfortably anchor or safely land, the shore was scrutinised from afar with the glasses. So we passed by many a ruinous mound, scarcely to be distinguished from the headland which it surmounted. Amongst them was Fort Kormantin, the first British-owned fort on the Gold Coast. This was the origin behind the appellation Coromantee, which the British planters in the West Indies used for any slave coming from these parts. Coromantee slaves were reckoned to be the best.

One evening we anchored off the town of Winneba, and before we had even put the boat to bed a canoe came paddling towards us through the light chop and the rolling swell. We rushed to hide away such attractive goodies as the fishing line, and the lead line, and any stray ropes, all of which at Axim, Elmina, and Mori had drawn our visitors' attention and provoked a deal of tiresome begging. However, as it turned out our latest visitors had no designs upon our property. They had come to take us ashore. A canoe like any other, this was apparently the "surf boat" often mentioned in our antique pilot book. On discovering that we had no wish to go ashore that evening, the eight-strong crew turned their vessel about directly and paddled away in quick time, one man singing all the while to keep stroke.

We have noticed before that when one or two boats in a traditional fleet get outboards, the others soon follow suit. The everybody-else-has-got-one syndrome is by no means unique to school children. Doubtless this was the reason why every single one of the boats at Axim and at Elmina was power-driven. At Winneba, we were delighted to note, not one crew had discovered the need for mechanical propulsion. Waking at dawn the next day I counted no fewer than 86 canoes drifting down from the town under sail, and the exodus continued for another hour so that there must have been something in the order of 150 boats, all told.

To be able to go to windward a sailing boat must have some kind of keel. This is one of the main reasons why even the poorest of fishermen finds it cost effective to buy or rent an outboard motor: with a motor he can go fishing even when the wind is contrary or very light. One of the Sierra-Leonese fishermen in the Bijagos, having realised that he would save money if he did away with his outboard, had asked us to design him a keel for a one man canoe. We suggested that the simplest solution was a set of leeboards - boards which hang from the gunwhale on either side of the boat - but leeboards are inefficient. Moreover, as soon as the canoe heeled (as it would be bound to do, on the wind) then it would probably fill up and sink. A Polynesian sailing canoe has an outrigger to stop it from capsizing. A modern, racing canoe has a sliding seat and a trapeze for her crew. Our Sierra Leonese friend later wrote and told us that the experiment was "partly successful".

The Winnebegan approach to the problem of leeway was completely different. These canoes had no keel, but because they were big twelve man affairs, heavily laden with nets, they were much deeper in the water. They were also far less likely to heel, because their rig was a low one. The spars consisted of a V-shaped frame, and the sail was a huge white balloon, almost like a spinnaker, which was held out by a third pole. To be honest, the canoes did not look at all weatherly - perhaps the wind always blows along the shore hereabouts, meaning that the canoes only ever need to reach - but they certainly seemed to provide a fast and exciting ride, and their crews waved and cheered gaily as *Maamari* passed them by on her way to Tema.

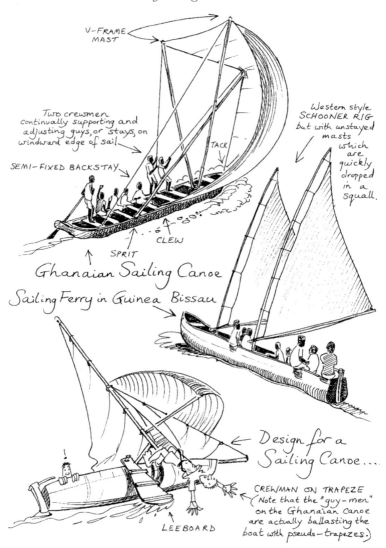

V-FRAME MAST

Two crewmen continually supporting and adjusting guys, or stays, on windward edge of sail

SEMI-FIXED BACKSTAY

TACK

CLEW

SPRIT

Ghanaian Sailing Canoe

Western style SCHOONER RIG but with unstayed masts which are quickly dropped in a squall.

Sailing Ferry in Guinea Bissau

Design for a Sailing Canoe...

CREWMAN ON TRAPEZE (Note that the "guy-men" on the Ghanaian canoe are actually ballasting the boat with pseudo-trapezes.)

LEEBOARD

The capital of Ghana is Accra, but Accra is an open roadstead - a useless place from the modern navigational point of view - and so neighbouring Tema has become the first port of the nation. Night had long since descended and Caesar and Xoë had just fallen asleep when we arrived off Tema. The wind was good and the entrance to the port wide, so that we had no qualms about sailing in. Nor were we the least bit troubled when we met a ship coming out; there was oodles of space.

Although it was dark we could see that the man-made harbour was about the size of Takoradi but very much busier. We were well within its waters before caution suggested that we start the engine - if it would deign to start. (We had not used it since that day off Sekundi.) The engine started - and we proceeded, following our noses.

It was at about this stage that someone turned a spotlight on us. We gave the glare a friendly wave and went on with our business. We soon found the end of the port - a tight cul-de-sac, or so it appeared in the gloom. Since there was no space for us to turn we were obliged to reverse, and since the boat, like any other long-keeled boat, does not go very well astern, we had to lean on the throttle. To the reader who has journeyed with us along the coast the result of this action will be apparent. The air all around was at once filled with black smoke.

And suddenly there was a patrol boat alongside us. Careless of our predicament her crew announced that we were under arrest, charged with having illegally entered the port. They took us in tow – which was just as well, for it was plain that the engine was on the point of imminent and everlasting decease.

By now the cabin had filled with acrid smoke, and I hurried to bring Caesar and Xoë out into the cockpit. Their appearance caused the usual stir. Henceforth our welcome was assured, and by the time we reached the security of the naval berth we were being received with the usual Ghanaian enthusiasm. No further mention was made of our arrest. Instead, we were told that we had been brought to this safe, snug berth as honoured guests.

"Hello? Hello? I want to have a word with you. Come here, please, I want to ask you some questions."

We awoke, the next morning, to find an audience of two dozen dockers gawping down at us from the wall of the quay. Ours was not the first yacht to visit Ghana. No, there had been another one - a big one - six or seven years before. Had we come to visit the British Ambassador? Would we like to be interviewed for the local television?

The onlookers crouched down, the better to be able to peer into the zoo. We heard them discussing our kitchen arrangement as if it were an exhibit in a museum. Sooner or later somebody would start to whistle or to call, "Hello? I want to talk to you."

Good grace and, besides that, good sense demanded that we respond to each new caller. Aside from any consideration of etiquette there was the fact that any one amongst them might turn out to be the official that all, by their manner, seemed to be. "Where are you from? How long did it take you to get from Britain to Ghana? How many people are aboard? How long are you staying? Do you have visas? Where will you be going next?" The questions were always exactly the same. Soon we were begging the port authority for permission to anchor off.

The final straw came with a "tornado". Like the earlier ones we had known, it struck with sudden violence, and it drove the placid, grey-brown waters of the harbour into short, steep waves which lay furrow upon furrow. With the wind came a heavy rain, and Nick, Johnnie, and I were left to fend for ourselves while our audience fled to the shelter of ships and a warehouse. And fend we must, quite literally, or else *Maamari* would have been smashed to pieces on the wall.

For more than an hour we braced the boat away, and not even the navy came to our aid. Faces peered down at us, each from their chosen refuge, but once again there appeared to be a lack of comprehension. After this adventure we were doubly eager to be away from the wall and gained permission to join a flotilla of derelict fishing craft, in the middle of the harbour.

The time had come when we could no longer push to one side the task of finding a new engine for *Maamari*. We have vowed to tread lightly on the earth and on the water, leaving behind us in our wake nothing but froth and foam. Nevertheless, an engine is, as we see it, an important safety feature. Had it not been for the engine *Maamari* would certainly have been lost in the squall at Sekundi, for example.

Ever optimistic, Nick reckoned that it would take him five days to rip out the old engine and replace it with a new, or rather, a reconditioned replica. In fact, he spent two weeks searching in Accra before he even found a suitable engine - one of the same make and model (a Peugeot 404) and in good working order. In the interval, two other engines were brought home, ferried out, craned aboard, and installed - only to be returned to the vendor as unserviceable.

Caesar and Xoë adapted much better than I to life in a mechanic's workshop. The old engine was propped up against the table and we had to pick our way amongst oily tools. Johnnie very wisely took time out to visit Togo. The entire project actually took six weeks, during which time we had abundant opportunity to make many good friends - without some of whom the job would never have been finished - and to get to know, in intimate detail, the road between Tema and Accra.

As someone had once said, on hearing of our fears of malaria, "If you're going to die in Ghana it will be on the road." The standard of driving in this corner of the world is, indeed, atrocious - with the bus drivers being the worst offenders - and almost every vehicle is a wreck.

"These cars would never be legal in England," Nick commented to a taxi driver, employed to ferry one of the engines from Accra.

"They're not legal here," was the prompt rejoinder. "We just have to keep dashing the police. It's 1,000 cedi (50p, at that time) every time they stop us."

The man went on to explain that this was how most policemen earned their ordinary living. "And they do very nicely," he said, pointing out an off-duty policemen of his acquaintance who was driving by in a relatively smart Volvo.

"Dashing" - or bribing and tipping - is a way of life in Ghana. A driver keeps the appropriate note folded into his licence so that the dash can be offered without comment when the police ask to see his paperwork. 50p might not seem much, but it makes all the difference if you are only taking £5 a day. This was the sum which one particular taxi driver named - and he reckoned that he was doing very well, thank you. One young man whom we met earned a daily wage of 30p for his work in a boutique. Shop rents in Accra were about £2 annually, and even the city's biggest cinema only paid £25 a year rent. By now they will be probably be paying even less, in terms of 'real money', because the value of the cedi was falling by the day.

Poverty, then, is also a way of life in Ghana. Yet, although the people whom we met were living in an entirely industrial conurbation, where they have no opportunity to grow their own food and where the culture of the car is dominant, still we did not see anyone in serious want of food or in want of a roof for the night. When it comes to finance and figures in the bank, Ghana is terribly poor, but no one is starving because Ghana is rich in terms of its traditional, family-structured social security arrangements - arrangements which are made out of a sense of duty rather than any law.

Ghana is also rich in terms of its farmland, and its people's ability to feed themselves. Yams, tomatoes, bananas, papayas, cassava flour, peanuts... all these and other locally grown fruit and vegetables were as cheap as could be in the noisy, vibrant market at Tema. Gin, if it came from the local distillery, was 50p a bottle - although, unless one took along the said bottle, an extra 30p was charged for that. Three gallons of peanut butter cost £5, but we had to provide the bucket to carry it away. Best of all, from the point of view of the reluctant cook, was the discovery that I could feed the whole family ashore for little more than £1. True, one had to be content with stodgy, slimy lumps of fufu - the local staple - swimming in a plateful of ultra-spicy soup, but the fare was filling. And that £1 included a pint pot of beer each, for Nick and me.

Tema was to be our last port of call on the African continent before we set off across the Atlantic for South America. In the last week or two of our stay I spent much time rummaging around in our lockers, listing the goods still in store, and I spent a great deal of time shopping, with Johnnie my reluctant porter. Johnnie would not be coming all the way across the pond with us but wanted to go as far as the twin-island state of São Tomé and Principe. After that we planned to stop at Ascension and then at Trindade, an island 780 miles offshore from Rio de Janeiro, but I could not count on being able to buy any more imperishable food in any of these three islands. I had to be sure that we had enough provisions and sufficient water - not to mention gin and beer - to see us through for at least nine weeks.

Maamari's lockers are capacious. My problem was not in finding room for the stores but in finding stores to fill the room. Fufu is fine, but I have not the time and patience to be pounding plantains and cassava to make it myself - and certainly not whilst at sea. Certain imported English goods such as Marmite and HP Sauce were available in the town's one grocery store, but our usual standbys - things such as baked beans, corned beef, tinned sweetcorn and tinned tomatoes - these were not to be found anywhere. Eggs we could get, but cheese and butter were just something remembered from years gone by. We had not seen any since we were in the Canary Islands.

Denied a supply of these staples of a Western itinerant's diet, we filled up, instead, with local goods. In the sprawling open air market we bought thirty big yams, a sack of roasted peanuts, and a sackful of dried maize, to be boiled and served in the Cape Verdean way. Chilli peppers were abundant, and so I pickled hundreds, and there being no other kind of cooking oil available I invested in several gallons of palm oil and coconut oil.

Xoë's eyes lit up when she discovered that I had bought half a dozen buckets filled with peanut butter, and chocolate was so cheap that I purchased 150 bars and let the kids have free access to them. Within a fortnight they had scoffed the lot - and for years afterwards they had only a very slight interest in chocolate.

Nick and Johnnie, for their part, humped home hundreds of beers - begrudging the generous deposit due on the return of each bottle - and then they got hold of four five-gallon jerrycans which they took to the market and filled with gin.

Bagfuls of smoked, dried prawns were sifted, and numerous beetles removed. We bought plantains, tomatoes, yellow aubergines, and some kind of spinach so abundant that the women were giving it away at the end of the afternoon. We bought all of this and stowed it away; and then we left. According to Nick, the engine installation was still not complete - but the thing would run; what more could one need? The exhaust emptied, temporarily, through the main hatch, and the starter had to be manually engaged, but these were just teething problems. I had seen enough of Tema.

Friends from the port turned up to see us off and amongst them was Abbey, the manager of the engineering shop. Without this gentleman's kind assistance it would have taken even longer to re-engine *Maamari*. He it was who had made sure that the higher authorities turned a blind eye while the various drivers of the crane and the launch ferried the various engines to and fro, for just a dash. Abbey had also come up with some suitable nuts and bolts, and a used heat-exchanger, and some galvanised pipe for our exhaust.

After we had said our farewells, we sailed out of the port. The walls and the cranes faded in our wake into one universal grey - and then, from out of the grey, came a speck which grew at a remarkable rate. Soon we could see a figure waving on the foredeck, and we realised that it was the yard launch storming towards us. Had

we done something wrong?
No, Abbey had just come to say one more goodbye.

Our first few days at sea were uneventful. After so many weeks spent on the even waters of a walled harbour Caesar and I were predictably queasy, but Nick and Xoë both remained in rude good health. Neither has ever known the awful sensation of mal de mer.

We idled along at about three knots. Clouds hid the sun, so that in determining our position we were obliged to depend on dead reckoning. Dolphins came to see us each black night but were never with us by day.

We had left on the 3rd of August, and on the 7th the weather changed: we hit a patch of wind and rain. Down came the main. We reefed the genoa. Waves broke on the deck, and spray came flying over into the cockpit. That evening the sun showed his face all too briefly as he fell towards the sea, but we managed to take a quick sight. The clouds then parted to give us a brief glimpse of the moon, and so we took a sight on that, too. Using both sights we were able to calculate our position. We were 45 miles from the island of Principe.

"We'll be in by mid-morning," we said to each other confidently.
Some people never learn.

The night passed, and all the next morning we strained our eyes for a glimpse of Principe. It was not a low island, this we knew from the chart, and it ought to be visible by now. Around midday the sun shone for long enough to allow a couple of decent sunsights, and to our dismay we discovered that our progress from yester-evening was almost negligible.

How could this be? The wind was light and contrary - we were limping along, close hauled, at no more than three knots - but still this should have put us a little further forward. And the current was supposed to be with us.

We looked again at the old Admiralty pilot. Yes, the diagram of the Bight of Biafra clearly showed a favourable current here. But, wait! The arrows, to be sure, were going our way, but when we read the text we learnt that this was no more than "conjecture"! Are the Admiralty no better than the originators of the Mappa Mundi? Is their knowledge no more to be trusted than that of the folks who led Cabot and Cook to go hunting for the North-West Passage and for Terra Australis Incognita? Now, as then, nature refused to imitate art: we had current against us and there was no arguing with the fact. We plodded on, and another day slipped by.

"9th August. *Caught a big dorado (54 inches) which was first observed overtaking the boat, trailing the line on which she had already become hooked.*"

No wonder the fish were swimming faster than us. During the night we had picked up a little bit of a breeze, but by morning time our speed through the water had fallen to about two knots. Nevertheless, the gain of the night had given us a few miles, and at midday, according to our sunsights, the island was 35 miles distant.

Again we scoured the horizon. We looked into the crystal glass of our radar, too. (The radar had a 35 mile horizon, so we were pushing our luck.) The island remained invisible. Perhaps it had sunk. I mused on the tales of the lost isle of Atlantis and of the Celtic island called Mag-Mell. Mag-Mell, land of the gods, was all around the explorer, Bran, and yet it was hidden from his eyes.

Then again, perhaps this was some kind of trick island. If we sailed away from it perhaps we would arrive, in Looking-Glass style.

Or could it be *we* who were not real? Could we have sailed over the edge of the world or gone through a time warp? I could well understand the anxiety of those mediaeval men who sailed out of the cosiness of the known world into... into who knew what? The isles of the dead were said to lie somewhere out there to the west, just over the horizon. And the gods were supposed to live below the sea. To men who had no knowledge of the earth's extent, and even less idea of their own position, the odd ghostliness of the empty ocean must have been quite as terrifying as the storms.

So, here we were: lost – it would seem – and alone. No ships had crossed our path in all the while since the continent fell away over the stern. Our only companions were a score or more of sooty terns who performed aerobatic feats close by. Sometimes at night they startled us with a sudden, shrill squawk. Their presence, at least, was a firm indication of an island somewhere nearby.

"10th August. *Sunsights taken this morning put Principe to the west, 45 miles away! This is a cause for celebration, or some other kind of commemoration.*

Never before, in 13 years of ocean sailing, has Maamari ever gone backwards in the course of a day and a night..."

At least the westing put the wind a couple of points further aft.

Late in the afternoon, Nick saw 'blows' of spray in the distance. We watched them for a minute and then saw a great fluked tail wave in the air, in a gesture of farewell. Its white underside was towards us.

In the next instant the humpback whale had sounded and gone – to who knew where? Not for the first time, I wondered what went on in that unseen world far below our keel. The whale belonged down there; he could only glimpse the surface of our world. And I, meanwhile, knew all about trees and birds and houses and tower blocks and aeroplanes; I knew all about chocolate, potatoes, books, and cutlery; I knew all about the Beatles, Margaret Thatcher, Henry VIII, and Neolithic Man; but if I tried to take more than a glimpse at the world of the whale I would die. When the whale came to the surface to breathe, our worlds overlapped – and perhaps he wondered about me – but then he was gone. Perhaps he had gone to that land of the Celtic gods.

A short while afterwards, amidst derision from the others, I turned on the radar and found a vague smudge on the screen. Possibly it was just a rain cloud. Nick was summoned to take a look, and he peered into the black, vinyl cowl.

"That's it!" he declared. "Clear as a bell! Land at 26 miles."

We did not sight Principe with the Mark-1 eyeball (as aviators are pleased to call it) until we were within two miles, and then its uneven black shape suddenly towered above us in the darkness of the night. By one in the morning we were at anchor in the lee of the strange, dark mound. It had taken us a record breaking three days to cover 45 miles.

Now follows the tale of the pirates of Principe.

In the morning we awoke to discover a lush island shrouded in rain clouds.

"It looks a lot like Dominica," I said.

"It looks exactly like the Marquesas," said Nick.

A couple of dug-outs appeared and came diffidently alongside. Frail craft, these, with tacked-on gunwales and a curious clipper bow. Instead of a many-coloured coat of paint they were covered only with tar. Some, indeed, had not even a covering of tar but were coated only in green algae.

"Have you come for the festa?" the fisherman asked us. "Big festa - Festa São Lorenzo - in a couple of days time."

Well, that was good timing!

We had moored in the mouth of a narrow inlet, which inlet was the island's only harbour, and after breakfast we hoisted the sails and weighed anchor again. Making our way up towards the little town at the head of the inlet was difficult because the only wind was the one coming down towards us in squally gusts sent by the mountains. Rocks waited, here and there, beneath the murky waters, and in the absence of waves or very much swell only swirling eddies published their position.

When the harbour grew too narrow for us to continue tacking in this fickle and contrary wind we began to kedge. We are not such purists or masochists that we would have chosen this means over mechanical propulsion, but the engine... well, as I have said, its installation was not quite complete.

At first we used the anchor only to stop the boat and bring her about, but then, when the wind failed altogether, we proceeded in the old-fashioned way, carrying the anchor forward in the dinghy and then hauling ourselves towards it. We were in the midst of this energetic exercise when a launch came out from the quay, up ahead. The skipper brought his craft alongside *Maamari* and five dour-faced gentlemen boarded us and marched, uninvited, into our cabin. One, it transpired, was the port captain, one was the immigration officer, another represented the police, and the fourth the custom authorities. The last was from a state owned company called Enaport who were in charge of all shipping through the port.

The spokesman for the group asked to see our passports, which were duly handed over for inspection, but rather than look at them the man slipped them into his pocket. We were to come ashore within the hour. No, we could not accompany the officers in their launch.

"What is this going to cost?" we asked, as the five men, on one impulse, vacated our cabin. We had heard that our visas would cost $25 U.S. each.

"Is there any entrance charge?" we wondered, but the men all shrugged or shook their heads. "We do not know. Come soon to

collect your passports."
We worked our way a little further up the inlet and anchored. Then
we hurried ashore.

In the port captain's office we filled out forms bearing the crest of
the Empresa Nacional da Adminstracao dos Portos. The forms were
in Portuguese, but beneath each question was printed the English
interpretation:

> *Nome da barco* - The name of the boat.
>
> *Capitaõ* - The captain.
>
> *Dono* - The owner.

Having filled out these two last we were not quite sure what to put
for *Qualidade de Navio*, which was supposed to mean "King of the
ship". Then there were other queries such as "If putted into an
harbour and if any cargo aft there", "Average protest or declaration"
and "Miles the ship can yet steam at its declared speed." That one
got a definite zero.

Then came the bill. It was for $24 (U.S.). We were not
accustomed to having to pay to clear into a country, but we paid
anyway. Someone had once warned us that there was a charge for
this in São Tomé. The port captain handed Nick a receipt and then
he led him upstairs.

A few minutes later we heard the sound of voices raised in
anger, and our leader returned – still without our passports. He had
just encountered the other four men, each of whom had also
presented a bill for $24. Besides that, we were to be charged $44 each
for the three visas, making a grand total of $252 U.S. (about £168).

"Forget it!" Nick had declared. "Just hand me our passports. We're
leaving."

"Impossible," was the port captain's flat rejoinder. "You have set
foot ashore and now you must pay."

So *that* was it. That was why they had all been suffering from
amnesia when they came to visit and to carry off our passports.
Now they could all remember well enough what dues we were
supposed to pay!

Nick cast his eyes over the officer's desk, but the man gave a
sly smile and inclined his head towards a safe in the corner of the
room. He had laid the trap well, with attention to the slightest detail.
Perhaps, in the past, a victim of this deceit had managed to snatch

up his passport and run. Ours were securely locked away. The Pirates of Principe held us in their sway.

A mantle of dark cloud had moved away from the mountain above us to hang in ominous threat over the little town of São Antonio. We paced the cobbled streets, striving all the while to come up with the answer to our predicament. We were the unwitting, innocent victims of a treacherous deceit – and we were absolutely certain that the sum demanded was no more than a bribe. Quite clearly, these charges, if they were due at all, were due only from commercial craft. What did we owe to Enaport? Nothing! We were not importing or exporting. And what involvement had we with the police? Absolutely none.

Never in all his years of travelling had Nick been faced with any such charges. And in Guinea, The Gambia, Ghana, Senegal, and the other West African countries there had been no official fees at all. Recalling our adventure in Cacheu, we vowed not to part with one penny, save for the visas. A phone call to the capital isle of São Tome soon confirmed that $44 was, indeed, the cost for these, but the same officials assured us that there were no other fees to be paid.

Besides our natural tendency towards parsimony, and besides our reluctance to be taken for a ride, we had another problem: we do not carry much cash aboard *Maamari*. In a bid to persuade the oppressor to lower his demand, Nick had explained that we simply did not have $252 - and, in truth, we did not. All throughout our travels in West Africa we had relied on using the magic plastic card, but the little bank in Principe did not take credit cards. The five conspirators wanted American dollars, and American dollars only; they were not interested in receiving a motley assortment of French francs, pounds sterling, Portuguese escudos, and so forth. Nor would they even accept payment in their own currency.

Word quickly gets about a small town, and soon the story was spread abroad. We had the support of all to whom we spoke; all agreed that the charges were wholly outrageous. One of the 'gang of five' backed down and settled for a bottle of gin. Another settled for half the fee, in the local currency. We got this by cashing one of Johnnie's travellers' cheques in a small guest house. That left three crooks, two of whom were wavering until a glower from their ringleader brought them into line. No matter; we had been advised by the people to put our case before His Excellency, the island's president.

The president of Principe is available to anyone. This is but one of the many boons of life in a self-governing village; anyone can have their say, and democracy is real and visible. Led on by one Carlitos, a young man who had taken our troubles upon his own back, we went to the town hall and mounted the grand staircase, part of the island's inheritance from the old colonial days.

But, alas, the president could *not* see us. He was in bed, suffering a bout of malaria. We were told to come back in a few days time.

Now into our tale we must weave the sub-plot - a little light-hearted interlude in the midst of the general comedy. The day of the Festa São Lorenzo had arrived, and while their president sweltered and shivered beneath the sheets, his people made merry with an elaborate pageant, bequeathed to them, once again, by the Old Colonial Master, and dating from the late mediaeval age.

In the streets of São Antonio the story unfolded. The participants were divided into two armies, the one clothed in red and pink tunics and bearing shields adorned with a crescent moon and a star, the other attired in costumes of green and blue and bearing shields emblazoned with a cross. The reds were The Muslims, and they represented the force of evil. The greens were God's army: the Holy Crusaders. The goodies had their HQ outside the church and the bad guys faced them from several hundred yards away, at the other end of the street.

Now began the action, or rather - before the action - a series of rather long speeches. The chief of the good guys was a man who, in spite of a tinfoil and cotton wool crown, a green satin skirt and a blue sash, still looked like a town councillor. Perhaps it was the black-rimmed glasses. At any rate, the man was perfect for the part. When an emissary came striding up the street from the Muslim redoubt, the councillor took the proffered, rolled declaration and read it quietly to his committee. This body of men also performed their part in an extremely life-like manner; there was a great deal of twittering and discussion, none of which could be heard by the audience standing about - but then, the councillor and his men were not performing for the crowd. They were playing, exactly as children play at being soldiers.

The Muslims - or Turks, as some called them - were made of an altogether different kind of stuff. When he got the dispatch, delivered by a huffy representative of The Power of Good, the Muslim leader strode to and fro, waving his arms dramatically as he shouted his well-rehearsed lines. He was An Actor; a marvellous over actor. He was quite perfect for the part of arch villain, right down to his arch villainous smile and his blue-mirrored sunglasses.

So, the spectacle continued. Before our eyes was enacted the conquest of Iberia by the enemy Moors. Wooden swords clashed as the armies moved up and down the street and each and, for all I know, every separate battle was recalled. At the end of the day the baddies were finally victorious.

Just a moment! Surely that could not be right?

Ah, but that was just day one of the festa. The pantomime went on for the whole of the following day, with the good guys finally usurping the evil Muslims, and also slaying a number of strange, scarecrow-like demons, who were clad in welly boots, and masks made from egg boxes. These chores having been completed, the heroes of the piece finally marched down the street and reclaimed the town hall - with more lengthy and completely inaudible speeches.

This fantastic drama was quite obviously a relative of the Moors and Christians festivals still celebrated, with processions and fireworks and "battle" marches, in various Spanish towns. It was evidently brought to this African outpost by people for whom the reconquest of Iberia was still vital and relevant; it may even have been performed here since the earliest days of the island's settlement, in the 15th or 16th century. And no doubt in the old colonial days the ruling class took the heroes' role and gave their workers the weekend off so that they could play the part of the losers.

Perhaps the most remarkable thing about the play, besides its survival, is the irony of the modern actors' sentiment and stance. Here they were - all of them black, all of them descendants of a people enslaved by the Portuguese - and yet they happily portrayed unquestioning support for the position of their erstwhile rulers and tormentors.

Let us hope that the good people of São Antonio continue, for a long time hence, to dwell happily in socio-political ignorance. One day some misguided activist will arrive to stir the people up to

Rightful Indignation, and then this precious antique play will be destroyed.

Although it rained hard throughout most of the two day Festa São Lorenzo, this did nothing to dampen anyone's enthusiasm; the people were all quite used to the rain. Our visit actually coincided with the dry season – or, at least, we had been under the impression that this was the dry season. Carlitos confirmed the fact.

"But it rains cats and dogs every afternoon," we complained.

"In the rainy season it does it every morning, *and* every afternoon, *and* all night – cats and dogs, and cows and elephants."

Nobody bothered to follow the São Lorenzo drama throughout its whole course, and between battles the actors themselves could be found taking refreshment in one of the several bars. We also took time out, in an interval of our own choosing, to climb the muddy, rain-soaked, lushly forested, mosquito-infested hills behind the town. We wanted to meet the folk who live off the land on the 'rosas', or old plantations.

Until the Portuguese imperialists were finally obliged to quit, back in 1975, the economy of São Tome and Principe was dependent entirely on cocoa. Since the workers did not live long in the unhealthy climate, new ones were needed all the while. Many of them came from the Cape Verde Islands.

Even before they left their homes, the Cape Verdeans knew that conditions down in São Tomé were terrible. A stretch in São Tomé was spoken of colloquially as a prison sentence, and it was common knowledge that, even in the 1950s, the workers were still driven towards their quota by men wielding whips. Yet for many this was their only chance to avoid death from starvation in their drought-stricken homeland.

With the departure of the Portuguese the cocoa industry folded, and the islands quickly became financially bankrupt. But the Cape Verdeans stayed. They continued to live on the old abandoned rosas. The slave drivers had gone, and there were no longer any jobs for them, but the land was now theirs for the taking.

Oddly enough, the people did not move into the fancy houses which had belonged to their masters. These are now mouldering and ruinous. Instead, they continued to inhabit their workers' hovels, and this was where we found them: men, women, and hordes of children all dressed in filthy rags or even in their birthday suits. The Cabo Verdeans have not integrated with the other islanders, and they are still regarded as immigrants – but the ones that we met didn't seem to care. They were very happy with their life and lot. Ignoring the old cocoa plantations, they had become subsistence farmers, living off the land. Besides producing their own vegetables and gathering fruit from the trees, they also grew sugar canes and like their cousins back in Santo Antão and Santiago they made grog.

Would they like to go back - back to the motherland - we asked the people whom we met on the rosas?

"Never!" came the swift reply. "Why would we ever want to go back?"

The contrast between their parched, barren homeland and this phenomenally lush and wet one was dramatic.

"If you drop a seed here, it grows. Life is so easy!"

The Cape Verdeans of Principe are poorer even than their brethren to the north. They have no money, no income whatsoever, and none of the ability of a traditional or 'primitive' society to weave its own cloth or light a fire with two sticks. Nevertheless, despite their absolute rock-bottom poverty, these people were the most contented that we had ever met, anywhere.

Of course, they were also completely ignorant. Cape Verde is still brown and naked, and ever more will be so, but life there is very different from what it was when the parents and grandparents of these immigrants left. Would that knowledge be of benefit to them? Clearly it would not, we decided – and rather than give them the news of the world we gave them two dustbin bags stuffed full of cast off clothing.

Now the interval is over and the house lights dim. We take our seats once more, for Act II: - in which the president, with whom we still seek audience, is called away to São Tomé, the president of the mother isle having been deposed in an armed coup. Only in the pixie-land republic of São Tomé and Principe could an armed coup be performed as a light-hearted comedy.

The curtain rises on Father Elias, a long-haired eccentric who dresses in sandals and a long sack-cloth shirt.

"*Him*, a priest!" Nick was raised as a Roman Catholic, and he found it hard to make room for this hippie amongst the purple and gold robed incense shakers of his recollection.

Father Elias was Swiss-born but he was fluent in both Portuguese and English, and this made him the ideal man to act as translator between ourselves and the president. Our smattering of Cabo Verdean creole coloured with snatches of faltering Brazilian dialect was not always intelligible to the people of these parts. Added to this, the padre was the perfect, unbiased go-between for - as he frequently told us - he loved everybody. Around his neck a rough-hewn cross hung on a leather thong. All that was needed to complete his image was a wooden staff.

It was from Father Elias that we learnt about the coup d'etat. True to the usual "third-world" form, the usurpers were a bunch of junior army officers - kids in their early twenties - but in this case the absence of involvement from any of their seniors was due to the fact that these had all been pensioned off. Perhaps the juniors feared similar treatment. The entire army was said to consist of no more than 200 men, eight of whom were responsible for defending the island of Principe.

Having locked the president away - some said in his home; some said in a cupboard, gagged and bound - the leaders of the coup then turned to his deputy. They had nothing against the party in general, it seemed, just a personal grudge against the main man. Now the way was clear for the number two to take over, if he would. He would not. Nor would the leader of the opposition, who was also invited. The leaders of the coup put out a general invitation. Would anybody like to come and run the country?
No takers.

From the minute that the coup was announced leaders all over the "civilised" world had condemned it. They had universally declared their intention to pull out their aid if the Democratically Elected Representative was not returned to the throne. All this was obviously a touch embarrassing for the young lads. They had got hold of something much too hot to handle and now nobody else would play ball. With elections due in only a couple of months time, was it really any wonder?

News of the coup d'etat in São Tome did not exactly grab the world's headlines. The BBC mentioned the affair on the World Service but not on the telly, so that our parents were not to know that we were impotent hostages held to ransom by a terrorist regime. In fact, even we did not discover until it was all over that the ports and airports had been officially closed. As for the criminals who truly held us captive, they were working to an independent charter.

"Perhaps we could get in through the window."

"Perhaps, but what about the safe?" I pictured a trail of gunpowder leading across the floor of the harbour master's office, and the safe going up with a puff and a bang. Butch Cassidy and the Sundance Kid were lurking somewhere at the edge of my imagination.

"We could just do a runner. Do you think they would give us new passports in Ascension, if we explained?"

"And what about all that flowery chat in the front of the passport? Doesn't it say that the document is the property of the British Crown?"

"How does that help us?"

"It's a pity there isn't a British Consulate around here."

Along came our young friend, Carlitos. A mulatto man of about twenty years, he was one of the few in this place who had heard the singing of the sirens and who looked beyond his own little world. Carlitos knew that there was a bigger, better life beyond the limp forest and the village where he was born, and he wanted to be part of it. Hence his attachment to us. He loved everything Western; he loved to listen to Michael Jackson and would sing along, believing that he knew the lyrics. He had called his house "Sunset Beach". ("Is beautiful, no? What is meaning?")

With Carlitos walked Father Elias, who brought news of the comic drama still continuing in the mother isle. The deposed president had announced that he was going on hunger strike and would "defend democracy with his life." Meanwhile, the cast had been augmented by a party of Angolans who had arrived to mediate with the soldier boys. The boys were having one last go before they agreed to back down; they had discovered that, in the absence of the president, the Speaker of the House was constitutionally obliged to take over, whether he liked it or not. As a bid to save face it was feeble in the extreme. It fell flat when the Speaker refused to do his bit.

"But it is not funny," said the padre, as we fell about laughing. "One man is dead."

"Who is dead? Not the president?"

"No. One of the officers is dead. He shot himself accidentally while he was cleaning his gun."

Father Elias wandered away down the cobbled street.

"I fancy him," said Carlitos.

After another couple of days the two men who had instigated the coup d'etat were persuaded to step down, which they did on condition that there be absolutely no recriminations. The president of São Tomé went back into the palace and ate dinner. The moral of the story is that little boys should not be given guns.

Our own saga had a less satisfactory finish. On his return, the president of Principe declared that the charges which we had been seeking to avoid were legal and proper and must be paid. He did not address himself to the theft of our passports. We left - having paid the ransom - still under the impression that there must be some mistake. Or else, perhaps, His Excellency was in league with the conspirators?

When we reached São Tomé and told our sorry tale to the only expatriate (Portuguese) yachtsman, he just nodded and said, "Yes, that's the way it is." Even as a resident of the country he and his wife had to pay the full charge - less the cost of the visas - every time they entered the country. I repeat, for the sake of anyone who may be thinking of heading that way: in 1995 it cost $252 (U.S.) for a yacht and three yotties to enter the state of São Tomé. By the time you read this, it might cost even more.

But I digress. We were not yet done with Principe. We trickled on around the island to Ilha de Bom-Bom, a little pile of rugged rocks buried beneath a dense thatch of trees. Bom-Bom was joined onto the main island by a long wooden jetty, slippery with rain, and where the jetty reached the little islet there stood a hotel restaurant, also built of wood. Wooden chalets with shiny wet, wooden verandas peeped from the sodden forest which carpets the whole of Principe. Around a little swimming pool, dimpled by the downpour, were other chalets shrouded by dripping palm-fronds. And this was the dry season, remember!

"I bet they don't mention the weather in their brochure," I said to Nick, and he agreed.

"Anyone who forks out to come and stay here must have been conned!"

We were met on the yellow sand beach by a South African gentleman who said that we had anchored within the hotel's domain.

If we wanted to enjoy "the facilities" we would have to pay $15 (U.S.) per person. Actually, the hotel did not like yachtsmen, the South African continued: "Yachtsmen dump their rubbish overboard and pollute the water with their effluent."

This was rich, coming from one who spoke with his feet planted on either side of a strong-smelling stream of diesel. Swirling, rainbow-coloured patterns of the man's own making painted the halcyon bay.

Just around the corner from Bom-Bom is Baia das Agulha - Bay of the Needle. The said "needle" is a stunning monolith - the remnant of a great volcano - which pushes its way up from amongst the lush foliage and overlooks the bay. In truth, it is more like a cathedral spire than a needle. Clouds swirled about the mighty shaft and a prism of light bound a halo to the summit. Surely, in the minds of the primitive African slaves who saw it, this stone must have been the abode of a god?

The minds of the men who now live below the megalith are not primitive, but their dwellings are as humble as those of the Pygmies or the Bushmen. With trees all around them for the taking, the fishermen are nevertheless content to live in huts the size of a wendy house, built out of no more than sticks and leaves. We found two families living together in what could not even be called a cave; it was just a great, overhanging rock. Its face - their living room and bedroom wall - ran all the while with rain.

But were these fisherfolk unhappy? On the contrary; they seemed quite content with their lot. They were not in the least bit covetous. They sold us salt fish, bread-fruit, bananas, coconuts, and matebala - a delicious kind of coco-yam which grows rampantly here. All of these things we could have gathered for ourselves freely, had we been of such a mind, but this was no sacrosanct culture which we feared to trample with even the most meagre generosity. Money having little meaning here, there being no shops, the bill was paid with fish hooks and plastic margarine tubs.

On then, to São Tomé. This is the bigger, by far, of the two islands and a place of an altogether different character. Here the land was still worked, and coffee, cocoa, and coconut palm plantations covered all. The people, although they were by no means affluent, at least had shirts on their backs and roofs to keep out the rain.

In Principe there were no cars, but here we were able to hire a car and explore. We found that the climate in this tiny place was surprisingly diverse, with much of the island being as damp and verdant as Principe but with one corner being so dry that the grass was yellow and there were baobab trees growing.

After six months, Johnnie had finally had enough of our company. He did not want to cross the ocean with us, and so we bid him adieu. We left the port and limped south against a light breeze. At the far end of São Tomé there is an islet which has the distinction of lying exactly on the equator. As its grey outline rose above the grey horizon we could say for sure that we were looking at the equator. The children, however, looked in vain. Concepts are as invisible as fairies.

At the close of the damp, dank, dreary day we turned away from the auspicious line of latitude and drifted into the bay of São Joaõ, still a few miles to the north. This was a pleasant anchorage, nestling between two headlands – but, as we were soon to discover, it had something more to offer besides good holding and ample shelter.

At the back of the bay was a yellow, rain-soaked beach, and beyond the beach, a sodden forest of palm trees. Now, there are many different species of palm tree. There are date palms, which grow only in hot dry places, and there are coconut palms, which are far less fussy and grow all throughout the tropics. There are oil palms, whose nuts are used to make cooking oil, and rhum palms, whose timber is good for building jetties; there are raffia palms, whose fronds are good for weaving baskets, and there are wine palms. Yes, wine palms!

During our travels in West Africa we had often been proffered a gourd full of the milky white nectar of the wine palm tree, but never had we seen it so abundantly available as it was in São Tome – and never had we encountered such a *grand cru*. Palm wine is not very strong, and it is not remotely like the produce of the vine, but it is just as variable in taste. In Guinea Bissau it is rather thin and "green". Here, in São Tome, it was both sweet and astringent; and it was enjoyed by all.

Padre Elias, though he cursed the demon grog, spoke in tones of near rapture concerning palm-wine. Caesar and Xoë had never shown any interest or curiosity regarding red wine or beer, and they knew that strong drink could be lethal - in Principe we had witnessed the wake of a little boy who died after he got his hands on a bottle of grog – yet, although the children knew that alcohol was dangerous, they begged for a sip – "one more sip, just one more" - of this forbidden fruit. Johnnie, meanwhile, had become a true palm wine aficionado, and whereas it would have been completely impossible to persuade him to go ashore and buy bread or potatoes, throughout the week of our stay in the town of São Tomé he had gone each day to the market place with an empty litre bottle in either hand. If only he had known what awaited us in São Joaõ...

In São Tomé, this tipple is so important that whole acres of forest are devoted especially to its production, and there were even men, known as tapsters, whose sole employment is the collection of palm sap. The sign of a bottle protruding from the spiky foliage of a tree is evidence that the tapster is somewhere around, or soon will be. It takes a day for the bottle to fill. And whereas in Guinea Bissau the sap has to be left to ferment for at least twenty four hours, here it is ready straight away - no messing. Just imagine! While lovers of the hard stuff must work away, with mill and fire and still, and whilst even the beer drinker has to wait a week for his potion to brew and the connoisseur of the grape even longer, the Africans have booze on tap! And here in São Tomé it cost only 20 pence for one and a half litres.

The only snag with palm-wine is that it must be consumed within a few hours, or else it turns to vinegar. Oh, alas and alack! We *must* finish the bottle within the evening. Of course, this also means that palm wine cannot be popped into a can and packaged-up for overseas supermarkets, which is why most people have never heard of it.

"If ever I live ashore it will be beneath a wine palm tree," I told Nick.

We had been anchored for two days in the bay of São Joaõ before we discovered its greatest virtue. On the third day we were gathering fallen coconuts on the beach when along came a little gaggle of women carrying empty jerry cans. We had seen the women before. Each morning they carried their empty cans along the beach, and then, an hour later, they carried back again on their heads. Naturally, we at first assumed that the women had gone to get water - but it seemed strange that in this most moist corner of the globe they should have so far to walk. We would have expected to find at least one well up in the village. The truth of the matter was that the women were visiting the fountain of Dionysus. The fact is that São Joaõ is the palm-wine capital of the world.

It grieved us no end that Johnnie had left before this discovery, which must have been beyond his wildest dreams. Still, perhaps it was just as well. If he had found the place, he would probably be there to this day. To make up for his loss we toasted him, as an absent aficionado, each and every time the wine flowed.

15

STEPPING STONES

*In which we find friendship and entertainment
at a couple of 'stone warships'.*

"9th September. *Grimly overcast but with little actual rain. Depart São
Tomé, under sail, at about 10.30.*"

Beyond the shelter of the deeply indented bay the wind was south to
south-westerly, force three or thereabouts. We tacked southward,
along the coast, our attention taken up with the "Seven Rocks" - of
which there seemed to be only six. And then there were eight, nine,
and finally ten, as more appeared over the horizon. Cartographers of
old seem to have been inspired more by poetic licence than by the
desire to provide accurate navigational information. Or perhaps they
were just innumerate.

Towards the southern end of São Tomé we saw another
mighty spire of rock, remaining from another antediluvian volcano.
This one reached up towards the low cloud which carpeted the
whole island, now and then snagging it and tearing off little, woolly
wisps. The megalith is called Grand Caõ, which means Big Dog, but
it was probably named for the explorer, Sebastian Caõ. It was odd to

think of his having been here when the New World was still undiscovered and even the bottom end of Africa had yet to be located.

Our preparations were under way for an equator crossing party, and our eyes were on the equatorial island of Ilheu Gago Coutinho, when suddenly we realised that we were, even now, crossing the line. Poseidon was hastily invoked and his might remarked upon. We toasted him (in palm-wine, of course), poured libation upon the sea and paid the toll in dobras, cedis, Guinean francs and Cape Verdean escudos. Prayers were also offered to The Creator and to his saints and other minions, for a safe crossing, fair winds, and no storms.

Ten minutes later, we tacked in towards the shore and crossed the line again. Then we tacked out and crossed it for a third time. Caesar and Xoë found this an excellent excuse for repeated drinks of apple juice although, for the life of them, they could not see this magical median. A year later, their toy sailing ships were still struggling over ridges in the carpet to accompanying cries of, "Hang on tight! Here comes the equator!"

That evening we hung up all our old African courtesy ensigns - from Cape Verde, Senegal, The Gambia, Guinea Bissau, Guinea, Côte d'Ivoire, Ghana and São Tomé - and we had a farewell party. Our stay had been three times longer than we intended but had still been something of a whistle stop tour. We vowed to return, someday.

As for the mosquitoes and the malaria: these were so dreaded by the folks at home that they had chided us for exposing our little ones to such danger and begged us to think again - so putting us in a very uncomfortable position. In the event, although we had seen plenty of mosquitoes after the beginning of the rainy season, our diligent preparations and nightly vigilance proved effective. In ten months Caesar had been bitten just once and Xoë never at all.

By the time the canopy of darkness came creeping over the world from the east, Africa was but a memory in our wake. Lost in the gloaming were the little grey specks floating, forgotten, in the Bight of Biafra. We were on our way towards southern South America.

"Cape Horn, or bust."

"Yes, here's to Cape Horn. And we're only three years behind schedule. No more diversions now," I said. "We're going to get there this time."

We had planned our route: Uruguay, and the Rio Plata were our first destination. Then, having got the boat ready for bad weather, we would head south to the whale breeding ground of Peninsula Valdez. Our adventures in the Southern Ocean would commence with a visit to the Falkland Islands, after which we would cross back over to the mainland and to Tierra del Fuego and the Horn. It was all worked out and there would be no more dallying.

Above us the quilted sky fell to pieces, like an ice-flow fractured by the thaw. Jove hung his lantern upon the head of the scorpion, and then the full moon rose, burning away all with her radiance.

"10th September. *Intermittent sunshine. Wind from the south, force four to five. This morning we were joined, suddenly as ever, by some kind of 'black fish'.*"

All cetacean sightings made from *Maamari* are recorded in a separate log dedicated exclusively to that purpose, and the following excerpt describes the visitors:

"*16.00 hours. Sunshine. Cloud 4 octas.*
Boat speed 4 knots. Course 260° (Hard on the wind.)
Fin of a "dolphin" seen beside the boat. Observation immediately showed it to be that of either a melon-headed whale or a pygmy killer-whale.
7 individuals. One was seen to 'spy-hop', exposing a white chin or chest. Heads seemed to resemble those of pygmy killer-whales rather than melon-headed whales. Very faint, v-shaped cape below the fin. One animal seemed to be swimming upside-down beside the boat. She had white markings all along her length.
Accompanied us 10 to 15 minutes. Windward side. Disappeared very suddenly"
- as such beings are wont to do.

Towards evening time, on that same day, I saw a tremendous splash on the far horizon. Then I saw another splash... and another. The action went on for about half an hour, but still I was unable to solve the mystery of its cause. Was it a whale jumping? If so, I never actually saw him; even through the glasses I could only see the huge splashes. To be all alone in this great ocean and yet to see evidence of other, unknown life leaves one with an odd, slightly eerie feeling. What would the mediaeval mind have made of this one, I wondered?

That night - the night following our second day at sea - I studied the dim horizon in the usual way and my eyes fell upon the light of a stranger. The bleary beacon grew, as it tracked slowly across the sea. It looked as if it would pass ahead. Then it altered away from us, perhaps by as much as 90°.

"So, it's a fishing boat," I thought to myself.

I do not much like to share the ocean with a fishing boat. Where there is one there are usually many more, and their movements are wholly unpredictable. In Biscay I have been almost run-down by the terrorist activities of the master of a trawler, and early one morning off Sierra Leone a huge purse-seiner had caused us considerable alarm by circling about *Maamari* at great speed. It had only gone away after I stood the children on deck.

I searched the horizon all around. There were no other lights. I turned back to look at the first - but he was gone... Quickly now! The radar! I hurried below to turn it on. But not the tiniest blip marred the even, green circuit painted by the scanner.

Throughout the rest of my watch I peered apprehensively into the black depths of the night. What could it be that vanished even from the radar screen? The thought that there might be a submarine creeping along just below our keel made me cringe. Submariners are not awfully good at spotting yachts and have been known to emerge beneath them.

We pressed on to the south, beating still, in search of the south-easterly trades. On the 11th we saw risso's dolphins (known in this family as rissoles, I'm afraid). They surged towards us purposefully - two great white shapes under the water. Blunt heads, but none the less beautiful for that. It was plain that they had searched us out and come to see us, yet they kept their distance, repeatedly diving deeply under the keel in the manner of orcas, and reappearing ten or fifteen yards away on the opposite beam. As ever, we felt almost apologetic about our inability to communicate with the creatures.

Another entry in the cetacean log records another visit, later that same day, by four or five risso's dolphins. Their markings were different from the first two, whose mottled white hides had borne scarcely a scratch. Their behaviour was once again recorded in depth.

We were four days out from São Tomé before we slipped from beneath the cloud coverlet which had been spread over the African continent. Now the sun fell fully upon us again, as it had not done since we were in Guinea. The wind, too, was finally blowing like the trades, although not from the appropriate direction - we had a steady sou'-sou'-westerly. Most telling of all, for the first time in months we were back in the big, long swell which one only finds on the open ocean.

Unfortunately, although her crew were happy to be back on the high seas, our ship seemed to have gone to seed. The fresh breeze tested gear which had seen no strain for almost a year, the first in the firing line being the sails.

"Nick! Come quickly! Come and give me a hand," I cried as I ground away at the winch. "Curse this sail! Come and give me a hand, Nick! The genoa's splitting."

Even as I spoke I could hear the stitching on the sail open - pop..pop..pop..pop..pop - and before my eyes the cerulean blue of the sky burst through between the panels. "Confound it!"

The genoa was a beautiful sail, but shoddily made. For months now it had been giving us trouble, although it was less than three years old. By contrast, our mizzen was a marvellous piece of workmanship. It was now approaching its sixth birthday but the only attention that it had ever needed was to one chafed pocket.

We dropped the genoa and Nick sat on the foredeck on a folding chair, the hot sun on his bare back and a sail maker's leather palm on his own. It takes quite a bit of strength to push the wedge-shaped steel needle through two layers of heavy-weight terylene sail cloth.

While Nick worked, a company of little spotted-dolphins came to see us. Although *Maamari* was almost stopped they played around us for about twenty minutes, gathering off the windward side of the boat and surging towards us in ranks of four and five. Others charged about around us at great speed, jumping and slapping their tails on the water. At any one time there were around thirty individuals close by, but there seemed to be a trend across our path and we reckoned that, in all, more than a hundred went passed.

We had now been at sea for less than a week, but already our meal times and the children's sleeping schedule had become erratic.

Although Nick and I followed our usual, fairly inflexible routine, Caesar and Xoë had succumbed to chaos. It was as if they did not notice or understand our new arrangements, or perhaps they had not been able to absorb them or decide how their own patterns might be slotted in. If they woke in the night and realised that one of their parents was up and about, then the children would want to come out and join in the fun. Meal times were equally inconsistent, for if they got up in the early hours and found Daddy tucking-in, then they would want to eat too. After that, they would have no appetite for breakfast but would be hungry again at about ten-thirty. Following on from this, lunch might be a kind of tea, eaten at half past four. Supper would then hold no interest, but a midnight snack would be called for.

Provided that we all got enough food and sleep, the lack of order did not matter much, so far as I could see. The galley was open all hours and the bed was always there. Often, Mummy or Daddy were already in it, providing the perfect environment for a quiet cuddle and a snooze.

On the afternoon of the 13th we were about to have some sort of meal when someone - I forget who - sighted the tell-tale blow of a whale. The animal was underway and set to pass close by. We timed the intervals between those steamy gasps and studied their shape. The blows were inclined forwards - the certain trademark of a sperm whale. Where was he going, with such purposeful intent, and did others of his clan lurk beneath the waves?

Nick ascended the main mast for a better view off the action. Every eight to ten seconds there was another tall cloud of spray - we counted about twenty such blows all told - and then, while he was alongside our beam but still a little way off, the whale issued one final shower of spray. As he did so he revealed the leading edge of his square-shaped head and we saw his blow-hole flap. The sea parted as his brown back sailed by, and then the flukes waved, and he was gone. For an hour, Nick remained aloft. *Maamari* was bound in precisely the opposite direction from Moby, but neither one of us was doing more than a couple of knots.

It is my ambition someday to shout, "Thar she blows!" at the top of my lungs - but in the excitement of the moment I always forget and cry, "Ooh, look everybody! There's a whale!" On what seem like promising days, or after a whale has recently been seen, I stand with eyes strained to catch the first distant spout. But whales are like kettles; they never let off steam while you are waiting. The hour passed but the whale, if he surfaced within that time, surfaced far, far away.

Later in the day we received another visitation, from a community of spotted-dolphins, and they came to see us several times over the course of the next few days.

"16th September. *Blue sea. White crests. Sunshine pouring from a bright blue sky. Gloria in excelsis Deo! It is so good to be a part of this world.*

Caesar and Xoë have made no complaint about leaving the land behind them, but this morning they showed that they do not have any comprehension of the time and distance involved in our journey: they asked whether we would arrive today!

In the afternoon the wind gradually rose. Maamari was chundering through the foam, ploughing a straight furrow across the short seas. But, no - I do her wrong in comparing her to a plough horse; she was a wild mare galloping, and I let her have her head. Froth flurried past the cockpit, but below decks there was little sensation of increased speed - no pitching, no crashing from wave to wave - only an increase in the inclination of the cabin floor. Maamari was a thoroughbred thundering evenly over the turf.

Ah, but Maamari, you are not a flighty quarter tonner, frisking about on the Solent. You are an old lady, with a precious burden to carry across the great, empty ocean. Steady there! Woah! It's good to be hurtling along, kicking away the miles, but what if something breaks? Perhaps it's time to drop the main..."

Finally awoken by the fluster of the water dashing past the hull, Nick came on deck with bleary eyes. If one has been sleeping and then comes outside, the wind always seems windier, and the water wilder, and everything generally more radical and out of control. Or is it simply that things creep up on the other fellow? White hair is a sudden surprise to the returning wanderer, and white water weltering by alarms the chap who has been fast asleep.

Nick hurried forward to drop the main. Poor *Maamari*. She stopped as surely as if she had run into a brick wall. Well, no, not quite; in fact, she was still making a good three knots. At least, this way, we should arrive in one piece.

"19th September. *No ships, no whales, no birds. Just shoals of flying fish...*"

On the 22nd September our midday sights showed that we had only fifty miles still to run to Ascension Island, and in the afternoon I saw a booby, with striking black and white plumage and a yellow bill. This confirmed our arithmetic findings, for such birds are not often seen far from land. A while later, a frigate bird sailed overhead and looked down at the boat.

At a quarter past four we sighted the island, a pale grey cone printed at the foot of a great sheet of pale blue sky. A tropic bird came out to welcome us with shrill shrieks. He circled about and tried landing on the tip of the mast, as it whipped to and fro and roundabout, but like all the others of his kind who have attempted the same trick in the past, he failed in his effort.

Sometime after night had descended, I stepped out into the cockpit and was startled by a little white ghost who flitted away from the guard rail and into the opaque black. The tropic bird again.

As ever, we had no idea what to expect of Ascension. It was British, that we knew, and it was a military base. Unexpected guests are not always welcomed with open arms in a military base. Worse yet, memory suggested that the place might have been leased to the Americans - in which case we would be "aliens".

"Wait a minute! What about Wideawake; isn't Wideawake here?"

Nick looked blank and said, "Who's Wideawake?"

"Let me see. Ah, yes - *The Story of the Falklands War*." I took the book form the shelf and flicked through the index. "Wideawake. Yes, it's here, in Ascension. They used it to fly that raid, you know?"

"No."

"It says here that it's the second biggest air-strip in the world."

So what did that tell us? Not a lot really, but now we envisaged an island bristling with guns and radar and radio beacons. There would be two dozen Tornadoes and Harriers and Hercules waiting in neat lines upon acres of black asphalt. We wondered why they had not come out to say hello. Aeroplane pilots like to buzz little boats. Surely, if this was a military base they must have spotted us by now?

As night advanced we passed beyond the most northerly point of the island and sailed into something of a wind-shadow. We pressed on until we reached Georgetown. We could see a couple of rows of street lights; nothing more. Nick dropped the main and spent the night casually drifting to and fro. There was a ship anchored off, but it was in water far too deep and rough for *Maamari*. The chart showed reefs close by the shore and since there were no leading lights we had no choice but to stand off until daybreak.

What was it like, this far-flung tropic isle? Darkness hid the answer, but to judge from the chart it seemed a rugged place. I pictured an island as luxuriant as São Tomé, but dawn took Ascension out from beneath the night's cloak and revealed a red-brown mound almost as bare as the Cape Verde Islands.

We anchored and waited to see if anyone would come and tell us to push off. Eventually, a man came by in a little dory and we exchanged greetings. Was he a fisherman, we wondered? The limpid, azure water was thronged with jet black trigger fish as voracious as piranhas.

"Lord, no! There are no fishermen in Ascension," our visitor declared. "Everybody here has a job!"

Ascension lies almost 1,000 miles to the north of St Helena - that other last toehold of the great British empire - yet although distance divides them, these far-flung flecks on the pale blue page of the atlas are sisters. More than the mere fact of British possession binds them together, for a large sector of the Ascension Island population is St Helenian. In fact, at the time when we were visiting, there was no such thing as an Ascension Islander, and nor was there any opportunity for people of private means to settle here. The residents of the island were there to work – just as our first visitor had told us. They worked for either the British or the U.S. government, and when their contracts expired they had to go home.

Nick and his parents had stopped off in St Helena in 1985, but in those days the word was that yachtsmen were not the least bit welcome in the northern isle. Fortunately, the official line has been loosened a little in recent years and visitors are now allowed ashore in Ascension. According to the official who cleared us into the place, we might wander as we pleased amongst the myriad golf ball aerials and under the VHF wires; we could even go into the U.S. base, or amble onto the immense military airfield (where there were no planes at all) - but we were only permitted to stay for 48 hours, and we must obey a seven o'clock curfew and be off the island by that hour. Those were the rules.

Happily, the residents of the rock were more open hearted than the anonymous, invisible originators of the rules. They were proud to display their "island hospitality" and we were soon adopted by a lovely Scottish couple who took us on a tour of the island. The man was a spy. He introduced himself to us as, "the fellow who sweeps the floors at GHQ", but in Ascension the job of sweeping the floor is only available to a "Saint" - or St Helenian - and British-born employees spend their days with their ears glued to the radio, listening intently to each and every radio transmission that comes tripping across on the international airwaves. Either that, or else they man the vast empty airfield and await the arrival of the once-weekly flight from Blighty. Others work for the BBC, whose aerial field carries health warnings. ("You don't stop your car, while you're driving through here," said our floor sweeping friend. "If you do, that's it: you're sterile.")

Then there were the yanks. They numbered about 200 at the time of our visit and were there, ostensibly, because Wideawake is the emergency landing place for the space shuttle. On a high hill above the island's south-west coast, remote from any gaze, stood a big empty building. The Americans formerly used it, and a notice on the door says that it was the shuttle-tracking station.
"Take a look through the window," said the spy. "See all that space? They had twenty men up here, and loads of machinery. Do you think they'd need that lot just to keep an eye on the bloomin' shuttle?"

Many months later we heard that the Americans had been firing missiles from their own land all the way out to this stone warship, only dropping them just before they hit the shore. I wonder whether any of those fellows up on the hill were keeping watch for folks like us, who might be innocently sailing by? I have my doubts.

Xoë and Caesar loved Ascension. Our Scottish friends had a television, and Caesar thought this a wonderful thing. Xoë was fascinated by the taps in their house, which worked without anybody pumping them. The children were both thrilled to bits with the corner-shop sized supermarket in Georgetown, and they ran up and down pointing out this or that gaily coloured packet or tin; there had been nothing like this in West Africa. After a time, however, something else caught Xoë's attention, and she cried, "Mummy! Look!"
I was a bit tired, by now, of being shown wonderful packets and tins,

but I looked round anyway. Standing in the queue at the checkout was a woman with a child a little bit bigger than Xoë, and Xoë was staring at her in complete astonishment.

"Mummy!" she said, "There's a girl just like me!"

According to the observations which she had made during her two and a half year's existence, the world was filled with black people and we were the only whites. Thinking back, I now realised why it was that Caesar had sometimes complained, "Why didn't you make me black?"

Our 48 hours "shore leave" was soon up, and we were preparing to get underway, when the captain of the oil tanker, *Maersk Ascension,* came to call. Would we care to join him for lunch, he asked? Certainly we would.

Maersk Ascension was a kind of floating bunker, permanently anchored about half a mile off the island. Rumour had it that submarines could lie alongside the tanker and refuel without betraying their whereabouts to the world. An unlikely story, but no more far-fetched than the whole fanciful world of Ascension.

Captain Browne carried us out to his ship in a big semi-rigid inflatable, and when we came alongside a hydraulic arm reached out and we were hoisted aboard, boat and all. Lunch was excellent, and then, eventually, the time came for us to leave. But, alas, the crane was no longer available; it was being serviced!

60 feet below the deck, the rubber boat waited impatiently, bouncing about in the waves. Xoë could cadge a ride on Daddy's hip, but poor little Caesar must climb all the way down the sheer metal wall under his own steam. And so must I.

The rope ladder swayed as the ship heaved gently up and down. The rungs were spaced for the long legs of the pilot, not for a little chap of four and a half years. Slowly Caesar and I made our way down it, with me descending just below and behind to give moral support. When we reached the end of the ladder, the dinghy rose up to meet us on the crest of the wave. I jumped. On the next wave, Captain Browne plucked Caesar off the ladder, with the words, "You're the bravest little lad I've ever met."

In just a few months time, someone else was to have reason to speak the same words.

We left Ascension at 18.00 hours that same day, the 25th September.

The wind was blowing a good force six, and we carried only the mizzen and most of the genoa, but we assumed that the rude weather was some kind of local effect, related to the wind-shadow that we had found on our arrival. The leeward shore of a mountainous island can often become windswept through the slightest change in the direction of the wind "outside", for such a change can send a breeze whistling into a ravine, or over a saddle. Like a draught blowing through a half-open doorway, the breeze is sucked through the narrow gap re-emerging at double its original strength.

Approaching the edge of the island, we rounded up and hoisted the main in anticipation of calmer weather ahead, but when we peeped out from behind Ascension the wind hit us like a hammer blow. Down came the main, and swiftly! We also furled half of the genoa. Even under such reduced canvas, *Maamari* went hurtling along.

The wind was actually very inconsistent, and strangely so. For ten minutes it would blow stink, and the air would be filled with spume and spray, like lashing hail. Then it would lower its tone and rumble. For a while, we answered the whims of the wind. In the first few lulls we raised the reefed main or unfurled a slice of the headsail. However, we soon learnt that the lulls seldom lasted very long. For perhaps a minute - and never so much as two - the wind would lie idle and sulk. Then back it came with another angry outburst.

So it went on all night and for the next two days. It was as if in stepping from behind Ascension we had stepped out of the world of blue seas and tropical sunshine. The wind's direction was more or less consistent - it blew from the south - but the strength was so variable that every ten or twenty minutes we had to be fiddling with the wind-vane, or the wheel, or the genoa - or all three. It was a frustrating, tiring business.

Sometimes it rained. Sometimes the sun peeped through and we rushed to take a sight. Occasionally there was even a patch of blue, but never one big enough to make the proverbial pair of trousers for a Dutchman. A discordant medley of squall clouds, fronts, and low stratus clouds hurried overhead.

On the afternoon of the 27th we were bowling along under full canvas when we were hit by a big squall. The lee deck dragged in the sea. I called to the children and told them to wake their father quickly. In a wind of this strength I could not manage to reef the genoa on my own without letting it flog for an age. The genoa winches were the biggest second-hand ones that we had been able to find - new ones were wholly unaffordable - but they were not big enough for me.

Nick was on deck in a matter of half a minute, and as soon as he arrived I let the sheet out a little way, to take some of the weight of wind out of the sail. As the sail began to flog, Nick leant his whole strength to the winch handle and ground the drum around and around - but even as he did so another seam began to open. He furled faster. I slowly released the rest of the sail... and watched the split march across the canvas, as if by the unclosing of a zip.

Now what? Well, obviously we could not unfurl the sail and drop it in this wind. That would have to wait. In the meantime we did need some kind of headsail. Already the fury of the squall had passed and *"Maamari"* was beginning to slop about aimlessly. Should we raise the stays'l on the inner forestay, we wondered, or would it be too much in the next sharp blow? Our only other option was to use the storm jib, a much stronger and far more diminutive item of our wardrobe.

"A waste of time," was Nick's prognosis. "The storm jib is so small that the mast, on its own, has more windage."

"But," I argued, "the mast does not have the same pulling power. At least let's get it out of the bag and see."

For almost an hour we dithered, our ideas alternating as the wind rose and fell, and rose and fell. At last we plumped for the pocket handkerchief storm sail, and to the captain's surprise it pulled us out of the gutter wherein we had been wallowing. Naturally, we were no longer cracking along at six knots - we were hardly making three - but at least we were on our way.

"28th September. *Wind-vane breaking up. We replaced it with another, smaller and tougher than the first. Wind force still six, with squalls of gale force eight, but these are much less frequent now, so that we risked using the stays'l. Our performance improved right away. Now we are making the same sort of progress that we would under furled genoa.*

The seas are getting bigger. They must be 15 to 20 feet at times. Leaping, dancing, white crests. Turquoise peaks, as clear as coloured glass. Sometimes they sink beneath us as they cross our path. Sometimes they surge beneath us, carrying us sideways and rolling us until the lee rail is awash.

Sometimes they slam into us with all the force of solid rock and with the sound of thunder. I find this very stressful and my nerves are frayed - I have this crazy notion that one almighty wave will smash through the egg-shell of the cabin side - but the kids are quite unperturbed and laugh gleefully each time."

It was odd that the sound of the waves should amuse the children so, for the *sight* of them no longer pleased even Xoë. Neither she nor her brother would do more than peep outside nowadays. Their time was entirely spent in playing with Lego and toy boats, and in reading.

The following day the wind and sea both abated and the swell changed direction, so that the waves were no longer arriving on the beam but on the port quarter. One huge wave landed on the aft cabin and the cockpit, burying everything for about two seconds and keeping the windows under solid water for a count of five. It gushed over the bottom board, which was the only one in place in the main companion way, and leapt down into the saloon. It even forced its way between the boards in the aft hatchway and soaked the corner of the bed.

To stop the water from getting into the aft cabin again, I took out all three boards from the hatchway, and then put them back in place together inside a plastic dustbin bag.

When the wind moderated further we hoisted the main with the first reef, but it was still too windy to unfurl the genoa and get it down to be mended. Another wave smashed off a length of the rubbing strake which had been damaged, many weeks earlier, by African canoes thumping up and down alongside us.

We flipped through Moitissier's book, *The Long Way*, and found that on this same day, many years before, he was off Trindade - which was our next destination. But he had been fighting not through gales but through light, variable winds and calms.

That day we had flying fish for lunch, several fine specimens having landed on our decks in the dark. One of them was as big as the ones which the Cape Verdean fishermen catch in their nets.

The weather was becoming chilly now, and I found that our coconut oil was solidifying in the bottles. Our other African stores were lasting well. Besides the yams and the maize we still had eight or ten brown coconuts which rattled about together on the side deck. They had been gathered in São Tomé, off the beach, and they had very thick, very sweet meat and plenty of sweet water. We were rationing them carefully, so that they would last us until we reached South America.

As we floated along, all alone - a mere speck on the surface of the vast ocean – I again found myself pondering upon the lives of the denizens below. "How big are the fish which swim out here?" I asked myself. "And do they just "hang out" in this almost infinite deep, or are they bound somewhere? If so, how do they know which way to go?" Questions of this nature trickled through my mind as I contemplated a smallish dorado which we caught on the 1st October. It was the first fish that we had landed for some time, but we had lost several lures. I wondered about the size of the fish who had managed to bite through the wire leaders or break our heavy-duty line.

That night, I again heard the peg on the fishing line snap shut. I pounced on the line as it shot out over the side of the boat. The beast which I hauled in was a most strange one: all head and teeth, with a long, skinny body. I thought that I might have found a living relic from the age of the dinosaurs, but Nick said that he had caught things like this one before. They were edible enough, he said. After a little bit of thought he decided that they were called snake fish.

During the night we sailed over the invisible line which marked the half way point between São Tomé and Punta del Este (which was to be our first port of call on the far side of the Atlantic). The children and I had made some little cakes, in preparation for a party, and in the early hours of the morning Poseidon provided another small dorado for our celebration.

Caesar and Xoë spent the morning washing and dressing their dolls and combing their hair. Then, they too were showered, and they put on some clothes and some African bead necklaces. The preparations were more meaningful than the actual, rather trivial do. I had made some crackers, each with a balloon and a toy rainforest animal inside, and these were a fantastic hit, but the party-poppers turned out to be party-poopers; Caesar had heard that smoke is dangerous, and so he fled from the cabin when the first one went off.

It was a glorious day. The wind had at last come around to the south-east and we were romping along. When night fell the sky remained clear and the moon poured its cold light upon us. Foam surged past the hull. White horses galloped by at a steady rhythm. The stays'l rolled and heaved, from side to side, and the main and mizzen strained at their preventers and banged and pumped.

Two days later the wind changed quite abruptly in the night, to the north-east, and we had to gybe. The swell was now east-north-easterly, and it was becoming bigger and shorter. *Maamari* lurched and rolled to and fro in a tedious, uncomfortable manner.

Our eyes now were upon the chart, and upon a little speck of rock called Martin Vaz. It belongs to Brazil - in as much as an uninhabited lump can truly be said to belong to anyone - the claim being based upon the ownership and occupation of Ilha Trindade, 25 miles to the west. As evening approached we began to gaze earnestly at the horizon, as if by hunting diligently we could bring the islet nigh. It was quite a high rock, we knew, for its altitude is given on the chart, and we also had a drawing sent to us by some French friends who had been here.

"Nous avons perdu le bateau." We have lost the boat. So, quite without emotion, began the letter from our French friends. It was at our instigation that the young couple had decided to take a look at Ilha da Trindade and Ilheu Martin Vaz. Without our encouragement, they would have gone straight from the Cape Verde islands to Rio de Janeiro. This was to have been their first ocean crossing. They had not been sailing for long.

With a mixture of shock and guilt we had read our friends' brief account, telling how *Roi de Harengs* had been carried ashore onto Trindade. "This is a beautiful place," Dabrice had written, "but I cannot recommend it to you. It is really very dangerous."

Besides the little sketch which Dabrice had sent, our only information for Trindade and Martin Vaz came from an Admiralty chart surveyed back in 1913. The Frenchman, in his letter, called this a wild flight of fancy.

"5th October. *Going by our performance over the past week we could have expected to make Martin Vaz by daybreak, or even before, but throughout the night we were thwarted by calms and contrary winds and squalls. We also encountered an easterly set.*

At daybreak we took star-sights - and in the midst of that urgent activity had to stop and land two snake fish, one after another. The star sights showed us to be still 26 miles off Martin Vaz. Despite the fact that we were aiming, all throughout yesterday, to overstand the place we now find ourselves obliged to beat."

It was not until midday that I finally sighted Martin Vaz. Its outline was as clear and clean as the chime of a bell, but it was also as pale as a harebell in the wood. For some reason it was still not visible on the radar, although it was quite obviously within the line of sight of the confounded machine.

Dolphins came and circled around the boat at great speed. Then they left abruptly, and in the same moment I saw a big fish, almost as big as they, come surging towards us down a wave as clear as glass. The fish came to check out our lure, but he was not fooled by pretty strips of yellow and silver plastic. He was coloured blue, like a dorado, but in shape he looked more like a shark - although I did not notice any fin.

By mid-afternoon the faint grey outline of Trindade was also visible, but that island was still more than forty miles distant. Martin Vaz was about 15 miles away. Its sides looked to be completely sheer. We wondered if anyone had ever managed to land there. And who was this fellow, Martin Vaz? We didn't know, but Caesar had just been given a new Lego man - a soldier on horseback - and when he asked what he should call him I answered at once: "He's Sir Martin Vaz, that's who he is."

We ploughed onward, against the wind. It was as if we were not destined to approach the rock. An unseen army held us at bay, hindering our advance with a force almost as sure as the repellent power of a magnet. Yet, we could continue to fight. And this invisible power might finish us off all together, by some means, or else it might suddenly back down and let us draw nigh.

Ah, there she goes again, with her own notions even more fanciful than the impression drawn up by the Admiralty! Out on the ocean, minds run free. Out here, man has not put his mark on Nature and trodden her beneath his heel.

The sun fell into the sea and set fire to the low clouds behind the unattainable rock. Or was it unattainable? Had Dabrice and Elena dared to profane the sacrosanct shore? Was their misfortune the anger of a god? Come now! Put down Homer; this odyssey is not to be governed by omens and fairy tales!

There seemed to be little point in hanging about, all night, by Martin Vaz. If we pressed on, we reasoned, then we could probably make Trindade by dawn. But once again our expectations were unfulfilled. This time we were hampered both by the light, contrary wind and by a big swell meeting us on the bow. By mid morning Trindade was still ten miles distant. Since sunset, twelve hours earlier, we had covered only thirty miles. My thoughts turned to lightening our load.

"Nick, why are we lugging all this gear around with us?" I asked. "You've got so many engine spares that you'll never need. Why have we got three spare heat exchangers, for example?"

"We might be glad of a new one, some day," the mechanic answered defensively.

"Yes. But these three are all too small for our engine. What are we carrying them around for?"

"There's nothing wrong with them! It would be criminal to throw them away!"

"You take after my father."

"What?"

"You're just like my dad. He's got a whole garage full of junk. The only difference is that you haven't got the garage..."

"Alright! Alright! I'll throw the whole lot overboard. But you'll be sorry when..."

"When we need one, two days later."

"We might!"

"And I'll be to blame."

"Of course!"

Stalemate. Then he said, crossly, "Your books weigh a ton. Why don't we throw some of *them* overboard?"

"Don't be stupid. *My* books; they're your books too!"

"And the heat exchangers are yours too."

I resisted the temptation to pick up *my* heat exchangers - not to mention a small, but weighty motor, long since seized solid; two seized-up 4hp Evinrude outboards; two Seagulls in similar condition; three alternators of unknown capability, and much, much more besides - and hurl them into the deep. Instead I pointed out that the books weighed nowhere near so much as these rusting lumps of iron.

"I'll bet they do! You've got hundreds of books! Thousands, probably!"

"Rubbish."

I changed tack. Ever since leaving Tema we had been hauling around the old engine, on the aft deck. No, I stand corrected; it was not the engine block itself - we had given that to Abbey (lucky man) - but we were still in possession of a full set of "spare" pistons, of a different size to the new ones, and we also had the cylinder head, the crank-shaft and the old, hopelessly corroded heat-exchanger. (Yes, a fourth "spare" heat exchanger.)

"For heaven's sake, what is this? If you want to start a scrap metal business we'll buy a nice bit of land and a nice, suburban semi..."

"Alright!" Faced with that horrid, below-the-belt threat, Nick capitulated. He went out onto the aft deck and threw the old engine spares into the sea.

The load having been lightened just a fraction, I unlashed the helm and took upon myself the task of easing the old girl up wind. Even out on the open ocean there are shifts in the wind's direction, and certainly there are waves to dodge. Left to herself a ketch will trot along, but the hand of a friend can help her to do better. And, anyway, on a day such as this what greater pleasure could there be? The sun shone and the fresh breeze pushed up pretty little white caps all over the blue sea. Ahead of us the island was an amazing, rock fortress emerging from ambiguity. As we drew nearer, some of the pale grey slopes which we had taken for vast plains of sand acquired a vaguely greenish hue. The peaks were fabulous castles of the wind, with giant grottos. On the most southerly tip of the island there was a tunnel - a pin-prick, from the distance at which we now viewed it, but said to be 300 metres long and tall enough for our mast. Deep enough for us too, if our French pilot book was to be believed, but doubtless strewn with rocks throughout, and probably subject to a tremendous surge.

As ever, we were approaching an island about which we knew almost nothing. Like Ascension, Trindade is a military base. In this case, it is a stone warship for the Brazilian navy. One tends to recoil from the idea of wandering, unannounced, into the arms of the South American military - it has about as much appeal as a social visit to a maximum security prison - but having already met the Marinha Brasiliero in Amazonia, we had fewer qualms than most. It was a pity that Dabrice had written so briefly of the island. He had given us little idea of what to expect in terms of our reception by the natives. On a sudden inspiration, Nick turned on the radio. Soon, somebody called us up - although we were still four miles off. Would we be stopping, the voice wished to know?

Yes, we would like to. Could we?

"Oh, *yes!*"

We were told that the anchorage was quite safe, at the moment. There was mention of a ship - or had we misunderstood? If there was a ship then it must be a naval supply ship. At the moment we were still too far off to see.

"Seabirds everywhere all of a sudden. Dark brown Trindade petrels, squealing like terns, and boobies, storm petrels, pomarine skuas - or perhaps they were arctic skuas - and a pair of delicate white terns."

We put in a tack. A helicopter appeared - a speck in the distance playing over the island. It rushed out towards us and circled round and round *Maamari*. It was painted battleship grey and the words Navio Brasiliero were emblazoned down the side.

By now we could see the ship, which was a little grey one. It was anchored just beside a village, or settlement, which consisted of half a dozen huts at the foot of the beautiful jagged mountain. We beat towards the shore on the draughts coming down over the rock. Right beneath the island there was little wind and the water was scarcely ruffled.

So this was the little bay where our friends had lost their yacht. It looked quite tame at the moment, but we knew that the slightest change in the wind's direction would send the swell sweeping onto the shore. Three sets of beacons identified the exact spot considered to be the best and safest place to anchor – and, naturally enough, the warship was sitting plumb on that patch.

Nick got out the lead line and we lowered the mainsail, the better to manoeuvre in this tight corner. And then I saw it - our friend's little, yellow boat. We had imagined her to have been sunk and smashed to smithereens, but there she lay, just above the high water mark and beyond some great, rounded boulders. Later, we were able to climb all over the boat, and we found that the hull was broken open all along one side.

I handed the helm to Nick. I rather fancy myself with the lead-line. Outside the warship the water was obviously going to be far too deep. We passed inside and I immediately swung the weight and let it fly. No bottom. To find the bottom, and the appropriate depth for a yacht to anchor, we were obliged to go quite a bit closer to the shore and well inside the transit marks. If the weather changed for the worse then we would have to get out fast because, according to the pilot book, we were now inside the area where the waves break.

The radio squawked back into life, welcoming us to Ilha da Trindade. This was pronounced Trin-daadj, or Trin-*daaD*, with a lot of emphasis on the final d. No mention was made of passports. We got the impression that the 'real world' and its trivialities did not exist here. Instead, we were invited to join the commandante for breakfast on the morrow and were told that there would be a party in the evening. Our anchorage might be rather unsatisfactory, but still it was a most contented crew who turned into their bunks that night.

16

MOLLYMAWKS

In which we intrude upon the world of the albatross.

Jth Dickin Schinas

We had timed our arrival at Trindade quite perfectly. The island is manned on a four month rota, so that only on three other days in the year could our coming have coincided with the change-over celebrations. Better still, the 7th October is Nick's birthday, and on this occasion it was the big four-oh. The gifts presented by his nearest and dearest were, I regret to say, few in number and rather paltry, but whatever wonders we could have produced they would all have paled into insignificance beside the excitement of a visit to this most special place.

By morning time the anchorage was as calm as a mill pond - and according to the pilot charts there is only a 2% chance of that happening here. After breakfast we set off for the shore. There were small waves breaking onto the nearby slip, but it looked fairly safe.

As we approached the slip, two men came running towards us and out into the shallow water. They caught hold of the boat and as we began to get out cried, "No! No!" Then we saw that the concrete slip was pock-marked and speckled all over with spiny, black sea urchins, some living in tiny craters but some on the surface. We got back into the dinghy and put on our flip-flops, and then we trod very, very carefully - because flip-flops are as ineffectual against the needle sharp, barbed spines of black sea urchins as they are against cactus spines. It was a marvel that we did not puncture the dinghy.

Having safely gained the shore we were taken directly to the commander of the base, who was in one of the little cabins nearby. We were welcomed warmly, and then one of the younger men was appointed to show us around the island.

So far as we could see, the naval base existed purely for the sake of maintaining a presence on this far-flung islet, and the sailors' duties were concerned entirely with the hum-drum chores of daily life. 32 men are stationed here, but because this was the changeover day there were actually 64 men on the island. Still, it did not seem at all crowded.

Throughout our visit to Trindade the crew of *Maamari* were all treated like royalty and we all experienced tremendous warmth and hospitality, but the children were an especial centre of attention. They were, of course, the only children on the island, and here were 32 fellows who had not seen a toddler in four months, and 32 others who had just left their own families behind and who were feeling a little bit homesick. (Now I come to think of it, I suppose that I was the only woman on the island but this seemed to be of no consequence!) Many a sorrowful family man came and patted either Caesar or Xoë on the head and declared that he or she was the exact likeness of his own little one, all those miles away in Rio. So far as they were concerned Trindade might be on another planet.

Celebrity status has its advantages. Young Brazilian men do not suffer from the need to be seen to be macho, and they came running up to give the children packets of biscuits and chocolate. Their kisses were rather less well-received, but most tedious of all was the media attention; everyone wanted a snapshot of the two cute little blondes. Besides the sailors, there were also two journalists and four professional photographers who were on the island for the day. One of these must have shot half a film of 'The Family and Their Yacht', and not for one of them could Xoë be persuaded to smile.

In the officer's mess, which doubled as the commandante's cottage, we were fed the traditional Brazilian dish of feijoada - black beans and salami sausage, cooked in a sauce and served with rice.
But what about the party, the sailors asked? Were we coming to the party?
Naturally, we replied, we would love to join in the celebrations, but how would we find our way back out to the boat in the dark? We had

noticed that the little waves lapping the shore were already somewhat bigger.

Not to worry, the commandante said. We could sleep ashore. Dabrice and Elena had arrived, like us, on the occasion of the quarterly change-over. Funnily enough, their visit had coincided with Elena's 24th birthday. And *they* had slept ashore.

An alarm bell rang. Was that, by any chance, the night that their yacht went up onto the beach?

Indeed! How had we guessed? They had woken and found their boat already lying on the beach.

So *that* was it! Dabrice had not told us the whole story, and we had been left with the impression of the swell arriving suddenly while he and Elena were walking in the mountains. Someone produced a Brazilian newspaper cutting which told the sorry tale of their misadventure. The commandante brought out the visitors book and we read the remarks written by Dabrice. We also saw that, in the last five years at least, no other yachts had called here.

"Many sail past," one man told us, "but they do not stop."

In just a little while we were to discover a second reason for giving the island a miss.

When the time came for us to return to our ship we found that we could not launch the dinghy at the ramp. The waves breaking here were now three feet high and they were steep. On the advice of the commandante, we headed for a little beach on the far side of the village. The sailors carried our boat up the slope and down again to the shore. The waves breaking onto this second beach were considerably bigger - some of them were as much as six feet tall - but whereas on the ramp they were stacked up in ranks, here, with a bit of luck, we could slip out between two breakers. But our luck was running out.

A wave caught the dinghy, overturning it and tipping us all into the surf. It had happened before, but familiarity had not bred indifference and the children howled in dismay.

What could we do? Somehow we must get off the beach and get back to our boat, still lying calmly in the mill-pond-flat bay. On our second effort we were successful, and we left the shore with Caesar and Xoë still sobbing and yelling in alarm. We vowed that if we went ashore again it would be under the auspices of the navy. They had a big semi-rigid boat with a powerful outboard motor and could nip in and out quickly between the waves.

The officers aboard the supply ship, *Felinto Perry*, were eager to be of assistance to us in any way that they could. A young lieutenant captain called Renato took us under his wing. He was a handsome, fair-haired man who was thoroughly pleasant and well-liked, but who carried himself with an air of inborn, unspoken contempt for his inferiors.

Strapped to Renato's right calf was a dagger, and one imagined that he probably slept with it there at all times; it was part of his persona. Nevertheless, he was a perfectly charming fellow. He had done a bit of sailing, and when we asked if we could have a look at a chart of Montevideo he fetched the said chart and gave it to us, with the Navy's compliments.

It was Renato who was in charge of ferrying the sailors to and from the stone warship. In the matter of actually handling the rubber boat he ought, presumably, to have delegated, but the activity was so much to his liking that no one else got a look in. He was delighted to offer us a ride ashore on the morning of our second day in Trindade. We piled into the boat, I with my camera wrapped in a plastic bag. The other matelots looked first at the bag and then at the beach, and then they all held out their own cameras for my care.

Renato unwound the throttle and the boat carved an arc across the sea. Then, when we reached the beach, he said, "Okay. Jump."

The sailors began to jump. Some were tall enough to keep their heads above the water, but others disappeared from sight.

"Jump!"

What? Us, too? And the children?

"Jump! Jump quickly!" Renato pointed at the wave, building astern. Then, since we had now left it too late to jump, he turned the boat swiftly away. The wave passed under us and broke. We came back for a second try.

In fact, Renato had the right idea; the only safe way to get onto the beach was under one's own steam. But the children did not think much of the swim and wailed piteously. The cameras survived the adventure remarkably well.

If the Brazilians had not claimed it, who would be living on Trindade, I wonder? Or would it be home only to the seabirds? The landing is tricky - it is completely impossible for more than half of the time, we were told - and there is very little water on the island. The naval base is built beside the only spring. The soil is poor and the vegetation sparse - although legend has it that there were once trees growing all over the slopes. This virgin forest is said to have been destroyed in a bush fire which was started deliberately by some maroons.

Oh yes, the ancient mariners knew of this place. Pirates are said to have hidden their treasure here. A Victorian adventurer by the name of E.F. Knight came looking for the loot, and having finally managed to get ashore he spent three months digging trenches in the orange-brown soil. An earthquake had buried the cave wherein the silver chalice and candlesticks and coins were said to have been hidden. Eventually, the treasure seeker found the place - or what seemed to be the place - but the cupboard was bare. One never hears from the people who find and recover these caches of ill-gotten goodies; they keep quiet about it. And so others go on optimistically hunting.

Knight sailed away, in search of other excitement. He reckoned Trindade a loathsome place. It was infested with huge land crabs which attacked him and his men - until they killed several score and so decimated the population. Knight was glad to see the back of the island. He was a great sailor, and he wrote beautifully - his descriptions of Trindade inspired Arthur Ransome to write "Peter Duck" - but his must have been a callow, unromantic soul. How else could he have overlooked the fact that Trindade *itself* is the real treasure?

Islands have always held for man a special allure. Yes, I know, I have mentioned it before - just once or twice - but whenever we come upon another noble, sea-girt shore then I am moved to contemplate the matter anew. As if my own intuitions were not enough, there is a whole wealth of primitive and historic thought to support my half-baked notions. People as diverse as the Bijagos and the Sioux used certain sacred islands for their burials. So, too, the Greeks had their Islands-of-the-Blessed, and then there were the Celts, whose gods were sometimes said to dwell on an island lying just beyond the western horizon. And Arthur retired to the isle of Avalon. And so on.

In the Middle Ages, pious people were still making pilgrimages to holy islands such as Lindisfarne, and three trips out from the Welsh peninsula to the island of Bardsey were said to equal one visit to Rome and the Vatican. To any present-day seeker of grace or a cure, I recommend Trindade. The task of getting here ought surely to score more Brownie points than the coach trip to Lourdes, and getting ashore is certainly a very much tougher assignment than crawling up all those steps.

Marooned mariners and treasure seekers may have hated Trindade, but I am not the only one to have sensed something sacred in this island so little touched by man; this island beloved of the white tern and the turtle, where the wind whistles through cathedrals and caves of its own carving; this island assaulted and safe-guarded by a wild ocean, where the sea rolls in great glass arches onto a white sand beach. Someone else has also felt an aura of the sacred here, and high up on the rugged hill above that same white beach he has painted a white cross. Beneath the cross a black gape marks the entrance to one of those wind sculptured caves, and this one is dedicated to Nossa Senhora - Our Lady.

As we climbed the steep hill towards the holy cave, we paused. Far below us, far away on the sea, we saw a disturbance. There were no rocks out there, so what could this be? While we watched, lo and behold, the tail of a whale appeared and waved. Then a littler creature hurled itself into the air, right beside the first.

A great white arm, as large as the smaller animal, was waved aloft - and it was this which gave us the identity of the creatures, for only a humpback whale has long white flippers. Far below us on the ocean the mother humpback was playing with her baby.

We turned our faces upward again. Above us the sky towards which we climbed was an intense blue. In the distance the white terns tore round in circles, shrieking. The whole island was one vast cathedral, and every creature, every rock, every particle of light seemed to be shouting praises to their Creator.

Outside the holy grotto, our friends held back. One crossed himself and muttered a prayer. The other sang a psalm, in the manner of a priest. The ritual words having been uttered, we went within, clambering around a boulder which stands guard in the threshold. We found ourselves in the first of three chambers, each higher and smaller than the last, and each one absolutely filled with devotional offerings and memorabilia placed here during the last thirty years. Before three separate effigies of Mother Mary - one in each cell of the triocular chapel - there were placed such things as a hand-made model of the supply ship, a model of the mess-room at the foot of the mountain, and a rope ladder with sixteen rungs, each one signed by the one-time members of the station's crew. There were T-shirts signed by the erstwhile wearer, there were photographs, and there was one big canvas painted with the portraits of another sixteen man crew.

With only hours to prepare our offering, or petitionary souvenir, we were not able to come up with anything so splendid, but I painted a little picture of *Maamari* and we framed it and gave it to the commandante to place in the chapel. Whether Our Lady of the wind-hewn caves looked favourably upon us thereafter is a matter open to interpretation.

The hospitality of the Brazilian Navy knows no bounds. Besides feeding us for two days they also showered us with gifts when we left. The whole family was kitted out with *Felinto Perry* baseball caps, and there were T-shirts and a handmade set of oars. Tins of salami and packets of biscuits were thrust into our arms. More to the point, the resident welder had repaired a broken rod from our self steering.

Our actual departure from the island was even more fraught than our arrival. We were required to jump from a wave-swept rock into the rubber boat, which Renato brought in and out as the waves permitted. Renato should be working with the SAS. "This is such fun; I *love* it!" he cried, as two men were bowled over and battered about in the surf.

With Xoë perched on my hip I stood even less chance of keeping my balance, but my yell of alarm brought the assistance of two stout marines and together we made it to the precarious safety of the boat.

No, Caesar did not think that this was any fun at all. He screamed hysterically until the boat had safely escaped from the break. And this was Ilha da Trindade on a quiet day. Heaven only knows how anyone gets on or off in normal weather.

We motored away and then, on the far side of the island, we shut down the infernal combustion engine and sat. There was not a breath of wind and no swell whatsoever. At one in the morning I could still hear the roar of the sea breaking on the shore, and I knew that when the sun rose Trindade would still be there on the horizon; a distant grey shape full of intrigue and magic, even more alluring now than on the day when we arrived.

I think that Nick and I both felt a little out of sorts during the last third of our crossing to South America. An unhappy change in the mood of the weather was largely to blame for our slight dispiritedness, but our state of mind was also affected by the mood at Trindade. When we had arrived at this island paradise, we had envied the men their four month vacation. We had supposed that the matelots must be queuing up to come to Trindade. But the new arrivals had tears in their eyes, as they thought of loved ones left behind, and the island suddenly seemed incredibly lonely. After four months, even paradise could begin to feel like Alcatraz.

Certainly, the home-going crew were jubilant at the thought of returning to the mainland. They would be there in a couple of days. We still had a long passage ahead of us - and we had no home. It had never mattered before - we did not want any home other than the boat - but seeing the sailors' joy, we suddenly felt as a vagrant must surely feel if he were to peer in through the window of a happy home on Christmas morning.

Perhaps it was just the weather. For the first two days of the final leg of our journey we were confronted by calms and light head-winds, a fine rain fell intermittently, and everything was really rather dismal. We were out of the tropics, even if the line on the map was still a few miles further on. Keeping watch by day was simply dull and a little chilly, but the nights... for me, the nights were somewhere on the margin of Hell.

Night watches are never my favourite, partly because I prefer to spend the hours of darkness in sleep, but also because I get scared. And throughout the last third of our crossing from Africa, the nights were especially ponderous. Moonlit nights on the ocean can be absolutely delightful, and starry, starry nights provide challenging entertainment; amongst that myriad of bright specks are old familiar friends, such as Boötes and Corona Borealis and Camelopardalis (one of my favourites, if only because of the name), but can I find them amongst this dazzling, awesome array? Nights such as these are refreshment for the soul and spirit - but not so the long, black nights when the moon has gone to bed early. Not so the nights when thick, louring cloud conceals the ceiling of the sky and even the horizon is only a vague idea. If God is light, then on nights such as these the Prince of Darkness surely has the upper hand.

These are the nights which fill me with dread; I am even tempted to shirk them altogether - perhaps I could feign a sudden, severe bout of seasickness - but that would leave Nick to carry the can, and Nick, although superhuman, is not quite as indefatigable as a robot. No, I cannot evade my duty. But when everyone else is asleep and I am alone in the world of primeval chaos, then I shrink and cower.

I cower on the top step of the companion way. The cabin lights are burning brightly and I cling to the circle of their warmth. Only my head peeps out into that Otherworld, and then only when it must. I scan the dark, searching for a light and praying that there will be none. And please, God, don't let the sails shake. Don't let the wind veer. Don't let me have to step *OUTSIDE*.

Imagination runs wild. Who knows what lurks beneath the sea? No one knows. Yachts disappear - ships sometimes, too. Perhaps they did not all run into storms or sleeping whales. Perhaps some of them met with... something worse. The oceans are said to be littered with containers washed off the decks of ships, but come the night and this does not trouble me half so much as the unknown. People fall overboard too. If no clear reason can be found, then the usual verdict is that the fellow tumbled in while he was at the rail, having a pee. But just suppose... suppose something pulls people into the sea! Perish the thought. But the thought will not wither away. It has taken root and now advances through my mind like a rampant weed. It chokes out the frail blossoms of rationale and common sense.

I take a step down the ladder so that only my eyes peep out. After a furtive scan of the horizon I dive for cover, for the snug security of the cabin. I stick my head in a book and am carried away to another place. But in ten minutes time I must force myself to stick my head outside again - and if the sails rattle...

Oh, let the sails rattle! But the wind has changed; the helm is too high; something will have to be done or the boat will try to put herself about. At the last moment I dart outside, crouched like someone evading a sniper's bullets, and rescue *Maamari* from luffing onto the other tack. Hysteria has all but taken over my mind and I can think of nothing but the giant kraken. Its body is the size of a circus tent. Its long, white arms feel their way blindly into the cockpit; the suckers grope about in search of... *ME*!

"She cowered behind the wheel, stricken with horror, and prayed that the creature would somehow pass her by - yet it was not to be. The tip of one giant tentacle waved in the air, like an antenna homing in on its prey, and in the next moment it lashed out and latched onto her back. Horror stifled the scream which rose in her throat, but as the beast secured its grip, coiling its arms around her, she, in turn, weaved her arms between the spokes of the wheel..."

Blind panic takes me over; I lash the wheel with the hook, and in two strides I am on the stairs and scuttling down into the cabin. *Maamari* is now too far off the wind and sailing below her course - but at least I will not have to go out there again.

Calm down, Woman! Get a grip on yourself. You're as crazy as little Caesar, who won't go near the forepeak at night, "because of the lion". So I tell myself. But my mind is not convinced. I know for sure that there is nothing lurking in our forepeak, least of all a lion, and I also know that there really *are* strange creatures living undiscovered beneath the waves. The ocean's depths, and not outer space, are the final frontier to man's inquisitive mind. There *are* giant squid as big as a circus tent, and people *do* disappear.

Perhaps tomorrow, if the weather remains miserable, my bogey man will be an extra terrestrial in a UFO. I have never seen one, but there is always a first time. Fortunately Nick has no imagination at all and loves the night watch.

The passage from Trindade to Punta del Este was no sunshine cruise. As surely as we had stepped over the Tropic of Capricorn, we had stepped into the ever changing weather of the temperate zone. *Maamari* could no longer be left to herself for days and weeks at a time - on the contrary, she needed constant attention - but all was not bleak. The low, grey clouds had a silver lining. *We* might not think much of the climate, but it was very popular with the birds. We were used to seeing shearwaters wheeling in the distance, and we had often been joined by little storm petrels and tropic birds, but here was a whole new avian world. Now we sailed amongst southern skuas, giant petrels, and white-chinned petrels.

Esoteric seagulls gliding about over the ocean were of little interest to the children, but despite the change in the weather and the nip in the air, Caesar and Xoë were not suffering any kind of despair. After a life lived in the nude, sweatshirts and socks were received as something of a novelty, but without complaint. The children built boats out of their Lego and called them *Maersk Ascension* and *Santa Maria*. They sent them sailing across the equator and down the Meridian Passage into the forepeak. Their curiosity concerning the seabirds was limited to obliging their excited mother ("Look, children! Come and look!") but they were rather more interested when one of our feathered followers came aboard:

"12th October. *We have been joined by a tiny, black and white swallow - or rather, a martin. At first she fluttered about the deck, trying to find a steady piece of string on which to perch. Then, finding none, she flew in and out of the cabin. I hung up a pencil. When the bird came back, this was the first place she chose to settle, but it proved too slippery and unsteady. She could not keep her balance while it flicked to and fro. After fluttering about for a while longer she chose the flat top of an African shaman's rattle, which is wedged in place on top of the barometer, and here she spent the night."*

Swallows and such like might hitch a ride with us, but we were having to work our passage now. In the tropics the wind and weather are consistent, but in temperate latitudes these things vary from hour to hour and sometimes even from minute to minute. Thus, on the 13th October, for example, the wind was recorded in the log as blowing South-Easterly, force four. It was blowing from the same direction the following day, but only because, in the intervening 24 hours, it had backed in a complete circuit. Whenever the wind changed its force or direction, Nick and I had to alter the set of our sails and our self steering, so that we were now kept constantly on our toes.

"15th October. While it was still night, the wind rose quickly and Nick shortened the sail. He was still putting the ties on the main when we were hit by a tremendously fierce squall which put the side deck well under water. The sea gushed down into the cabin through the bathroom port-hole, absentmindedly left open.

Within five minutes the squall had passed and in its wake we were virtually becalmed. After a time, a light wind filled in from the south-west, which is also the direction of the swell."

More martins came flitting around the boat on this day. One came inside and perched, first on the head of our statuette, Nan, and then on my head. She seemed so unafraid that the next time she settled I reached out and stroked her gently with my finger. She looked at me askance and prodded the finger once with her pointed beak. I picked her up.

At once the little bird let forth a stream of terrified cheeps - but when, immediately, I tried to put her down again I found that she could not stand! She was rigid with shock and fear. I had to lie her on her side on a cushion, and I was very much afraid that she would die. After two or three minutes she recovered sufficiently to fly around the cabin, after which she hid for the night amongst the sail bags. The children picked out a dozen weevils, from the dried beans, and put them close by the bird in a saucer of water, but she seemed to have no appetite for such things.

An hour after the arrival of the first martin we were joined by another, and then another, and I found myself wondering where they all came from, and whither they were bound. Surely they were not crossing from Africa?

If I were offered the gift of wings, I would never choose to be a swallow or a martin, that is for sure. Those same draughts which fuel the flight of the shearwater and the petrel only batter their poor, timid cousins. I cannot imagine how any swallow survives the awful passage over the vast ocean plain.

The wind continued to swing around us in lazy pirouettes, and now we were met by a big, long, westerly swell put up by some distant storm. While the wind was in the east this encouraged a nasty, contrary chop.

On the afternoon of the 16th I saw the dark clouds which foretold the approach of another squall, and we began to furl the genoa. Furling the genoa takes no time at all - a matter of half a minute - but by the time we were through, the sail had opened another seam and the wind was about force nine. The sea was streaked all over with white spume. Little gusts ran hither, thither down the waves, like hobgoblins trailing scarves.

We hoisted the storm jib and contemplated lowering the mizzen, but the wind soon abated somewhat. The westerly swell had been completely obliterated but we were left, instead, with a lumpy sea splattered with breaking waves. It was raining, and keeping watch in the rain and spray is a tedious business, particularly at night. We had not seen a single ship since leaving São Tomé, so that it was difficult not to become half-hearted about the chore.

"17th October. *Flat calm all day with an almost constant drizzle. A giant petrel, or "stinker", came and sat on the water beside us. Truly, he is a giant, with a wingspan of more than six feet and a massive head. Three more little swallows, on deck this time, in the rain.*

"18th October. *Flat calm again, with occasional draughts from the north. In the early hours we caught a snake fish, in spite of the fact that we were hardly moving. Nick has been hard at work stitching the genoa, but it is still not done.*

At about 10 o'clock that same morning the sky cleared and we got our first sunsight in three days. A gentle wind arose from the south-east, but the sea was a mess of conflicting swells. Going on deck to scan the horizon, I suddenly caught sight of a huge seabird shearing over the waves on wings as long as a plank. My first albatross. It was not the king of seabirds himself - not a wandering albatross - but a grey-headed albatross or mollymawk. It soared about the yacht and never once flapped a wing.

In the afternoon three chocolate-coloured white-chinned petrels came to pay us a visit, swinging round the boat with awesome grace and ease.

"*They circle us; they double back in knife edge flight; they come straight for us, like jet fighters skimming low over the sea. Every different facet of each rolling wave necessitates minute adjustments of trim. A wing tip shears the sea and seems to caress it, but never actually does - not quite. To see one bird performing thus is thrilling, but to see three dancing together in an unchoreographed ballet is simply awesome; it is an honour to behold. One feels that one has trespassed into a private world and witnessed an indulgence of the divine."*

But why am I down here, I asked myself? I was anchored to the deck. My heart and mind soared with the albatross and with the white-chinned petrels, but I was trapped in the prison of my own mortal frame and my spirit could only strain to be unleashed.

After a time, I lost the three petrels. I waited in vain, in the chill damp, for them to reappear. I was just going below when, happening to glance at the water creaming past the hull, I was startled to see them all sitting there - three brown ducks, beside us for a moment and then gone in our wake! To judge by their expressions, the petrels were equally surprised.

By now we were eight days out of Trindade. We had caught a couple of fish but we had seen no cetaceans, which seemed odd. If all these seabirds congregated here, then surely it must be a place of abundant food. At first light on the 19th we discovered a school of small dolphins, who were fishing some distance off the bow, but although they travelled with us for three hours or more they never came close enough to be identified.

For some time now we had been accompanied by half a dozen great shearwaters, birds with beautiful, speckled plumage. They kept scrabbling their feet on the water, in the manner of storm petrels, and then landing and sticking their heads below the surface. *Maamari* appeared to be a great attraction for all the birds, perhaps because she stirred up the plankton. I expect that we were also "towing" a colony of fish and other, smaller creatures who were attracted to our rather foul bottom. The boat had not been out of the water since we were in Portugal, and during our stay in Ghana she had acquired a crusting of white, coral-like weed, five inches thick. The worst of the fouling had been scraped off, of course; Nick and Johnnie had gone round the boat in the dinghy, wielding a palette knife tied to the end of a long deck-brush. No doubt we would have travelled faster if someone had gone over the side and given the boat a decent scrub, but we rather preferred to idle along in the company of the birds.

After having hobbled along for three days on the merest ghost of a breeze we were feeling very sorry for ourselves. Our spirits rose on the 20th when we were at last blessed with the very wind we wanted - a steady force four, sou'-sou'-easterly. If only it would last! The sea was a dark, serious blue studded with white caps. The pale-blue sky was patterned with white fluff. The birds picked themselves up off the water, where they had rested and dabbled during the calm, and today even the tubby "cape pigeons" managed to shearwater.

Why is the ocean of the tropics a stunning, brilliant blue, whilst down in the South Atlantic it is very much darker? I sat watching the sea and wondered about such mysteries. And while I mused, there went wheeling-by, only feet from our sails, a most magnificent white-backed bird with a huge, pink bill. The Wanderer! The king of all seabirds! To be honest, he did not appear to have a wingspan more than twice my height, but beside him the grey-headed mollymawks began to seem like mere gulls.

By midday the wind was already increasing and so we dropped the main. By evening we were riding along in a full gale with gusts of much more. We dropped the mizzen. The stays'l hung on all night but took a real hammering. Rain swept by in icy squalls; waves smashed down on the cockpit. By now we had two hatchboards permanently in place in the companion way, for one of the waves had found its way down into the cabin. Rain drove through the remaining open slice, below the sliding hatch. The visibility was so bad that we needed to go outside every five minutes, and this would have been difficult with the topmost board also in place.

Below decks all was calm - we could have been romping across the English channel in a stiff breeze - and the children slept soundly. When we stepped outside, however, the wind and the noise hit us with brutal force. White foam raced past the hull at seven knots - nothing to some, but plenty for an old girl getting along under one small headsail. Waves and spray leapt into the black air and were illuminated dramatically by our stern light. Meanwhile, the bi-colour light on the bow split the headwaves into two garish red and green halves. Rain like hail stung our faces when we tried to look to weather.

None of these theatrical effects was to be compared to the noise, which was simply exhausting. The incessant howl of the wind passing by was like a whole pack of depraved hell-hounds unleashed. A hundred distraught eldritch spirits whined in the rigging, their anguished voices accompanied by the discordant percussion of halyards rattling wildly against the masts. Indeed, rattle seems like something of a euphemism; the halyards were vibrating with such manic vigour that there seemed to be no pause between one staccato hammer beat and the next. Blackness exaggerated the drama.

At about 06.00 the next morning the wind began to ease, and at 08.00 the glass stopped falling. At dawn we discovered that the vane from the self steering was gone. *Maamari* had held her course so well without it that we did not notice the loss before sunrise. The boat would not manage so well with the wind aft of the beam, but fortunately we had a spare vane already made.

By afternoon the glass was rising rapidly and the wind had fallen to a southerly force five, so that we decided to hoist the second-reefed main. While we were casting off the ties I suddenly glimpsed, close by the bow, the brownish-black fins and then the curved back of... I knew not what. Perhaps it was some kind of a seal.

"22nd October. *Fewer seabirds today, and quite a lot of flotsam on the water, both of which suggest a change in the current. The wind is at present in the south but is backing.*

In the evening I heard the fishing line go, but there was nothing on the hook. The fish had evidently just bitten the tip of the streamers. A white-chinned petrel was just taking off from the wake astern. Ten minutes later I again heard the peg snap-to - and this time I was on deck. Up from the water came that same bird, with a look of shock and puzzlement on his face. Thank God we didn't hook him!"

The wind backed all throughout the following night, following its usual, tedious pattern. Next would come a calm, with a few puffs from the south, and then, when the glass first began to rise, we would get another blow from the south. The predictability was very tiring.

That night, while I was in the cockpit, I was startled by a sudden crash from aloft in the mizzen. Sensing something falling, I dived for cover fast - and a big flying fish landed at my feet! He was the first that we had seen for weeks, for his kind do not belong in the cold, southern sea.

"24th October. *Wind force two to three, but increasing. In the afternoon the visibility fell as we were swallowed up by a light misty haze. The wind backed, heading us, and the glass fell slightly. According to our various books, these are all the classic symptoms of a pampero, a strong south-westerly wind born on the Argentine pampas. But none came. The wind reached about force six by daybreak, but then it quietly faded away."*

"25th October. Damp and grey. Less than 200 miles to run, and no chance of a sight. Between 21.00 and 24.00 there was absolute calm, and then the wind came hurrying across the sea from the west and quickly spun around into the south."

This *was*, in fact, the pampero. We had not understood that it can take a few days to come. Fortunately, it was only a little one - bigger ones can take the mast out of a sailing ship with their first, vicious blow. This one only reached about force seven.

By now the sea was the cold-green colour of an ice-fed river, and the air was tinged with the same chill. Never mind what the calendar may have to say on the subject, it was still winter over here. In spite of this I had no inclination to hide away in the cabin. I stood in the cockpit, absorbed in every detail of this new world that we had found.

A shiny, brown seal darted away from the bow, showing us his back, and then peeped around in curiosity. His face seemed to say, "What in God's name was that?" Chocolate coloured petrels hurtled round the boat, like spitfires on a raid. Sometimes there were as many as thirty in the air and another couple of dozen resting in our wake. Grey mollymawks wheeled by, and wheeled away. Pied petrel-pintados fluttered about, and a great shearwater skimmed past. A small grey tern and one lone arctic skua completed our entourage on this particular day.

The weather really was very cold now. On deck, we needed gloves even when we were only standing about. I was doing just that, on the afternoon of that same day, when my eyes fell upon a black, white, and grey head with a big bill. It looked surreal - a monochrome toucan, up to his neck in the waves and watching me! Later I saw two more such creatures and realised that they were magellenic penguins, the first penguins that any of us had ever seen.

The day seemed to grow colder still with each mile that we advanced towards the shore. That evening I wore two pairs of trousers, a pair of gloves, my boots, a woolly hat, and my coat - yet, I was still cold. In the afternoon we had seen our first ships - and plenty of them - making their way along the South American coast. Now, in the night, we raised the loom of Cabo Pollonio's light - and by daybreak on the 27th we had discovered the new continent.

17

SILVER AND COLD

*In which we journey from the Rio de la Plata, or
the Silver River, on down the Argentine, or Silver
coast, and towards the wintry Southern Ocean.*

Jru Dickin Schinas

"What's that? I didn't hear... Mum, if we... Look, don't talk while I'm talking!"

"I'm sorry, Mum... No, no, I *didn't* mean for you to shut up. Listen, I just mean that we mustn't talk together. You see if we both talk together then... What's that? *Mum!* Don't talk at the same time as I'm trying to answer!"

Curse these satellite communication thingys. Trying to hold a conversation with England is like doing that peculiar little waltz of two strangers trying to pass on the street. Except that, in this case, we have our eyes on the clock because these particular minutes are money.

"Yes, we got here... Uruguay... It's just south of Brazil... Yes, they're fine, and so is Nick... What's that?... A niece! Well, that was pretty damn sneaky!"

All the while that we were trundling around the bulge of Africa we had been incommunicado, and now we learnt that during this time my sister had managed to produce an entire baby. Had we really been out of touch with our kith and kin for ten months? It was amazing to think that a whole new person could be magicked into the world while we just turned our backs for a moment.

Punta del Este was cold. We had known that it would be cold down in Patagonia, but we were not expecting to find it still winter when we arrived in the Rio de la Plata. The sky was a hard, icy blue. The sea was as cold and hard as steel. The sun merely glittered, its rays like the sparkle from a cut stone, and the wind slashed and wounded us like a knife.

"Error! Error!" There must be some mistake. Caesar's internal computer tells him so and my chattering teeth agree. We are creatures of the Tropics. What the devil are we doing here? The kids have no coats and no shoes - only flip-flops - and the temperature in town is only 10°C (50°F).

What a cruel shock this was to children born in the sunny Caribee. But the folks of Punta del Este were whingeing, too. Some of them were shivering in shorts - *shorts!* - their knees a pretty shade of blue. They had come to the seaside for their annual holidays. Three days ago, they told us, the temperature was 35°C (96°F).

So, *that* was it. We were sitting on the inter-tropical convergence zone - the battle frontier between winter and summer. When the wind was in the north the days would be so hot that the beaches would be covered in bikinis, but while the wind was in the south we would all be huddled up in duffel coats. I had seen this before, in Canada, and the extremes really have to be felt to be believed.

Punta del Este is the rich man's Vilamoura - a seaside resort purpose built for the well-to-do of Uruguay and Argentina. In fact, to be perfectly honest, Punta del Este is *exactly* like Vilamoura, right down to the endless ranks of junk-food restaurants and the street vendors selling hand-made leather masks and jewellery. This is an artificial town, a huddle of tower-blocks parked on a long, thin, sandy peninsula. The tower blocks overshadow a few cottages belonging to an earlier age, when fewer folks could afford a holiday by the sea.

There is no doubt that Punta del Este was built looking out over the Atlantic, but nowadays it is turning its attention towards the river. There is now a marina tucked just inside the spit, and it was here that we washed up, leaving behind us the world of the albatross and the petrel. But we had certainly not come here to holiday. Far from it. We had an urgent appointment with the summer solstice in the deep south, but before we could head for the roaring forties and the archipelago of Cape Horn we must prepare.

In West Africa there is little or no opportunity to buy chandlery. We had not even managed to buy a decent piece of rope to replace the length that was stolen in Côte d'Ivoire. After two years out in the sticks there was a great deal to be done aboard *Maamari*. Had we stuck to our schedule, and left Africa before the rainy season, then there would have been plenty of time to get all sorts of things done. We might even have finished rebuilding the bathroom, which Caesar and Xoë had never known as anything but a wood store. Perhaps we would even have got around to plumbing in the heater, bought almost five years earlier. As it was, time was short and we would only be able to do the essentials. The priority was to get *Maamari* ready to face the southern ocean.

Down at the bottom of the world, where there is no land to impede its progress, the wind is free to chase its tail round and around. And when the wind is up and the waves are monstrous, then a little sailing boat is nothing more than flotsam. Down in the Southern Ocean a knock-down becomes a distinct possibility. We knew that the journey ahead would be the toughest that we had ever made, and we needed to be sure that our boat was fit for the challenge.

From Punta del Este we moved on up the river, to Montevideo. As we picked up a mooring buoy inside the little, shallow Puerto del Buceo our thoughts were on Bill Tilman, the sailing mountaineer, and on Joshua Slocum, the first man to sail alone around the world. Slocum spent Christmas here in 1895, so that our arrival coincided almost exactly with that centenary. The place must have changed quite a bit even since Tilman's days, but it still gave us a good feeling to know that we were sailing in the wake of our heroes. The interval of time may have kept us from sharing a glass of wine, but we could re-read their books and know their thoughts, and at least raise a glass to absent friends.

In Montevideo we were joined, once more, by Nick's father. Jim knows that he is always assured of a warm welcome from all aboard *Maamari,* but when he produced from his suitcase a little hand-held GPS then we were doubly pleased to see him. Much as we like to get by on our own wits, and without recourse to modern magic, there is no denying that a satellite-navigation-system can make sailing much safer. It comes in jolly handy on those days when the sun hides his face, and we knew that there would be many such days ahead of us, down south.

On then, to Colonia, said to be the oldest town in Uruguay. Cobbled streets; veteran cars on every corner; a lighthouse; a drawbridge; bougainvillaea overflowing from walled gardens. It was a pleasant corner.

By now it was late in November. We celebrated Xoë's third birthday, and the planets - Venus, Jupiter, and Mars - all got together in a neat isosceles triangle above Scorpio, which is her sign. Retrospectively, I would love to know how the astrologers interpreted this event. At the time, it seemed so special that we took it for a kind of blessing. Xoë was very pleased to hear that the great planets were shining especially for her.

We had been sent to Colonia by the local Uruguayan yotties, for Colonia is a free-port and has two chandleries, but neither store could provide very many of the items on our long shopping list. Next stop, Buenos Aires, just a short hop away across the river. From one town to the other is only 25 miles, and Argentinean yachtsmen nip to and fro in the same way that English seafarers trot back and forth twixt the Solent and Cherbourg, yet the journey is not so straightforward as it sounds. First we had to wait until all the water came back.

Time and tide may do funny things in Southampton water, but at least they do it to some ordered pattern. The scientists can tell us exactly when it will be high tide, and they can even give us some idea of how high the water will be. Time and tide govern the English Channel, and the Straits of Magellan, and the River Geba. They even have a say in what happens on the Amazon - but they cannot dictate to the Rio Plata. Here, it is the winds who are master, and when they blow from the north the water all goes rushing across to Buenos Aires. Contrariwise, in a Pampero or in a Sud-estader (a south-easterly gale) the water all whistles away and floods Uruguay.

We are talking, here, of an unpredictable rise and fall of around five metres. Before setting off for the opposite shore one does well to consider whether it will be possible to get into the harbour, over there, - but the harbours are not the only problem. The whole of this river is very shallow. Ships can only reach Buenos Aires via a narrow and strictly controlled channel, each awaiting the direction of a river-traffic controller before he proceeds. The channel is dredged constantly and the slurry is dumped on either side, building up gravel banks which hinder the passage of even a shallow draught yacht. When the river is low, these man-made banks can actually dry.

There is only one place where it is possible to cross the busy juggernaut trail, and even this pass is too shallow when the water has gone elsewhere. Add to this picture a sprinkling of several dozen flashing beacons and the wrecks and rocks which they mark - and there you have it. Not the most relaxing place to sail.

Obstructions to navigation and the tedious, cyclic weather pattern notwithstanding, the Rio de la Plata is, in fact, a very popular spot. One seldom encounters either Uruguayan or Argentinean seafarers abroad, but certain reaches of the river which they share are almost as busy as the Solent. Take, for example, the Rio Luján, which joins the Plate just above Buenos Aires. The mouth of the Luján has fragmented the land, much in the same way that the Niger has fragmented the Nigerian coast. Pictorally then, the river is like a frayed cable - and each of its separate strands is lined on both sides with yachts moored gunwale to gunwale.

When we slipped over the bar of silt and into the strand of the river known as the San Isidro the water level was a little bit higher than average. It had to be, or else we could not have carried six feet. The sight of so many hundreds of boats within the river was astonishing. "But why are they tied to such enormous poles?" we asked ourselves. "If the river were ever that high, the banks would flood and this land on either side would be underwater." The message had still not got through.

We motored on up to the head of the narrow channel and squeezed into a vacant space. One morning, a few days later, we awoke to find that the river was, indeed, over the quay. Sometimes it goes up over the road. Two days later, its level fell so low that we were aground and wallowing in the mud. Come the next northerly, and it was over the quay again.

In San Isidro we finally found shops with the merchandise which we needed. There was a sailmaker, too, and so we were able to have the genoa completely re-stitched. We overhauled the self-steering gear, and Nick examined every inch of the rigging and bought a lot of beefy, stainless-steel shackles. In Africa we had only been able to buy galvanised shackles and they had rusted.

We bought rope. We bought oilskin jackets. With the purchase of a new echo-sounder we completed our return to the 20th century. In the company of a crowd of interested spectators we pulled the cord on our liferaft and watched it inflate to our satisfaction. Then we packed it carefully away again.

After living like hermits in West Africa we now enjoyed the contrast of being part of a little community. Besides the day boats and little racing yachts, which belonged to the local Argentines, there were also half a dozen other foreign cruising yachts. Like us, most of the foreign yotties planned to nip through the Magellan Straits or the Beagle Channel and then hurry back up into the tropics, but a couple of the boats were going to be based in Ushuaia. From there they would run charter trips around the legendary Cape Horn islet.

Our intention was a little different from the other yotties in that we were not rushing headlong south for Christmas but wanted to stop on the way at the whale breeding ground in Peninsula Valdez. We were also going to make a detour out to the Falkland Islands - and that piece of news provoked raised eyebrows and pregnant pauses in any conversation with our Argentine hosts. The war was an embarrassment, they told us; it should not have happened. There should not have been a war between friends. And Galtieri, he was a drunk. But the Malvinas - "Well, *of course*, they are Argentine! You have only to read the history books to see the truth about that!"

Later, in the Falklands, we were told about a forthcoming book in which it is planned to cover the history of the islands in a manner satisfactory to both sides. A very short book, it would seem.

In San Isidro we made some good friends. First there were our neighbours, Gustavo and Marcela, young Argentines whose ambition was to set-off in their boat just as we had done. Caesar was forever clambering over to visit Gustavo, who took very good care of his young visitor and taught him words of Spanish. But Gustavo's boat had sloping side-decks and, of course, it had no netting around the rails. One day the inevitable happened: Caesar tumbled in - to be quickly retrieved by his host. He was not the least shaken, but came back for a change of shorts. "Mummy," he said as I towelled him down. "How does Jesus walk on water?"

On our other side was Jean, a French citizen of Brazil. He had lost a leg fighting for the legionnaires in North Africa, but it was not going to stop him from trying to sail around The Horn. Lastly, there was Max, whose attentions and friendship we at first firmly rebuffed. Max was a down-and-out who lived on the street, but he had his eyes on the comforts of our cabin. He loved to be with our kids. Time and again we shooed Max away, but he always returned and the children welcomed him with open arms. "We want Max to live with us. He can sleep in the saloon."

Max was a young, black and white cat.

It is easy to walk on by past a pet shop and say, "No, Dear, we don't have room for a doggy. No, I can't stand goldfish. No, Darling, you can't even have a mouse." It is very much harder to send away a creature who has already taken up residence and charmed his way into the hearts of the whole crew. Max was an alley cat, but it was plain to see that he had not always lived rough. Once, somebody had loved him and he wanted some more of the same attention, please. His fur was clean and he elected to do his business always in one particular spot on the aft deck, never sullying the cabin floor. He ate anything that was offered but disdained milk, preferring to lap water from the loo. He could hold his own with the children, who soon learnt not to pull his tail. In fact, he could even hold his own against the entire assembly of the local pack of stray dogs.

All well and good, but did this cat really want to come sailing? And did we really want him along? Max was decorative and amusing, but there were problems. Would it be right to let him go ashore, as he would undoubtedly wish to go, in foreign parts? How would he have faired in the Bijagos, for example, where cats are unknown? Would he come back home - and when? I could see us, slaves to the feline whim, forever awaiting him with the dinghy or running about yelling, "Here, puss! Come on, Max!"

In the end we decided that Max would be better-off staying put. We bought him a last dinner and plonked it on the deck of a neighbouring boat. As we motored out, the cat cast occasional puzzled glances, from us to the watery space that we had left, but his main preoccupation was with the nosh. Perhaps this was not the first time that his home had upped and offed.

"14th December. *Depart San Isidro. We crossed the dredged channel in the appropriate place and shortly afterwards we ran aground in a patch where two dredgers were at work. We had to back-track to find our way out of their trap. We anchored for the night."*

"15th December. *Light wind, glass falling quickly. Tonight we sailed on, although we were still in shallow water. We want to try to reach Peninsula Valdez in time for Christmas, and every day counts.*

While I was keeping watch, in the busy river mouth, I saw a weird, flashing, yellow light about the size of my fist which flew an erratic course amongst the rigging. It behaved as an insect might, but what insect could be so big?"

The identity of this UFO remains unknown.
In the early hours of the following morning we left the river and set off southwards down the coast.

"16th December. *Wind north-westerly, three to four, but gradually backing - as usual. The glass fell to 29.62 inches (1003 mb) and then sat. In the instant that it rises, the wind will strike..."*

"At 15.00, a great gust of wind came, quite literally from out of the blue, from the south-east. Within minutes we were beating into a force nine. During the night the wind gradually moderated to force seven, and as daylight came it backed into the east and began to diminish still further. In the moment of that first gust, the glass leapt up and then afterwards it climbed steadily."

"17th December. *Wind continuing to back and to fall, until by nightfall it was virtually calm."*

Oh, the everlasting cycle which the wind follows in these parts is horribly tedious! In England people moan about the unpredictability of the weather, but here we had soon learnt to detest the predictability. It makes one forever expectant of the next stage. If it was calm, then it must be just about to blow hard - and so we would be waiting anxiously for that. As the wind died down again, we knew that it would soon be calm, and that the calm would last for the next day or two - so now we lived with the dread of that. If, by some accident of the gods, the weather happened to be just perfect, then we might be certain that the error would at once be put to rights. After all, it could never be more than a passing interlude while the wind wound its way back round the clock.

During the southeaster we discovered an advantage of the GPS hitherto unforeseen. My plan had been to turn it on briefly, as and when the sun failed, but Nick reckoned to leave it ticking away all the while. As long as the machine was there, it was impossible to resist looking at it every hour or so - and certainly, Nick did not see this as a temptation but as a duty. Thus it soon became plain, as we beat about in the gale, that one tack was more favourable than the other. And it was not the tack which, taking into account the current, we would have expected. The wind had evidently put up an invisible set into the river, now lying astern of us, so that although we were heading 105° on the inshore tack, we were actually only making good 150°! Thanks to the advice of the GPS, we did not lose any ground at all during the blow; we tacked out to sea.

Nick was immediately hooked on the GPS and began to think like a racing man, but my admiration for the machine was unashamedly grudging. I picture a world where astro-navigation is a lost art, like that of lighting a fire with two sticks. And what will happen when civilisation as we know it winds down, and we are back to counting on our fingers and sighting the moon and sun? What then? Yes, I know, I would have resisted the invention of the steam engine and seen it as a demon. In fact, I do. I reckon our mistake was in coming down out of the trees...

"18th December. *It continued calm and beautifully sunny and warm until about 14.00. Several petrels and albatrosses were sitting about on the water, and shearwaters went flapping round about. The rigging was perfectly clear, and then quite suddenly it was covered in silken strands of spiders' web. These webs are the parachutes of tiny spiders which are dispersed in the manner of seeds, on the wind. A charming design, of Mother Nature - but Tilman sights this as a sure indication of a coming sud-estader.*"

Since this had already happened twice before we knew that it was not such an infallible sign, but the wind did rise, albeit quite slowly. It reached gale force and then at once began to decline. During the height of the gale the halyard winch fell off the mizzen, and with such a crash that from the aft cabin, directly below, it sounded as if the mast itself had come down.

The next morning all was calm again. The water was a glassy green plain scattered with birds. As usual, *Maamari* seemed to be the focus of attention. The birds congregated around her, perhaps out of curiosity. Sometimes there were up to twenty "chocolate petrels" bobbing about just astern, and every now and then one of them started chirruping like a canary. At first I could hardly believe that this delicate little noise was coming from so big a bird!

An inquisitive giant-petrel, with his ugly great beak, came paddling towards us as fast as he could. The mollymawks settled individually or as a family group, and sometimes there were birds of two or three different species gathered together. Sometimes an albatross seemed to play follow my leader with a chocolate petrel and a great shearwater, and although I am sure a behaviourist would say that this was mobbing, or intimidation, it really did not look like that. The birds all appeared to be the very best of friends.

While the birds were milling about around us, the tips of the tower blocks at Mar del Plata were peeping over the horizon as if to see what was going on out on the ocean. They looked quite bizarre intruding into this world.

Late in the afternoon the horizon grew indistinct - which, we had found, was usually the sign of a pampero. However, as night fell we saw lightning far away over the horizon, and we recognised the pattern: we might expect sudden squally gusts, interspersed with calms and light rain, but nothing more would come of the doomy portent.

"21st December. *By mid-morning the wind returned - a south-westerly force five. The glass is rising very fast.*
Nick watched the sunset and saw the famous green flash, which made me suitably green with envy. Why him? He's seen it twice before and I've never seen it at all!"

"22nd December. *The glass is falling again...*"

Oh, how wearisome was this monotonous weather pattern! I made up a silly rhyme, the better to remember the cycle and see where we were "at a glance":

Glass falling: the wind is in the north.
Keep watch on the pressure, as you sally forth.
For when the glass stops, the wind will back
And the sud-estader will hit us with a whack.

Glass rising: the south wind blows.

It fades as it slides round the compass rose,
And when the glass stops, the wind will back.
Then comes the calm - oh, alas and alack!

(Repeat endlessly)

Throughout the day the wind rose and it was gloriously sunny. Just what we ordered - so it was obviously not going to last. The sea was blue with crisp, snow-white caps. The birds were quite stunning. Amongst today's little brood there were a dozen mollymawks, some of them grey-headed albatrosses and some the exquisitely beautiful black-browed albatross.

At about midday, with the wind rising, I dropped the main. As it tumbled down a fearless mollymawk came and landed right beside us, not ten feet away. "Hi, Diome'dea!" I called, and Nick, from the cockpit, shouted, "Hello there!" We both waved cheerily.

The bird turned himself around, down-wind, to take a look at this curious, flightless life-form. His face seemed to say, "What are they, I wonder? Whatever they are, they lack proper decorum."
"One day," I said to Nick, "you'll build that steel yacht that you're always dreaming about, and we'll name it after this fellow."

Until now we had seen no storm petrels on this particular journey, but this morning we were joined by a little flock. They pattered about in our wake, fluttering to and fro, scattering away from a wave and flitting nervously from this side to that, rather like agitated robins. The bigger birds sheared amongst them without seeming to intend any menace, and nor did the little petrels appear the least afraid.

We sighted the light at Peninsula Valdez at three o'clock the following morning, from a distance of twenty miles. As we closed the land the albatrosses and the shearwaters abandoned us, but one giant-petrel stayed. The sealers used to call this bird Stinker, or The Vulture, because of his habit of eating dead seals, but having never seen one with his head all covered in blood we still regarded him with affection; such a clumsy-looking, cartoon-style bird. He followed us right into the entrance to the Golfo Nuevo, which was our destination.

Peninsula Valdez is a hammer-shaped pendulum of desert land sticking into the sea. In its interior there is a natural salt-pan which is said to contain the lowest point of land on the American continent. On its either side, encircled by the peninsula itself and by the curve of the mainland shore, there are two gulfs, both of equally remarkable depth. Here, since time immemorial - and perhaps from the beginning of their creation - the right-whales have come to breed.

If any whalers knew of this place they kept it a close secret, and the breeding ground was not discovered by cetologists until the 1970s. Nevertheless, the record written in the soft rocks of the peninsula bears evidence of whales who came to the Golfo Nuevo and the Golfo San José while man was still swinging in the trees.

Today the gulfs are still largely the domain of the whales - and of sea lions, and penguins, and a resident pod of orca, or killer whales - but whereas the only two-legged mammals who may intrude into the Golfo San José are scallop fishermen and professional whale watchers, in the Golfo Nuevo a little modern industry has arisen. Each year several thousand tourists come to see the oldest and most primitive cetacean of them all. And we had come with the same ambition.

As we entered the gulf my eyes were already peeled for an early sighting of a whale, but the only ones to show themselves were the orcas.

"Quick! Come and see, children! There are two... no, three of them. Over there, a long way off."

Caesar and Xoë came tumbling out of the cabin to gaze in the direction of my outstretched arm. Three tall, black fins far away in the distance. "Big deal," their expressions seemed to say, and they hurried below to resume their play.

The bay was wide and quiet, and so desolate that we were at first disappointed. Perhaps we should have stayed a little longer with our friends at Buenos Aires. It looked as if this might be a lonesome and even a rather depressing Christmas.

"Penguins! Come quickly, they're going to dive. Too late; they've dived."

Caesar preferred the warmth of the cabin, but Xoë had once more come scurrying up the ladder. Penguins were her passion. Ever since she had seen the pictures in our bird books, and heard that there were penguins as big as herself, she had longed to find one to cuddle. These, who swam like swamped ducks in the cold, grey water, were only little fellows. They were magellenic penguins, which stand about 18 inches tall.

"Too late, Xoë. But there'll be more."

Xoë looked hopefully at the empty lake and then scuttled below again.

Dusk was approaching. The town of Puerto Madryn was some distance away and the village of Pyramides, although closer, was upwind. And where would we be most likely to see the whales - or had the whales already gone south? Here, it seemed, was an empty stage; a vast stage left vacant after the cast had finished their piece. Even the orcas whom we had seen in the distance were now gone. As for the penguins, they were like little, frightened mice in this great, eerie, silent auditorium.

But why go thrashing up the bay by night? We had come here to see it. We might as well anchor now, on this lonely shore, and press on again in the morning. As we approached the beach which sweeps around the southern jaw of the Golfo Nuevo, we saw that it was smothered in terns. 50 yards off the steeply banked pebbles we found the preferred depth for anchoring and we dropped the hook. All at once we were in the thick of a scolding, screeching mob, who flit about in a silly panic, telling us to be off yet not daring to back up their threat with a massed assault. They soon settled down again.

Thousands of terns sat, all head to wind, on the shingle beach. No, not thousands; Nick climbed the mast and returned with the news that there must be *tens* of thousands of these South American terns, with their stunning crimson bills and legs, and their crisp white wings and trim black caps. The whole beach, from this place until the jaw of the bay, was white with terns. My attention was caught by one small patch amongst the great sheet - a patch so far off that it was about the size of postage stamp held at arms length. While I watched, the patch grew swiftly darker - like a yellow-brown stain seeping into white cloth - and in the same moment the patch of blue above the beach became filled with a fluttering snow-storm.

Perhaps a skua or a fox had come amongst the birds. Or perhaps it was a false alarm. Certainly it was not a man. In all this great desert of shore and sea we were the only men. *Maamari* was as intrusive as a spaceship and we as alien as extra-terrestrials, in a world of hysterical birds.

The next day was Christmas Eve, and as soon as we had eaten our porridge we went ashore. Nick led the children along the wave-lapped pebbles at the foot of the beach, for to amble up over the top of the shingle bank was to wander through a minefield - although with the opposite kind of effect. Any careless foot-fall might terminate the life of an unborn chick. After a while, however, I realised that the tern's eggs, although wonderfully camouflaged, were betrayed by the artistic instincts of their parents. Each nest was decorated by strands of dried seaweed and a few wisps of tangled net. Big sun-bleached crab's claws were all the rage, but some of the birds had gone for a modern look and employed bits of plastic crate, or a light bulb, or a coca-cola can. One hoped that this formative influence would not have the same deleterious effect upon the young terns as it does upon human offspring.

As we studied our surroundings from the yacht, our eyes had lit upon what seemed to be a length of fat rope. This, rather than a desire to cause further alarm amongst the terns, was our reason for going ashore. And there it was, sure enough - the very thing that we wanted: a piece of fat, black rope, 95 feet long; it would be ideal for use as a fender and very much more practical than the old, wooden rubbing-strake which had been smashed about by African canoes. We claimed our prize from the tide line and towed it back to the mother-ship.

The wind was still in the north, so that to reach Pyramides, 22 miles away, we had to beat. While I prepared lunch, Nick got *Maamari* under way and all afternoon and throughout the night we slogged to and fro. The wind was restless and inconsistent, vacillating between a zephyr breeze and some quite ferocious squalls. We never seemed to be carrying the right amount of sail. The sea was short and steep, slapping *Maamari* on the nose.

As darkness fell we discovered a beckoning light. Our chart showed it to be sitting on the point beside the village. Home and dry - or so we thought - but as we entered the bay Aeolus unleashed a truly savage attack, so that it was all we could do to hold our own. While I sat on the floor and parcelled-up Christmas presents, Nick, wrapped in his new oilskin jacket, fought to and fro.

"Happy Christmas," he greeted me, as the clock chimed the midnight hour.

"Not again! Not another one at sea!"

Well, not at sea as such - and by the time the first fingers of sunlight groped under the grey canopy of dawn we had reached the anchorage. Even while we were arriving the wind fell away, as if to say, "Well you've beaten me this time", but we knew that it was not the north wind but the southerly which would cause us the most angst here; the southerly wind had a 22 mile fetch. This would not be a good place to be in a pampero. In a sud-estader it would be even worse, for the entrance to the gulf was now directly to the south-east and so the little bay would be open to the ocean swell.

In that case, why had we come? We had come because Pyramides and Puerto Madryn are the only ports - the only settlements, indeed - throughout this entire desolate lagoon. And Puerto Madryn brings to the seafarer its own share of problems as we were later to discover.

The light of day revealed a hamlet vaguely reminiscent of São Pedro, in Cabo Verde. The bay was about the same size as that one; the headland was on the left, and it was about as tall; and some gigantic dunes behind the village echoed the brown, rubble hills of that other desert land. Most familiar of all, of course, was the wind's acceleration. In one respect, however, this place was quite unlike São Pedro, for whereas that is a fishing village it was obvious, from a mere glance, that tourism is the sole industry in Pyramides.

The children awoke without a thought of Christmas and rushed on deck to see the new land. The scent of warm sand was borne towards us on a hot wind. The sun beat down. Xoë scurried below to look for her spade and only after some very heavy hinting did either she or Caesar recall that they had put out stockings for Father Christmas.

"No. 'Hasn't come," said Xoë, who had forgotten where she put her stocking. There was no trace of disappointment. What was this Christmas-thing all about, anyway? Caesar was more persistent and soon found both socks. Now there was great excitement as they explored the knobbles and bulges and unwrapped each new delight. No mention had been made of presents, and so I kept quiet for the time being and we went ashore. Christmas dinner was a parilla - a great chunk of beef steak in a hamburger bun. In Africa we had lived chiefly on vegetables, but in Argentina beef is the staple. I have never much cared for meat and this over-abundance set me firmly on the road towards vegetarianism - or rather, fishytarianism - but for the festival day I put my scruples aside and tucked in.

By the luncheon hour the breeze blowing off the dunes was so hot that one looked around for a source. My mind insisted that there must surely be a bushfire. Had we been out on the water, we knew, we would have needed to be wearing our coats, but in the shade of the bar where we ate our meal and sipped cold beer it was 45°C (113°F).

It was far too hot to go exploring amongst the sand dunes, and so after lunch we retreated to the beach. The little resort was surprisingly quiet - it seemed that the whales had all left, and this was therefore the "off" season - but there were one or two other sightseers milling about on the sand. As we made our way back towards the dinghy, I realised that one of their number was making a bee-line to intercept us.

"Is that your sailing yacht?" The voice was an American one and the speaker was fair-haired, but he introduced himself as Rafael. His wife was called Belem and they had an eight year old daughter called Sami.

"Where have you come from?" the man asked.

I gave him a brief run-down.

"Wow? So, you just... live aboard. And travel around. Wow! That's amazing."

It was going to be one of those, do-you-anchor-at-night conversations, I could tell. Never mind, this was the season of goodwill and mellow fruitfulness, or something, and anyway the sun seemed to have softened my brain, or perhaps it was the beer. Nick raised his eyebrows as I invited these complete strangers to come aboard.

"We'd love to come, but we still have one more trip."

"One more what?"

"One more whale-watching trip. That's *my* boat, on the beach, over there." Rafael pointed and then, as the inspiration struck him, he said, "Tell you what: why don't you come along, too?"

"For free?" We had already discovered that the usual fee for the whale-watching trips was $25 (U.S.) per person.

"Well, of course! For free."

In August, Rafael told us, the bay at Pyramides is just about paved with right whales. "When they're all here, we could just about walk out to your boat on their backs."

Now it was our turn to express astonishment.

"Yes, they surface under your dinghy," Rafael went on, "and you find yourself high and dry for a moment. Sometimes they get tangled in the anchor chain and make off with the boat."

Not so good - for either the boat or the whale.

Rafael and his brothers were half-American scallop fishermen who had spent years diving in the other gulf - the Golfo San José - and they knew the right whales and the sea lions as friends. They knew each whale by name, and knew his age and his parentage. They had untangled curious right whales from their airlines, sometimes needing to climb over the great leviathans to perform this delicate feat. Even the professional cetologists came to talk whales with Rafael and the other members of the Benegas family. Few people could be more qualified to run whale-watching trips than they.

Rafael's speed boat pounded out through the short steep seas, kicking up clouds of spray. On the point, at the western jaw of the bay, were a number of sea lions who had arrived to stake out a claim over a patch on the rock. In the boat we could approach them without any trouble, but woe betide anyone who tried to walk amongst them. Sea lions are as aggressive towards man as they are to each other, and they have very sharp teeth.

There were not so many sea lions as there should have been on the flat, rock plateau. Nobody knew why, but they were late in coming. By December they should have moved across from their rookery, a few miles further along the bay, and there should have been a couple of thousand animals, but as it was there were only a few score. One dominant male had collared most of the females and they lay around him - an adoring harem of five corpulent females for one fat slob. One or two of the other males had a female apiece - one had even pulled two girls - but most were bachelors still. While we watched, there were sporadic confrontations between the espoused and the various unattached males, so that the sound of fighting was almost constant. With snarls and roars, and with the fur which rings their fat necks erected, the bulls really did seem like aquatic lions. When they walk, however, they are more like grizzly bears and when they lie down they look like nothing so much as gargantuan, overweight slugs.

Sea lions in the water are beautiful animals, but the affection we had hitherto felt for them disappeared swiftly as we regarded their behaviour on terra firma. The males attacked one another so viciously that they drew blood. Even the females were fractious, those in the harem constantly bitching and snapping like jealous suitors.

After a while we noticed that there was a little newborn seal pup bobbing about in the waves beside the rock. He must have been swept off the shelf, and as he was too weak to swim for long he would surely drown if not rescued. The adult members of his family were just above the pup, yet they did nothing to assist him in his plight. Not five feet away from her distraught newborn, the mother sea lion basked in the sun, seeming to have not a care or a thought in the world. We knew her by the blood still staining her fur and her hind flippers.

Every now and then the tiny pup let out a high pitched squeal - a plea for help - but his mother scarcely raised her head. Then the pup was carried along in the light surf until his little body lodged between the bodies of an adult couple. They were sitting, like Western holiday makers, gazing rapturously at the sun. Either one could have picked up their nephew with their mouths and put him on the rock, but neither so much as glanced down at him. It occurred to us that although man wages war on his fellows and is sometimes said to be worse than an animal, any man who behaved in this callous way towards an infant would be labelled psychopathic and locked up.

We expected better things of the right whales. Rafael turned his boat away from the rocky headland and went in search of them. As we skimmed along he explained that most of the 200-strong tribe who use the Golfo Nuevo had already gone south, and disappeared into the Antarctic Ocean, but the late breeders were still hanging around and he reckoned that there were about thirty animals remaining. Eight or nine miles off the beach we found a mother and her young son lounging about in an affectionate embrace; she, black and shiny-wet, and perhaps as much as 60 foot long, although hardly visible above the waves; he, half her length and therefore even harder to find.

It was the blow of steamy air and an oily texture on the sea's surface which showed us the whales' new position after each dive. They would hang below the surface and then, after a few minutes, the long, black backs would slowly move forward and first the mother and then her child would raise their great tail flukes. Rafael said that he had once seen a female hold her flukes aloft for twenty minutes on the trot.

Back aboard *Maamari,* our guests shared our Christmas fizz and made themselves maté, a pungent and highly caffeinated tea. Across the bay, storm clouds were looming and lightning flashed, yet the glass foretold no disaster. Our friends predicted a blow from the south, but we expected just the usual squally puffs and some short, sharp showers; nothing to worry about. We poured another round of drinks and then sat back, soaking up the peace of our surroundings.

It was Nick who first saw the strange disturbance on the water, nearby. Could it be...? Yes! - "Thar she blows!" - and a right whale came ambling right into the bay where we were anchored! I ran to fetch the glasses, and Caesar clamoured for the first look. There now, I'd almost forgotten: time for the presents, quickly, before the sun set.

Xoë unwrapped a cuddly penguin. It would be a while before we met a real, live, fluffy, Xoë-sized chick.

"Hurry, Caesar, or the whale will be gone."

"Help me." He struggled with the sellotape. "Now I've torn the paper. What is it? It's binoculars! Look, I've got my own binoculars!"

Side by side we sat at the rail and watched the right whale wave her tail. It had been a very odd, un-Christmassy Christmas, but one of the best, ever.

When the wind went into the south and blew a gale, a few days later, we had to get out of Pyramides fast. We had to beat out, and we had a close call with the rocky cliffs when we missed stays on the first tack. By the time we reached the little town of Puerto Madryn the wind had gone into the east, so exposing this anchorage instead. Whoever governs this reach of the South Atlantic must be a close relative of Biscay's troll.

Off Puerto Madryn, *Maamari* rolled and bucked, tugging at her tether like a panic stricken horse. There was a big launch prowling about the wild anchorage, but the man who drove it wanted $30 just to run us over to the adjacent pier. We sat it out until the next day and then went ashore in a lull.

Madryn is nothing to write home about; a small, drab seaside resort with a very North American feel to it. Perhaps it was the grid-plan streets and the big cars, or perhaps it was the Indians, looking very like North American Indians. We sensed mild but deep-seated racism. There was not much mixing. The Indian youths hung out in gangs and spent their time preening and posing on street corners.

The wind rose while we were exploring the town, and by nightfall there were waves breaking around *Maamari*. She was only 50 yards off the pier but it would not have been safe to try rowing back to her. Nor did we want to spend the night ashore; the anchor might easily drag in these conditions, and we needed to be aboard, just in case.

"I'll have to go by myself," Nick said. We were standing in the ferryman's office and he looked down at Caesar and Xoë, who had spread themselves on the floor. "You could probably sleep here, too. I'm sure this chap won't mind."

The idea of sleeping on a stranger's office floor was fairly grim, but it was nowhere near so alarming as the thought of Nick trying to row back to the boat.

"You must be kidding! You'll never make it! - and you aren't exactly a champion swimmer."

Fortunately, at this point the ferry man's pity was aroused. There is nothing like a couple of little, sleepy, blond kids for stirring up sympathy.

"Come on! Come on!" We followed the man aboard his launch. He fired up the engine, and in the safety of his snug wheel-house we crossed the small divide.

But that was just the first part. The real problem was going to be getting from the launch onto the yacht. The launch was bigger than *Maamari*, and she was made of steel, and both boats were rolling wildly.

The launch could not possibly go alongside. The decks flicked towards one another violently as the two boats rolled. If the ferry-man messed this up, our home was going to be match-wood.

Nick jumped the gap. A leap of faith.

The next roll - and I swung Caesar across to his dad, who grabbed him around the waist.

Now Xoë, by one arm.

"I've got her! Let go!" Nick shouted. Too much caution was as deadly as none. If we both hung on to either arm then our child would be injured, or pulled into the sea, as the boats rolled apart.

That just leaves me. Oh, I hate this! Can I time it right, or will I mess it up and be mashed between the boats? One wild vault, as the decks lunge down towards each other... and I'm home and safe, and we're laughing.

"Just one thing, Nick," I said, as we hugged each other tight. "Let's *never* come to Puerto Madryn again."

18

THEY THAT GO DOWN TO THE SEA IN SHIPS

These see the works of the Lord and his wonders in the deep.
Psalm 107, verses 23-24

I had the vague idea that something amiss lay ahead, in our path. Was it only a cautious respect for uncertainty which led me, when speaking of our plans, to call them hopes? Some kind of fatalism caused me to say, "We intend," and not, "We *will* go south." Yet the feeling which I now had in my head was less nebulous. It all had to do with our windsurfers.

"We can't possibly keep them while we're down there," I said to Nick. Two windsurfers sitting, as they had always sat, lashed on the cabin top. It was ridiculous really; we had not used them in ages. Since Caesar was born, we had used them only once. When waves swept the deck, they sluiced over and between the boards to no effect - but down in the Southern Ocean it would be a very different matter. Down there the waves would be bigger. "We're bound to lose them."

"Well, alright then. We'll sell them."

That much had been agreed over a year ago. The problem was

finding a buyer. Much as I hated to see the boards cluttering the deck, I was aware of their value. Mine alone had cost £500, and we had another £300 worth of sails. I could not bring myself to let the whole lot go for peanuts.

Trying to sell a windsurfer in West Africa would have been like trying to sell a computer in the stone-age. No one had a use for something 'useless', and no one had even a tenth of the cash. Buenos Aires was the obvious place, and so we had tried selling them there. One or two people came to look at what was on offer, but nobody bought anything. In Pyramides we finally raised a bit of interest, but once again cost was a problem. "Look," I declared, "We might as well give them away, rather than just take pin money."

And then it began to occur to me that we should, indeed, give the boards away. If you have something that you no longer need then perhaps you *should* give it away. Rafael and his brothers would be delighted to have a couple of windsurfers and some smart sails. Life had been generous with us. Perhaps it was our turn to hand on some of the luck.

It was our turn to reciprocate - but we failed; we followed rationale. Money was as tight as ever, and it went against the grain to give things away. The devil sat on my shoulder and said, "That would be spendthrift! Prodigal! Insane!"
How was I to know one little voice from another?

"You promise you'll send us a postcard, hey?"
"We'll send you lots, Rafael. Are you sure that you don't want to change your mind?"
"I'd love to; I'd love to come. Maybe in a few years time."
The faces in the launch were all smiling - there were no fears or worries in the minds of our friends - but I felt uneasy. Did they not understand that this was to be no sunshine cruise? I was sorry that neither Rafael nor his brother could join us, but at the same time I was relieved. This would be a lively passage. It would not be a good introduction to the life on the ocean wave.

It was on the 4th January that we left Pyramides, bound for the Falkland Islands, and to outward appearances our departure gave no cause for concern. The wind was light, and sometime after Rafael had turned his boat back towards the shore it fell away altogether. We drifted out of the gulf in an absolute calm.

A little after midnight, while we were still sloshing about in the entrance, a light north-westerly arose. By daybreak it had risen to force six or seven but during the morning it faded and backed.

"Here we go again." The usual cycle. Soon it would be calm and then would come the gale - or worse. Over the past few weeks we had listened often to the weather forecasts. Sometimes they would give hurricane force or more for the area of the Falklands Islands.

"Mummy, we should put the bungies over the crockery." As he spoke Caesar began to hook down the shock-chord straps, newly made for the purpose. I smiled to myself. They were certainly not needed yet. The sea state was no more than average, and we had never yet lost a plate or a bowl from the rack. But then, of course, we had never been laid right over. Now there were bungies and nets everywhere to cope with that eventuality. Meanwhile, out on deck everything was lashed and lashed again. If we went over we would probably lose the dinghies, but there was not much we could do about that. As for the windsurfers - I already knew in my heart that the sea would have them.

I was contemplating such things when I suddenly realised that the wind was *veering*, to a north-north-easterly. Could it be that we were leaving the region of the tedious, predictable pattern? This was the first time in weeks that we had seen the wind veer, rather than back.

A few hours later we were suddenly buzzed by a twin-propeller, high-wing plane labelled Prefectura Mail. It flew past from astern at no more than 40 feet - certainly it was lower than the mast - and then it turned round to come back and beat us up again.

In the last seconds of the plane's final approach the pilot seemed intent on landing on the foredeck, and with collision imminent I was considering jumping into the sea with Xoë in my arms. The starboard wing tip, when the plane passed, was no more than a boat's length away from our port side and we saw the man's face, his cap, and his round sunglasses. Nick turned on the radio and after hearing our destination the pilot wished us good luck.

The day continued to bring its surprises with first one, then two, and in the end, by supper time, five decent-sized fish spread out on the cockpit floor. Then there were the birds, one of whom had evidently strayed all the way from Patagonia. He was a little, tubby, chocolate-brown bird with a rust-coloured cape. He was scarcely bigger than a wren. I saw him catch two blue-bottles in flight, in the manner of warbler or a fly catcher, but his curiosity and fearlessness were that of a robin. He even let me touch him once, and many times he hopped over my foot.

We also had a black backed gull land on the radar scanner and stay for a time. There were a couple of albatrosses, but they were rather shy. There were little flocks of magellenic penguins, startled to find *Maamari* looming above them. There were mats of kelp, drifting by - but there were no whales - or, at any rate, we saw none though we sought them diligently. After our ride in Rafael's boat we had become more aware of how difficult it would be, in a big sea, to spot a right whale which happened to be hanging about in our path. And a sudden impact with one of these leviathans might be terminal for both parties. We kept an almost constant watch, but there were no whales to be seen and nor were there any ships or fishing boats. The sea was blue-green - beautiful, but icy-looking - and the horizon was empty.

"6th January. *Wind very variable in both direction and strength, ranging from calm to force six. Maamari needs constant help and attention and there have been frequent sail changes and plenty of gybing. We are now crossing the mouth of the Golfo San Jorge and the sea has changed to a sombre, green colour. The swell, which was in the north-east, driving us along, is now coming from the west and meeting us on the beam.*

In the afternoon we were suddenly struck by a ferocious pampero, or a squall of that type. It was a south-westerly gale which arrived with great violence but then, after half an hour, gradually faded away. Afterwards the wind backed to east by south and there is now a swell from that direction also, opposing the westerly swell. The result is a very messy sea."

So it went on, with never an idle day for *Maamari's* crew. Throughout the 8th the weather continued variable. We battled, and then we romped along, and then were left to roll and creak in a calm. Gone, long gone, but by no means forgotten was the indolent pleasure of being carried on a warm wind and the current.

Besides the fact that we now had to work at sailing the boat, we were also feeling the cold. Whereas in the tropics we only needed to pop outside every ten minutes, here we were spending most of the time in the cockpit. The perpetual changes in wind strength made us feel the need to keep an eye on things; but there was more to it than that. There was something compulsive and almost addictive about the new and very different world into which we had stumbled.

"9th January. *At 02.00, when I turned into my bunk, the wind was north by west, force six, and we were storming along. The waves met us on the quarter. The glass was falling, as it had been all day, and the wind was backing. During the night I heard the wind rise and we gybed.*

In the morning, when I took over from Nick, the sky was intensely blue with clouds piled up here and there. The glass had just stopped falling at 06.00. The wind was in the south-west, blowing a gale and gusting quite a bit more."

"You know, we really need an inside steering position."
Nick hardly bothered to acknowledge the remark. It was one which I had made often in the past few weeks as we went further south and the weather grew colder. An inside steering position would have enabled us to put all the boards into the companion way and shut the hatch whilst still keeping an eye on the world from the comfort of the cabin - but, of course, it was just another one of those things on a long, long list. Anyway, it was not worth hacking the boat about when we would only be down this way, and needing such a thing, for a few months. Soon we would be turning the corner and heading back up into the tropics. I pulled on my oilskin trousers, my jacket, boots, and gloves. I climbed the steps, slid open the hatch and clambered out over the two boards which were in place.

Maamari was galloping across an endless plain of dark, blue-green waves which were stacked up, like the lines of an advancing army, to the west. The waves met us just aft of the beam, either sweeping under the boat while their crests took a short cut over the top, or else spending their energy on our deck. In the squalls, foam filled the air and adorned the weather face of the waves like loose scree on a steep hillside.

I had tightened the hood of my new oilskin jacket around my face, and now I pulled down the peak and taped the visor over my cheeks and nose. Only my eyes, peering out through the slit, were exposed to the weather. Still, if I tried to look upwind I could not, for the cold wind stung my eyes and made them water straight away.

Ahead of the boat two giant petrels landed together, carefully and gently, on the crest of a wave. At our advance they opened their wings and took off - backwards! Today there was no need for even these great birds to go paddling over the water, like planes on a runway. Today they were jump jets.

Black-browed and grey-headed albatrosses soared by. Emboldened by the wind they passed within a wing beat of the boat - yet on this day there was no need for anyone to actually *beat* his wings. The birds swooped across our wake and swung by; then they turned and crossed ahead of the bow in knife-edge flight. The music from an old movie came to my mind. Was it 'The Dambusters'? And then I found myself humming snatches from 'The Flight of the Valkyries'. An albatross swept past my head, like a Spitfire beating-up the enemy airfield.

Amongst the big waves there were some really huge ones. They rose to a peak, boiling with foam, and then surged down - crashed down - leaving a broad, white train on the concave sea. Sometimes, rather than surge down the slope, they tumbled over themselves and were hurled straight down onto the plain beneath the mountain. Then, afterwards, a vast, white patch remained printed on the ocean, and that little piece of the ever-changing landscape lay still for a while, as if in shock.

When the waves chanced to explode onto our hapless, helpless boat, then the sprayhood trembled beneath the weight of water and the cockpit brimmed over. Fingers and arms of white froth reached into every crevice and poured down from the dinghies on the aft cabin roof. And only the day before I had been lying atop the rubber dinghy, watching the birds glide by!

I went below to warm myself, and because the children wanted a story, but how could I think about the Elephant Child or Anansi the Spider, when my whole mind was taken up with the ocean? Today I could not even tell a tale of adventure on the high seas.

I climbed the steps again, and for a little while peeped out through the slit at the top, between the second board and the hatch. I saw another wave dump a ton of water onto the boat, filling the cockpit to the height of the seats. Yes, that amount alone must weigh a ton. These waves, what must they weigh in their entirety? And their weight was not the only factor; their force was compounded by motion and speed. Another one landed, and I watched the foam boiling over the dinghies in exactly the same way that a wave landing on a rock at the seashore gushes down its cracks and fissures for such an impossibly long time afterwards.

Caesar and Xoë could find sufficient amusement in each other. I went outside once more, climbing over the two boards and afterwards bolting the sliding hatch behind me. I stood on the weather side of the cockpit and clung to the rim of the sprayhood. There was no sense of danger. In fact, I am ashamed to say that I was not even wearing a safety harness.

The waves enthralled me; those blue-green mountains with their white veins. But, it was not their size so much as their purposeful passion which absorbed me. Today the seas were not playing with *Maamari*. They were not teasing or even threatening us. We were simply irrelevant to their design. Today the seas had not even noticed *Maamari*, and this frenzy was not rage but religious fervour. Ranks of waves; ranks of devoted muslims, all following the sheik's command. Leaping seas, crashing seas; like voodoo worshippers intoxicated and hypnotised by the drum.

As for *Maamari*, she was as out of place here as a tourist trespassing through the Kaaba during the Hadj. She was as out of place as a peeping-tom - yet for the time being our presence here went unremarked. The ocean and the gale were utterly absorbed in each other and in their own business.

"If this sea gets any bigger we'll have to run before it, won't we?"

"Maybe," Nick answered, "but it's quite okay at the moment."

We were going along very nicely under only the storm jib and the mizzen. I peered at the glass. "Still falling."

"Yes. This is just the beginning. Plenty more to come."

The wind was now in the south-west and I put its strength at force nine. More to come... but *Maamari* was strong and sure. We had put her through force ten before now.

"An albatross soars by, his shadow an obsidian cross on the chiselled, chipped surface of a wave. Clouds slide overhead but seem irrelevant to what is happening here below. Their form and behaviour bear no relation to the strength or direction of this wind.

My hands and feet are numb with the cold. And I keep thinking of the sailor on Magellan's ship who blew his frost-bitten nose, only to have it come off in his handkerchief!

One little grey prion - like a soft, grey tern - flits about in the distance. One tiny storm petrel, patters about beside the boat, looking so vulnerable

amongst the huge seas.
In another 24 hours, if all goes well, we should be off the Falklands."

I awoke, the next morning, to the sound of our Aerogen self-destructing. Over the course of time the wind generator had evidently worked its way loose on its rubber mountings and now the blades were hammering against the mizzen mast. Even as we watched, the machine shed five of its six blades and I cursed inwardly. The ever-faithful Aerogen was one of the few things in this cruising life that I took completely for granted. It supplied all our needs for power and I pictured dark nights ahead. Either that, or else we would be having to run the engine every other day.

"Never mind," said Nick, who was more inclined to look on the bright side. "We're only forty miles north of the islands now. We'll soon be in Port Stanley. Aerogen are a good crowd; they'll have some new blades flown out to us in no time."

Caesar and Xoë pursued me out of the aft cabin. Caesar, in particular, was still very sleepy and I began to suggest that he stay put. Then I thought better of it. Why not let the kids do as they liked, for once? They took up their usual stations, at either end of the dinette. Fortunately it was on the leeward side at the moment. Soon they were fast asleep again.

During the night the wind had risen, as expected, and Nick had first reefed and then dropped the mizzen, so that now we were going along under storm jib alone. After 24 hours of constant south-westerly gale, the seas were quite a bit bigger too - and they were very long - but there was nothing in the motion of the boat to suggest any kind of danger. Without the mizzen up, the bow had fallen away so that the seas were now meeting us on the quarter. We were no longer making our destination, but prudence suggested that it was better not to try pinching and so slow the boat. Moreover, it was obviously better not to take these bigger waves on the beam.

"No problems," Nick said. "We haven't had a wave on deck for about three hours."

I had dragged on my foul weather gear, both in preparation for my watch and because it was so cold in the cabin. I was feeling pretty glum and unenthusiastic. I had not slept at all well. Nick handed me a cup of hot soup and I took it with my mittened hands. I said, "Just before you undress, do me a favour. Stick your head outside, one more time."

Nick put his foot on the bottom step of the ladder.

In the next instant the boat began to roll and I found myself being tipped backwards. My eyes met Nick's, and in that momentary glance we both raised our eyebrows in surprise. I was fighting to remain upright. In the same moment there was an almighty crash, as the wave evidently smashed the cabin-side to pieces, and bits of wood and sundry other objects came tumbling down onto me, borne by the sea. I struggled against the deluge, thinking as I did, "Am I going to be able to get out through the hole, before she sinks? And am I going to be able to drag Xoë out?" Xoë was behind me and, as someone once said when asked which of his kids he would save from a fire, in a crisis you just grab your nearest dearest. In my mind there was no panic, nor even any thought for our future. In that instant there was no time for me to consider how hopeless would be our situation, bobbing about in an icy sea.

Then the boat very suddenly jerked upright again and I was standing where the cabin sole had lately been, saying, to myself and to Nick, "What happened?"

To my complete astonishment I saw that there was no hole in the cabin side. *Maamari* had been knocked through 180°, but she had sprung up again before I even had the chance to realise it.

My mittens were gone and the cup of soup had vanished, never to be seen again. Everything that we owned seemed to have been taken from its home and deposited on the leeward side of the boat, in a pile. The scene can best be imagined by picturing what would happen if a giant hand picked up a house, turned it upside down violently, fired a hose inside, and then slammed it down again. The pieces of the cabin-side which I had been fending off were actually the floorboards, and everything that had once been within the deep lockers below those boards was now on the saloon seats, on top of the children.

In the aftermath, the children were obviously our first priority. All that could presently be seen of them was their legs waving about above the extraordinary pile of rubble. The fact that they *were* waving was a tremendous relief. We hauled them out and shuffled them into the relative safety of the passage which joined the saloon to the aft cabin. There, if we went over again they could not be hurled around or buried. I was amazed to see that they were unhurt. Neither one was crying. They had no idea what had happened.

All this thought and activity took place in mere seconds. As I pushed the children into the corridor there was a loud hiss and the cabin began to fill with white smoke.

"Gas!" But it was not the calor gas. What was it?

Nick cried, "Get them into the aft cabin,"- but I wavered. I knew that the aft cabin hatch was bolted from the outside - (actually, the hatch was no longer with us, but we had yet to discover this) - and I had no mind to be trapped by the gas. Should I get the kids outside? I hesitated.

How unfair! To be confronted not with one disaster but two. Would I rather have my children drowned or gassed? Then I realised that none of us was showing any signs of expiring. After what was probably less than a minute the air cleared, but the smell of ammonia remained, and mingled with it was the stench of chlorine. We could hear something spitting and crackling as an electric current took a short cut through the water.

"The batteries!" Nick had been hunting in the debris to find the source of the first gas leak - it was not a fire extinguisher, nor was it the fridge - and now he hurled fallen tools and bolts and boxes away from the batteries and disconnected the leads. Again, it was only moments which had passed but they were valuable moments. Nick grabbed a bucket and began to bale. The water was up over the floorboards, so we probably had five or six tonnes of the stuff weighing us down.

It was at about this stage - still only a minute or two after the capsize - that we realised that the mizzen had broken in half. All that now joined the upper section to the lower was the bracket supporting the radar scanner. Looking up at the mess I found myself scarcely able to believe that all this had happened to *us*. I saw that the rubber dinghy and my little sailing dinghy were both gone. The sprayhood had been buckled and bent and generally smashed to pieces. The lifebelts, the danbuoy, and the water-activated man-overboard raft were all missing.

Much later, when we had time to analyse the remains, we found that some of the dinghy lashings were actually still with us. A half inch diameter rope had been passed around the rubber boat, through a set of plastic eyes, and some of the lashings had been made up to this. The force of the wave was so great that it simply tore out the eyes from the dinghy, leaving us like a man with the lead and collar but no dog. Besides these lines there had been one other - a rope of at least one inch diameter - which went over the dinghies twice and was fastened at either end onto the mizzen chain-plates. Of this rope there was no trace. It had obviously broken at the knots. Others, amongst the spider's web of lines, had snapped or had torn out their fittings. The grab rails, for instance, had been wrenched from their aluminium end-fittings, and stainless steel lacing-eyes had been broken in half by the pull on the lines which they held. A massive aluminium fairlead was snapped in two.

But all of this we learnt only later, as I say, for in the immediate aftermath of the disaster we concentrated all our efforts on saving our boat and ourselves.

While Nick bailed, my attention was with the children. In this climate it was a matter of urgency that I change their sodden clothes. Next, I helped them into their life jackets. I took down the emergency grab bag and got out the EPIRB. Then I lashed it onto Caesar, saying, "This is very important. It's a radio beacon. If we press the button, here, it will start to send a signal, and people will come in ships and planes to find us. Don't press it now. Just keep it safe."

"I want a cuddle," said Xoë.

"Pump!" shouted Nick. He had just been outside and discovered the loss of the aft hatch and the lazarette hatch. Now we had a huge hole - four foot by two foot - open to the waves landing on the aft deck.

The lazarette was sealed off from the rest of the boat by a water-tight bulkhead, but if we left it that way - if we let it remain water tight - then we would be carrying around almost two tonnes of water at the stern. Nick dived back into the engine room and I heard him rummaging about.

"What are you doing?" I shouted.

"I'm going to cut the tube which carries the steering cables." One slash with a knife from the kitchen drawer, and I heard the water begin pouring into the engine room. In the passage on the other side of the plywood wall I redoubled my efforts with the pump.

From where I sat I could talk to the children. I could also see into the aft cabin and view the devastation there. Before this event, I had always considered the aft cabin to be the safest place in the boat, and if ever I had feared for their safety I would have sent the children to play on the bed. Now I saw that the lashings which held the mattress down had not been able to hold it against the weight in the lockers below. Where Caesar had been sleeping, only minutes before the capsize, there was a pile of junk which touched the deck-head. Prominent amongst the rubble was the old Singer sewing machine, in its big, black box. In spite of our predicament I could see that their guardian angels had certainly been keeping watch over the children. That thought, at least, gave me hope.

Above my head I caught glimpses of Nick, as he worked to fasten a locker lid over the hole where the aft hatch had been. With the grab rails and several lacing eyes gone or broken there were few places to which he could lash the necessary ropes.

"Nail it down!" I shouted, but Nick had already thought of that.

"'Can't find any nails. 'Can't even find a hammer. The drawers in the wooden chest came open, and everything is in the bilge."

As for the tool box, itself - this was a steel trunk, bolted through its base to the floor. Not only had the lid burst open when it was turned upside down, but the bolts which affixed it had simply torn through the metal. The contents were under the engine and the box was flying about on its own.

Nick came tumbling back down the ladder - or rather, down the companion way. The ladder itself had torn out the bolts which fastened it and was lying on its side on the floor. He tried to find something with which to cover the lazarette, but we had no floorboards or locker lids big enough. Besides that, there was simply nothing left, back there on the aft deck, to which he could have lashed the boards.

Our attention turned to the mizzen, and Nick hurried back outside to release the triatic stay - the piece of rigging which leads from one masthead to the other. We had always wondered about this stay. Its purpose is to guy the main mast, but it had always seemed to us that if one mast broke, the triatic could actually cause the destruction of the other. We had thought ourselves pretty smart in rigging up a rope triatic which, in an event such as this, could be released from the deck. But with the mast folded in two, the line jammed. It needed a release point not just at one end but at both.

"I think it's going to be okay," Nick said, as he came below. "It doesn't seem to be pulling on the main mast."

I took a quick break from pumping the bilges and we gazed up at the injured spar. The top half was flailing about as we rolled. Nick wondered if he should try to cut it loose, but he was afraid that it would fall onto the deck, or even on his own head. Was there any way in which to save the radar, we asked ourselves? Of all the modern aids to navigation this was the one we most cherished. It was an expensive piece of kit and we would not be able to afford a replacement.

"The jib is still pulling." It seemed amazing that the sail could be unharmed, and still carrying on its work, after it had been dragged through the sea. The anchor hatch and the forehatch were also undamaged. Although the wave had seemed to strike us on the beam, its force had obviously been spent on the after half of the boat. "Perhaps we should bring her further off the wind and take the next one on the stern" - but the self-steering vane was gone and the gear itself was buckled, and we were much too busy to steer by hand.

The sea was still breaking over the aft deck. After one short burst the electric bilge pump had failed. With more water arriving aboard the whole time, through the open hatchways, it was imperative that we keep a pump running, and so I hurried back to my station. While I worked I realised, with numb astonishment, that one of my nightmares had been realised. We had been knocked down. We had been turned right upside-down. Psychologists sometimes say that a person who prepares himself, mentally, for a given disaster is less likely to suffer shock if that particular drama actually happens. This seemed to be the case, for there was none of the terror and panic expected.

While I worked, I prayed, too; I prayed aloud and Caesar joined in. "Please, God, look after us. Look down from your heaven and help us." I called upon friends who have gone before - for it seems to me that "primitive" peoples may be right to believe in their power - and I asked them to pull some weight on our behalf, in the manner of ambassadors and agents at the court of the most high God.

"Come on, Moitissier. You've been here. Lend us a hand! Captain Slocum, help us if you can. Send us guidance."

Above all I cried out to our creator, begging him, "Help us, God. If we ask it in the name of Jesus will you calm the waves?" Romantic notions of Poseidon, spirit of the sea, were at this stage very far from my mind. Christianity has given such beings a rather dubious image, and in time of crisis we turn to what we know best.

"One of the windsurfers is gone."

A premonition fulfilled - but what about the other?

Everything having been thrown out of the under-floor lockers, the boat was now ballasted in the wrong sense; everything had landed up on the leeward side. Nick began to hurl things back into the bilges until the space was all filled. His mind was still on the lazarette and on a means of covering that huge hole.

To say that we were ready for the next capsize would be an exaggeration, but certainly we were awaiting its arrival and we had done our best to prepare. Again, the deadly wave arrived unseen and unannounced. This time we had all three of the hatchboards in place, in the companion way, but it was to very little avail.

"Here we go again! Hang on tight." I was still at the pump and, as the boat went over and down, I felt myself rolling up the passage wall. My head and upper-back were on the deck-head. Once again, it all happened too quickly for any kind of fear or panic. I never doubted that *Maamari* would bounce back up again - such a thought never even entered my head - and when she did, I landed on my knees amongst a pile of half a hundred music cassettes. Caesar was beside me - I remember hauling him to his feet - and in the same moment I shouted, "Where's Xoë?"

Xoë was nowhere to be seen. She was not in the passage. She was not in the saloon. In an instant I saw that the main hatch had gone and realised, with a kind of numb disbelief, that Xoë must have fallen out through the gaping hole. Nick hauled himself up the companion way and looked at the debris floating all around *Maamari*. "She's not here."

"She must be! Look again! She was wearing her lifejacket!"

"She's not here."

But she *must* be. My mind was completely blank. It absolutely refused to accept the possibility that my little girl could simply disappear as if she had never existed.

I seemed to hear a little squeak - but I must have imagined it. We were calling her name - helplessly, stupidly - but there was no reply. We were just standing here, doing nothing, when there ought to be action. But, what action?

Then we heard a little gasp. We both heard it this time. It came from the rubble in the bilge. How could she be in amongst that lot, which Nick had only just replaced? I scrabbled at the pile of junk and found Xoë's little face, peering up at me with an expression of horror and shock. Besides the junk, she was up to her nostrils in water. She can have had no idea where she was. (She later told us that she thought she was at the bottom of the sea.)

All those cans of paint and shackles and screws had flown out, and Xoë had somehow tumbled in before their return. In her trajectory from the passageway across the deck-head she must have missed the companion way by only inches. And had she fallen into the locker head first, and then been buried in the same way, we would never have found her; why should we have thought to look under what seemed like undisturbed stores? Imagine the awful horror of finding her hours later...! But no, try not to imagine anything, except our survival. Get her back into the passage and hug her tight. Then set about saving the boat.

As I hurried Xoë back into the corridor, I happened to notice the main mast lying on the deck outside the port holes. "Did you know we'd lost the main mast?"

"Yes."

This time there was no surprise or chagrin. Compared to the loss of our main hatch, the loss of the rig was of no consequence. Now we knew that we were fighting for our lives. With all these hatches gone another knock-down would surely sink us.

"Shall I set off the EPIRB?" My finger hovered over the switch. All those who go down to the sea go at their own risk - or so we have always believed. What right did we have to summon others into this maelstrom? What right did we have to alert the world and expect them to spend thousands of pounds in coming to our aid?

But what about the children? Why had we got them into this mess? Xoë was unhurt - by an absolute miracle - and still she did not cry, but she was soaked to the skin and, as I soon discovered, so was every other article of clothing in the boat. Even the blanket and tracksuits in our waterproof grab bag were sodden. Had the roll-down top or the seams failed, or had I forgotten, when I took out the EPIRB, to reseal the bag?

Perhaps we could dry some clothes. Learning from Nick's misadventure in Biscay, I had always kept some matches in a waterproof tub. We could light the stove and... But no, we couldn't. The second capsize had swept the gas bottles off the deck.

"Shall I press the button?" Are we really in such peril? If the sea and the wind would only calm down... But the glass was still low, and still steady. When it rose it must bring an even mightier blow. How long could we survive, cold and wet as we were (all except Caesar)? How long before Xoë was suffering hypothermia?

"Shall I press it, Nick?"

"Yes! Yes! For God's sake, press it! What the hell do you think it's for?"

As I pressed the switch, the strobe light on top of the EPIRB began to flash. An invisible message hurried across the airways, through the hollow ether, to find a passing satellite. Or so we hoped.

"Hang on tight to this, Caesar. This is going to save our lives." I checked to see that the beacon was still securely lashed to his lifejacket.

If ever a stricken yacht stood a good chance of being rescued then it was us, I knew, for just 100 miles away was a British military base equipped with planes and helicopters. In my naïve ignorance I believed that our mayday message would be with them in minutes. A spotter plane would set off, with exact news of our position. It might be overhead within a couple of hours!

It was now eight o'clock. Our rescuers would surely be with us by midday, and then the burden of our ordeal would be shared. In the meantime, we were on our own. For a few hours more we must fight to stay afloat.

Already I was back at the pump, and from the passageway Caesar and I kept up an unceasing prayer vigil: "God, please help us. Don't let us be rolled again. Please let them hear our beacon. Please send a ship or an aeroplane. God, please help us. Don't let us be rolled again..." Soon our chant took on the form of a mantra.

Nick, meantime, was occupied in trying to do something practical. If they were not to batter a hole in the boat then the fallen masts would require some attention. The main mast was in three pieces, only one of which was still aboard, and both halves of the mizzen were dangling in the sea. However, since the masts were not yet hammering and clamouring for any action, the first chore must be to deal with the great gaping hole left by the companion hatch. Whatever was lashed over the top, in place of the hatch, must be lashed in such a way that we could release it from below, to get out.

But, wait! "Nick! Why don't we use the aft hatch, instead? It's smaller, and we don't have to worry about the ladder." The ladder below the aft hatch was bolted through the bulkhead and so it could not budge.

"Or, what about the forehatch?" If we used the forehatch then we could put more permanent lashings over both the main and the aft hatches.

No, the disadvantages of using the forehatch outweighed the benefit. It was distant from the passage, beyond all the rubble in the saloon, and besides that the foredeck was now a very dangerous place. The pulpit and the guard-rails had all been swept away and with the rigging also gone we were left with only the jackstays, running along the side decks, for a hand hold. No, when the final moments came we could not possibly send the kids out through the forehatch.

Nick revised his plans and set about putting a permanent lashing over the big, main hatch. A floorboard sufficed to fill most of the space, but the lack of any lashing point was once again a problem. What could we possibly put in place that would withstand another capsize? The hatch had been built of ¾ inch teak, but the wave had simply smashed through it, tearing the grain apart.

As for the three hatch boards, they were made from ¾ inch marine ply, but the might of the sea had actually fractured one, as if by a karate chop. The metal tracks which carried the boards had been buckled by the blow. How could we hope to create anything which would withstand another such wave? But we must at least try to do so. Over the floorboard Nick lashed a windsurfer sail, which was sufficiently big to cover the whole hatchway. It was tied off to various distant winches and cleats.

While Nick worked outside my prayers became even more fervent, for it was pretty clear that if the boat should happen to be rolled whilst he was on deck, his chances of survival were slim. No sooner was the jury hatch completed than the pieces of mast, which were still fastened to the boat by the rigging wire, began to make trouble. The precise whereabouts of the bolt-croppers was by now a mystery, but in any case Nick preferred to cut the rigging with a hacksaw. By great good fortune, rather than any clever forethought, we had stowed a set of spare tools and spare blades in a little locker behind one of the saloon seat-backs. These were at once brought out.

Again, it was Nick, with his greater strength, greater skill, and far greater courage, who must risk his neck for us all and go outside on deck. We were reluctant to let the masts go altogether- they acted as a very effective sea-anchor - and so he sawed away only the starboard rigging. The pieces of mast now hung down below the boat, suspended by the rigging on the port side. (None of the rigging had failed. Compression alone had been responsible for the fracture of both masts.)

His work complete, for the time being at least, Nick came below and took a spell at the bilge pump. While he pumped, he gave me a brief rundown of our circumstances.

"I hate it out there. There's just nothing left to hook onto."

"What about the masts? Are you happy about the masts?"

"Yes. At the moment. The main mast is in three pieces. The tabernacle is torn out of the deck."

"What if we go over again?" No need to answer that. If we went over again then the masts would fly around with us, like iron flails on a whip. They would cause utter calamity. But we had to go for prevention. If we went over again, then the jury-hatches would come off and the boat would probably sink. We just could not *afford* to go over again, and the masts were essential in preventing the act.

"At least the deck didn't budge."

"No, the compression strut is fine." We had heard of boats - even steel boats - whose deck had been split when the compression strut failed. Nick's handiwork had been tested to the limits and proven.

"What about the liferaft? Have we still got the liferaft?"

"Yes! Incredible! It's the only thing that's left. But the eyebolts have been bent over. It's bound to go next time."

We discussed unlashing the raft and bringing it below. "It's so heavy I can hardly carry it," Nick said.

"We might lose it while you're trying to carry it."

"We could inflate it now, and tow it."

"No way!" That was no solution. We might as well throw the thing away as inflate it now. It would never survive a knock-down, inflated.

"Let's get it below," Nick said. "I think I'd rather we had it below,"

"I'm not so sure. Look at all this junk. It could get buried if we went over again."

"And we'd have to man-handle it up through the hatch again if we needed it"

"Hang on a minute. It won't fit through the aft hatch." End of story. We were certainly not about to undo the lashings on the main hatchway, so the liferaft must remain on deck.

The main mast began grinding against the hull again. The mid-section of the three was trying to batter its way inside. We slipped the lashings on the aft hatch and Nick hurried outside, once more to intervene. He sawed away the port lower shroud. In his absence I waited by the hatch, ready to unlash it again at his call.

And what were the children doing while their parents fretted and scurried about? They sat quietly in the passageway, the urgency in our voices holding them in restraint. The presence of our children in this ordeal was a crushing weight, straining us both physically and emotionally. Their presence kept me tied up in catering to their needs - their chief need being my company - but the vessel, too, had needs.

I cursed myself for my stupidity and gross parental negligence in bringing these little ones into a place of such danger. Why couldn't we have played safe and stayed in the tropics? Why not a nice little house by the seaside? Anxiety and guilt gnawed at my insides.

At about ten o'clock it occurred to us that the EPIRB signal might not be getting out through the glass-fibre and wood of the deck. We knew for a fact that our GPS would not receive a signal through the deck. Amidst great fears for its safety, we took the radio beacon and Nick lashed it outside, on the compass pedestal. We had already tried to put out a mayday on the VHF, but with the mast down there was no aerial. Moreover, I could hear water sloshing about inside the radio.

Time ticked by. Still no one came. The anguish of not knowing whether the EPIRB signal had even been heard was very hard to bear.

In fact, although we could not know it, the emergency signal had been picked up by a satellite, and at midday the rebounding message was received by a station in Falmouth, England. The mayday was swiftly relayed back down to our part of the world, and at 13.00 hours a fishery protection vessel left Port Stanley, capital of the Falklands, to begin a search. Nor were the RAF standing idle - or rather, they were, but through no fault of their own. At Mount Pleasant Airport, the four man crew of a search and rescue helicopter were pacing the mess-room floor like caged tigers. The wind was blowing 75 knots, and RAF regulations forbade them to take off in anything over 45 knots (Force nine).

Throughout the afternoon we became increasingly stressed, both mentally and physically. Nick made repeated visits to the deck to saw at the rigging. I pumped constantly. Xoë grew more miserable by the hour. I had found a coat and a hat of mine in which to wrap her, but the hat kept falling over her eyes and making her cross. Likewise, I had to cut off the sleeves from the coat, at the elbow, otherwise she could not find her hands. The aft cabin was in such chaos that I could not find her shoes or her wellies or even some wet socks.

After hours of sitting huddled in the passageway boredom became, for the children, the hardest thing to bear. Xoë could not understand why I would not let her play in the saloon. She could not understand what was happening at all.

"Look, Mummy." she said. "Your sunglasses are on the floor! Oh, dear."

Possessions were of no consequence. Life alone mattered. Precious souvenirs of Africa were trampled underfoot.

From a shelf bearing a hundred sodden books I fetched one or two old favourites. As I pumped I read 'The Tale of Farthing Wood' and 'The Tiger who Came to Tea'. When he got tired of hearing me read the books Caesar said, "Tell us a story about *Maamari.*"

Was it a tale with a happy ending that he sought? I could not tell that tale, indeed, my whole being yearned for me to quit jabbering and just concentrate on prayer and positive thinking.

Caesar and Xoë were not for a moment allowed to doubt the fact that ships and 'planes and helicopters were all on their way to our aid. Caesar's only concern was for *Maamari.* If we left her would she be all right, he asked?

"Yes, she's big and strong. She'll be just fine."

Morale was becoming increasingly low as we grew colder and more tired. We had not eaten all day. We had been too busy. I now found some dry biscuits and a pot of honey, but no one was really very tempted by such unappetising fare. When she heard that there would be no hot dinner, Xoë burst into tears - for the first time since disaster struck. "I want a ship to come!" she wailed. "I want to eat ashore."

"Alright then. You get some sleep, and I'll wake you when the ship comes."

Caesar dozed, waking with a start each time a wave broke over the deck. "What will happen if *Maamari* sinks?"

"It's okay," I said casually. "We'll get into the liferaft."

I can imagine that a singlehander faced with a situation of this kind might easily become irrational and make stupid decisions. Certainly, Nick and I felt the need to discuss all the possibilities open to us before doing anything, and I am sure that we gained thereby. Would a singlehander have given in to the urge to get the liferaft ready, by inflating it? There was even the temptation - and a strong temptation - to abandon ship altogether, incredible though it now seems. We had flipped the dinghy in the surf quite often enough to know that a liferaft could never hope to remain upright in this sea, yet we had to keep reminding ourselves of this fact. We had to keep looking out of the window at the awesome breaking waves. While we stayed aboard *Maamari* we had to work at keeping her intact. It would have been so easy to just quit.

Then again, we had to face the possibility that another knock-down might send the boat to the bottom before we could get out. Again and again we reminded ourselves of the findings of the Fastnet Force Ten investigations. We had a copy of the report. We had read it again, quite recently. Many of those who died in that race died in their liferafts, while their boats were still afloat.

"Step *up* into the liferaft. Step *up* into the liferaft."

But suppose we got trapped inside, while the boat went down? The people who get trapped inside while their boats go down are never around to tell the story.

By nightfall we had pretty much given up all hope of being rescued. Perhaps the EPIRB was not working. 18 miles away to the east a Hercules and a SeaKing helicopter were now searching the inky black sea - but we were not to know it. Nor did we ever sight the ship which, since 21.00 hours, had been combing the same waters. At one stage I suggested that we might set off a couple of flares, but Nick was against the idea. Had we done so then, as it happens, we might easily have been spotted. But who lets off their flares on the mere chance that somebody might be around? We had seen no ships since we left Peninsula Valdez. Why should there be any around here?

The wind was abating and towards midnight the seas began to diminish. We knew that we still had the spinnaker poles, for we could hear them clunking against the hull, and my thoughts turned to the possibility of a jury-rig. Nick preferred to think of trying to start the engine. Either way, we had to get the boat moving somehow. We had to get to the Falkland Islands, or else we would be swept down towards South Georgia or South Africa. How long would it take us to reach land, I wondered? Even to get things organised might take a day. Would Xoë survive a whole day in those cold, wet clothes? The burden of concern for her was almost unbearable. It was by far the worst aspect to the ordeal.

By now we had cleared the passage-way of all its clutter and all the obvious dangers. Gone was my big pestle and mortar, souvenir of The Gambia. Gone, too, the smaller one, my birthday present and souvenir of Côte d'Ivoire. If the boat went over again these heavy lumps of wood, flying around, might kill one of us. Without emotion we tossed them into the sea. With them went a big stone quern, our coffee grinder and a souvenir of Cape Verde. Its weight was such that it could even have smashed a hole in the side of the boat.

Favourite souvenirs such as these were not the only things to go over the side. We had also rounded up every item of glass. A couple of the drinking glasses had escaped from their shelf and each piece was sought and sent overboard, through a cabin window. So too were the unbroken glasses. A half-length mirror in the aft cabin had broken into long, jagged shards, more dangerous than the sharpest sword, and these were all sent spinning down through the depths.

Nick needed to sleep. He had now been on his feet for almost 24 hours. He ate a few biscuits and then squatted down in the passage-way, beside the children. I continued to pump, forcing myself to do thirty or forty strokes before I broke off to peer through the portholes. And what if there *was* a ship? How would we transfer the children, or even our own selves, in this sea? Things were calming down, and fewer waves were landing aboard, but still the prospect made me shudder. It just would not be possible. Despite the odds, we would do better to stick with the boat. We could not swim or jump for a rope ladder with the children in our arms. It would be madness to try; it would be suicide.

I pumped and pumped. I began to worry about my own stamina. My arms ached from pumping and my knees from kneeling at the pump. My back hurt. During the first capsize something had hit me. I wondered if I had broken a rib. I wondered if I had damaged a kidney, for I was constantly thirsty and needed to urinate every ten minutes. That business, in itself, was a trial. It involved peeling off my lifejacket, my harness, my coat, and my oilskin trousers before I could even get at my damp clothes beneath. With the fear of another roll still filling my mind I hated to undress and be caught, quite literally, with my pants down.

38, 39, 40 strokes, and I broke off from the pump. I hauled myself to my feet and stepped over to the porthole. How could I possibly hope to see a ship when my nose was hardly higher than the sea? Again the nagging anxiety; the thought of trying to transfer the children. It made me feel sick with fear. If we got through this ordeal, I told myself, we would buy a farm. Even so - even in the deepest depths of our crisis - I was unable to imagine a life without sailing. I pictured a peasant farmstead, but it was beside the sea and there was a little boat anchored in the corner of my vision.

Back to the pump - no dallying - but first I forced down a couple of biscuits and a spoonful of honey. I was shivering and had white spots before my eyes. Was it hypothermia or just over-exertion and lack of food? I pumped, and pumped, and pumped, and my arm hurt, but the bilge never seemed to empty. I could hear the self-steering rudder grinding about on the stern and I wondered if it had made a hole. I kept on pumping. 23, 24...

It was two in the morning. I heard the ship's clock chime. And then I heard something quite unbelievable - the sweetest sound that I shall ever hear. It was the sound of an aeroplane. My heart leapt! "A plane!"

Nick was awake in an instant, and on his feet. Together we rushed to unlash the aft hatch and were just in time to see the beautiful silhouette of a Hercules go roaring low over the deck. It was the most marvellous sight in the world.

"Joy! Joy!" I was skipping about like a born again evangelist, praising God with glory-alleluias sent from the depths of my heart. "They've found us! They know we're here!"

The burden of our misadventure was no longer ours alone; it was a problem shared. Oh, the sweet relief! Odd though it may seem, one thing which had weighed me down all day was the knowledge that, if we sank, no one would know what had happened. Now, whatever happened, at least our folks would know.

The plane had banked and was coming back. We waved a torch, but it was obvious that we had already been spotted. Already there was a helicopter circling around us. It was like something from a movie. Here comes the task force! Once again I could not believe that it was little old us at centre stage. There must be some mistake, I found myself thinking. They surely wouldn't go to all this trouble for insignificant us? How embarrassing; they'll be so cross when they find it's no one important.

Everything now began to happen very quickly. The SeaKing hovered 50 feet above the deck, spilling pools of white light over the sea. The noise was indescribable and the down-wash was as cold as ice. I woke the children and got Caesar into the cockpit with Nick. Xoë became almost hysterical at the thought of being left behind, but her screams were scarcely audible above the racket from the chopper.

We gazed up into the dazzling lights and from amongst them there appeared an angel dressed in green overalls and with a crash hat for a halo. He arrived amongst us and it was so very odd to suddenly have the company of this absolute stranger. Even his attitude towards us, and towards our situation, was concealed by the impossibility of seeing his face or hearing his words. Putting his mouth to Nick's ear the man explained the rescue procedure.

Caesar looked up apprehensively at the lights which he had been told were a helicopter, but he uttered no protest when the visitor slipped the halter over his head. In fact, he continued munching on a biscuit. In the stranger's embrace he was lifted skyward and was gone.

Next it was Xoë's turn to be rescued - and once she was on the deck and knew that salvation was near, she became all calmness and co-operation. Her desire to get off the boat at all costs was made very clear. Without so much as a glance at Mummy, she went soaring away with the winch man. Then, to my horror, she came soaring back again.

In order that the pilot should be able to see what he was about, the chopper was hovering just upwind and to one side of the boat. Thus, the winch behaved like a pendulum. The helicopter was held in a fixed hover, 50 feet above the ever-changing surface of the sea. *Maamari* was also going up and down of course, and at this precise moment she was evidently going up while the helicopter was descending. As Xoë and our hero hurtled back across the black void and towards the stump of our main mast, collision seemed imminent - but in the last fraction of a second *Maamari* began her descent into a trough.

"That was close!"

"You're next," Nick shouted into my ear.

"You're coming too?" Throughout the day we had discussed this matter at length. Our priority was to get the children out of here, and if the children went then I must obviously go with them. Nick had at first said that he would prefer to stay with the boat and create a jury-rig, but many hours had passed since our last discussion. He was in no fit state to remain aboard alone. He was hungry, wet, cold, and very tired. He could not cope on his own.

"You're coming?"

"Yes." The sea and the wind may be calming down but the glass was still low and Nick had definitely had enough. We would say goodbye to our boat, our home, to everything we owned, and to our dreams.

For the third time in succession the load-master put his man down right beside us in the cockpit, with an ease and accuracy which belied the enormous difficulty. This time our saviour had two halters. It seemed to him that the yacht was on the point of sinking and he wanted to get us both off the deck fast.

As we were hauled up through the air we spun around and I looked down at *Maamari*, lurching to and fro in the pool of bright, white light. I felt a pang of guilt. After all that she had done for us we were abandoning her to her fate. We were letting her down. Her white hull - such a pretty hull - stamped on the ink-black sea; the deck, devoid of masts but a scene of such carnage and clutter. That image of *Maamari* remains etched like a photograph in my mind.

And then we were in the helicopter. Seated, and strapped in, and given hot tea. I looked out of the tiny window and tried for another glimpse, but our boat was gone. In our hearts and minds was no sorrow - how could there be sorrow when we were all safe? - but still there was not the least hope that we would ever see *Maamari* again.

Epilogue

AND THEY ALL LIVED HAPPILY
EVER AFTER

for a while…

Jon Dickin Schinas

"I'm sorry to disturb you." The nurse peeped her head around the door of our ward. "We've told them that you're resting still, but they're jamming the hospital switchboard and no one else can get through."

"Who are?" we asked. "Who's jamming the hospital switchboard."

"The Daily Express, and the Guardian, and the Daily Mail. And the BBC - they want to talk to you as well. What shall we tell them? Shall we tell them that you're resting still?"

It was six in the morning, and we had been ashore for just three hours, yet already the world had heard of our shipwreck and our rescue. The British press were fighting each other for a few words straight from the horse's mouth. Wild figures came flying in by fax and phone for the rights to an exclusive interview.

Here we were, at the other end of the world, and we a family of nobodies whose adventures were of no concern to anyone but ourselves - or so we had thought. Ah, but we had overlooked the Falklands Factor. And we had forgotten that our saviours were from the Royal Airforce. And once again, it was really our children who were the focus of interest. Put it all together and you have the plot for a bestselling lead story. For the tabloids, our disaster was a scoop.

"Wave struck us like an exocet missile." Not a bad analogy, but they were the words of a journalist and not ones ever uttered from my lips. Caesar and Xoë were on the front page of the Mail and there I was, in full glorious technicolour, breastfeeding in the Daily Star. "What the...? How the devil did they get hold of that?"

For 24 hours we were a one hit wonder, and all the bigwigs in the Falklands Islands flowed though our hospital ward. Hot on the heels of the journalists came the clergy, and then came the Red Cross, with armfuls and whole trolleyfuls of clothes. We had stepped from the helicopter with nothing to our names except the sodden clothes in which we stood. Some kind of superstition had prohibited us from taking anything at all from the boat, be it valuables, a souvenir, or even just our passports. No, not even the log. (In fact, although I did not know it then, the log and most of my other writings had gone over the side.) We must take nothing at all or else, like Lot's Wife, we might meet our end still.

On our arrival at Port Stanley Hospital, Xoë had been hastily stripped to the skin and wrapped in silver foil. A sack of warm water placed beside her heart soon had her back to normal and within half an hour she was running around and enjoying herself, much to the astonishment of the nurses. Besides my kidney, which very soon recovered, the only injury amongst us was to my right wrist. It had suffered the classic repetitive-strain-injury from 18 hours of pumping, and for the next three weeks I could not even hold a pen!

So here we were, with nothing - nothing except our lives – and yet our hearts overflowed only with joy. We had each other, and we had the children. There was no room for any regret.

Here was a brave new beginning. We had *nothing*, and it felt unbelievably good. Gone was the burden of our meagre possessions, and not a tear was shed. The feeling was quite remarkable. It was a feeling of lightness and freedom.

"What will you do now?" asked the governor's wife. We had no idea. We had no money for another boat. Perhaps we would go back to West Africa. Perhaps we might get our hands on some land, somewhere, and subsist.

I imagine that, with the passage of time, our euphoria would have faded. Life and life only is all very well, but in the end one has to eat. Absolute freedom is wonderful, but unless one is a nomadic Tuareg or a Bushman, a few possessions will be necessary; in this material, physical existence it cannot be otherwise. In time our happiness would most surely have been blighted - but before the day was through our life's course had once again changed direction.

"Your boat has been sighted." The harbour master tried to restrain himself and be terribly formal, but it was evident that he was bursting with excitement. He was delighted to be able to bring us the news. As for us, we were completely stunned. Suddenly, from having nothing and no direction we were turned right around and put back on track. Or, at least, we might be. The boat had been seen, but she was by no means home and dry. The next few hours were hours of uncertainty.

While the crew of the helicopter lifted us from *Maamari's* deck their activities had been under the observation of a fishery protection ship called *Cordella*. At the time when the *Cordella* first received the mayday alert she was at anchor in The Narrows just outside Port Stanley harbour. There was too much wind for the ship to go alongside - according to the captain it was blowing 75 knots - and as an added precaution her engines had been kept running. Thus, when she received the call, *Cordella* was able to get under way at a moment's notice.

At this stage the identity of our vessel was unknown and her position was reported as being 50° 29' S by 58° 52' W, whereas in fact we were 18 miles further to the east. *Cordella's* bridge is equipped with an electronic chart plotter. By studying it after the event we were able to see that, in steaming towards the given position, the *Cordella* actually passed within two miles of *Maamari*. But what is a little white boat, naked even of a mast, in a sea of white crests bigger than she?

All afternoon and into the night the search continued. To have attempted a transfer from the yacht to a ship in the conditions prevailing would certainly have meant disaster, as I have previously remarked, and given the knowledge of the final happy outcome we can only be glad that *Maamari* remained hidden.

At 22.30 the wind finally abated sufficiently to allow the RAF Hercules and the rescue helicopter to take off from Mount Pleasant Airport. Within an hour the two aircraft were circling around our reported position. They were disturbed to find that they couldn't pick up any mayday transmission on 121.5 MHz, for besides communicating with satellites in outer space the EPIRB should also have been transmitting on that radio frequency.

Meanwhile, the captain of the *Cordella* was searching his radar screen for a racon signal, which he expected the EPIRB to emit - but the screen was blank. And since the ship left Stanley there had been no new position report, although the 406 satellite system could have been expected to return the mayday signal on an hourly basis. Why was there no new signal, and why were there no radio or radar transmissions? The conclusion must have seemed inescapable. Nevertheless, the search went on into the night.

At about one in the morning of the next day - the 11th - hopes were very suddenly revived. A new signal had at last been received from the EPIRB. It put *Maamari* at 50° 29' 9 S by 58° 26' 5 W. This was very nearly our true position and, as they approached, the crew of the Hercules spotted the little flashing light atop our beacon. The light was first visible through infra-red, night-vision goggles from about five miles off. One can imagine the whoop of delight from the man who first saw it. At two miles distant, the Hercules finally picked up the 121.5 MHz radio transmission, but by then the signal was irrelevant and moments later they roared over our deck.

As for the folks aboard the fishery protection ship, *Cordella* - they saw the rescue, but they saw it from afar. They were too far away to follow the action, but they could see the brilliant white glare with which the helicopter lit the scene. The captain of *Cordella* was now able to take an exact bearing on the distressed vessel. Better yet, he also had the yacht's position to the last tenth of a second, as given to him by the navigator in the SeaKing, who read it straight off his GPS.

At 02.10 the rescue was complete. The lodestar vanished and the sailors were left alone in the mire of the filthy, black night. They must have felt a momentary pang of regret, but then they surely pressed on with confidence. When you know exactly where you dropped the needle then it is easy to find it again, right? Though the night was a blindfold and the ocean the most enormous hayrick it was just a matter of following the electronic eye; left a bit, right a bit. There! You're on the mark.

Cordella steamed on, and within the hour she came to that precise position. For the rest of the night her crew peered out into the blackness. By the light of the new day, they continued to scour the sea. The luminous trail left in her chart-plotter betrayed *Cordella*'s movements as surely as the glittering path left by a snail, and it would seem that the ship must have very nearly motored right over *Maamari*, yet still the yacht remained hidden. Our next yacht will have a great, big orange triangle daubed on the deck.

For 12 hours the crew of *Cordella* searched. In all that time there was no new signal from our EPIRB. At last the captain of the *Cordella* reported *Maamari* sunk, and no one was surprised at the news - least of all us.

So ended the tale. And then along came the harbour master. *Cordella* was back in harbour, but the fishery protection plane, flying its regular patrol, had sighted *Maamari* floating just as we had left her. "Are you insured?" the harbour master asked us.

"No," said Nick. Not after the last time. When he and Jim had lost their last yacht, off Papua New Guinea, the insurers had refused to cough up.

"Hmmm... that's a shame." The harbour master pursed his lips for moment. Then he said, "Of course, we'll have to move her, one way or another. She's a hazard to navigation; we can't just leave her out there. If it's calm, then we'll have a go at towing her" - and by now the weather was absolutely calm - "but if it blows up, then we'll have to sink her."

"We'll send Cordella out at 08.00 tomorrow," the gentleman continued. "Would you like to go along for the ride?" The question was addressed to Nick alone. Come and save your boat, or come and see it sent to the bottom. Either way, Nick wanted to be there and at 08.00 the next day he left Port Stanley aboard *Cordella*. Once again, the children and I could serve the cause only with our prayers. Another long day and another long night passed.

"Mummy, look! *Maamari* hasn't got any masts! We'll have to buy her some new ones before we can go to Cape Horn." Once again, our prayers were answered - the sea lay as calm as a mill pond - and with these words, and no least hint of fear or trauma, Caesar greeted the arrival of the yacht in Port Stanley.

New masts, yes, and much, much more besides. What a scene of devastation was our poor, dear *Maamari*. We were delighted to see that the hull and deck were basically undamaged; the soundness of her structure had been proven. And nor had the modifications to the rudder or the newly-built skeg suffered in the least. As for the deck, however - the deck told the tale of our adventures. Even the teak planks overlying the fibreglass had been torn off. The pushpit was a tortured mess, and the inch diameter stainless steel tubing of the pulpit had simply been snapped in two.

Gone, now, were the spinnaker poles with which we had thought to build a jury-rig, and gone was the self-steering rudder which I had heard graunching around. The stanchions on the leeward side of the boat had been folded over the deck. The mizzen mast was a stump the height of the tabernacle.

Amongst the debris were two things of note. One was the big, fat, black rope which we had picked up in Peninsula Valdez. It had not even been tied onto the boat, yet it remained there. The other was half a windsurfer. The prophecy had been fulfilled with far more drama than I could ever have imagined. I took the relic and threw it, without ceremony or remark, into a skip.

For a few days after she arrived in Port Stanley, *Maamari* was an object of curiosity to all. Amongst our visitors was Sally Poncet, who lived with her husband, Jerome, and their children on one of the most remote isles in the Falklands archipelago. The Poncets surely know these waters better than any other cruising folk, for with their yacht, *"Damien II"*, they have journeyed often to Antarctica and to the American continent. How could it be that in all their years on this perilous sea they had never been brought to grief?

Sally met the question with another. She wanted to know exactly where it was that we had capsized. Then it transpired that *"Damien II"* had, indeed, been knocked down - and in precisely the same spot, forty miles north of the Falkland Islands. At least one other yacht had been capsized and damaged in, or near to this same location, and Sally also told us of a ship which was damaged when it fell into a freak trough hereabouts. It would seem that this is a known, if *little known*, trouble spot.

The freak waves which were our undoing were probably caused by a meeting of currents. The tide which flows up between East and West Falkland might be a crucial factor. The relatively shallow depth of water and the proximity of the edge of the continental shelf may also be relevant.

By far the most highly esteemed of all the folks who came to take a look at our shipwrecked yacht were our saviours. We were acutely aware that, but for the efforts of the RAF search and rescue team, we might yet be drifting, and very much the worse for wear. Anonymous in overalls and helmets, they arrived at the port - by helicopter, of course.

Whereas we had supposed our rescue to be a run of the mill affair, the SAR crew told us that it was actually the most difficult they had ever attempted. For pilots, Mark Dennis and Tony Gear, it was the wave height which caused them most anxiety. It is always very difficult to judge the height of a wave, and on this occasion the waves were long, making estimation even harder. Earlier in the day we had put the average height at around 30 to 35 feet, but by the time the chopper arrived they were only half as big. So we said to Mark Dennis. The pilot shook his head.

Because the SAR SeaKing is equipped with an auto-hover facility, enabling it to be placed at a fixed height over the sea, its actual altitude will constantly vary. And that variation, between trough and crest, gives an accurate measure of the wave height. According to Mark, the waves at the time of the rescue were up to 35 feet tall - which suggests that the waves we had seen earlier in the day must have been over 50 feet tall; and the ones which rolled us were obviously bigger still. The auto-hover facility could not cope with 35 foot waves, and Mark was having to keep the chopper on station manually.

There is no doubt that our safe arrival aboard the helicopter was an exact measure of the remarkable skill and bravery of the whole crew but - "It was all thanks to my incredible skill" said the load-master, with a cheeky grin. Steve Larke was as pleased as punch with his success. Three times in a row he had hit the bull's eye - our small cockpit, heaving and rolling in the seas. We were under no illusion as to Steve's contribution, but our highest regard was for the 'dope on the rope'. To the one who had put his life on the line we owed the greatest debt of appreciation. Steve Labouchardiere was, in our eyes, the main man. When offered our visitor's book he wrote, "I'm sorry I couldn't sign it when I first dropped in."

We were surprised and relieved to find that neither the search and rescue team nor any of our other visitors scolded us for having put ourselves in so great a position of need. On the contrary, the lads from the RAF were delighted to have had the opportunity to put their skills to the test. Nevertheless, the good folks of the Falkland

Isles - landlubbers all - assumed that we would now have had enough. The news that we could not wait to be back out there on the briney had most of them scratching their heads. At home in England, we found that our friends and family felt the same way. We were forever having to explain ourselves.

Why *do* we still want to go to sea? By way of answer, I can only point to the sailor of yester-year. History and his songs portray the old jack tar as a man condemned to be forever putting to sea, but is this really the true picture? On the contrary! His three years pay disappeared in a one week binge - but doesn't that only go to show that the fellow had no other purpose in life? Believe him exploited and you are surely misled. No doubt the mate was a tyrant. No doubt the food was awful. No doubt that the sea can kill, and so could the scurvy. Yes, of course the man swore that he would never go back - "no never, no more" - but he knew that he would. He couldn't wait to set foot in the bar and the brothel, but after a week ashore he was singing a different song - singing "Shenandoah" instead of "Leave her Johnnie" - and his eyes were on the far horizon. The ancient mariner *lived* for the sea. Call the passion an addiction and you will not be far wrong.

What was true in the old days of sail is still true today. Mere words cannot even begin to explain the feeling of being at one with those two purest of elements, the wind and the sea. Intruders trespassing into this anarchic domain, we sometimes must pay the price for our freedom. Naturally, we hope and pray that we never have to pay the ultimate price... but there is salt water flowing in our veins, and our children have had the same salt water baptism.

Do people who have survived a car crash break right away from the culture of the car? They do not. If you live in the modern world you keep on with it, even after an accident. Well, the same is true of a shipwreck. If you live the life on the ocean wave, that's the life you live - and you just get on with it.

When I think of our capsize, I think also of the day before. I remember the albatrosses sweeping by on the wind. I remember the waves - and not with fear but with a thrill.

Steve Labouchardiere listened to our yarns, and we saw a little light come on. "I could do that..." In a few years time, Steve told us, he would be able to pick up his pension and push off. What a life for the kids! His own children were much the same age as Caesar and Xoë, whom he had already labelled "the bravest little children in the world." The spirited attitude, adaptability, and easy self-confidence of cruising kids is often cause for favourable comment. The lifestyle shines through.

Caesar and Xoë had no doubt about what they wanted. They wanted to go home, and as Caesar explained, when someone asked him, "Home is where the boat is."

NOTE

It has taken me a long time to finish this book, and that is largely because I have been too busy living in the present to look back at the past.

I started writing the book while Caesar and Xoë were babies. Household chores and maternal duties kept me from working on it during the day, and so I used to write while I was on night watch. I would sit in the main cabin, and every five or ten minutes I would go outside to take a look at our heading and check the horizon for ships.

The chapter which tells the tale of Nick's capsize in the Beneteau was written while we were crossing from the Caribbean, and the conversation with which it closes is a verbatim record of the things I remembered us saying to each other that night. Of course, I had no idea as I penned them that the words would prove so prophetic.

After *Maamari* was towed into Port Stanley we tried to get her back into shape, but it was impossible to do this in the Falkland Islands - the weather was inhospitable and the supplies which we needed for the job were not to be had - so we had to ship the boat back to England. Back in Birdham Pool once more, we set to work with a will; or rather, Nick did. I still had the chores and the children to attend to - and I still had my book to write.

Often, while Nick worked, I would take the kids round to my parents' house. They would spend the day playing in the garden and I would sit at a little desk in my old bedroom, upstairs. The log books having been lost overboard, I used my letters home as an aide memoire, but often while I worked I would find myself standing at the top of the stairs.

On each occasion, when I came to an awareness of where I was, I wondered what had brought me here. Was I on my way downstairs for something? I could never remember what it might have been, and so I would go back to my desk - but always, five or ten minutes later, I would find myself back at the top of the stairs. Eventually I worked it out. I was keeping watch for ships.

The Schinas family are still cruising. There are five of them now, and they have a new boat - named Mollymawk *- which they built with their own hands. They have still not made it to Tierra del Fuego - but they are still aiming to get there...*

If you would like to keep tabs on them, take a look at their website:

www.yachtmollymawk.com

GLOSSARY

For readers who are unfamiliar with the language of the sea.

ABEAM : (Adj) Directly off the side of the boat. (See also **beam**.)

AFT : (Adj) Towards the back of the boat, or behind it.

ALONGSIDE : (Adj) A boat which is alongside is moored (tied up) to a quay or to another boat.

ANTIFOULING : (N) A special type of paint applied to the bottom of the boat in an effort to inhibit the growth of marine organisms.

ASTERN : (Adj) Behind the boat.

ATHWARTSHIPS : (Adj.) Across the boat (as opposed to along it).

BEAT : (Vb / N) To sail into the wind **/** The zig-zags made by a yacht sailing to windward.(See also **Tack**.)

BEAM : (N) The beam of a vessel is her width, but the word is also used to refer to the middle of the side of the boat. Something which is off the starboard beam is off the right hand side of the boat.

BEAM ENDS : (N) A yacht which is on her beam ends is heeled right over, with the edge of her side deck touching the water.

BILGES : (N) The bilges are the part of the vessel which lies under the floorboards.

BLOCK : (N) That which is known on terra firma as a pulley.

BOTTLESCREWS : (N) A bottlescrew, or rigging screw, is a piece of hardware which is used to attach a wire **stay** to the boat and control its tension.

BOW : (N) The front end of the boat.

BULKHEAD : (N) A partition set **athwartships** across the boat. Bulkheads strengthen the boat and also serve to divide it into cabins.

CLEW : (N) The bottom, **aft** corner of a sail. In the case of a **headsail** it flies free, but in the case of a **mainsail** or a **mizzen** it sits on the boom. It is to this corner that the *sheet* is attached.

CLOSE HAULED : (Adj) A yacht is close-hauled when she is beating / tacking - ie. when she is sailing as close to the wind as she can without the sails flapping. (See also **Tack** and **Beat**.)

COMPANION WAY / HATCH : (N) The main hatch / hatchway which gives access from the cockpit to the main cabin.

COMPRESSION STRUT : (N) A compression strut stands directly beneath a deck-stepped mast, transferring the load of the mast to the keel. (See also **Tabernacle**.)

DANBUOY : (N) A floating pole fitted with a flag. If somebody falls overboard the danbuoy should be thrown after them to mark their position.

DECKHEAD : (N) The deck, as viewed from inside the vessel. A landsman would call it the ceiling.

DORADE VENTS : (N) Cowl vents fitted to the top of cunningly designed wooden boxes. The boxes are supposed to keep the sea from entering the cabin via the air vents – but unfortunately they are not quite cunning enough.

DRAUGHT : (N) (Pronounced "draft" – and spelled so in America.) The amount of water that a boat draws (ie. the amount of water that she needs in order to keep from bumping her keel on the bottom).

ECHO-SOUNDER : (N) An electronic device used for measuring the depth of water under the vessel.

EPIRB : (N) (Pronounced "ee-purb") Emergency Position Indicating Radio Beacon. A device which can be used to transmit a

mayday. All being well, the mayday is picked up by a passing satellite and bounced back down to a rescue centre.

ETA : (N) (Pronounced as three letters, and not phonetically.) Estimated Time of Arrival.

FOC'SLE : (N) ("Folk-sul") Aboard a yacht the word foc'sle is used interchangeably with the word **forepeak**.

FOOT (of a sail) : (N) The foot is the bottom edge of a sail. In the case of the **main** and the **mizzen** it is attached to the boom. (See also **luff**, **leech**, and **head**.)

FOR'ARD : (Adj) Towards the front of the boat, or ahead of it.

FOREDECK : (N) The **for'ard** (or front) part of the deck.

FOREHATCH : (N) A hatchway in the **foredeck** which gives access to the **forepeak**.

FOREPEAK : (N) The **for'ard** (front) cabin, in the bow of the boat.

FORESTAY : (N) See **stay**.

GENOA : (N) A large triangular sail set on the **forestay**, at the front of the boat.

GPS : (N) Global Positioning System. A means of navigation which depends upon satellites orbiting the planet in outer space.

GUARDRAIL : (N) A small fence around the edge of the boat.

GUNWHALES : (N) (Pronounced "gunnel", to rhyme with funnel.) The junction between the side decks and the side of the hull.

GYBE : (Vb / N) To alter course by turning the boat ahead of the wind, while the boat is **running**. During a gybe the sails will move across from one side of the boat to the other. If the gybe is not controlled they may do this violently. (See also **Tack**.)

HALYARD : (N) A rope which is attached to the **head** (or top) of a sail and used to hoist it (pull it up).

HEAD (of a sail) : (N) The top corner of the sail, to which the **halyard** is attached.

HEADING : (N) A boat's heading is the direction in which she is being steered.

HEADSAIL : (N) Any triangular sail set in front of a mast, usually on a stay. *Maamari*'s **genoa**, **stays'l**, and storm jib were all headsails.

JACKSTAYS : (N) Lines or wires running the length of either side deck. In bad weather the crew can hook their harness lines onto one or other jackstay, so securing themselves to the boat.

JURY-RIG : (N) A jury rig is a make-shift rig which is set up in an emergency after the proper rig has been lost or damaged.

KEEL : (N) A large wing sticking down from the bottom of a sailing boat. It is partially filled with lead. It has a two-fold purpose. It counter balances the heeling effect brought about by the wind pushing on the sails, and it provides lift and stops the boat from sliding sideways through the water.

KETCH : (N) A vessel having two masts, the larger one standing in front of the smaller.

LAZARETTE : (N) A large locker set into the **aft** deck of the vessel. It is also known colloquially as the garden shed.

LEAD-LINE : (N) A light line, or rope, to which is attached a heavy lump of lead. The line is festooned with a series of pieces of cloth and leather, set at measured intervals. Each colour or shape of cloth represents a different depth, and the initiated user can therefore quickly establish how much water is under the boat.

LEECH : (N) The leech is the back edge of a sail. (See also **luff** and **foot**.)

LEE : (N / Adj) A boat which is in the lee of an island is sitting in the wind-shadow formed by that island. Lee is also used as an abbreviation for **leeward** – thus the lee side-deck is the one which is to leeward (on the downwind side of the boat).

LEE CLOTH : (N) A piece of cloth set up along the side of a bed, or bunk, to stop the occupant from rolling out onto the floor.

LEE SHORE : (N) A lee shore is one which is to **leeward** (downwind). In a strong wind a lee shore can be dangerous, as the wind will be trying to blow the boat towards it.

LEEWARD : (Adj) (Pronounced "loo-urd" in England, and "lee-ward" in America.) On the downwind side of the boat. (See **Windward**.)

LEEWAY : (N) A yacht which is **beating** (sailing **close-hauled**) always makes some leeway. Although she may be pointing at a certain buoy or island, she will not really be heading that way; she will be "falling off" or "falling away". The difference between the course steered and the course actually achieved is the measure of her leeway. A **weatherly** boat makes less leeway.

LINE : (N) Any piece of rope of any size whatsoever which is no longer sitting on a drum. **Sheets**, warps (mooring lines), **halyards**, lashings, lanyards, and reefing pennants are all lines.

LUFF : (Vb) To luff is to manoeuvre a sailing boat up towards the wind until her sails begin to flap – at which point they can no longer pull her along. This point of sailing is the exact equivalent of the aeronautical stall.

LUFF (of a sail) : (N) The luff is the leading (front) edge of a sail. (See also **leech** and **foot**.)

LUFF GROOVE : (N) A groove in the **roller furling** stay which grips the **luff** (or leading edge) of the genoa.

MAIN / MAINSAIL : (N) The sail which is set on the main mast (the biggest mast).

MAYDAY : (N) An emergency signal or an emergency call transmitted over the radio (from the French, "m'aidez").

MIZZEN : The sail which is set on the mizzen mast, which is the shorter of the two masts. It stands towards the back of the boat.

OFF THE WIND : (Adj) Away from the wind. A boat which is sailing "off the wind" is **running** or **reaching**.

ON THE WIND : (Adj) Sailing **close hauled**, as close to the wind's direction as is possible.

PAINTER : (N) A line attached to the **bow** of a dinghy which is used to moor it, either to the mother-ship or to a jetty.

PORT : (Adj) The left side of the boat.

PREVENTER : (N) A rope or tackle set up to prevent the **mainsail** or the **mizzen** from inadvertently **gybing**. (See **gybe**.)

PULPIT : (N) The metal framework placed at the bow of the vessel and forming part of the **guardrail**. It is so-named for its superficial resemblance to the pulpit in a church.

PUSHPIT : (N) A word derived from **pulpit**. It is the metal framework round the **after** end of the deck, at the **stern**.

QUARTER : (N) If you are standing on the **port** quarter, you are right at the back of the boat in the left-hand corner. If the vessel is taking the seas on her **starboard** quarter, they are meeting her on the opposite side, on the right-hand side of the **stern**.

REACH : (Vb / N) Sailing across the wind, with the wind meeting the boat on the **beam** (side). When she is on a close reach the yacht is almost **beating**. On a broad reach she is going downwind and is almost **running**.

REEF : (Vb) To reef a sail is to reduce its area by folding or furling part of it.

RIG : (Vb / N) To rig a sail is to attach it to the stay or spar and fit the necessary lines.
A boat's rig is the sum total of her masts and sails, together with the **stays** (wires) and **lines** which keep them in place and functioning.

ROLLER FURLING : (N) A system whereby the **genoa** can be **reefed**, from the cockpit, by rolling the sail around a special **stay**.

RUBBING STRAKE : (N) A piece of wood set into the **topsides** just below the level of the deck. It is semi-sacrificial, being designed to protect the hull itself from damage.

RUN : (Vb / N) A boat which is running is sailing directly before the wind, with the wind pushing on her outspread sails. / The point of sailing during which the boat is sailing directly downwind.

SAT-NAV : (N) Satellite Navigation system. The predecessor to **GPS**.

SEA-ANCHOR : Any device used to stop or control the motion of a vessel which is not underway but which is in water too deep to permit anchoring.

SHEET : (N) A rope which is attached to the loose, **aft** corner of a sail and used to control it.

SHEET IN : (Vb) To haul on a **sheet** and so change the shape and angle of the sail.

SKEG : (N) A miniature **keel** sited immediately in front of the rudder and providing it with support.

SHROUD : (N) See **stay**.

SPRAYHOOD : (N) A contraption resembling a large pram-hood which is sited in front of the main hatchway. In good weather it is folded down. In bad weather it can be lifted up to keep the spray out of the cockpit. (In America the sprayhood is called a dodger, but aboard an English boat dodgers are pieces of cloth set up on either side of the cockpit, on the guardrail.)

SPREADERS : (N) The spreaders are little poles which stick out on either side of the mast. They help the **shrouds** to support the mast.

STANCHIONS : (N) The stanchions are a set of posts set up around the edge of the deck to support a **guardrail**.

STARBOARD : (Adj) The right side of the boat.

STAY : (N) Stays are effectively guy lines. They hold up the mast. The stays at the front of the boat are called **forestays**, the ones at the back are called backstays, and the ones on either side are called **shrouds**.

STAYS'L : (N) A relatively small triangular sail set on the inner **forestay** (behind the **genoa**).

STERN : (N) The back end of the boat. (See also **Transom**.)

TABERNACLE : *Maamari's* masts were deck-stepped. Instead of passing through a hole in the deck and resting on the keel, each one stood in a metal shoe which was bolted to the deck. These metal shoes are known as tabernacles. (See also **Compression Strut**.)

TACK : (Vb / N) Boats cannot sail straight into the wind, and so if they want to travel in that direction they have to do so in a series of zig-zags. These are known as tacks (N). At the end of each tack the boat is tacked (Vb). A boat which is tacking is being steered in such a way that her bow passes through the wind (at which point her sails flap). Having been tacked, she can begin sailing again on the other tack. (See also **Beat**, **Close-hauled** and **Gybe**.)

TACK (of a sail) : (N) The bottom, **for'ard** corner of the sail, which is attached just above the deck or towards the bottom of the mast. (See also **clew** and **head**.)

TENDER : (N) A dinghy belonging to a yacht and used to ferry the crew to and from the shore.

TOPSIDES : (N) The part of the hull which is above the water.

TRANSOM : (N) The flat, back end of a boat.

WEATHER : (Adj / Vb) Something which is "to weather" is to windward (upwind) of the vessel. **/** To weather a rock or buoy is to pass to **windward** of it. (See also **lee** and **leeward**.)

WEATHERLY : (Adj) A yacht which is weatherly goes well to **windward**. ie. She makes good progress whilst **beating**.

WINDWARD : (Adj) On the upwind side of the boat.

YAWL : (N) Very similar to a **ketch**, but with the **mizzen** (smaller mast) standing **aft** of the rudder.

Printed in the United Kingdom
by Lightning Source UK Ltd.
135822UK00001B/65/P